Transplanetary Americas

Transplanetary Americas

ART, OUTER SPACE, AND THE LATINX IMAGINATION

Robb Hernández

Duke University Press
Durham and London

2026

Printed in the United States of America on acid-free paper ∞
Project Editor: Lisa Lawley
Designed by A. Mattson Gallagher
Typeset in Minion Pro and Degular by Westchester Publishing Services

Library of Congress Cataloging-in-Publication Data
Names: Hernandez, Robb writer of supplementary textual contenta author
Title: Transplanetary Americas : art, outer space, and the Latinx imagination / Robb Hernández.
Other titles: Art, outer space, and the Latinx imagination
Description: Durham : Duke University Press, 2026. | Includes bibliographical references and index.
Identifiers: LCCN 2026004094 (print)
LCCN 2026004095 (ebook)
ISBN 9781478039228 paperback
ISBN 9781478034186 hardcover
ISBN 9781478062769 ebook
Subjects: LCSH: Hispanic American arts—Themes, motives | Hispanic American arts—20th century | Hispanic American artists—20th century | Science fiction in art | Cosmology in art | Astronomy in art | Science in art | Postcolonialism and the arts | Outer space
Classification: LCC N6538.H58 H4625 2026 (print) | LCC N6538.H58 (ebook) | DDC 704.03/68—dc23/eng/20260603
LC record available at https://lccn.loc.gov/2026004094
LC ebook record available at https://lccn.loc.gov/2026004095

Cover art: Leo Villareal, *Star Ceiling (El Paso)*, 2025. LEDs, custom software, electrical hardware, and aluminum, 18 ft. 9 in. × 135 ft. (5.7 × 41.2 m). El Paso Museum of Art, El Paso, TX. Gift of the El Paso Museum of Art Foundation. Photo: Alex Marks. © Leo Villareal.

PUBLICATION OF THIS BOOK HAS BEEN AIDED BY A GRANT FROM THE WYETH FOUNDATION FOR AMERICAN ART PUBLICATION FUND OF CAA.

In memory of
Robert M. Hernandez
(1951–2020)

For Lincoln

Contents

Illustrations

Figures

Plates

Acknowledgments

Perhaps my first "transplanetary relation" took place in the discreet corners of my childhood bedroom in Boulder, Colorado, in the 1980s. A space capsule toy box brought US Cold War politics into our Mexican American household. Between this plastic monument to Project Mercury and my dad's sojourns to the local video store, where cover art in the horror and science fiction section delighted my young eyes, these outlets stoked my imagination and unexpectedly opened strange new worlds for me. Besides kid amusement, space science and technology were always there. Rocky Flats was an ominous yet recurring name that provoked alarm and fear around my grandmother's kitchen table. Fabled stories about radiation exposure and "running hot" sparked anxiety among my mom and her sisters, who worried over brothers, husbands, and cousins working long hours at this nuclear weapons manufacturer. Though these family members all bought homes, purchased trucks, and raised families, many had unexpectedly short lifespans or compromised illnesses. Little did I realize that this toy box, an innocuous relic of NASA space boosterism, symbolized the human price of this labor that my uncles gave to the US defense industry. Certainly this fraught relationship among corporations, government agencies, and vulnerable ethnic populations is not new under the auspices of racial capitalism and settler colonial violence, the ways in which our backs and bodies forged US space industrialists' march toward the stars cannot be overlooked. My drive to look up or even occupy a plastic spacecraft with the fantastical desire to go skyward punctuated how outer space came home to us and other working-class Latinx households in ways left unsaid in the grand narrative of the modern space program. Could art history offer some answers? My efforts to crystallize that connection mark this book's "one small step," as Neil Armstrong put it, to reckon with Latinidades' deep entanglements with space, art, and politics in ways not yet told.

Getting to new plateaus and aerial fronts in Latinx studies required a launch pad with the necessary propulsion to go elsewhere. At the most rudimentary level, I want to thank Duke University Press and, in particular, my editor, Elizabeth Ault, for her patience, insightful procurement of fantastic peer reviewers, and overall stewardship throughout this publication process. Editorial assistant Ben Kossak resolved my innumerable questions with impressive finesse. Development coordinator James Moore was instrumental in securing a grant from the College Art Association's Wyeth Foundation for American Art Publication Fund. As well, a Fordham Publication and Book Award aided in the robust art program reproduced here, allowing access to many images for the first time. I praise estates, copyright attachés, galleries, and even caregivers who graciously lent work, waived fees, or aided in the image reproduction. I am forever grateful to Jacqueline Arias, Holly Barnet-Sánchez, Alayna Barrett Fox, David Botello, CalEarth Institute, Sharon Camhi, Cassils, Beatriz Cortez, Lincoln Cushing, Silvia De Biasi, Celeste De Luna, Kristopher Driggers, Ciara Ennis, rafa esparza, Elizabeth Ferrer, Nansi Guevara, Richard Haro, Bibi Healy, Elisa Leonelli, Ron Miller, Roger Minick, Rich Puchalsky, Vincent Ramos, Josué Rawmírez, Dario Robleto, Francisco Rovira Rullán, Carolyn Russo, Dan Solomon, Susanna Temkin, Rafael Vargas-Suarez Universal, Vincent Valdez, Simón Vega, Gaby Velasquez, and Sophie Winner for their support. The technological savvy of Karlyn Allenbrand readied several artworks for publication. My research assistant Quinn Findley remedied many loose ends. Last, and certainly not least, the copyediting mastery of Lisa Wehrle brought my prose up to code and added the necessary sparkle.

Residencies at key art institutions were consequential for this Latinx retelling of art, astronomy, and space history. A position as a Tyson Scholar at Crystal Bridges Museum of American Art in 2018 started this journey. A Smithsonian American Art Museum senior fellowship in 2021–22 and Ailsa Mellon Bruce senior fellowship at the National Gallery of Art in 2023–24 parlayed access to records, art collections, scholarly networks, and curatorial specialists that completed this investigation. Museum professionals enriched my stays in northwestern Arkansas and Washington, DC, respectively, and, at risk of overlooking the village that supports residencies of these kinds, I thank Sarah Battle, Angelica Becerra, Alejo Benedetti, Mindy Besaw, Sarah Bohannan, Kaira Cabañas, Josh T Franco, Amelia Goerlitz, Lauren Hayes, Melissa Ho, JP Jacob, Peter Lukehart, Steven Nelson, Jen Rokoski, Jeannette Ibarra Shindell, Stacy Weiland, and especially E. Carmen Ramos for their thankless efforts and enduring support. An award from the Andy Warhol

Foundation Arts Writers Grant aided in the preliminary writing of the earliest iteration of the project. More important, these fellowships also relied on the labor of written letters of recommendation, and I want to underscore my deep appreciation to Mary Coffey, Jennifer Doyle, David Getsy, Ricardo Ortiz, and Roberto Tejada for this time-consuming yet important service to scholars of color.

My collaborative work with Matt Shindell from the Space History Department at the National Air and Space Museum (NASM) on an oral history project entitled "Estrellas y Cuentos" (Stars and tales) gathered nearly twenty interviews with Latinx artists for whom outer space, space science, and science fiction were influential registers in art making and cultural expression. These dialogues took place under the unpredictability of pandemic lockdown when plugging into Zoom, computer terminals, and recording software ironically offered closeness through otherworldly suppositions and utopic outlooks. For that, I am deeply appreciative to Matt and the artist participants, whose words galvanized the transplanetary-relational framework that is the focus of this study, among them Elia Alba, Angel Cabrales, Beatriz Cortez, Hector Hernández, Dario Robleto, Clarissa Tossin, Rafael Vargas-Suarez Universal, Simón Vega, and others.

As the unpredictability of COVID-19 surges and upticks restructured how many interdisciplinary humanities scholars conducted research from afar, I must commend the virtuosity of special collections archivists, reference librarians, and historical society volunteers who rose to the challenge and humored my very precise questions bridging art and science divides. Their intimate knowledge of manuscript collections cannot be underestimated, and their attention to detail culled new findings. In particular, I am indebted to Claudia Romero at the El Paso Public Library's Border Heritage Center, Nancy Godoy at Arizona State University Libraries, Veronica Reyes at the University of Arizona Library's Special Collections, Traci Patterson at Rice University's Woodson Research Center, Erin Henry at University of Houston–Clear Lake's Archives and Special Collections, Mikhaila McCray at the Houston Public Library, Malia Van Heukelem at the University of Hawai'i at Mãnoa Library, Evan Fay Earle and Laura Linke at Cornell University Archives, Kevin Schindler and Alma Ruiz Velasco at Lowell Observatory, Emily Una Weirich at the Center for Creative Photography, Peter Collopy at Cal Tech Archives and Special Collections, Paul Spitzzeri at the Workman and Temple Family Homestead Museum, Rudy Martinez from the Boyle Heights Historical Society Advisory Board, and especially Christian Kelleher, a true gem at the University of Houston Libraries system. In addition, Sarah Cooper,

Laura Copelin, Jill Dawsey, Mia Fineman, Miki Garcia, Alexis Wilkinson, and Claudia Zapata took time away from hurried curator life to offer important exhibition details, enhancing my assessments. Also, collectors like Peter Kleeman, Jeremy Rowe, and Christopher B. Steiner finessed my scope and directed my attention to strange and popular amusements across the Americas.

Invited talks and guest lectures at the University of Nebraska–Lincoln, University of Southern California, Virginia Commonwealth University, University of New Mexico, Smithsonian American Art Museum, and National Gallery of Art offered critical forums in which my earliest ideas about transplanetary relationality were introduced. Key insights from these audiences and faculty improved my argument and enhanced the book's completion. In particular, I thank Katie Anania, Kathleen Chapman, Matt Goodwin, Ray Hernandez-Duran, Ryan Linkoff, Catie Merla-Watson, and Tobias Wofford for facilitating these visits.

My students were often the testing ground for lectures and art analyses, and I am deeply indebted to those astute visual readers from my ongoing Alternative Americas course at Fordham University. I am often reminded of our dialogues about looking up, and I hope that they see themselves in the prose centering this book. Also, faculty readers from Fordham's Race, Empire, and Colonialism Working Group offered feedback on my early book proposal. My colleagues in English, including Chris Gogwilt, Glenn Hendler, Stephen Hong Sohn, Julie Kim, and Jordan Stein, shared kernels of knowledge that improved this manuscript. Caitlin Meehye Beach, Anna Indych-López, Marisa Lerer, and Tatiana Reinoza carefully read chapters, and I am grateful for their precision and deft insight.

A book is also indebted to communities of practice and scholarly exchange. Peers from the university, museum, and artist studio anchored my ideas, raised my spirits, and encouraged joy under dire circumstances. Though lists are never fully complete, I want to thank (in no particular order) Tatiana Reinoza, Kency Cornejo, JV Decemvirale, Lois Rosson, Claudia Zapata, Joanne and Luna Flores, Marisa Lerer, Ranald Woodaman, Taina Caragol, Eddie Hayes Jr., Ricardo Ortiz, Mike Amezcua, Mireya Loza, Julio Capó Jr., José Centeno-Melendez, Tey Marianna Nunn, Eduardo Diaz, Bree Robertson Chen, Emily Voelker, Alejandro Anreus, Meghaa Parvathy Ballakrishnen, Justin Brown, Brian Goldstein, Pamela Lee, Kelvin Parnell Jr., Nancy Troy, Adriana Zavala, Emmanuel David, Jason Gladstone, Patrick Greaney, Cheryl Higashida, Kristie Soares, Maria Windell, Caitlin Meehye Beach, Mary Bly, Crystal Colombini, Chris Dietrich, Carl Fischer, Glenn Hendler, Asato Ikeda, Corey McEleney, Barbara Mundy, Tom O'Donnell,

Sasha Panaram, Aly Thomas, Dennis Tyler, Roberto Tejada, Jennifer Josten, George Flaherty, Christian Wurst, Francisco Pedraza, Donatella Galella, Emily Hue, Keith Miyake, Maile Arvin, Liz Przybylski, Scott Savage, and the indefatigable Jennifer Doyle. A recent retreat to Carmel by the Sea brought a dormant cohort of University of California, Los Angeles, girlies together decades after graduation, and to Elena, Burcu, Crystal, Hye Jean, and Françoise, I am honored, humbled, and grateful for your companionship. My friend and adviser, Mary Corbin Sies, instilled scholarly rigor and interdisciplinary acumen in me through her work on race, vulnerable heritages, and cultural landscapes studies, which I found myself returning to again and again. As she retires from the University of Maryland, College Park, I hope she sees her handiwork in this unexpected guide to space at cosmic and atomic levels.

Mary and I reunited in the aftermath of the sudden passing of our friend and colleague Angel David Nieves. Although he unexpectedly departed, I hope that this book is a testament to the lessons he shared with me in an ethnic studies classroom at the University of Colorado Boulder. Though as a queer of color scholar I am aware of the uncertainty of time, I was truly unprepared for the abruptness of his passing. Such precarity was a hard lesson that I, unfortunately, learned again. His death was shadowed by other losses: my dear cousin Rizzo Benavidez, former University of California Riverside English chair George Haggerty, exhibition designer extraordinaire Zaid Yousef, cultural visionary Adál Maldonado, personal trainer Jerry Christal, and Aunt Marianne Romero, a glorious matriarch in embroidered Mexican garments unafraid to remind me where I came from. One of my last conversations with Ricardo Ortiz was over boozy cocktails talking about this manuscript, my family, and the future. His loss is reexperienced with every trek down Fourteenth Street. Of course, the greatest of these travesties was my dad's passing from COVID-19 causes, sparking a search to rectify a story about art, space, and beyond in ways reflective of him. If anything, I surrender this visual archive as a testimony about his life and other kinfolk who turned to science fiction to remedy themselves and to better this and other worlds. Though his death opens this book, our journey does not end there as his presence pervades these pages and bleeds into my present in ways that inspire introspection and rediscovery every day.

To get through this, I found solace in a young man from Fullerton with the solidity of the Rockies and the buoyancy of a tennis ball. Stephen, little did I realize the unexpected journey we were about to find ourselves on. From the sand-dusted trails of Mt. Rubidoux to the lush hillsides of the Hudson

River, we imagine alternative futures together, and I can't think of anyone I would rather dream with. You remind me that "I tell jokes," and with side-splitting laughter this place becomes less grim. Your light conquers the folds and shines on me in ways that spell new adventure and invite the creature comforts of home, rich with plushies and the crackling sound of our fireside retreat. I look forward to each new morning with you.

Impressive in the aftermath of Dad's passing is my family's resilience. Mom is a boulder, and like her birthright, she refused to crumble when the rest of us did. She was tested in ways that seemed insurmountable, but when I see her toiling in the garden and sowing new seeds, she proves each new spore is precious. As she communes with the most ancient of ways, Mom knows that tomorrow is a gift that must be nurtured. I am honored to be her son. My brother, Lonnie, rose to life's challenges with the acrobatics of a Jedi knight growing at each new responsibility (*leveling up*, in gamer speak), becoming a husband to Margarita and stepdad to Hayden in ways that would have made Dad proud. Last, and certainly not least, our lives changed when we welcomed my nephew, Lincoln Hernandez, into the fold. His arrival came when we needed him the most, and like his namesake, he formed a link anchoring us through turbid times. With his boisterous laughter, flair for science, and technological wizardry, he is the best of us. I pray for you a future where monsters are tamed, bubblegum is plentiful, and wishing wells give you everything that your heart desires. To you, and your new sister, Savanna, a better world is dawning.

Introduction

ART AT THE OUTER LIMITS OF LATINIDADES

"Do not attempt to adjust the picture. We are controlling transmission. . . . We will control the horizontal. We will control the vertical. . . . You are about to experience the awe and mystery which reaches from the inner mind to . . . The Outer Limits," warns the hijacker as the oscilloscope frequency bounces at the backdrop of the TV show's title card. The sound wave crescendos over a booming score composed by Dominic Frontiere. The theme music's foreboding chords warn of something ominous over the horizon.

Indeed, something ominous was approaching as the man watched *The Outer Limits*, a short-lived science fiction–horror serial that ran from 1963 to 1965. The DVD played despite his ailments from a COVID-positive diagnosis in October 2020. What he saw before the paramedics pulled him away is a matter of speculation. However, what that show represented to me, his son, was haunting during the confusing period that followed when social distancing, hospital internet goodbyes, and probate attorney appointments occupied my conscious attention.

"Tourist Attraction," the first *Outer Limits* episode on the disc I recovered from Dad's DVD player, is set in a fictitious Republic of San Blas. The voice-over indicates that San Blas is located west of the Orinoco basin, a watershed encompassing Colombia, Venezuela, and Guyana.[1] However, the actual San Blas is an archipelagic chain of islands north of the Isthmus of Panama. The Caribbean tenor of the region is twisted and confused on-screen, as images of the Sierra Madre mountain ranges are shown instead of views of Central or South America. Thus, Mexico City forms the ambiguous "Pan-American" backdrop against which this creature feature unfolds.

The plot centers around US business scion John Dexter, who is participating in a science expedition to the ancient crater lake of Aripana. Using advanced sonar, hydrophones, and live feeds, his research team studies the depths of the water hole. When Dexter stumbles on a gilled beast hiding on the seafloor, he stops at nothing to capture it. His discovery, the *Ichthyosaurus mercurius*, is a rare primordial marine species that the country's resident scientist, Professor Arivello, compares to a cross between a coelacanth and an ichthyosaurus, though with evolutionary differences that allow it to survive on land. When San Blas dictator General Juan Mercurio catches wind of the find, a battle brews over the specimen, pitting a greedy US capitalist against a fumbling Latin American communist ruler inept at science and technology but crafty when it comes to leveraging the beast against the businessman. Alas, San Blas's feats of engineering and infrastructural modernization crumble by the episode's climatic end. The native creature's family hears its wails, rallies, and tears through the dam, thus returning the environment to a state where these ancient fish can live freely again (see figure I.1). With General Mercurio's regime underwater and US corporate capitalists terrified to export the *Ichthyosaurus mercurius*, like coffee, to the Global North, the real monster is not the gilled giant. It is us.

As a genre, science fiction is lauded for its ability to parallel social ills and wield political commentary in ways that are subversive yet encoded. As scholar Samuel Ginsburg notes, "Science fiction narratives are not merely a method of escaping current realities; they are also a tool for articulating their lasting social, political, and rhetorical effects."[2] Though he speaks in literary terms, can the same be said for art history's response to the field?[3] Certainly, science fiction's aesthetic expression has found its way into this scholarship through mid-century modernists' appraisal of the space age, and even recent curatorial evaluations about Afro-, Latinx, and Indigenous futurisms are germane to this conversation.[4] However, a science-fictional art theory and method are harder to come by. Art historians, I suspect, are careful not

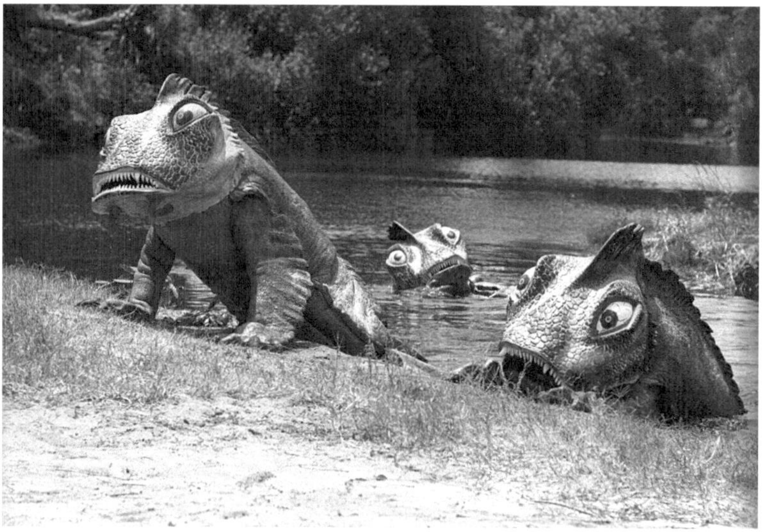

I.1 A scene from "Tourist Attraction" (1963), Season 1, Episode 13 of *The Outer Limits*, directed by Laslo Benedek. Production still.

to speak of the genre's lowbrow visual culture in the same breath as fine art. Traditional attentions to line, form, technique, palette, and other formal concerns are hardly bestowed on a man in a rubber fish suit, even though he arrived the same year as pop art cemented itself with the *Six Painters and the Object* show at the Guggenheim Museum in New York (see figure I.2).[5] Despite this surprising popular culture turn in contemporary art, it is impossible for me to ignore the attraction that my dad felt to a TV show such as *The Outer Limits*, even with its caricatured portrayal of Latin America or Latin Americans.[6] What was it about this low-budget genre and its cheap theatrics that resonated with him as a Mexican American at the alien edges of good health, wellness, and recovery? What indescribable pleasures did a nonsensical tale about the San Blas Islands rouse in him as he confronted life's end? More simply, what answers could a man in a rubber suit present to him about a world turned topsy-turvy by infection, lockdown, and quarantine? I like to think that Dad experienced this Latinx science-fictional representation as a malleable, adaptable, and recognizable site of identification that connected and empowered him, despite his ailments.[7] My hope in writing this book is that others, too, will *feel* a similar transformation, with something higher up that breaks the surface and articulates a way of being

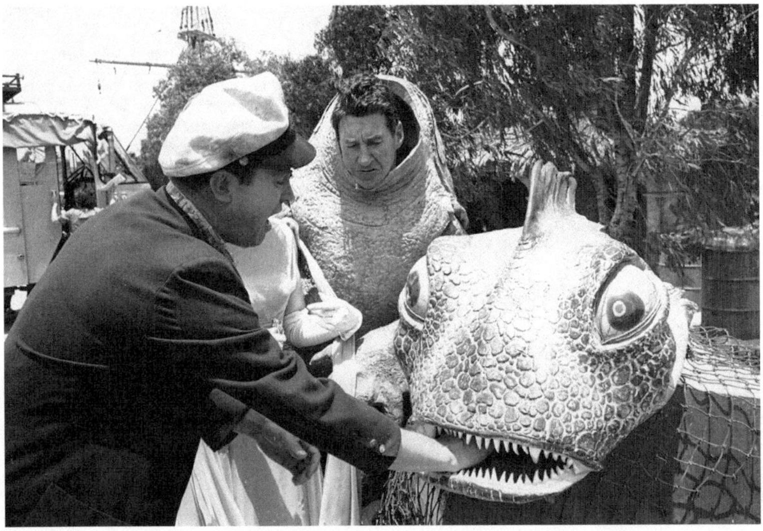

I.2 In a behind-the-scenes outtake, a puppeteer appears in the *Ichthyosaurus mercurius* rubber suit from "Tourist Attraction" (1963), an episode of *The Outer Limits*, directed by Laslo Benedek. Production still.

in communion with the speculative powers of this and other worlds, a topic rarely broached outside discourses of fandom or audience studies.

Losing Dad under such dire and chaotic conditions animated the outer limits, truer to life than genre fiction. Like Jayna Brown's own curious ride with her clairvoyant father in "the bleak and bloody dimension we are taught to call reality," I had not fully comprehended my parent's impact on my thinking, seeing, and feeling about what was speculatively possible.[8] I feel that my dad's hand is guiding me still, leading me to that errant DVD disc, begging me to ruminate on the complicated ways in which Latinxs invest in, think with, and respond to a genre in search of something *más allá*: seeking a beyond outside present realities, even outside Earth. To "adjust the picture" and reclaim not just the horizontal but the vertical, as the commanding voice control of the hijacker in *The Outer Limits* says, evokes another kind of Latinx culture making. Adjusting to an upward scaling allows for another orientation of Latinx creativity, one unbounded by the gravitational pull of the physical world. Rather, this expressivity emerges from the abyss like the *Ichthyosaurus mercurius*, arising in search of justice, liberation, and answers from up there. Turning vertically, this book offers a way to study the ascendant attentions of artists of Latin American descent that expand the terms of Latinx belonging, expressions which traffic in what I call *transplanetary relationality*.

Before I define this operational modus of the project, it is important to foreground an aerial redirection for the study of both art history and Latinx studies more broadly. This directional shift is necessary because of majoritarian presumptions that "defin[e] Mexico and Mexicans [and by extension Mexican Americans] as backward and technologically inferior," according to Curtis Marez, or represent technology as the "techno-colonial and techno-authoritarian alienation of the Caribbean in popular narratives of space exploration," as Samuel Ginsburg writes.[9] As a result, major and minor players in Latinx creative cultures are crudely left in the rearview mirror in the story about the modern space program and its art-science inflections. Such disjunction raises an important question: Just how does an art history of outer space, science, and speculation grapple with someone like Dad? As a child born in 1951, he learned, played, and grew amid the space race pitting the United States against the Soviet Union in a truncated version of the complex geopolitics at that time. Television shows such as *Captain Video and His Video Rangers* (1949–55) and *Space Patrol* (1950–55) captivated viewers of all ages, especially children. Fast-forward thirty years, to when Dad would wear his *Captain Video* baseball cap while rummaging through his rat's nest of wires, hi-fi components, and pirated VHS tapes, indicating his answer to the call of a 1980s home entertainment boom.[10] His stylish, self-labeled "system" of speakers and subwoofers was adorned in sequined fabric selected by my mom, adding sparkle to his latest cable channel interception (see plate 1).

These memories of Dad's art, media, and technology choices spur a new understanding: The nexus they share offers a minor yet profound insight into Latinx culture making in ways little considered in a US space-age corpus, science fiction studies, and Latinx media studies, all of which appear unaware of the domestication of home entertainment systems in ordinary Latinx households. Evidence of technology's intimate reach is observed from a 1982 snapshot (see plate 2). Dad, frequently seen at family functions with a camera in his hand, counters my uncle as Mom breaks into laughter at this dance of dueling photographers. This "mountain Chicano" precept precedes Graciela Iturbide's much-lauded urban portrait of a Chicana versed in her own image making (see figure I.3). These pictures capture a photographic vernacular, demonstrating how a Mexican American visual culture was taking shape under a cyclopic optic. More than hobbyists, these Chicanxs were equally technophilic and even alien-eyed in appearance, expanding how Latinx cultural producers responded to a racist and invasive camera culture where intrusive lenses, spy

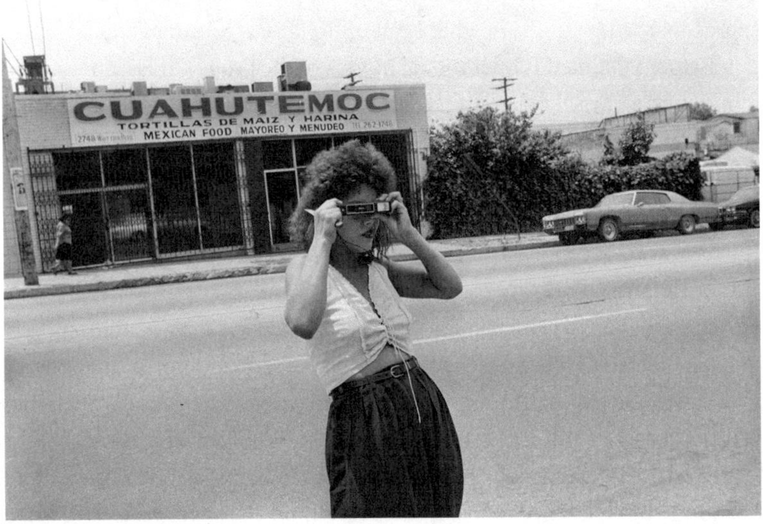

I.3 Graciela Iturbide, *Cristina tomando fotos en Los Angeles* (Cristina taking pictures in Los Angeles), from the series *White Fence, East LA*, 1986. Gelatin silver print, 16 × 20 in. Collection of the artist. Image courtesy of Rose Gallery, Santa Monica, CA.

planes, networked satellites, drones, and space probes articulated policing advancements affecting US communities of color and the immigrant populace.

Despite these kinds of portrayals of high-tech Hispanics, the image archive about this contentious period of US-Soviet hostility typically focuses on artworks funded by NASA (the National Aeronautics and Space Administration), a topic I take up further in chapter 1. These artworks were completed at the behest of NASA administrator James Webb and the National Gallery of Art's curator of paintings, H. Lester Cooke, in 1962. US artists like Fred Freeman, Robert Rauschenberg, Norman Rockwell, and Andy Warhol (among others) honed a visual language that boosted the technology and future design of tomorrow with little consideration of minoritarian subjects' place in it.[11] The artists who are the focus of this study dare to reset the terms of these spacefaring visionaries, with machinic monocles being redirected and refocused as seen in these photographs; they reverse the lens, crash zoom, and, with ocular enhancement, link this world to other versions of reality in heightened ways.

This book's point of view amplifies creativity in a threefold way: art, science, and speculation. In its many cultural variations, speculation specifically has stimulated gregarious forms of Latinx expressivity that embrace the interstellar traffic of outer space, prod celestial bodies, and propose astronomical idioms little explored in art history, cultural studies, science or technology studies, and cultures of media use and production. So why does art history—and, for that matter, *Latinx* art history—find it difficult to confront this multimodal register? One reason is that Latinxs have resided in the blind spot of the Cold War, portrayed as witnesses to but not participants in a battle for technological mastery and scientific superiority between so-called first-world superpowers. Keep in mind that although Arnaldo Tamayo Méndez was trailblazing, becoming the first cosmonaut of Afro-Caribbean heritage on Russia's Soyuz 38 mission in 1983, his symbolic flight on behalf of Cuban and Soviet cooperation did not alter the relations of power, technology, and colonialism. As Juan Toledano Redondo observes, "The country never created a similar aerospace industry. Its arrival to the stars was . . . by chance; a favor from our [socialist] brothers."[12] During the Cold War, devastation reigned over Latin American peoples, lands, and skies. US interventionism propped up dictatorships, reshaping the geopolitical terrain of the Americas throughout much of the twentieth century. This country's involvement was justified based on the threat posed by communist ideology. In particular, the United States as an agent of empire "had designs on Central American territory since the nineteenth century. . . . This land takeover would later produce the internal social upheaval of the 1980s, subdued to U.S. international interests in confrontation with the socialist bloc."[13] This history of US corporate, defense, and economic investments was not specific to the "Northern Triangle," a region composed of El Salvador, Guatemala, and Honduras; it also pervaded colonial efforts in the Caribbean, South America, and Southeast Asia. Often this is a story of hemispheric control over territory and sea. But as Tamayo's example reminds us, this story is also about air.

For these reasons I want to reset the representational terms of Latinidades beyond the ground and, instead, point the field toward its transplanetary relations. The book's premise is not predicated solely on the gestural act of looking up but, rather, on what that skyward turn means for being Latinx and on the artistic language calcifying in response to this cosmic alignment. In some ways, this study is about how Latinx artists engaged space science and the modern space race, specifically. As a result, this investigation traffics in unexpected junctures, like the founding of astronomy at Cornell University (see chapter 1), the first transborder telescope to traverse the United States and Mexico in pursuit of Mars (see chapter 3), and Latinx migration spurred by Halley's Comet (see chapter 1). It is also about the entanglements of space, time, and planetary matters when the human-centered lessons of Latinx humanities loosen and embrace the vastness of the universe. When Latinidades are linked within a planetary nexus of interstellar connection, new emphasis emerges around vision, scale, movement, and visual and material expression (areas I will expand on momentarily). In short, this book demonstrates how, since the nineteenth century (and even in the ancient Americas), Latinxs have had intimate knowledges of astronomy if not of the universe and responded with creative innovation. But how to understand this vertically inclined conception of Latinx studies broadly?

Since the 1990s a transnational turn has refocused this ethnic study in response to a critical moment of late capitalism. Passage of the North American Free Trade Agreement (NAFTA) in 1994 and the Dominican Republic–Central America Free Trade Agreement (CAFTA-DR) a decade later increased global circuits of US domination in economic, military defense, and geopolitical sectors. These cooperation agreements of expunged tariffs and trade production expanded a colonial project with devastating consequences for precious ecosystems, natural resources, and vulnerable populations dominated by the exploitative and corrupt forces of nation-states and corporations. The Americas are the "extractive zone," which Macarena Gómez-Barris calls "the colonial paradigm, worldview, and technologies that mark out regions of 'high biodiversity' in order to reduce life to capitalist resource conversion."[14] In a multinational corporate landscape, a workforce mainly composed of women and Indigenous laborers, vulnerable populations certain to expand profits and widen dividends, is plentiful. The growing manufacturing sector transformed the US-Mexico border region, for example, as well as the police state with militarized checkpoints, law enforcement, and private security firms concretizing regimes of legality/illegality. The transnational turn in Latinx studies affirmed how worldwide forces reshape immigrant lives in ways ill-conceived when ethnic studies programs were first institutionalized in US universities in the 1960s and 1970s. Whether making transparent Latinx immigration through stoop labor akin to the United Farm Workers movement or through factory work in predatory *maquilas*, the field conflates the Latinx body politic with land-based imagery as anchors, border dwellers, or mud people.[15]

Consider how South Texas artist Celeste De Luna's print *Breech Baby* (see figure I.4) draws on this connotation. Here she interrogates xenophobic anxiety over immigrant women's unborn children, which weaponizes fetuses as covert threats to a US citizen-body. These babies literally breach borders, trespass property lines, violate legal citizenship laws, and thus become the

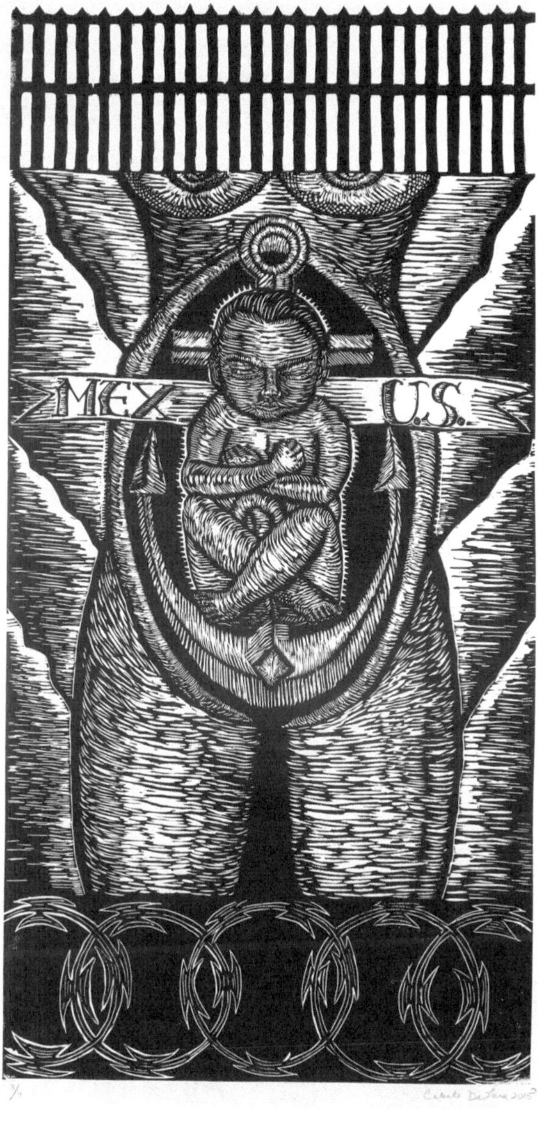

I.4 Celeste De Luna, *Breech Baby*, 2015. Woodcut print, 24 × 48 in. Image courtesy of the artist.

means to subvert deportation and legitimately *anchor* the undocumented family in the United States. The grounded impetus of her print crystallizes a visual vocabulary tying the cisgender immigrant woman and her womb to the land. Her imagery underscores an episteme that scholars like Frances Aparicio observe in terms of Latinx ethnoracial formation: "The condition of being Latina/o, today it is more strongly *anchored* in the social, everyday realities of our diasporic communities. . . . It now signals the mutual transculturations and *horizontal* hierarchies that emerge in these spaces."[16] Her comments implicitly point to the bidirectional axis that humanists and social scientists tether to Latinidades as a category, not to mention a preexistent and uniform reality.

These presuppositions aside, Latinx studies also scales upward, and this path is captured in concepts like the "vertical border," which describes the multiple checkpoints from southern Mexico to the US-Mexico border that Central American migrants experience, most specifically.[17] This northward transit is vertical "to critique the proliferation of immigration enforcement in Mexico's interior" and thus to imagine "state power in a spatially linear, ahistorical and top-down framework."[18] As a social science advance in the field, it is inadequately flat. Nowhere is the vertical border outside the properties of the physical world, and so its meaning is metaphorically relayed. This connotative language is equally reminiscent of Gómez-Barris's conception of "vertical seeing."[19] She articulates how colonial and state apparatuses operationalize "territorial oversight" into "visual regimes normalized [as an] extractive planetary view that continues to facilitate capitalist expansion, especially upon resource-rich Indigenous territories."[20] Her point curiously pairs with the colonial surveillants mastering the land in a way that Nicholas Mirzoeff also observes (discussed in chapter 1). My position is not to diminish how this hierarchal visual arrangement or what Gómez-Barris calls the "extractive view" consolidates "an increasing planetary system of control."[21] However, aerial scaling in the broadest sense should not overlook the ancient Indigenous lifeways, cosmologies, and speculative discernments, which created sources of cultural knowledge indebted to intimacies, enmeshments, and looks toward the solar system.

Precedents of this transplanetary-relational shift exceed contemporary times. We need only consider how "[Hernán] Cortés was able to easily defeat the powerful Moctezuma, an accomplished astronomer and astrologer, in part because Moctezuma recently had witnessed eight omens that had come to him in a dream, suggesting the end of his reign."[22] One interpretation from the Florentine Codex predicted that the collapse of the Aztec civilization came on the tail of a comet that the emperor observed in the sky. Visions, visionaries, and reenvisionings animate a relationship with outer space that complicates the status of verticality in transnational approaches in Latinx studies. To grasp this directional transformation for the field, another framework is needed to shift this ethnoracial population's Earth-bound definition elsewhere. But what are we to call a Latinx study in community with celestial bodies, astronomical phenomena, and other worldly realms? More specific, what happens to a racialized visual field like Latinx art when faced by the alternative terms of representation that I am describing? And what approach to take?

This book proposes a theory and method of doing an art history of the Americas that I term *transplanetary relationality*. The four modalities that support its operation—aberrant vision, elevated scale, star-powered movement, and scientific visualization/materialization—I explore more fully in the first chapter. For now, I introduce the historical and cultural scaffolds undergirding my rationale for a transplanetary-relational turn. I explain why Latinx artists practicing at the cusp of art, science, and speculation are little regarded—obscured, even. And I explore the whys behind this veil: a triangulation of how "science fiction art" mediated lowbrow channels in the first half of the twentieth century, how the Apollo program galvanized artistic responses that contradicted or fit uncomfortably around the political tumult of the civil rights era, and how identitarian discourses of nation and period in US and Latin American art historical canons struggled to assimilate the propulsive pathways produced by these artists who frustrate categories of time and place. The introduction closes by elucidating how transplanetary relationality pairs with scholarly alternative futurity projects, which have yet to grapple with Latinx creatives' space-based thinking: artists for whom aerospace technology, ancient cosmology, astronomical data visualization, or modern space history is central to their practice.

Could lunar regolith simulants or outer planets ever be as important as an aerosol spray can is to Latinx creative expression? The artists centering this study believe so. This art-science and speculative overlap nuances how the dispersed group of Latinx visionaries discussed here are linked because of viewpoint and vertical orientation: being in community with the vast expanse of outer space. Together, they find alternative forms of expression in transplanetary relation, reclaiming and remaking a place between this and other worlds.

Toward Transplanetary Relationality

Transplanetary relationality presents an ongoing yet little-conceived approach for art history, a field with not only less favorable views about science fiction as art but also remarkably little discussion about how these artists access speculative expressions and what to discern from that extrapolation. This simplicity misses the transformative process that results when we invite the possibilities of trans- or trans-ing the planet into the art-making fold. Because the Latin root of *trans-* refers to "across, to or on the farther side of, beyond, over" in the *Oxford English Dictionary,* I am compelled to think about the way this prefix traffics in *change* in ways proposed by Afrofuturist writer Octavia Butler, who argues that science fiction, "more than any other genre, deals with change—change in science and technology, social change. But [science fiction] itself changes slowly, often under protest."[23] Although Butler exposes the genre's perpetuation of whiteness, she also lauds the field's historic courtship of change, advancement, and, more to the point, transformation. In this way, her advocacy for minoritarian intervention in science-fictional customs curiously pairs with both transgender studies and visual culture studies as areas inherently interested in speculation and the beyond. Francisco Galarte makes this conjunction clearer because "transformations that are material, discursive, and affective . . . might describe forms of attachments, disciplining, and enmeshments that are not solely attributed to bodies that subjectively identify and/or are identified as being transgender."[24]

These "enmeshments," as Galarte describes them, could also be "temporal practices" that align alongside higher, metaphysical, and celestial bodies.[25] To be in *trans*ition with this and other planets, we are afforded "expansive forms of difference, haptic relations of knowing, uncertain modes of being, and the disaggregation of identity politics," according to Jack Halberstam.[26] The strange shapes that emerge from that kind of communion with the universe's vastness are less preoccupied with an "abstract ball covered in latitudes and longitudes, cut by virtual lines, once the equator and the tropics and so on," as Gayatri Spivak observed about the globe.[27] By grasping the trans-ing potential of Latinx art and speculative study, our attention is no longer about a colonial project of conquest or mastery of territory and less still about an exploration of space for extractive capital purposes. Rather, the relationality provoked here is akin to Spivak's "species of alterity"; as "planetary creatures," we belong to biodiverse systems, remap our social worlds and even elevate our viewpoint to the outer limits with an aerial climb.[28] By dethroning a human-centered domination of this and other planets in ways that underwrite astronomical knowledge, a transplanetary relation covets the solar system to sidestep a "techno-dominance" posturing, which Ginsburg refers to as "the ways technologies and technology-based rhetoric or imagery interact with, maintain, and facilitate colonization and authoritarianism."[29]

Rather, it espouses a linkage to outer space to elicit another kind of transitioning when the body adapts to, aligns with, and even feels the cosmos.

While I expand on specific modes of transplanetary relationality in vision, scale, movement, and visual/material expression in the first chapter, this trans-ing enmeshment reoccurs and has critical consequence for the meaning, interpretation, and making of Latinx art as it cuts across other worlds, timescales, and bodies (of physical and cosmic proportions). Because this creative register negotiates with astronomic objects of grand immensity, what is perceptually legible and thus categorically recognizable as Latinx art must transform. Timothy Morton's argument about hyperobjects as "things that are massively distributed in time and space relative to humans" is insightful in this regard.[30] *Hyper* in that they "occupy a high-dimensional phase space that results in their being invisible to humans for stretches of time," these "entities," as he calls them, "cause us to reflect on our very place on Earth and in the cosmos."[31] Whether we consider the ancient geoglyphs of the Nazca people in the Andes or even that oscilloscope frequency bouncing on my dad's flat-screen television, we confront "scalar dilemmas" in which our coexistence with geological, climatic, ecological, or planetary dimensions envelops us in ways that complicate an anthropomorphic centering of the universe.[32] According to Morton, "Hyperobjects have magnified this weirdness of things for our inspection: things are themselves, but we can't point to them directly."[33] Because the magnitude of the universe is something that we are always in, these trans-ing "enmeshments," as Galarte calls them, hint at how the art practices centering this study bristle at Latinx art's present space-time orientation.[34] Even as I employ this art category in my analysis, I do so to encourage a means of visual study that embraces Latinidades' immensity, strange shapes, and "weirdness of things." By thinking speculatively, art historical operations about artworks in observable reality or mediated by firsthand visual investigations destabilize, change, and even ascend. As a result, pursuing a study of this type inherently questions what can be satisfactorily assessed with the naked eye and, in turn, considered a "good object" to submit to visual study's evaluative protocols.

With a transplanetary-relational approach, we expose fine art's frustration to make sense of "bad objects" that upset aesthetic experience, linear chronology, scope, and first-person assessments contrary to our grounded surrounds. In this way, a meteorite is equal to Salvadoran art as both become reflections of a common liminal place in art historical discourse. Such comparisons grow more salient in Beatriz Cortez's *Cosmic Mirror (Sky over Los Angeles)* (2022), where steel boulders plot dual pathways to the stars and

Central America, a biomimicry of Latinx art that, like rafa esparza's adobe platforms, sends audiences into a relationship with the planet that is transitory (see chapter 3). As A. Joan Saab puts it about ways of seeing wondrous and fantastic curios, "The viewer must simultaneously suspend rational belief systems yet also maintain certainty in the authenticity of the object on display or the site in question and their transcendent powers."[35] While she is mainly speaking of devotional or divine objects, the art-science and speculative intersections germane to my study pose methodological quagmires because this kind of relationality and its expressive articulation complicate a Latinx art grounded in present space-time. This investigation assembles cross sections of artworks in transplanetary relation to show how these unusual pairings, combinations, and co-conjugations demand another approach for a creativity that weirdly entangles with other timescales, expanses, and cosmic bodies beyond the Western colonial foundations of the seeing world. This approach is necessary to explain how other folks of color like my dad transform being in touch with or touched by otherworldly existences. By transitioning Latinx visual culture study toward its outer limits, we can delimit which lane is suitable for arts research from the ground up.

When we move toward these artists' ascendant reach, the terrestrial definitions of Latinx creativity retract, as previously discussed. Instead, this art making's scientific and speculative potency is enhanced and accentuated. As my father's obscurity as a purveyor and custodian of the finest "bad" science fiction media foretells, speculative expression is innovative, and Latinxs, as this book reveals, have long participated in image making versed in the genre traffic of science fiction, fantasy, supernatural horror, the paranormal, weird tales, and, in a Latinx context, the satirical and political narratives of the "illegal alien." These gregarious proposals are unevenly addressed in Latinx art history and even visual culture studies more broadly despite their pervasive presences. When they appear, they are typically under the guise of graphic novels, cartoons, comic book illustrations, or slash fiction (areas worthy of study but unrepresented in this book because of this tendency in literary studies). Even scholar John Morán González underscores the genre's political efficacy because it empowers Mexican American writers "to articulate their most pressing aesthetic and social concerns," a trajectory he predicts will trailblaze the future of Chicanx literature.[36] Since the time of his writing, a spate of publications, special-themed journal issues, anthologies, monographs, art exhibitions, and conferences have posed bold questions about not only Chicanxs' but also Latinxs' "collective futures" where "the hoary ghosts of colonialism and modernity . . . continue to exert force through globalization and neoliberal capitalism."[37] According to Cathryn Josefina Merla-Watson and B. V. Olguín, "Since at least the 1970s [Latinx cultural producers] have continued to repurpose and blend genres of sci-fi, horror, and fantasy to defamiliarize the ways in which the past continues to haunt the present and future."[38]

Of course, situating Latinx science fiction in terms of a post–civil rights timeline obscures its precursors in not only literature but also visual arts. Had these genre aficionados turned to the artistic record, they would have seen an incredible image archive complicating claims like those lauded by Christopher González, who asks, "Why are there so few such [science fiction] works created by Latinos in the United States?"[39] To examine artworks or performance arts would unveil a Latinx penchant for space science history, technology, and extrapolations about the universe that spans the Americas in several watershed moments from the history of Latin American art. Some readers may consider works not extensively analyzed in this book, such as Rufino Tamayo's steel sculptural ruminations on the cosmos, Raquel Forner's "astrofauna" spacefaring adventurers, Édgar Negret's "aparato mágico" (magical devices), and Remedios Varo's flying contraptions. While these creatives could be called "science fiction artists," their citations are manifold in postwar art history, though they are often appraised opposite their Latinx counterparts in the United States.[40]

This divide aside, I want to underscore how speculative fiction and popular science have dually excited the creativity of the artists centered in my study. Again, these literary forms combine image and text in ways that influence not only Latin American readers but also stateside Latinx creatives. These encounters through the printed page bolster interdisciplinary visual vocabularies with great impact for these visionaries. *Transplanetary Americas* points to the ways in which science fiction writing inspires artistic questions and practices. One might consider how Clarissa Tossin read Octavia Butler for the writer's speculative attention to a dystopian Amazon (chapter 5), Vincent Ramos exchanged correspondence with an aged Ray Bradbury and found Venice anew (chapter 4), Dario Robleto was drawn to the popular science writing of Carl Sagan in his production of nineteenth century–inspired vitrine displays (chapter 2), and Vincent Valdez and Ry Cooder were exchanging ideas through the dime-store paperback illustrations of Gerald Gregg, the airbrush trailblazer who coincidentally was born in my dad's hometown of Lamar, Colorado (chapter 4).[41] Simply, the way speculative print culture was bandied about by artists of the Americas demonstrates how transplanetary relations were nurturing viewpoints from literature to the sky.

Artists like those included in this study remain neglected not only in Latinx art history but across other disciplines as well: literary studies, performance studies, speculative studies, and popular science studies, to name a few. This myopia more than demands an interdisciplinary rebuttal. Such obscurity persists because studies of race and genre in literature and visual culture confront a triple bind.

First, because science fiction circulated in the commercial channels of the wonderfully distasteful record of cheap paperbacks, periodicals, and pulp magazines (a shorthand referring to the pulpwood paper they were printed on), the cover art that formed a "gateway" for readers is deemed too lowbrow to merit attention.[42] In addition, despite the early contributions of Latinx creatives such as Ale de Cañedo, Alex Schomburg, and Luis Senarens of *Frank Reade Library* fame, most cover artists worked for hire.[43] Their contributions to short fiction writing, design, cartooning, and graphic arts are rarely tracked as Latinx cultural texts; and so, their legitimacy as arbiters of the field since the first half of the twentieth century is missing or minimized. As a result, the history of science fiction cover art and illustration is remade into what Merla-Watson and Olguín call "historically . . . a largely white, male, Eurocentric, and heteronormative genre."[44] Catherine Ramírez concludes that the genre cultivated "a middle-class, white, male, adolescent nerd" culture, exactly the group whose preparation for meeting Cold War threats was considered vital.[45] Minoritarian subjects were left out of the equation entirely, while no one seemed aware that these fictional gateways to elsewhere were cultivated by artists of Latin American descent.

Second, the US space program was created in the image of white heteromasculinity, with cisgender men composing the earliest astronaut recruits. The Anglocentrism of the Apollo program, in particular, eclipsed gender and ethnic minorities from the nation's pictorial history of astronautics in image and photojournalist archives. As historian Neil Maher concludes, "Strong, masculine, physically active astronauts appealed to Americans because they symbolized a nation of strong, masculine, physically active men."[46] Scholar Sean Topham also notes, "Their pictures were all over the press, they were used to endorse products from cameras to cars, and they even appeared on television chat shows . . . [bringing] a human face to the space age."[47] Indeed, that human face was without racial or gender differences even though NASA subcontractor Dr. Randall Lovelace had thirteen women undergo the same rigorous testing that the *Mercury* crew candidates endured in New Mexican facilities. His efforts were thwarted by order of Vice President Lyndon B. Johnson, who told NASA, "Let's stop this now!"[48] What did emerge were pictures of the Mercury 7's wives as domestic window dressing in the pages of *Life* magazine.[49] Instead of mirroring the many civil rights actions during this period, the astronaut program perpetuated a vision of space rife with misogyny and gender exclusionism.[50]

Third, this myopia further extends under a modern and contemporary art museum and culture industry suspicious of aesthetic expressions predicated on any of the elements just discussed: lowbrow amusement, dime-novel illustration, and scientific data visualization. Although exceptions are found, the reach of Latinx and Chicanx creatives is largely omitted from this repertoire.[51] Part of this book's intervention reintroduces artists who over the past three decades have responded to or practiced in the United States. However, this study thus extends this orbit from the perspective of US racialization to an art-science and speculative conjunction. What happens to "being Latina/o" when *racial formation*, a term that scholars Michael Omi and Howard Winant define as the state structures, laws, and other apparatuses of oppression that organize race into social hierarchies, extends to the cosmos?[52] Emphasizing how these artists' heterogeneous connection to science fiction and space science twists and turns makes it necessary to complicate the identitarian rubrics in which Latin American and American art are based, the nation-period organization of art historical study, and terrestrial definitions of national belonging. Arlene Dávila crystallizes the affordances that "national privilege" provides Latinx artists, which grants access to an art marketplace broken into categories by country, chronology, or even national movement.[53] Such saliency allows uncomplicated or "geographically bounded definitions of authenticity."[54] As a result, one's national identity can enhance access to promotional circuits in which art dealers, gallerists, festival programmers, curators, and tastemakers improve an artist's standing and legibility. Dávila's point further crystallizes the terrestrial investments of major art establishments predicated on geopolitics and territorial delineations.

While I do not dispute the powerful material regard for mobilizing "Latinx art history," I also forward "art of the Americas," aware of the unsatisfactory application of terminology for artists whose space-time, viewpoint, and outlook on reality are transitory and thus incompatible with a US system of racialization in the present. Artist Beatriz Cortez captures this sentiment when she argues, "I don't have an investment of having a US centered identity, even though I see myself as a US artist, I don't have an investment of imagining Central American nationalism. . . . I'm interested in the Central American experience of people."[55] For Cortez, like other artists in this study, the imaginative project of Latinidades makes speculation a profound contribution to cultural identities in its trans-ing capacities, its strange shapes, and its aerial standpoints. Cortez and others in this book do more than create art about outer space; they demand institutional regard for alternative experiences and expressions that are "more of a hyperobject than a human life."[56] Her comment underscores Sjoerd Van Tuinen's supposition that "whereas aesthetics already binds the contemporary to the empirical status quo of its immediate past and implements the hermeneutic relations between the object and its observer or reader, only a new, speculative proposition can make us grasp contemporary art in its heterochronic contemporaneity."[57] The challenge that this expressivity presents to the field of art history and Latinx cultural studies writ large is how affiliating with outer worlds "cause[s] us to reflect on our very place on Earth and in the cosmos," as Morton writes.[58] A transplanetary-relational approach strives to understand how and why these artists' propensity to look outward and upward is an important cultural reset because it nuances Dávila's contention that national categories "[make] Latinx creativity impossible to imagine."[59] In fact, impossibility is invigorating here. If one recognizes art practices that are simply at the outer limits, the definitional categories matter less and Latinidades takes ascending forms.

Many Futures | *Muchos Futuros*

The artwork I describe here may appear to represent a more traditional return to the genre's origins when Hugo Gernsback's "scientification" discourse from the US interwar years boosted "anecdotal tall tales spiced with technically inclined questions" and, in turn, forwarded "new methods of story-telling" with plausible techno-science outcomes.[60] More important, these visual vocabularies also reflect on what Cortez refers to as "untimely conversations." She argues, "We can create a community across time. . . . The idea that we can choose our own contemporaries, they don't have to be the people next to us, our contemporaries can be the people that we decide . . . including the ancestors that were building in stone."[61] Building with the ancestors is another way of accessing "new methods of story-telling" and "new technologies" of space, time, and futurity that aren't so new after all.[62] Artists focusing this book establish how transplanetary-relational approaches in art making are done. Less about replicating first-world science with its firm grip on planetary resources and extractive colonial intent, they work in collaboration with and on behalf of the planet, universe, and ancient epochs.

Understanding Latinidades' outer limits means that the hierarchical powers of aerospace technology are subverted. Earth's atmosphere democratizes as Latinx creatives enable a vertical borderland for liberation and imaginative possibility. Kapton tape, lunar regolith simulant, solar panels, capsule modules, and shiny exterior plating may appear to be the inventory for a NASA space mission, but these items also form the material register through which these artists commune with the cosmos and remake the US space program in the image of themselves and their communities. By reclaiming the skies and speculating on space histories detached from the grip of Westernized space-industry capitalists, they articulate other ways to express political concerns and to stage actions that commune with the planetary systems to which they belong.

These transplanetary-relational pathways are made with an anticipatory impulse that echoes what Catherine Ramírez dubbed *Chicanafuturism* in 2002.[63] Her influential neologism forwarded a way of doing Latinx science fiction closely inlaid with art and feminist of color differential consciousness that "permits functioning within yet beyond the demands of dominant ideology"; like "kinetic motion," it "maneuvers, poetically transfigures, and orchestrates while demanding alienation, perversion, and reformation in both spectators and practitioners," according to Chela Sandoval.[64] By transfiguring the hegemonic voice of *Chicano* cultural nationalism, Ramírez equally ponders, "What happens to Chicana/o texts when we read them as science fiction?"[65] Her work covers a swath of important visual and literary publications. She locates science-fictional tendencies in the writing of Gloria Anzaldúa but also contemplates the work of Hispana folk artist Marion Martinez, who salvaged circuit boards and computer waste from New Mexican landfills to re-create Indigenous and Catholic icons in a wired technofuturist image of tomorrow. Ramírez writes that Chicanafuturism is "Chicano cultural production that attends to cultural transformations resulting from new and everyday technologies (including their detritus); that excavates, creates, and alters narratives of identity, technology, and the future; that interrogates the promises of science and technology; and that redefines humanism and the human."[66]

Her definition is indebted to the important foundations established by *Afrofuturism*, a term first coined by Mark Dery in 1994 and later operationalized by Alondra Nelson, who grew an online community connecting people for whom "technology, fantasy, and ideas about the future could advance

Black life" in the early days of the Web 2.0.[67] Ytasha Womack clarifies how Afrofuturism operationalizes Black epistemology, ontology, and aesthetics, identifying the concept as "another dream tool in the arsenal to contemplate what may be coming."[68] Such preparedness expands on the forward-sighted foundations of Afrofuturism because "artists . . . invoking space through sound, word, and visuals that appear to collapse time to help us reexperience ourselves—unveil a new lens on the potentialities around us."[69] Her commentary complements that of Ramírez, who concludes that Chicana futurist art "dares to imagine new ways of being in the future," affirming that these futurity projects are in close proximity as both praise the empowering promise of dreamers, whether as a toolkit for social justice or a legislative compromise for foreign-born children raised in the United States seeking citizenship.[70] Although these open-ended outcomes anticipate "freedom" in different ways—"terrestrial bondage" signifies differently for an African diasporic population than a Mexican American one—both frameworks "imagine a future as such within the limits of the here and now[,] ultimately rais[ing] speculative questions about how material conditions would have to be transformed in order to support widespread expectations of the future," as Curtis Marez notes about the "imaginative labor" farmworkers forged in pursuit of better tomorrows.[71]

In their mutual investigations into the elsewhere, the imaginary, and the impossible, artists of color are jointly aware of the politically empowering promise of the genre and, as chapter 4 makes clear, are proposing their own speculative cycles in film and other media arts. Certainly, transplanetary relationality also attunes to the "potential blueprints of a world not quite here, a horizon of possibility, not a fixed schema," as José Esteban Muñoz puts it.[72] However, as a theory and method, it differs through its emphasis on the gestural language of looking up, a radiant arc for Latinx futurity that reconfigures the terms of art making and accentuates the meaning of celestial bodies, planetary systems, constellations, and star clusters for the study of Latinx creativity. As this skyward comportment once stirred an eagle-eyed Moctezuma, who foresaw the fall of the Aztec empire in the stars, these artists do the same linking themselves in stretches of generations, species, eras, and even worlds. Although the future has always been present in civil rights movements, mobilized in ways that "dream and enact new and better pleasures, other ways of being in the world, and ultimately new worlds," as Muñoz argues, a transplanetary-relational approach for Latinx art and cultural study separates from that "horizon," seeking answers through the enormity of the universe.[73] What is demanded is another way to do art history, to seek appraisals that deliberately transgress the bounds of progressive time and cogent realities, embracing expressions that activate Earth's terrestrial stage through unapologetic ascent.

As a result, a traditional art history committed to Western progressive chronologies must be rethought, emptying terms like *modern*, *contemporary*, *new*, and *now*. Artworks of a transplanetary relationality propose a "futural vector outside of historical time and chronological determination," making "all those forces that never cease to invert the whole system of the fine arts and its orderly linear progression into a simultaneous multiplicity of virtual becomings."[74] This temporal patchwork invites the "suspen[sion] [of] rational belief systems," as Saab argues, and illuminates the invaluable role of the not-yet, the to-be-seen, and the what-is-to-come.[75] To practice visual study in this way allows for classic counterfactual questioning to grow in importance for cultural assessment. By applying "what if" inquiry to categorical definitions of "contemporary art," "contemporary performance," and "contemporary craft," we find that "the temporal tangle" of artists in transplanetary relation ultimately resets the terms of Latinx art and art of the Americas more broadly.[76] Just as Armen Avanessian observes that "despite [art historians'] interest in and engagement with contemporary art, most . . . have trouble evaluating art that is being created in their own time, art that points the way, i.e. the way to the future," the unevenly heterochronic or asynchronous orientation of these creatives' ascendant orientations demands speculative ways of evaluating art making on pace with different existences, different clocks.[77]

A mélange of artists in this book fits uncomfortably around Western and colonial timescale, reality, and becoming and thus illuminates other relationships with Earth that place as much emphasis on ancient Mesoamerica as on future outer planets. By honoring their "knotty and porous relationship to time," I advocate for a transplanetary-relational approach that allows these image makers' experimental questions about the inner workings of the universe to guide a more robust and counterfactual art history. By looking up, unveiling how the tools of visual study may have more in common with those of astrophysicists, aerospace engineers, and practical effects technicians than of fine-art arbiters and aesthete gatekeepers becomes possible.[78]

This ascendant viewpoint remains the most profound yet unsaid register of Latinx creativity in the twentieth and twenty-first centuries. "Where to go, if not up?" the creatives investigated in this book appear to ask. Think of a transplanetary-relational approach as the star map outlining the routes Latinx cultural responses to the outer limits have taken, still need to take, and will use to get there.

Structure of This Study

Four case studies ruminate on Latinx creatives' art, science, and speculative scaffolds. This book offers a transdisciplinary theoretical and methodological framework indebted to a cross section of fields: art history of the Americas, speculative studies, cultures of science and technology, critical ethnic studies, performance studies, queer of color critique, transgender studies, Chicana and Latina feminist thought, Latinx cultural studies, and museum/exhibition studies. The approach showcased here further benefits from other fieldwork practices: close and comparative picture reading, literary analysis, media narrative analysis, art ethnography, curatorial study, and archive historiography. The voices of artists enrich this study, drawn from interviews conducted by space historian Matthew Shindell and me for the Smithsonian National Air and Space Museum.

As for the origins of speculative studies, literature and motion pictures foreground case studies with four foci elucidating how media-specific practices like public art, installation and spatial aesthetics, practical effects technology, and art activism sharpen Latinx transplanetary-relational approaches with respect to image, materiality, and scale. Chapter 1 establishes the theoretical and methodological underpinnings of a transplanetary-relational framework. It explicates how this art, speculation, and science fulcrum is made possible through four modalities rarely explored in Latinx art, performance, and visual culture studies. Aberrant vision, elevated scale, star-powered movement, and scientific visualization/materialization enhance different scaling, showing how looking up is attuned to viewpoints that are vertically aligned, scientifically proficient, and perceptually aware of encounters with the universe from present astronomical resources and ancient Indigenous perspectives. Artworks by Amalia Mesa-Bains, Celia Alvarez Muñoz, Alexander Maldonado, and Simón Vega nuance a vocabulary of art making about celestial phenomena. By bringing aerial surveillance, telescope history, stargazing, and scientific visual renderings into an important amalgamation, they debunk terrestrial definitions of Latinidades and show how migration and border discourse share much with space-based thinking.

Chapter 2 pivots on Ernest Hogan's urban science fiction adventure *Cortez on Jupiter* (1990) to unfetter the future of street art. *Barrio futurism*, as I term it, was no work of fiction but an important strand of post-1960s Chicanx public art practice. Transporting multiethnic publics in Southern California to outer worlds, mural activations like Richard Haro's *Outer Space* (1977), the lunar surface in the East Los Streetscapers' *Moonscapes* (1978), and stars' natural longevity, featured in Vargas-Suarez Universal's *Starcycle* (2014), bring this form of postrevolutionary Mexican political communication someplace beyond material reality. In turn, Latinx viewers arrive at other points of departure that necessitate another evaluative language for murals placed in the vastness of outer space. These futurist musings reveal the muralists' stakes in astronautics, further demonstrating a Latinx cultural politics invested in human spaceflight and off-Earth address.

Beyond the static expression of painting on walls, chapter 3 addresses site-specific installations where stairways, portals, and platforms sensorially cohabitate with deep space. The chapter focuses on Central America as an uncanny playground of Cold War violence and a terrestrial landing from which the NASA Artists Cooperative Program pontificated on the United States' astronautic future in the 1960s. Artists such as Beatriz Cortez, rafa esparza, and Jacqueline Arias reverse these aerial surveys and engage in an "untimely conversation" with ancient Indigenous worldviews that undercut Western and colonial definitions of timescale and progress. Here immigrant laborers build the physical pathways to the stars by "terraforming" the gallery. By recodifying a device familiar to science fiction writers and planetary geoengineers, they resurface sanitized white cubes with extraterrestrial grounds. Together, they rejoin the hands of the builder, toilers of soil, and keepers of the planet in muddy incubators. Whether calcifying these interventions in adobe bricks or oxidizing metals, they stand to remake the museum into a more hospitable environment, one in the image of a great brown world to come.

B-movie rubber suits and flying saucers on strings punctuate an important register combining Latinx creativity with art and technology in chapter 4. Turning to not the sophisticated annals of fine art but instead the pulp archive from the first half of the twentieth century, artists such as Angel Cabrales, Vincent Valdez, and Vincent Ramos revisit science fiction's penchant for gimmicks and low-budget scares to interrogate the monsters stoking atrocities experienced by Latinxs, like border violence, mass deportation, and gentrification. Working in what I term a *Latinf/x sensibility*, they reinvest a rarely considered cultural register—B-movie practical effects—to combat social inequity with lowbrow flourishes and unapologetically bad amusements. Written like a drive-in billing dubbed "Tequila Sci Fi" after Cabrales's poster series, this chapter invites a reading with 3D glasses where the illusory realm stands out to expose the volatile spectacles targeting multiethnic populations. By bringing pulp art into proximity with Latinx art, these creatives dare to make distasteful media palatable and thus propagate a racialized visual language more conversant with late-night cable creature features than with international biennials.

Chapter 5 examines the artistic responses to the "second space race," where private aerospace corporations spearheaded by billionaire tech giants are revitalizing a for-profit defense industry with direct impact on the local Latinx residents in Texas. While companies like SpaceX and Blue Origin are merging their corporate entities into recognizable cultural registers, some Latinx creatives are reacting to the future of spacefaring and spacecraft in ways that their postwar Mexican American predecessors could not have foreseen. Women and queers of color are on the front lines of this battle. Using their incipient Latina space feminist knowledges to reignite art activism, they protest the environmental threat these organizations pose to delicate ecologies, housing markets, and healthy biosystems. With a specific look at the insurgent curatorial and exhibition programs of Celeste De Luna, Nansi Guevara, Josué Rawmírez, and Clarissa Tossin (among others), new fault lines and threats mount, which results in a space art resurgence among Latinx communities. Here a burgeoning cultural field arises from which Chicanas and Latinas defend home, land, waterways, and, more important, airspace. Together, they fight for a future free from impending devastation.

In sum, the art, science, and speculative conjunctions harnessing Latinx creativity in this book are by no means complete. The scope of transplanetary relationality is expansive. The speculative aesthetics underwriting it overlaps with the subgenres of cybernetics, robotics, magical realism, comic book narratives, fantasy, and utopia/dystopia, though these tenets are little rehearsed here as they have been explored to different degrees in other important Latinx cultural studies investigations.[79] However, the approach I present here shows how, despite the sprawl, artists throughout the Americas continually turn skyward for answers. And yet no book-length study has addressed this overlap for Latinx studies, science and technology studies, or art history. Suffice it to say, the synergistic dialogue documented in *Transplanetary Americas* is a first step proving how any position apathetic toward or dismissive of Latinx creative responses to the US space program and its adjoining technologies is willfully misguided.

If anything, this project strives to move us closer to Carmen Lomas Garza's *Camas para Sueños* (*Beds for Dreams*) of 1985 (see plate 3). Here two young women retreat to a roof, moongazing into a humid Kingsville night. Dual variations about dreaming appear in the work: One site is an enclosed preparatory interior space, the girls' bedroom, and the other site is the exposed landing on top of the house, where wondrous dreams also happen. As the gazers recline, visions stir among them as they stare at what lies beyond the clouds. Flecks of white paint add dimension to the darkened vista, appearing as stars, light probes, planets, or even satellites that imbue the sky with fantastical possibilities. The figures in Lomas Garza's work comport in transplanetary relation, tilting their heads and pointing up as they give physical vibrancy to this extraterrestrial sighting.[80] Together, this pair asks the viewer to grasp other perceptual realities in tandem with the universe. What do these young women see beyond their earthly existence? What life exists outside the terrestrial arrest of South Texas and the oppressive grip of gravity, of time and reality? Daring to go to the outer limits at the tips of trees, the arch of asphalt roofing, and the depths of the solar system, this work asks the viewer to dream of life beyond what may seem possible. With a turn of the neck, as Beatriz Cortez gesticulates in chapter 3, these Tejana girls embody an extrapolative act perhaps intended only for Anglo-Texan readers of the *El Paso Herald* in 1927, decades before this scene. "Well, a little star-gazing by El Pasoans now and then won't hurt," it reads. "It's better to look upward than downward."[81]

1

Planet Anew

TOWARD A TRANSPLANETARY-RELATIONAL APPROACH

"Do you suppose that there will ever be Mexicanos in space?" asks Tiburcio Mendez, an enlistee from Tijuana in the US Army. He cases the Vietnamese jungle in Alfredo Véa's wartime novel *Gods Go Begging* (1999).[1] His inquiry breaks the silence of his platoon, as they erupt into a cacophony of chuckles, snickers, and sounds of disbelief. The group of army men more than welcomes this diversion from hunting for enemy soldiers on the ground, not realizing that "a hundred yards away North Vietnamese regulars lifted their heads when the laughter reached them."[2] A collective vision develops within the group, beginning from Mendez's "brown eyes . . . glued to the darkening horizon" and moving toward the other soldiers' upcast looks. "Is that one of those . . . *como se dice . . . satélite . . . uno de los esputniks*?" he asks, to which "some necks craned upward to look. A few tired eyes pulled away from the dull green light of starlight scopes and lifted to the heavens."[3] With eyes driven up, their Cold War paranoia sets in ("It's a spy plane," one remarks), demonstrating that the threat they are facing is coming not only over the "darkening horizon" but also from the sky.[4]

Forming a mutual vision of an advanced Soviet spacecraft elucidates just how this multiracial and multiethnic platoon creates through the night sky a kind of social collectivity which speculates on space, technology, and plausible futures. Although this scene of looking upward invokes mixed reactions ranging from fear to amusement (Cornelius, a solider of African descent, jokingly retorts, "Let's suppose on something real crazy . . . like a bunch of Mexicans flying around in outer space!"), it also captures a shift of vision created by Cold War alarm.[5] Another kind of awareness grows in an "upward . . . look[ing]" direction, moving them from a jungle in Vietnam to the expanse of the solar system.[6] In Véa's novel, the sky is a fantastic but also a terrifying space from which an omen looms predicting the astronautical technology to come.

Another scene of looking up, set on a beach in Mexico a decade before the events of Véa's wartime novel, proved influential in the biography of artist Chaz Bojórquez, whose vision was stirred by a sighting with his uncle in 1957. The young East Los Angeles graffiti artist, equipped with a telescope, caught a glimpse of Sputnik, a symbol of Soviet aerospace engineering and sophistication. What he saw through that telescopic aperture made him realize that "the manmade object was 'designed to look down over nations. [It] saw the entire world as one.'"[7] What that technological surveillance raised for Bojórquez as well as for that US Army platoon in Véa's novel was an existential question about the "interconnectedness of humanity" and the power differentials of being on the ground.[8] Through this self-reflection Bojórquez gazed skyward to experience himself as a Chicano, an artist, and a citizen-subject on the planet anew. "It was that night the world changed for me," he remarked.[9]

Change is a planetary matter for Bojórquez, and as the introduction elucidates, change has been impactful for social movements, speculation studies, and transgender theory as they are mutually preoccupied with the imaginative possibilities of the unknown, of elsewhere. Bojórquez's viewpoint literally *trans*itions and attunes to the world differently at the end of a telescope. This sensory experience of feeling the planet's enormity says something about scaling. With breakthroughs in optical technology, a kind of "techno-wonder," as Joan Saab calls it, "[even] microscopes . . . reveal entire worlds within a drop of water."[10] In seeing with "technological vision," according to Saab, Bojórquez vacillates between scientific discernment and wondrous extrapolation, and thus an alternative outlook on the universe is brought to bear on an ordinary beach in Mexico.[11] Certainly, "the possibility of wonderous encounter within a rational, scientific frame" is a part of the optical instrument innovations that are outlined here.[12] However, what must be emphasized is that this Chicanx artist's recollection is about more than just looking up, a familiar comportment for any novice stargazer. It is about what change is possible as the artist climbs through Mexican skies and embodies an "interconnectedness" to the planet and beyond.[13] As these literary and biographical examples suggest, being Chicanx and affiliating closer to the Kármán line (where outer space begins) suggest entanglements that move Bojórquez and Mendez—and the platoon, for that matter—to ascendant points that unhinge Latinx expressivity from a terrestrial platform on which the study of Latinx art and culture is typically staged.[14]

What to do with these scenes from literature and an artist's biography? Another approach is needed to comprehend what in the introduction I termed *transplanetary relationality*. This theory and method allow for a way to grasp expressivity that mediates the cultures of science, courts speculation, and thus creates a community within outer space. This is not to say that all cultural workers making art about the cosmos in iconographic terms fit in the categorical framework for this study. It is more complex than this. Rather, as the introduction stresses, by understanding how these artworks imagine in their "supposing" work and "crane upward to look," we see how they alter the terrestrial boundaries of Latinx art with alignments that *trans*ition across worlds, timescales, and bodies of aerial and interstellar proportion.[15] We find relations that complicate, if not surpass, Latinidades as a horizontally defined multiethnic and multiracial social collectivity shared by people of Latin American descent. That is, how might we comprehend a Latinx study of art and culture unbounded by gravity, apprehended in its strange becoming and ascendant shapes?

The creatives who are the focus of this book are forwarded not solely for their speculative intentions but also for their art and science conjunctions. They share positions, outlooks, and viewpoints that do not reject US space history as neocolonial fodder but regard its archive as theirs. This study rectifies a gap, showing how Latinx artists have long responded to the modern space program, including its historical precepts, and even rehearsed astronomical thinking germane to the ancient Americas. Through this nimble regard for timelines and imaginaries, these visionaries think with, against, and alongside the vast scope of the universe. Whether we ruminate on Clarissa Tossin's collaboration with the Lunar and Planetary Institute at Rice University in Houston, Texas, or Vargas-Suarez Universal's residency at the NASA (National Aeronautics and Space Administration) Ames Research Center in Mountain View, California, we see that their aerial and outer planetary outlook is cause for another framework to do Latinx art history widely because of its otherworldly expanse. To apprehend this propulsive upward pathway, this chapter explicates the four distinctive features undergirding transplanetary relationality. Why a transplanetary-relational approach in Latinx studies? Simply, transnationalism alone is an insufficient framework for the astronautic and aerospace technological activities that are reformulating the late-capitalist flows of labor, migration, natural resources, and economies circumscribed by global trade and extractive colonialism in the Americas.

Consider, for instance, that the United States and Canada invested $75 million in Mexico in the first quarter of 2022, making the country a pivotal site for the production of aerospace equipment.[16] Border maquiladoras and other manufacturing chains formed "aerospace clusters" with Collins Aerospace, Safran Group, and Beechcraft by opening production campuses there.[17] As Mexico supplies the Global North with the component parts for liftoff, albeit in aviation or nanosatellite assembly, another border region like the Rio Grande Valley in Texas is experiencing rapid changes in tech industry infrastructure as billionaire space baron Elon Musk sets up camp at Boca Chica Beach, a longtime recreational playland for working-class Valley families and Matamoros transcultural residents on the border. As chapter 5 makes transparent, Musk's SpaceX headquarters is sharply redefining the cultural landscape, with spacecraft and launch ports dotting the skyline. The threat of the liquified natural gas (LNG) pipeline through Brownsville, which connects to the Gulf of Mexico, hints at the latest ways in which this burgeoning aerospace enterprise threatens delicate biodiversity and presents environmental risks.[18] Also, locals report harmful physical, psychological, and biological consequences from failed rocket tests and calamitous launches, with domestic landscapes in the borderlands rattling with each blast. If Musk's tumultuous time in Donald Trump's second administration is any indication, then new battles are being waged that are weaponizing the sky and intensifying a billionaire space tech's Martian dream. Of course, people of color have intimate knowledge of racialized and colonial state violence that extends from above.

The transplanetary-relational approach lauded here reverses this polarity and, as a result, attends to ascendant fields that place new demands on Latinx stakes in space-based thinking, creativity, and speculative trajectories. As discussed more extensively in the introduction, these artists look up only to be enmeshed in distanced heights, depths, and "scalar dilemmas" that, Timothy Morton muses, "provoke *irreductionist* thinking" and delimitations of Latinx expressivity's magnitude.[19] In this way, celestial objects, astrogeology, cosmic phenomena, and even a blanket of stars are credible media in need of greater address. This methodological quagmire asks the question: How does one interpret transplanetary relationality, especially as the hermeneutics holding these artworks together operate like a "drop of water" that Saab proposes, a world in which other worlds exist outside the rational circuitries of reality and chronology?[20]

As the introduction establishes, the competing contexts of and discourses over Latinx art, science, and speculation perpetuate blind spots that obscure this pervasive yet understudied visual field in its interdisciplinary traffic. This chapter more closely unfurls transplanetary relationality as a way of doing art history of the Americas that, as Morton contends, enacts a "pull focus . . . simultaneously zooming and pulling away" to make space for aerial forces that push the Americas into vertical alignment, nudging them toward other spheres of knowing in the grand architecture of the outer planets.[21] Like Bojórquez's upward gaze on the beach, this approach is cause to adjust the eye and appraise this visionary work with an equally nimble interpretative skill set for its literalizations.

Four modes represent transplanetary relationality's operations: aberrant vision, elevated scale, star-powered movement, and scientific visualization/materialization. Each locus is given added explanation through correlating artwork by Felipe Dante, Amalia Mesa-Bains, Celia Alvarez Muñoz, Alexander Maldonado, and Simón Vega. Although these modalities build scaffolds articulating transplanetary-relational episodes shaping the field, aspects of each mode (to a greater or lesser degree) yield a coterminous language of Latinx art, science, and speculation. To study an expressivity that spans the universe and communes with proportions that crisscross borders on and off Earth, Latinx art historical and visual culture readers find themselves in positions that are contrary to empirical measure, observation, and diachronic timescales championed in more conventional humanistic inquiry. The vastness of Latinidades expands in ways that place new pressures on Latinxs' cosmic depths. This book considers not only what looking up means for cultural analysis but what the transplanetary-relational contours of an artwork mean for scholarship and for the museum field. This chapter closes by contemplating how curating this material challenges cultural institutions that have either grounded Latinx art in discernible reality or bounded its definition in terms that order and distinguish art from science, highbrow from lowbrow, presentism from temporal disorder, and factual representation from the fictional beyond. Ultimately, this chapter unlocks the stakes of transplanetary relationality and demonstrates how looking up foregrounds this study's gateway out of this world.

Aberrant Vision

Interpreting a transplanetary-relational framework first necessitates understanding why racialized ways of becoming and looking must be separated from earthen terrain, which pervades the foundations of Latinx studies. As outlined in the introduction, social theory, immigration policy, and policing and border studies are deeply entrenched in terrestrial thinking about citizen subjectivity. Such predispositions crystallize in Myrriah Gómez's study of nuclear colonialism in the "third space" of northern New Mexico, where life exists in an "atomic" zone "between the bomb and the bean fields."[22] As she counters hegemonic narratives of the Manhattan Project, which privilege a US "nuclear empire" during World War II, the Latinx and Indigenous laborers and nearby residents of the Los Alamos National Laboratory are "from the land where they farmed, ranched, and remained in tune with the earth."[23] In Gómez's reading, Earth is an ancestral and sacred site that Nuevo Mexicanos tune in to, suggesting a kind of environmental consciousness that is land-based and potentially planetary, though not stated in these terms. This connection is "a nuclear *facultad*" that riffs on Gloria Anzaldúa's ideas about "sensing" deeper realities.[24] In Gómez's use, Nuevo Mexicanos feel their polluted valleys and waterways in a kind of land sense. This idea is visually conveyed in Celeste De Luna's *Breech Baby* (see figure I.4). Her woodcut print of border wall and fencing motifs depicts the image of a faceless immigrant woman and her womb. Seen from above, her body binds to the land masses beneath her. Literally anchored between the physical borders of US and Mexican territory, this figure's land sense is shaped from directional viewpoints above and below. It also shares a vertical outlook, a guideline drawn from art and technological histories of aerial sight and aviation photo technology.

Not long after the colonial atrocities of the Spanish-American War of 1898, which led to the United States' annexation of several Spanish territories in the Caribbean and Pacific (including Cuba, Puerto Rico, Guam, and the Philippines), the Wright brothers made their first successful flight at Kitty Hawk, North Carolina, in 1902; with it, the human flight era began. The airplane marked modernization, avionic technology, and new visual relations that also enforced racial disparity and social control. Aeronautics radically shifted how a security state galvanized the "emergent practices of aerial looking and thinking," as art historian Jason Weems puts it.[25] The airplane's mechanized gaze empowered agricultural industrialists to barnstorm the Great Plains. Cameras mounted onto the wings of aircraft allowed for advancements in the way publics viewed their relationship to land and sky. Flattening the terrain from above empowered government scrutiny, leading to prescriptive determinations from these images with consequence for landscape regulations, city growth, and future real estate prospecting.[26] These photo surveys proffered visual information systems from which agribusiness corporate capital, crop production, and profiteering organized ways of seeing broad and unencumbered terrain with a machinic eye. Weems concludes, "Together, photography and aviation allowed people to radically reconceive their ties to the earth by affording them real images of the land from the new elevated viewing positions created by flight."[27]

However, when Weems speaks of "people," to whom is he referring? The terrestrial stages from which these aerial photos were taken also reinforced racial hierarchies and settler colonial domination and control over tribal lands. To Weems's credit, he acknowledges how an "all-seeing vertical view" is continuous with what Michel Foucault calls the "panopticon," which engenders a "field of visibility" that is tied to modernity and later clearly aids state systems of incarceration and policing.[28] Under the panoptical view, authority is exerted through the intrusive eye as prisoners' placement in honeycombed rooms organized around a security tower expands the state's capacity to control and inspect.[29] This type of surveillance technology structures captive persons within an ocular field of domination. Institutional authority polices and dominates from above while the inmate internalizes and self-disciplines because the omnipotent eye of the state watches.

Although Foucault was speaking in the context of the nineteenth-century prison system, Macarena Gómez-Barris extends his visual theory to "the enclosure, the plantation, the ship, and the reservation, quintessential colonial spaces where power was consolidated through visual regimes."[30] Her position boldly points to the settler colonial and white supremacist authority in this kind of racialized looking, which is intrinsic to the grounds of the plantation complex and the transatlantic world. Not only did plantations materially organize indentured servitude with exploitative systems of slave labor, but they also alienated the workforce from the means of cash-crop production. This "ordering of [plantation] reality," as Nicholas Mirzoeff argues, was made possible through a "system of visualized surveillance" where "oversight," a charged complex of governmental and corporate authority, monitored laborers and dispossessed them from physical, legal, and natural domains.[31] For Mirzoeff, "separations and distinctions" were enforced through overseeing techniques "of mapping that separated and defined slave space and 'free space,'" redrawing a racist enterprise, which organized the landscape on behalf of colonial power.[32]

By asserting ocular authority, these technosurveillants also mastered the environment. Monocrop systems like sugar manufacturing in Barbados left a destructive mark on island habitats where forests were ravaged to produce fires to heat sugar production, resulting in irreversible devastation for delicate ecosystems. Since the seventeenth century, resource extraction and spatial politics have remained a consequential part of visuality's authorial prowess because, as Anna Tsing notes, "plantations dispossess both Indigenous people and indigenous ecologies," making displacement and dislocation another matter of tactical warfare.[33] No one knows this kind of violence better than racialized laborers such as migrant workers, who are "an essentially coerced labor force that's highly vulnerable and kept vulnerable by law and by practice," according to Donna Haraway.[34] She clarifies that "plantation conditions" apply to the exploitive system farmworkers endure. Under the violent duress of a corporate agricultural industry that detaches its workers from autonomy and land and dehumanizes them, the plantation is simply about "out-and-out exterminism."[35]

Haraway's comments second how the plantation system's invasive surveillance dually oversees laborers and resource-rich lands to aid extractive capital, deforestation, mining, and other violations of natural habitats under an elevated, coercive gaze. For Gómez-Barris, this way of looking is akin to "vertical seeing [that] normalized violent removal" with consequences for "capitalist expansion" in aid of "an extractive planetary view."[36] How this is done, she says, is innovated by technologies "enabling a grand-scale view from above."[37] These systems of technological domination are foreshadowed in satellites, telecommunications, and space probes that take "large areas of the planet to convert them into commodities for utilitarian market ends."[38] For her, vertical scale is a mode of seeing that has profound material and physical consequences for Indigenous and ethnoracial publics.

Gómez-Barris's warning, much like Gómez's alarm about a contaminated New Mexican cultural landscape devastated by weapons of war, is predicated on aerial scale and in keeping with a way of looking that bonds the racial other to the ground in a flattened nexus of panoptic state control. "Vertical seeing" may be further observed in the scopic practice of social domination in Curtis Marez's discussion of the physical strains and mutilation that migrant farmworkers experience through stoop labor in the United States.[39] His argument magnifies how aeronautics structured visual relationships between the corporate farm and seasonal worker. Using short-handled hoes (*cortitos*), these farmhands would harvest crops, keeping their backs bent and bodies low to the ground. An upright stance meant fewer profits and less work, and so this draconian piece of farming equipment produced relations of domination and control over the body, maximizing production and increasing profits. As Marez points out, it was a "means of surveillance," reconstituting body politics so that the corporate planter's vision ensured a "sort of panoramic perspective . . . reproducing an unequal set of visual relationships whereby big growers were the subjects, or we might say 'owners,' of the gaze, while farm workers were its objects," anchored by these archaic hand tools.[40] The way in which agribusiness corporations kept ocular order, disciplined the body, and tamed the wilderness is further comprehensible from the photographic archive of Latinx farmworkers.

Felipe Dante's image *Migrant Farmworkers Picking Cauliflower, Stamford, NY* (1973–74) (see figure 1.1) is taken from *Portfolio 1*, an artwork generated for En Foco, a Bronx-based camera club and nonprofit fostering mainly Puerto Rican image production that was founded in 1974. Dante's snapshot unveils the physical hardships of laborers from Puerto Rico picking cauliflower crops in Stamford, New York. They are stooped, hunched, and angled close to the ground. The strain of five farmhands lends a sense of exhaustion as we view their backsides bent close to the soil. Dante shares the same visual plane, and his footing is equally squared up. His camera records faceless workers recoiling from the sun, conveying a sense of anonymity and indifference. The sky was apparently no place for them as they toiled among the crops. However, Dante's photography is traced by Operation Bootstrap. These workers were the by-product of a US neocolonial enterprise stimulating the industrial and agricultural sectors with a surplus of manual laborers. Government-sponsored flights resulted in the largest air-led migration from the Americas by way of "la Guagua Aérea" ("the air bus"). Around World War II, sky traffic facilitated the movement of approximately 760,000 Puerto Ricans who left their island for New York. They shored up US labor shortages and transgressed a "figurative border zone float[ing] above the ocean."[41] Though Dante's image is not an "aerial photograph" in the traditional sense, it does show how these workers' presence in Stamford is a representation of an island agro-economy decimated by US corporate capital investments and an aeronautics industry advancing the migration and deployment of ethnoracial workforces. Labor was renewed as an airborne commodity coming from the island's "modernization" period overseen by the newly elected Governor Luis Marin Muñoz. With the elimination of corporate tax, an industrialized manufacturing market grew. Economic growth predicated on US consumer goods in crops and factories caused a workforce

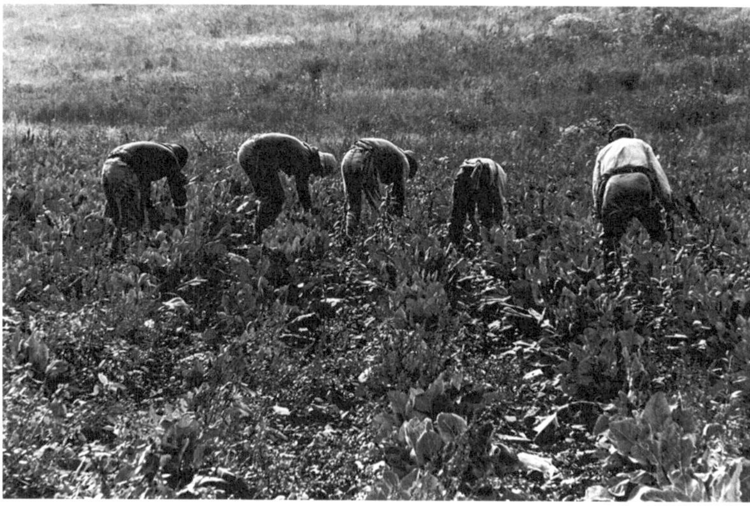

1.1 Felipe Dante, *Migrant Farmworkers Picking Cauliflower, Stamford, NY*, ca. 1973–74. Gelatin silver print, 5½ × 8⅝ in. Courtesy of El Museo del Barrio, New York. Gift of En Foco, Inc., PH92.137.71.

to accept incentives in garment, food service, and corporate farm industries with unexpected points of arrival like Stamford.

As Marez would surely point out, unseen from Dante's social activist lens are the crop dusters spreading fertilizers and pesticides, militarizing aeronautical technology to disperse toxic clouds that extend the life of produce and conversely exterminate the plantation system's vermin: pests, insects, and even immigrants. Their vulnerabilities are cruelly (and even ironically) underwritten by racialized "techno-dominance," in the words of Samuel Ginsburg.[42] Even though Puerto Ricans are a preeminent Latinx population in the State of New York because of plane travel, their aerial sophistication is undercut by an aeronautical subordination. They remain under the tyranny of "terrestrial bondage," and as Dante's image shows, a horizon of neocolonial punishment and visual surveillance arises in the distance.[43] Bound to the ground, these farmworkers' bodies are refused the privileged sight of vertical alignment despite their airborne arrival, hinted at in the photo. The "horizontal gaze" that Weems contends "anchors itself to the fixed position of a singular viewer" is experienced differently from these laborers' perspectives.[44]

As this study unfurls, Latinxs who refuse to be overseen and, in turn, look up counter visual power, subverting scopic dominance allied to the history of colonialism, slavery, racial capitalism, and aeronautical technology where people of color are subjugated from above. But more than sensing the land with *cortitos* under the authority of corporate growers (to borrow from Gómez), they traffic in otherworldly elsewheres.[45] By collectively raising their gazes, they provoke questions about speculative visions that extrapolate possibility from the stars. But how to understand this viewpoint, and why?

In the next section, artists' ascendant looks place renewed emphasis on what scientific instruments do to extend the eye and widen the scale of what is imaginatively possible. For this, some of these image makers turn to the telescope as a source of creative insight and sensory apparatus. With it, they breach the oppressive powers of surveillance and find empowerment in the promise of magnification and reorganization of reality.

Elevated Scale

Transplanetary relationality is not only a practice of aberrant vision but also a study of ratios. With greater attention to proportion, artists in the Americas speculate on other worlds by bringing distant objects close for analysis. These optical lenses introduce macroscopic and microscopic realms, altering how one perceives one's everyday environment and relationship to a tangible and observable reality. Scientific rational truths shift the visual world and do so alongside "speculative observation" or hoaxes affirmed by optometric instruments, according to Saab.[46] These "new forms of vision . . . could substantiate the existence of new worlds and wonderful things," as evidenced by different perceptual scales.[47] From the cellular to the atomic and enlarged, practicing transplanetary relations is a modality of elevated scales crystallizing other substrates that connect to this and outer worlds. As the oft-cited phrase goes, "Objects in the mirror are closer than they appear," and this meaning could not be truer for Latinx creatives negotiating dimension, size, and volume. To understand this outlook, we have to consider the scientific discourse of optics or optometry and its affectual consequences for Latinx artists' sensing of the universe.

Although mathematician Galileo Galilei is credited with discovery of the telescope, that honor precedes him, perhaps owed to other optic tinkerers, such as the German-Dutch craftsman Hans Lipperhey or Jacob Metius. As Fred Watson notes, "There seems little doubt that several spectacle-makers knew the secret of the telescope in the early 1600s," with activity occurring around northern Holland, perhaps taking advantage of Middelburg's glass factory.[48] "The modern consensus is that we will never know for certain who actually invented the telescope," Watson concludes.[49] According to Saab, Lipperhey laid "the groundwork for Galileo's design . . . [which] created a lens that could magnify objects up to twenty times."[50] With this new technology, an improved pursuit of ocular acuity transformed not only the visual but also the sensorial apprehension of Earth's satellites and celestial phenomena. Referencing the historical and political context, Watson observes, "The idea of peering through an eyepiece with one eye—familiar enough today—would have seemed unnatural and bizarre in the early seventeenth century."[51] Even Lipperhey would concede that his invention came in the form of rudimentary binoculars, not with the monocular view traditionally associated with the modern telescope.[52]

However, this "technological vision," as Saab called it, grew uncannier as viewpoints shifted skyward, allowing astronomical observations to rebut the geocentric cosmology popularized under Aristotle.[53] Again, before Galileo, Lipperhey's optical lenses were pointed up, causing a Thai ambassador to remark, "Even the stars, which ordinarily are invisible to our sight and our eyes . . . can be seen by means of this instrument."[54] His visual fascination was seconded by English scientist Thomas Harriot. As early as 1609, he was moongazing. His illustrations of craters on the lunar surface represent some of the first selenographic illustrations, revealing what the synthesis of art and science can visually render through the end of a telescope. That residual look drawn from the skies seconds Graham MacPhee's criticism of the "self-deluding, arrogant, and even potentially dangerous" activity of visual perception by presuming the ideal sighted subject conveying the natural world with clarity.[55] His contention nods to Charles Baudelaire's argument about "the artist as an optical instrument" because "knowledge of the world is built on its prior assumptions about its nature."[56] For MacPhee, this ideal perceptual reader potentially eclipses the opportunity "to think beyond the static nature of the visual form."[57] In the case of Latinx artists in this study, seeing vertically intensifies strange shapes and deep space entities that crystallize with aerial looks. More than perceptual acuity, MacPhee lauds "the prospect of different possible configurations of vision" that sees "through distortion, visual ambiguity, blurring, and dissonance."[58] Artists doing work in transplanetary relation enhance this sensorial counterknowledge, a dissonant scaling for Latinidades with extrapolative questions about the unknown.

This, combined with a modern space program that would expand "technological vision," shifts how the "model of engagement with the world" transforms "the sensory apprehension of appearances."[59] Satellite telescopes and astrophotography create a conundrum for telescopically assisted viewers who gaze upon celestial bodies they may never physically encounter.[60]

Outer space upends the "beautiful appearance" of artistic composition at least in a way unsatisfactory to most formal art historical analyses predicated on firsthand accounts.[61] Pointing skyward, "vision [that] has come to imply a paradigm of meaningfulness based on clarity and coherence" elevates in ways that partake of an "image-world" yielded because of a lack of acuity and a distorted view. "Cast as aberrant, incoherent, and false," that deviant perception imbues the technological field of sight with fantastical proportions.[62] In turn, the perceptual body recasts its sense of belonging, leading an "image of the world that jars with the expectations of the eye" to some extrapolative, extraordinary, or even extraterrestrial place.[63]

As a result, this perceptual work is akin to the "planetary imagination," according to anthropologist Lisa Messeri, practiced by scientists. Her point suggests the creative play-work astronomers enjoy through "an imagination of being on/within/alongside, of experiencing, the planet." Despite a self-proclaimed "placeless" existence in the quiet hum of the mountaintop observatory, they forward "experiential ways of knowing" as an episteme that speculates on existences inspired by science fiction.[64] In this mutual negotiation of rational and irrational belief, they engage in an aberrant casting where their eyes ponder the beyond in ways also reminiscent of the visionary work of creatives.[65] Such echoes of space-based thinking are rarely considered together as astronomer and artist share in similar cultural imaginaries, a practice of elevated scale. Some differences are harder to reconcile. Gómez-Barris's claims of "colonial visual regimes normalized [as] an extractive planetary view" stand, and some artworks in this study may appear to subscribe to this critique and blunt the material consequence of aerospace industries.[66] However, the vertical scale with which Latinx embodied experience climbs to remote outer planetary vistas—ones that were otherwise consequential for Indigenous cosmologies, I might add—invites aberrant directions for those optics. The sensorial resonance aids in other translations and transitions against material worlds that bound, seal, and gag. To scale vertically, these agents working on behalf of transplanetary relations raise incursions against expressivity that reaffirm Westernized colonial knowledge and aesthetic regimes. These aerial looks—whether retrofitted with assets from a telescopic lens or astrophotographic zoom—eye expanses in ways that unfix "terrestrial bondage" and contest gravitational oppression.[67] By raising sight lines that punch through the sky, Latinx creatives relate to the universe with a range of optical measures and haptic experiences that are unaccounted for in the predominant European retelling of art, science, and optometry intersections.

The negotiation of vision and ratio is a proportional shift, a mediation critical, though understated, in Chicana feminist artist Amalia Mesa-Bains's installation *Vanitas: Evidence, Ruin, and Regeneration*. Her scene was featured in Chon Noriega and José Piedra's 1993 exhibition *Revelaciones/Revelations: Hispanic Art of Evanescence* at the Herbert F. Johnson Museum of Art at Cornell University (see figure 1.2). Synthesizing found objects, tchotchkes, and the bricolage of everyday life, Mesa-Bains combines sacred and domestic relics into memorializing discards that resemble *ofrendas*, or domestic home altars. Infusing that spirit into constellations of organic and inorganic detritus, Mesa-Bains places Chicana atomic worlds in microcosmic scale. Whether she is transforming an ordinary vanity into a glittering homage to a Mexican movie siren in *Ofrenda for Dolores del Rio* (1984) or monumentalizing the interior plight of a Latina lesbian nun with writerly and scientific instruments topping her wood-carved desk in *Sor Juana's Library* (1994), Mesa-Bains uses banal domestic furnishings to unearth entry points that arrive elsewhere. These cluttered displays invite serious visual, scientific, even literary engagements "where women's intellectual endeavor[s] took place in parallel with, or outside of, a patriarchal logic of knowledge production and acquisition," as Jennifer González summates.[68] These artifactual arrangements, or what the artist terms "domesticana aesthetics," are versed in the modernist language of assemblage and collage of Kurt Schwitters, Joseph Cornell, Noah Purifoy, and Louise Nevelson, though ringing with mischief and even mockery.[69] "I just feel like museums need to be slapped around from time to time," Mesa-Bains commented in a 2018 interview with *ARTnews*.[70]

Her museum interventionist work and criticism of histories about colonial theft and Indigenous dispossession are often found alongside those of her contemporaries like María Brito, Mark Dion, and Fred Wilson. However, it is Mesa-Bains's skillful attention to the fantastical engineering of the *Wunderkammer*, or cabinets of curiosity, that demonstrates her scientific intentions. By subverting taxonomies of new science, Linnaean classification, and ethnological specimen gathering, she builds on "a collection and display milieu which attempt[s] to be encyclopedic, a microcosm of the entire known world."[71] Pre-Enlightenment technology meant to sample the new world as synecdochic fragments, approximations, and specimens destabilizes. Her presentational format interrogates global exoticism for European fodder and allows for many possible scales to stand in for "other worlds." Mesa-Bains's "overall understandings of the universe" extend, combine, and open other optometries and dimensions in dense layers and aggregations.[72]

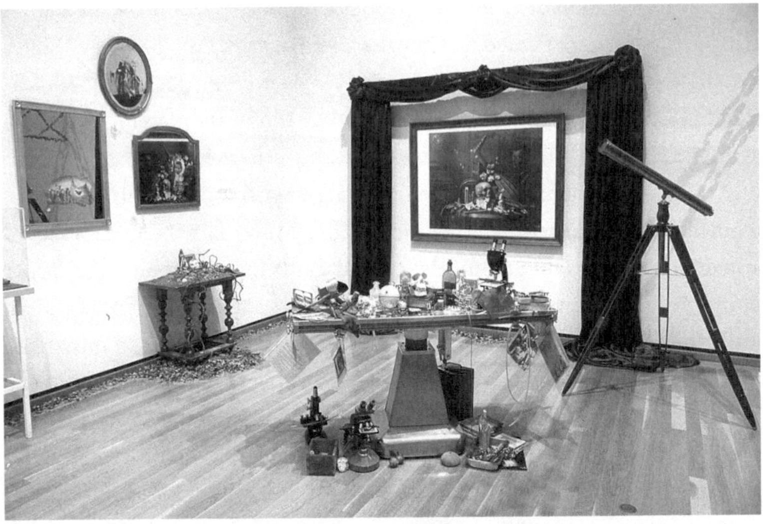

1.2 Amalia Mesa-Bains, *Vanitas: Evidence, Ruin, and Regeneration*, 1993. Installation view, Herbert F. Johnson Museum, Cornell University, New York. Courtesy of the artist. © Amalia Mesa-Bains.

Her aberrant vision honors wonder, scale, and proportionality.[73] Her installation at the Johnson Museum is most exemplary of this shift through its replica of David Bailly's seventeenth-century Dutch painting *Vanitas with Negro Boy*. The artwork hangs on and centers a gallery wall, surrounded by swaths of green satin fabric. Like in a hall of mirrors, authenticity and duplication are shrugged off, much like the Teotihuacán objects cast aside on the adjoining wall. The museum's decision to prevent the artist from using the actual Dutch painting accounts for a scholarly postmortem about the show, critiquing how Mesa-Bains's request for the original was denied although her use of the museum's pre-Columbian collection was unregulated. Critics point to this detail revealing the hierarchy used to evaluate objects with historical integrity and value to the institution. Little scholarly attention, however, has been paid to how the museum negotiated with the artist and instead reproduced a copy of this Dutch "masterpiece," measuring it "to scale." This facsimile suggests how the installation is a maze of institutional authority, art historical biases, and fastidious simulacra. Bailly's stand-in is a "trick of the eye," and so an important element of this installation is about how patrons assign trust to a rational and observable world framed in the museum. What appears to be true is also false. Mesa-Bains's visual culture dilemma—whether incidental or not—is little commented on, perhaps forgettable beneath the detestation that another artwork caused. Daniel Martinez's *The Castle Is Burning* sparked "class bias and racial hatred," thus "be[coming] the catalyst for heated debate on campus," according to Noriega, after its reported vandalization.[74] However, Mesa-Bains was equally confrontational in her take on the institutional past and (im)perceptual present, an exceptional maneuver magnified through a telescopic eye.

In *Vanitas*, optical tools, glass lenses, and scientific instruments cluster atop and at the feet of an examination table borrowed from the university's veterinarian school. Akin to *Sor Juana's Library*, which appeared one year later, its staging is a comparable display of microcosms where globes representing the earth and moon bring celestial and astronomical maps to the seventeenth-century proclivities of a Mexican lesbian nun. For Mesa-Bains, instruments of magnification are cause for audiences to marvel over the transformation of human perception. However, unlike in *Sor Juana's Library*, *Vanitas* adds one more instrument absent from this exercise in scale and proportion: the telescope. Here viewers read race in near and far "associative readings: the African diaspora and indigenous populations (represented by tiny figurines and historical images) [are] subject to devices of observation, speculation, measurement, and investigation," according to González's appraisal of the work.[75] The clustering of micro- and macroscopic technologies concretizes how light and refraction shape the eye with profound implications for how the natural world is perceived. Simply, vision is a matter of scale. How viewers experience that scale alters their sense of being and relating to the universe. This shift in scope has consequence for public appraisal of Chicana art, which is seen and felt at atomic and cosmic levels.

The gilded telescope juxtaposed with the examination table and the Bailly painting invites its user to access visual knowledge about the world's inner and outer workings. Mesa-Bains's environment organizes viewpoints less predisposed to nineteenth-century astronomy and the foundations of optometry; instead, she stations the telescope at the intersection of a memento mori still life and altar in memory of United Farm Workers cofounder and activist Cesar Chavez, who died that year. She presents a "dialogue" "between the terrestrial and the celestial spheres," as Tomás Ybarra-Frausto observes.[76] By hoisting her audience into dimensions near and far, Mesa-Bains suggests that with a telescopic lens transplanetary relations open vertical corridors that elevate Latinidades to its cosmic enormity. By tilting this astronomic instrument upward, she affords directional and proportional sight lines to a pursuit of Latinx visuality and visibility that was already in play at that campus long before her arrival.

The foundation of astronomy at Cornell University dates to the nineteenth century. In 1873 Estevan Antonio Fuertes was recruited under the leadership of university president Andrew Dickson White (see figure 1.3). Fuertes, who was raised in San Juan, Puerto Rico, and graduated from Rensselaer Polytechnic Institute in Troy, New York, brought the field to Cornell in 1874.[77] In 1882 he fought vociferously alongside the chair of the Physics Department, William A. Anthony, to demand that the board of trustees build the campus's first observatory. The $2,000 funding allotted enabled the construction of a "comparatively small building made of wood, and apparently unimportant," as the *Cornell Daily Sun* noted in 1885.[78] In the interim, Fuertes found his way to Europe under President White's charge, where he made "large purchases of apparatus, instruments, models, photographs, and diagrams of various sorts."[79] Fuertes was responsible for curating the instructional equipment for coursework in astronomy theory and practice. His students' summers were "spent in field work, surveying the Finger Lakes."[80] Fuertes's career shone as he worked "on public infrastructure in Puerto Rico, on the Croton aqueduct for New York City, and on early Panama canal surveys for the US Government."[81] He became the engineer in chief for an expedition to Nicaragua and Tehuantepec and other "enterprises in this country and South America."[82] His twenty-nine-year career ended following an illness exacerbated by Bright's disease. He died on January 16, 1903, just one year after his appointment in the newly established Astronomy Department, where he advised on the construction of the A. C. Barnes Observatory.[83] In the aftermath of his death, the new building was honorifically renamed Fuertes Observatory in 1904, affirming his significance in securing the necessary apertures to take that Ivy League campus to the stars. "Without the efforts of this colorful professor," Zachary Newkirk concludes, "Cornell's forays into astronomy may have been stunted."[84]

Though it is unclear whether the telescope Mesa-Bains installed in the gallery was purchased by Fuertes, the instrument was nonetheless borrowed from the university, according to the artist. Its presence in *Vanitas* is a racialized callback to this space science and technology history, perhaps reminding the campus how astronomy came to fruition because of the actions and training of a neocolonial subject, someone who lived under Spanish colonialization, bore witness to the inhumanity of slavery in the Caribbean, experienced the ravages of the Spanish-American War in 1898, and saw the US occupation of Puerto Rico before his death in 1903. In this

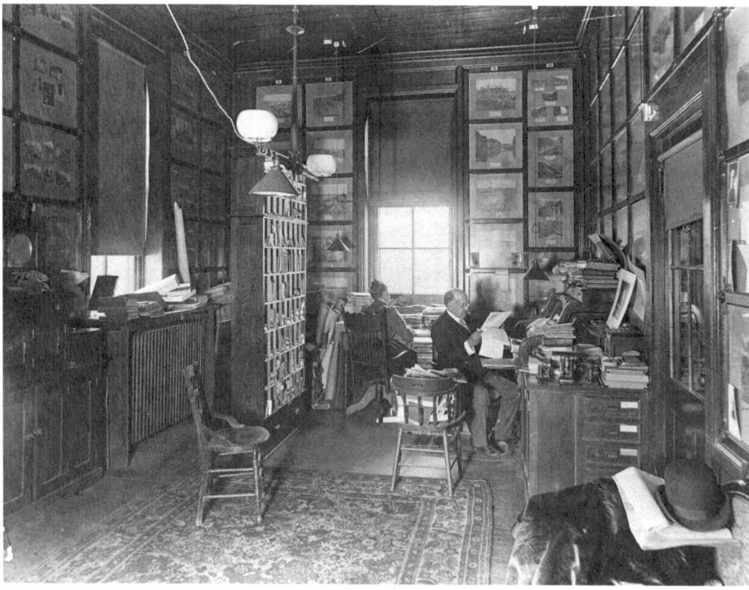

1.3 Estevan Antonio Fuertes, founding dean of the College of Civil Engineering and professor of astronomy at Cornell University, 1870s. Gelatin silver print; dimensions unknown. Archives picture collection, #13-6-2497, Division of Rare and Manuscript Collections, Cornell University Library.

way, Mesa-Bains's broader intellectual investments in Latina feminist and decolonial approaches within institutions that composed collections from enslaved and conquered people subvert sanitized white boxes. Instead, her site-specific approach to art restores the crucial role that a Puerto Rican played in realigning the horizontal and static constitution of the Latinx body politic as laborer, colonial possession, and evidentiary specimen. Her perspective aids in something ascendant, if not transcendent, in tone, transforming the Latinx viewer's perceptible world and relationship to reality. Markers from pre-Columbian ancient times, late nineteenth-century colonial conflicts, and atrocities of African diasporic enslavement in the Americas accrue in the display, showing how somewhere in this stratum of optical and astronomical material is a Puerto Rican scientist who likely not only thought about himself in relationship to a US empirical project but also sought off-Earth escape, tutoring his pupils' eyes skyward over the Finger Lakes. At an elevated scale Fuertes's aberrant looks brought them closer to the cosmos. More than mere stargazing, this astronomical activity is a kind of transplanetary-relational work in late nineteenth-century New York, an homage to a practice enabled by an instrument that holds Latinx historical significance for a campus nearly a century later. With its poetic positioning at the *Revelaciones/Revelations* show, the telescope delineates something truly revelatory happening in the visual translations of sight and transitions of scale.

What Mesa-Bains's installation accomplishes as a spatial aesthetic at the Johnson Museum of Art is rooted in a history of spectacular amusement and learned practices of modern science. Her work recalls a sensorial awareness about deep space performed by Mexican publics documented in the Casasola archives nearly a century before. These prescient scenes are apparent in Anita Brenner's classic study of the Mexican Revolution, where publics' visual literacy intensifies around the sky.[85] These serendipitous happenings of astronomical phenomena are caught on camera and preserved in the photographic archive. One occurrence takes place at the precipice of the revolution in 1910. In it, a couple gathers around the lens of a telescope, edging out a crowd.[86] The man's hands clasp in a concentrated gesture, performing popular science literacy for the camera. His companion pulls back her veil and leans forward, readying her gaze. It is difficult to know what they see at the end of that cyclopic apparatus, a technology of the "unnatural and bizarre" reshaping vision with a disordering squint and one eye.[87] With the promise to see Halley's Comet up there, this regal pair might delight in the opportunity to witness this cosmic happening. But more important, their comportment stands to question other forms of belonging. The scale at which they observe this celestial object and become excited over its fiery glow resets the terms of space-time as they relish something of cosmic magnitude, an ancient entity of the sky and modern to the eye.

Although this snapshot predates the Mexican Revolution of 1910, a conflict which led to the fall of President Porfirio Díaz's regime, the image anticipates philosopher José Vasconcelos's introduction of "la raza cósmica" (the cosmic race) into the Latin American zeitgeist in 1925.[88] Vasconcelos theorizes how European and Indigenous intermarriage would engineer a new race, a volatile project of ethnoracial transcendence that left little room for African and Asian diasporic difference, I might add. Vasconcelos's scope and sense of the world *beyond* a Mexico at war with itself hint at the kind of worldviews Mexican publics like the couple on the other side of that lens stood to see and envision for themselves in the early twentieth century. Vision and scale combine to unveil visual proximities to places beyond the couple's physical reach, and yet that reach is embodied, comported, and performed. The cosmos acts on them because of that beveled glass and a viewpoint that senses Earth on a vast expanse rather than a planar one. This expansive search gleans other ways by which Mexican publics even on the cusp of war sought to see and know their potentiality in transplanetary-relational ways.

Whether demonstrated in the gestural articulations of looking up or bursting at the novel sight, the eye scales up and moves in concert with and even on behalf of celestial pathways, voyaging closer to the origins of the universe. This kind of visual contact demands complicating a horizontal body politic in Latinx transnational studies of art and culture to better actualize those motions mobilized by vertical attentions.

Star-Powered Movement

Suffice it to say, stargazing resonates differently in a transplanetary-relational approach as starry night skies have organized not only aerial attentions in Latinx narratives but also the movement of people. This sentiment is conveyed in the docudrama film *Stand and Deliver* (1988), where, after being accused of cheating by the National College Board, cholos Chuco (Daniel Villarreal) and Angel (Lou Diamond Phillips) cruise East LA.[89] "That's the stars out there, Homie. Not too polluted," comments Chuco, gazing at the evening sky, to which Angel retorts, "The stars aren't really out there, Ese. What you're looking at is where they used to be. It takes the light a thousand years to reach the Earth. You know, for all we know they burned out a long time ago. God pulled the plug on us. He didn't tell nobody." An awkward pause looms between the pair. "The stars are out there, homeboy. I don't care what you say," Chuco replies defensively as they lapse into another beat of silence. The tense exchange serves multiple purposes in the narrative, showing Angel's self-reckoning with a barrio intellectualism at odds with his mathematical acumen, his growing alienation from a thug life ruled by codes of the streets and not astrophysics, his increased awareness of being seated on Earth. Looking up, the pair partakes in a kind of ascension that breaks away from East LA. However, sight is not sight. Space-time, gravity, and physics make that blanket of stars more than a vision to behold. It is aberrant and alien, even foreboding.

Angel's despondency is about optics, a branch in physics that tells us moonlight takes more than a second to reach the human eye, sunlight is delayed by eight minutes, and starlight from Alpha Centauri, the closest star system, needs four years. These principles model what Chilean filmmaker Patricio Guzmán in his widely acclaimed documentary *Nostalgia for the Light* (2010) calls "the trap. The present doesn't exist."[90] Therefore, the transplanetary relation modeled in *Stand and Deliver* redefines the temporal and spatial definitions of borders that constitute life in *el barrio*, where the divisions between territory and turf recede under the laws of physics. *Carnalismo*, or cholo fraternity, is thus recoded, brought closer to the algorithms of wavelengths and light particles.

The profound vertical alignments created in the embodied connection between the observer's body and the starry entity occurs with dire consequences in Guzmán's dramatic evaluation of Augusto Pinochet's dictatorship, the longest in Chile's political history. The filmmaker recounts the human atrocities at Chacabuco, a concentration camp converted from an abandoned nitrate mining town built in 1924 in the Atacama Desert, considered the driest place on earth. This desert's climate, altitude, and elevation make it not only a terrestrial analogue for the moon with its rich geological formations and mineral deposits but also the ideal setting for astronomical research.[91] Life, death, and the cosmos intermingle in Guzmán's film as he recomposes the galaxy through the pulverized bones of the disappeared. He offers what film scholar Elizabeth Ramírez-Soto terms a "deeply sensorial experience . . . [where] the gaze of the spectator seems to be touching the calcium of the dead bodies, the soil of the desert, and the dust of the stars."[92] This cinematic grammar underwrites the story of "Luis," one of twenty to twenty-five camp prisoners who studied the stars during his incarceration. Guzmán's interview subject described how, under the instruction of "Dr. Alvarez," the detainees took astronomy classes by day and performed fieldwork by night. Luis explained that because they did not have telescopic equipment, they used found materials and scrap wood to construct a viewfinder. The interstellar positions they observed partly alleviated the horrors they faced under Pinochet's military. "We all had a feeling of great freedom. Observing the sky and the stars, marveling at the constellations, we felt completely free," Luis reported, retracing footsteps and traumatic memories on the camp's grounds years after the dictator died in 2006. His death occurred as he faced trial for innumerable war crimes.[93]

Astronomy renewed the captives' hope by acting as a transplanetary-relational gateway toward other ways of belonging, a practice of liberatory movement with outer space. As these prisoners' stargazing sparked alarm and retaliation from the soldiers, who feared the stars would help these political prisoners map escape routes, Guzmán's film enunciates the threats that an ascendant reach posed for the Pinochet regime. This episode from Chile's history of genocide and authoritarianism accentuates star power, a sensorial register that orients how Latinx bodies traffic in skyward sources of cosmic meaning; with an elevated scale, their gazing animates a choreography attuned to planetary movement because freedom, like starlight, evades the trappings of detention, war, and incarceration.

In this way, star power is profound because of its transplanetary-relational capacity to cause action, change, and mobilization against majoritarian tyranny. One case in point is a story from conceptual artist Celia Alvarez Muñoz, who recalls her great-grandfather's turn toward the stars. Orphaned as a child in Mexico, he was raised in the care of Jesuit priests who taught him astronomy. Every New Year's Eve he would look to the constellations, and on one occasion he foresaw famine and moved his family north. Unbeknownst to them, the Mexican Revolution would break out later that year. When the artist's grandmother crossed the border as a young girl, her vision of El Paso electrified her eyes and stirred her imagination. She commented, "¡Mira nomás . . . Que Americanos tan mas inteligentes; hasta ya bajaron las estrellitas del cielo!" (Look at that . . . Those Americans are so smart; they've even taken down the little stars from the sky!).[94] The tale of her grandmother's migration is poetically rendered in Alvarez Muñoz's 1991 installation *Abriendo Tierra/Breaking Ground* at the Dallas Museum of Art (see figure 1.4). Like a memoir graphed onto the wall, the artist's family story spills out onto the museum's interior in vinyl text written over a pane of glass. At sunset her writing reanimates before the Dallas skyline, twinkling alongside those *estrellitas* that dotted her grandmother's passage to the United States.[95]

Such glimmers suggest how migrations and border crossings were catalyzed by the stars. Though the Muñoz family's move happened because of what was forecast through astronomy and prophecy, that was not the only predictor of coming tragedy. In 1910 Halley's Comet streaked through the sky, becoming an omen of the impending Mexican Revolution, a series of conflicts erupting between campesinos and Indigenous villagers opposing Porfirio Díaz's rule. His binational economic investments modernized the country through land seizures, labor exploitation, and political corruption. A broadside from draftsman José Guadalupe Posada illustrates the contradictory ethos of the time—an amalgamation of political satire, panic, and science fiction (see figure 1.5). "Don Halley" is an intrusive party crasher. He fires down toward a Mexican pueblo. The villagers scatter in fear with arms raised and faces braced for the alien threat hurling down from the dark unknown. Posada's comet is comedically paired with a daffy moon wagging its tongue in this theater of the absurd. Mother Earth pleads with the comet not to destroy her on the cusp of the Mexican centennial. The significance of the print captures competing views at that time. "The young were told by the old that it meant war, death, famine, plague," Anita Brenner recalls.[96] "The scientists understood it, everything was under control. But in the villages, where the glare destroyed the peace of the night and made the cattle

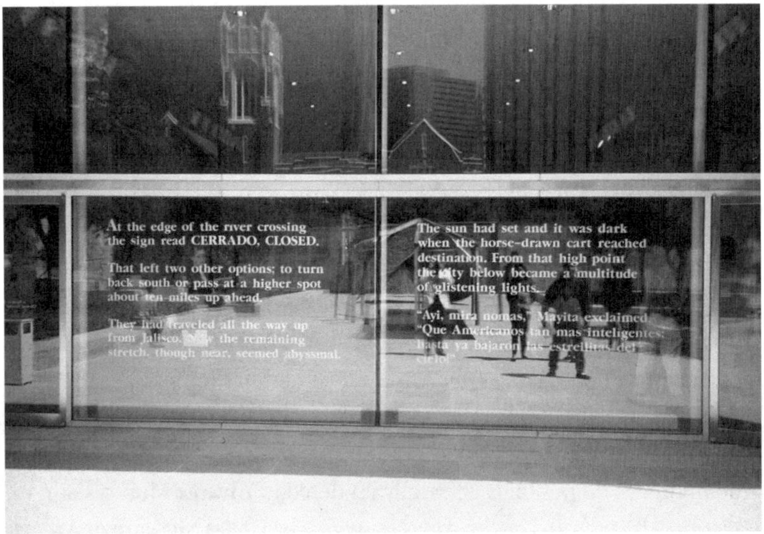

1.4 Celia Alvarez Muñoz, *Abriendo Tierra/Breaking Ground*, 1991. Installation view, Dallas Museum of Art. Photograph by the artist. Image courtesy of the artist.

uneasy, it was an announcement."[97] An announcement of *what* remained unclear. Was it an omen of change, a portent of destruction, or a symbol of even stranger things to come?

More important, the streaking flash of light does not know binational division, international diplomacy, or security zones. The comet was an extraterrestrial migrant of colossal scale. It was spotted over downtown El Paso on May 16, 1910, and stirred public imaginations with headlines like "Comet Can Be Seen in El Paso at Last" (see figure 1.6).[98] A sensationalist photograph by W. F. Stuart is a novel companion to Alvarez Muñoz's grandmother's story, showing how this border city opposite Ciudad Juárez is a place of amusement, cosmic things, and immigrant fantasy for better tomorrows. The astronomical object redraws this town's physical borders, driving a binational crossroads of migrants and residents alike toward that flaming star in the sky.

The aftereffects of this cosmic encounter are made more clear in figure 1.7, Alexander Maldonado's painting *Mexico (May 1910)*. In it, we see a horse-drawn carriage carrying a family across an arid vista. Mountainous hillsides in the backdrop offset a parade of constellations ornamenting a dark and vacuous void. A blanket of stars dominates the upper half of the composition, commanding the narrative. The travelers' ride is lit by not only

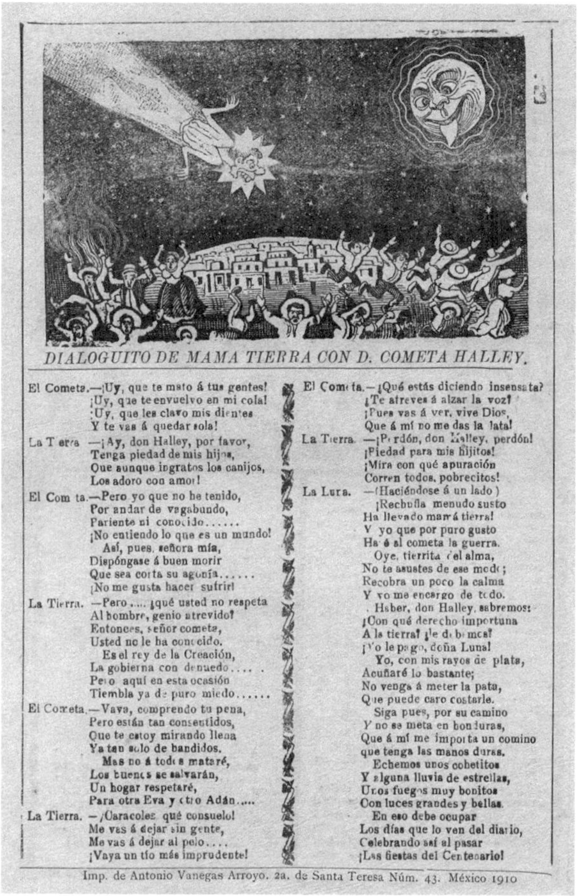
DIALOGUITO DE MAMA TIERRA CON D. COMETA HALLEY.

El Cometa.—¡Uy, que te mato á tus gentes!
¡Uy, que te envuelvo en mi cola!
¡Uy, que les clavo mis dientes
Y te vas á quedar sola!
La Tierra —¡Ay, don Halley, por favor,
Tenga piedad de mis hijos,
Que aunque ingratos los canijos,
Los adoro con amor!
El Cometa.—Pero yo que no he tenido,
Por andar de vagabundo,
Pariente ni conocido......
¡No entiendo lo que es un mundo!
Así, pues, señora mía,
Dispóngase á buen morir
Que sea corta su agonía......
¡No me gusta hacer sufrir!
La Tierra. —Pero ..... ¿qué usted no respeta
Al hombre, genio atrevido?
Entonces, señor cometa,
Usted no le ha conocido.
Es el rey de la Creación,
La gobierna con denuedo.... .
Pero aquí en esta ocasión
Tiembla ya de puro miedo......
El Cometa.—Vava, comprendo tu pena,
Pero están tan consentidos,
Que te estoy mirando llena
Ya tan solo de bandidos.
Mas no á todos mataré,
Los buenos se salvarán,
Un hogar respetaré,
Para otra Eva y otro Adán.....
La Tierra. —¡Caracoles qué consuelo!
Me vas á dejar sin gente,
Me vas á dejar al pelo....
¡Vaya un tío más imprudente!
El Cometa.—¿Qué estás diciendo insensata?
¿Te atreves á alzar la voz?
¡Pues vas á ver, vive Dios,
Que á mí no me das la lata!
La Tierra. —¡Perdón, don Halley, perdón!
¡Piedad para mis hijitos!
¡Mira con qué apuración
Corren todos, pobrecitos!
La Luna. —(Haciéndose á un lado)
¡Rechuña menudo susto
Ha llevado mamá tierra!
Y yo que por puro gusto
Hacé al cometa la guerra.
Oye, tierrita del alma,
No te asustes de ese modo;
Recobra un poco la calma
Y yo me encargo de todo.
Haber, don Halley, sabremos:
¿Con qué derecho importuna
A la tierra? ¿le debemos?
¡Yo le pago, doña Luna!
Yo, con mis rayos de plata,
Acuñaré lo bastante;
No venga á meter la pata,
Que puede caro costarle.
Siga pues, por su camino
Y no se meta en honduras,
Que á mí me importa un comino
que tenga las manos duras.
Echemos unos cohetitos
Y alguna lluvia de estrellas,
Unos fuegos muy bonitos
Con luces grandes y bellas.
En eso debe ocupar
Los días que lo ven del diario,
Celebrando así al pasar
¡Las fiestas del Centenario!

Imp. de Antonio Vanegas Arroyo. 2a. de Santa Teresa Núm. 43. México 1910

1.5 José Guadalupe Posada, *Dialoguito de Mamá Tierra con Don Cometa Halley,* 1910. Newsprint. Image courtesy of the Jean Charlot Collection, Archive of Hawai'i Artists and Architects, University of Hawai'i at Mānoa Library.

moonlight but also the resplendent flash of Halley's Comet jetting across the sky. Most actors portrayed mid-drive in the piece cruise undeterred. Their looks are a consummate arrangement of profiles and face-forward turns, with one exception. One child looks away and out the window. His flat and unspecific rendering makes his sight line difficult to discern. Although the work is a part of Maldonado's earliest entry into painting, after he took up the practice at sixty in 1971, his characters' backsides are a recurring shorthand, a recognizable signature for a body turning skyward.

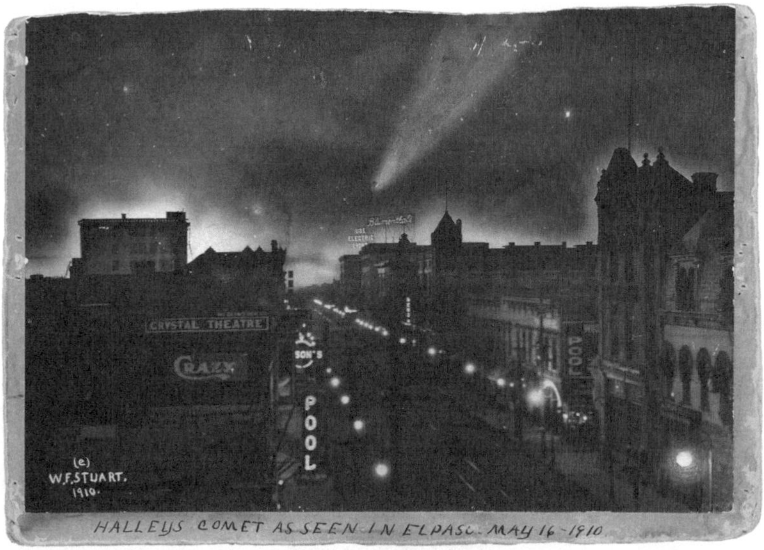

1.6 W. F. Stuart, *Halley's Comet as Seen in El Paso, May 16, 1910*, 1910. Photograph; dimensions unknown. Courtesy of the El Paso Public Library, Border Heritage Center, Picture File Collection.

This motif is found in later paintings like *Watching Halley's Comet* and *Planet 2-Suns 4.3 Light Years from Earth*, a reference to Alpha Centauri, the closest star system to Earth. In the latter piece, he reworks the foreground, placing starry-eyed spectators from the past and future into a familiar body idiom. Their backs turn to the viewer, part of the artist's vocabulary to suggest gazes pointed upward. This discernment is made clearly in Ames Gallery of American Folk Art ephemera promoting Maldonado's 1989 show, the last he would attend before his death that year at age eighty-seven. "Sometimes the backs of spectators' heads appear on the bottom of the frame, *looking up*," it comments. "His work is occasionally reminiscent of his early boyhood in turn-of-the-century Mexico."[99] This flattened abbreviation, also found in *Mexico (May 1910)*, centers a child peering out into the Mexican night sky in a way that recalls a personal memory involving outer space. Maldonado remembered seeing the comet from his family's stagecoach on the way to visit his uncle's ranch; he was nine years old. "He never forgot it," wrote his sister Carmen about the painting.[100] "You thought it was daylight," Maldonado noted.[101] "The whole world was lit up; but the light was different—from another world."[102] It is difficult not to imagine how that "different"

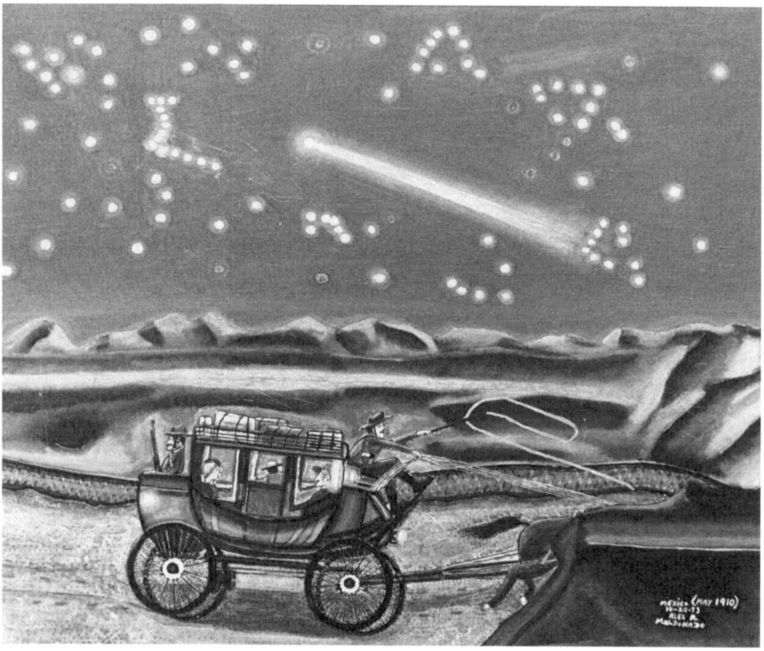

1.7 Alexander Maldonado, *Mexico (May 1910)*, 1973. Acrylic painting; dimensions unknown. Collection of Bonnie Grossman.

luminosity activated a transplanetary relation, connecting a way of seeing and being to an extraterrestrial light that transgressed the geopolitical divisions of the United States and Mexico. His aberrant sight aligned with someone like Miss S. E. Church, who first saw Halley's Comet in 1835 from her girlhood home in Ogdenburg, New York, another border town but one near neighboring Ontario, Canada. "It was so brilliant that it filled about one-third of the sky and covered our house with light," she recalled to the *El Paso Herald*.[103]

For Maldonado, that cosmic experience of visual apprehension, sparked by a radiant comet in the Mexican sky, set him on a life course in the United States, where, amid the outbreak of the Mexican Revolution, his family migrated, eventually settling in San Francisco. After careers that took him from amateur boxing to Bay Area shipping yards, his late-in-life adoption of painting allowed for a rehearsal of cosmic memory through which his speculative architectural designs established him as a preeminent figure in the art of Latinx futurity in the 1970s, even though he is little acknowledged in these terms.[104] His self-taught art and science education favored visual source material from encyclopedic entries on "petrified bones, astronomy, galaxy and nebulas."[105] He even recalled, "I once saw Mars in 1925 on a 10″ telescope," adding to his deep-space zeal.[106] Maldonado's *Mexico (May 1910)* presents a transnational immigrant experience that cannot be disarticulated from transplanetary relationality in its vision, scale, and comet-led voyage. Although his life story is consistent with the kinds of push-pull factors outlined by Latinx social scientists that clarify how social unrest, economic instability, government turmoil, and coups d'état culminate in migration, his move, like that of Muñoz's grandmother, was entangled with starry guideposts. The sensorial feedback born of cosmic light shaped the movement and bodies of artists who blended these extraterrestrial experiences into their familial border narratives. This transmission of Latinx otherworldly knowledges is further honed in another monument to the United States–Mexico borderlands in vertical alignment.

In West Texas, artist Leo Villareal presents *Star Ceiling (El Paso)* (2025). This 135 by 19-foot canopy projected nonrepeating abstract patterns of constellations and cosmic happenings just twenty-five feet above patrons entering the El Paso Museum of Art. Through a twinkling overhead screen of nearly fifteen thousand LED lights which contemplative visitors recline on benches to gaze upward and observe, Villareal's artwork brings the stars down from the sky in a way that recalls the awe and inspiration that Muñoz's grandmother experienced a century prior—through a light field presenting migration stories across horizontal and vertical divides. In this restaging of community in a perpendicular strait, stargazing is not only a practice of everyday astronomy or an exercise of art appreciation; it is also an empowering act of border crossing, of transplanetary liberation, a lesson that Chilean political prisoners in the Atacama Desert knew all too well.[107]

These movements on behalf of astronomic objects like stars, comets, and constellations suggest how nation-state cultural politics that centers its evaluation of Latinx art (not to mention transnational Latinx studies) on the ground must also reconcile what the stars pose for creatives working in tune with, or even on behalf of, entities beyond Earth. When Latinxs' movement in solidarity with the sky is honored, what becomes of citizenry? An aerial view pushes the creative imagination upward; as a result, interpretive analysis must also look upward. Transplanetary relationality suspends gravity-centering explanations and, through a discernment of art of the Americas beyond our present grounding, fosters a vocabulary that accounts for the observant body ringing to the universe's cosmic radiance and borderless expanse. Like the pulverized skeletal remains juxtaposed with the cracks and crevices of the lunar surface in Guzmán's documentary, we are specks. At a granular level, we are particles of elemental matter as ancient as the cosmos. Migration is attached to those life signs and pulsars that originate from the coordinates of the universe "belonging to another system," as Gayatri Chakravorty Spivak puts it.[108] Factoring in a modality of star power in art appraisal suggests that humans may flow at land's edge, but also they flow at planet's edge with visual discernment from above.

Transplanetary relationality's negotiation of vision, scale, and movement empowers an aerial arc that exceeds Latinidades' terrestrial demarcations on the ground. In response, Latinx artists' investment in a modern space program is an expected outcome as it not only revises the erasure of the Americas in historical assessments about spacefaring and the space age generally but also crystallizes how the migratory and imaginative work of these vertical pathways finds expression in technologies and infrastructures building the gateways to an interstellar elsewhere. How this bridge is made in Latinx visual and material articulations outlines this framework's final modality.

Scientific Visualization/Materialization

As chapter 5 elucidates, Latinxs' regard for the US space program likely dates to President John F. Kennedy's administration. The president's courtship of mainly Hispanic voters congealed with Viva Kennedy clubs formed throughout the US Southwest. After all, Kennedy's famed "We Choose to Go to the Moon" speech was delivered at Rice University Stadium in Houston just one year prior to his being named an honorary member of the League of United Latin American Citizens (LULAC) at a mariachi-accented event hours before his assassination in 1963.[109] The impact of this national tragedy animated assimilative, patriotic, and militaristic rhetoric for a postwar Mexican American generation that paired with the Kennedy-Johnson administration's broader commitment to the Apollo missions. Without rehearsing the global repercussions of the president's slaying, it is important to stress its implications for a contentious Cold War, which placed the United States opposite the Soviet Union in a pursuit of world and, potentially, interstellar domination. As I explain momentarily, Latinxs were a part of this social upheaval.

It is difficult to disentangle NASA's origins in 1958 from Russia's space program. The year before, on October 4, 1957, the Soviets launched Sputnik 1, the first human-made object to orbit Earth. As historian Patrick McCray points out, "To Western military and political observers, Sputnik's launch signaled that the Soviets possessed rocket technology sufficient to hurl large objects over thousands of miles."[110] The threat of nuclear annihilation aside, it is equally disingenuous to minimize the impact of the modern space program on art, architecture, design, and popular culture at mid-century. In fact, art was constitutional to much-needed space boosterism to promote US technological superiority, scientific achievements, and "new frontier" ideology.

This combination of art, space technology, and vision—of what could only be compared to "the future"—dovetailed with a plan by James Webb, NASA's director. In 1962 he worked with the senior curator of painting at the National Gallery of Art, H. Lester Cooke, to launch the NASA Artists Cooperative Program. It was based on the US Air Force Art Program, established in 1950, and the possibility of using "fine art as a form of documentation" proved invaluable to Webb's greater aims to capture an enduring and faithful testament to American ingenuity.[111] This initiative resulted in a number of popular exhibitions. Cooke curated *Eyewitness to Space*, which opened on March 14, 1965, at the National Gallery of Art and featured fifteen creatives, resulting in the production of seventy artworks. On December 4, 1969, he presented *The Artist and Space* (see figure 1.8). This engagement was an apotheosis of this art-science endeavor and featured seventy artworks by forty-seven artists, demonstrating its growth. The accomplishments of the NASA Artists Cooperative Program would aid the Smithsonian's Traveling Exhibition Service (SITES) companion show, *Mission Apollo*, in 1970 with a national tour. Alas, Cooke's attentions to these space matters would soon end. He passed away in 1973 at fifty-seven years of age.

Despite the contentious Cold War backdrop against which "space art" arrived, its cultural legibility relied on long-standing aesthetic and compositional forms characteristic of military painting, battlefield illustration, and the Western landscape genre. This analogue is raised in the work of art historian Elizabeth Kessler, who concluded that since the Hubble Space Telescope launch in April 1990, its astrophotography "proposed that the dramatic features and vistas of the unfamiliar landscape were best represented and understood through the aesthetics of the sublime[;] the images established a visual standard for seeing and representing the American West that endures today."[112] This nineteenth-century formula leads Kessler to contemplate "the astronomical sublime," a conclusion made possible by a generation of "astronomical art" makers like Ron Miller, whose work is compared for its scenic qualities to that of the Hudson River school acolytes, such as Albert Bierstadt, Thomas Moran, and Thomas Cole (for more, see chapter 3).[113] This observation is enshrined by Miller, who also self-reflects, "Words were

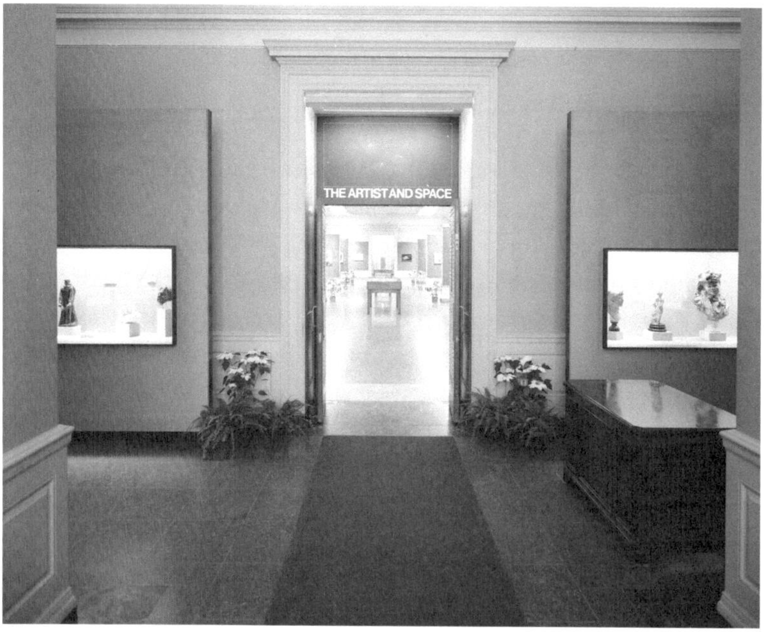

1.8 *The Artist and Space* installation, on view from December 6, 1969, to January 4, 1970, at the National Gallery of Art. Documentary photography courtesy of the National Gallery of Art Archives.

one thing, but romantic images of the West's fantastic landscapes made them both real and unforgettable. I hope that I can do the same for our neighbours in space."[114] His and Kessler's sentiments seconded Webb's impetus for the NASA Artists Cooperative Program, substituting journalism with the artistic feats rendering "ordinary gestures with a heroic elegance."[115] Thus astronomical art's search for recognition was wide-ranging and drew from an art historical tradition in the Western picturesque.

Forerunners of the field, like Chesley Bonestell, Robert McCall, David Hardy, Paul Calle, and Ron Miller, prided themselves on data visualization or scientific accuracy, sometimes at the expense of the formative visual language of science fiction birthed in the pre- and interwar years. For example, Bonestell criticized any image maker who took liberties with sound astronomical data. Such inaccuracies, he believed, needed to be condemned because "so many 'artist' frauds succeed."[116] Scholar Patricia Allen Dreyfus took the middle road in her evaluation of McCall's oeuvre in a way satisfying to critics like Bonestell, noting, "Despite painstaking detail, his paintings do not freeze into flatness. . . . His knowledge of space technology enables him to visualize the various pieces of equipment from every angle, giving him tremendous freedom of composition."[117]

These perspectives illustrate how space art discourse developed with two objectives in mind: to preserve art and science legibility within aerospace and national defense industries while also repudiating criticisms like those launched by James Elkins, who wrote that "the colors and compositions of astronomers' pretty pictures are clearly dependent on such things as science fiction paperback covers, Maxfield Parrish works, fantasy art, Hollywood special effects, and the gaudy colors of popular magazine illustrations . . . sources that have virtually nothing to do with contemporary art making."[118] His accusations were not far-fetched considering Bonestell's and McCall's foray into Hollywood special effects and set design, visual resources so viable and creatively agile that even Latinx artists reclaimed such "gaudy" expressions in something I term a *Latinf/x sensibility*, as discussed in chapter 4.

Unable to wipe away the stain of lowbrow pulp, they had to deal with other contradictions that undermined a scientific empiricism legitimating the field. Consider how the range of media and technical practice shaping this "genre," like pen and ink, airbrushing, pastels, graphite, photography, and acrylic and oil paints, added to it multisided visual definition. Is it a style, a movement, or an accurate depiction of scientific fact? Or might it boldly share some aesthetic symmetry with that bastion of 1940s vanguardists known as the New York school, trailblazing painting with brushy abstractions and frenetic splashes? As McCall attests, "I can propel myself into outer space looking at a DeKooning [*sic*] . . . but even more so with Franz Kline. I can enter his pictures and imagine that I'm standing on one of those broad, black swaths of pigment, and it's another world, an extraterrestrial environment."[119] His words linger with consequence for the study of art, modernism, and speculation. One might ask, What would it mean to think about modern art as an alien visual language? How would its proximity to the lowbrow realm of actors in rubber suits devalue its standing as high art and aesthetic refinement? These questions were certainly being proposed by at least one space artist in the 1960s. However, the thought of modern art as belonging to "another world" is little pursued in the field.[120] Art historical evaluations instead privilege analyses closer to the landscape genre and the sublime when it comes to space. In either case, art history cannot shake how wonder and amusement stimulate extrapolative thinking and provoke visions about the unknown in ways that make lowbrow creature features, astronaut portraiture, and abstract paintings part of a broader extraterrestrial milieu.

And yet the colonialist implications of space exploration cannot be disentangled from these idyllic portrayals of spacefaring and otherworldly discovery. Afrofuturism is a tremendous resource in this regard. For example, Shelley Streeby assessed Octavia Butler's archive, in which manuscript excerpts and abandoned stories revealed how "intellectual, practical, and ethical questions about colonization and the difficulties of creating a truly mutualistic symbiosis between people from Earth and other worlds" perpetuated settler colonial violence in ways that shaped her Afrofuturist prose about Black relations to outer space.[121] Although trailblazing writers of color like Butler, Samuel Delany, and Russell Bates were negotiating the racist implications of US empire building in the solar system, this ethical dilemma was opaque for many astronomical artists.

Artists rehearsing scientific visualization during the space age, in particular, sidestep the ongoing sociopolitical realities of the civil rights, feminist, and queer liberation movements of the 1960s. This obfuscation, combined with the mainly cisgender men in the astronomical art pantheon, which defined art-science liaisons as the province of a homogeneous majority, promoted a vision for the space program in the image of the country: a white one. If the main impetus of this cultural imaginary is predicated on "space-related subjects and styles . . . spurred by the creation of NASA," as Lois Rosson and Ron Miller suggest, how do we reconcile Latinx creatives who fit awkwardly around this definition?[122] How do we make sense of artists of color for whom astronautics, aerospace industries, and advanced space technologies were sources not only of inspiration but also of the visual and material means to enable social critique? An instructional example in response to these questions is merited.

Such profound retorts pervade artworks featured throughout this book, and yet none comes close to the shantytown charm of mixed-media artist Simón Vega's space modules. Born in 1972 in Panama and raised in El Salvador, Vega blends a trans-isthmus perspective with a view on space tied to the Cold War, ideological conflict, and military defense technology with hints of science fiction panache. These factors focused a young life in which an amalgamation of "weird things" stoked his childhood imagination: bazaars with lizard tail flooring, ornately gated food stalls resembling spacecraft, and a friend's swampy courtyard where fantasy, war, and film intermingled in a restaging of Yoda's retreat from *The Empire Strikes Back* (1980). For a young Vega, just beyond those walls another kind of empire was underway. Armed soldiers and death squads aimed to disappear suspected dissidents and communist sympathizers when civil war broke out in 1981.[123] Even as that mossy playland was an allegory for

El Salvador's oscillating existence through separate if not dire realities, those bricked-up walls harbored an inner sanctum for young Vega. Like Yoda's forgotten world, Dagobah, the force was plentiful and protective there.

El Salvador's fissures in space and time are something Vega dates to La Matanza, the 1932 massacre of nearly thirty thousand Indigenous people who contested an exploitative wage-labor system and the government's refusal to seat a popularly elected candidate from the Communist Party. Their genocide left the Pipil Indigenous culture ravaged and paralyzed in historical erasure. As Kency Cornejo notes, "Many Pipiles in El Salvador hid their indigenous clothes and languages out of fear of execution, concealing not only their existence as a people but also their cultural legacy."[124] This atrocity created temporal repercussions for the present, fortifying Vega's belief that "the future is in the past."[125] To remedy this disjuncture, he intensified his attention to the world's ancient technologies, keyed to dolmen megalithic portals, precision stonework at Tiwanaku in Bolivia, and the colossal Incan ruins at Machu Picchu in Peru. Finding future possibility in the remnants of the ancient Americas empowered astronomical art in ways that decoupled Western colonial science from a formative architectural record in service to the cosmos. Vega's references are reminiscent of other diasporic Central American and Mexican American artists in this book, like Jacqueline Arias, Beatriz Cortez, and rafa esparza (discussed further in chapter 3). However, his take on this space-time nonlinearity activates a counterfactual device from speculative literature. He asks, *What if* the militaristic and political turmoil in El Salvador led not to genocide but to a space program?

His answer boldly offers a way to understand the country's war-torn trauma through its entanglement with global superpowers that simultaneously mastered rocket science in conquest of the stars and painted it above this region like a passive backdrop for defense technology might. Because the space race is intended to intimidate if not to educate audiences in the Global North and Global South about US and Soviet aeronautical superiority, Central America is the most suitable place to propose an alternative space project of this kind. For Vega, this trans-isthmus serves as a connective tissue between first world and third world, between global economy and resource extraction, between Earth and outer extremities. He seeks restitution not from the familiar Central American diasporic art strategies memorializing the wounded and disappeared in comparable works from a foundational generation of US-based Salvadoran artists like Juan Edgar Aparicio, Victor Cartagena, or Muriel Hasbun, for example.[126] Rather, Vega practices a speculative Latinx visual vocabulary in three dimensions. Like a 4D printing device, he arises from the ideological unrest and terrestrial "playground" of temporal irregularities with out-of-whack contraptions that rearticulates genocidal mass disappearances in ways reminiscent of unexplainable alien abductions. Confronting how everyday life in 1980s El Salvador was experienced in terms of fantasy and destruction, his corresponding collection of aerospace machines makes tangible a Salvadoran space program, though never realized. With humor, his lo-fi improvisational versions of "high technological robotic systems," using repurposed found materials and beachside clutter, concretized astronomical art in ways unimagined in the NASA Artists Cooperative Program from decades before and, more important, conveyed the exploitative power of transnational global capital and colonialism in the region.[127] It is a great irony that his largest and most accomplished installation to date occurred not in Central America but at an international destination for art aficionados, trendy millennials, and Gen Z music devotees tucked away in the low desert of Riverside County, California.

Palm-3 World Station (2018) was featured in the public art and installation program for the Coachella Valley Music and Arts Festival in 2018 (see plate 4). Otherwise dubbed "Beychella" by fans because of Beyoncé's historic headlining, the event nestled away in the arid surrounds of the Coachella Valley was a magnet for celebrities, TikTok influencers, and other tech-savvy bon vivants. The atmosphere was one of exuberant fashion statements—part postapocalyptic party wear meets Thunderdome chic. Vega's 150-foot-long structure complemented other large-scale and interactive artworks, provoking Instagram-ready selfies and hashtags in a screen-addicted field of image-conscious hipsters.

Unbeknownst to festivalgoers, Vega's artistic landmark represented a replica of the Mir space station, an advanced piece of Cold War–era aerospace engineering that existed even after the fall of the USSR in 1991. As such, Mir reopened international collaboration until its decommissioning in 2001. Basing his vision on the original low-orbit outpost that consisted of seven unpressurized modules, Vega expanded on the spacecraft design by giving his piece thirty compartments, some with discreet views of Salvadoran tienda interiors, like museum period rooms resurrected from the 1980s. While meeting Coachella art programmers' expectations for an enlarged public artwork in scale and look, Vega took liberties with history and speculated on a future and much-expanded version of the spacecraft, encapsulating what he observed to be the literal translation of the Russian word *mir*: "world," "peace," and "village."[128]

His resulting "world space village" towered at fifty feet; its fabrication was humble and cheeky in tone. Constructing it from corrugated metal sheets, scrap lumber, PVC roofing tile, and other junkyard detritus, Vega "Latin Americanized" this fortress of technological superiority, translating the architectural know-how of Salvadoran *colonia* design into a recognizable symbol from Cold War conflict: the spaceship.[129] Vega's insistence on a shantytown aesthetic synthesized first-world building techniques with a validation of slapdash logics in construction and sensibility. Even if US safety codes prevented him from fully realizing a Salvadoran vernacular of snaky wiring and faulty cables, he achieved a look "as if" Mir were improvised with Central American spit and grit (see plate 5).[130] He further relays other authentic touches through a shabby facade built from hand-painted signs, fabric curtains, and a lighting system replicating the rolling brownouts emblematic of El Salvador's scattershot infrastructure. From design to inception, Vega's practice is science materialization composing a spaceship from the vernacular know-how of his team's Mexican builders, accomplished in "work[ing] in a shantytown way."[131]

According to Vega, audiences were convinced that the large-scale installation was fabricated from Salvadoran imported materials, not items mined from Southern California scrapyards. Christian Morales, an attendee of Salvadoran descent, told the Inland Empire's *Press-Enterprise*, "This is just an amazing piece. . . . He did this as an homage to basically what happened during the Cold War and how it affected Central America."[132] By creating the impression of Mir crash-landing in the Coachella Valley, Vega does more than rehearse a polarizing drama on a music festival stage. Rather, his artwork retells the United States' and Soviet Union's harm to the Salvadoran diaspora with ruins of the past. This injury remains part of the present, earmarked in a symbol of humanity's future: astronautical machinery remade in a visual lexicon in which Vega and his community are fluent. Despite this ambitious accomplishment, he is not entirely convinced that his public statement will remedy a Central American futurity on the brink of planetary collapse. "If the world ends . . . who will get on the space station? Most likely, we are not. Salvadorans are not, so we will build our own."[133] By announcing the arrival of a Salvadoran space program intent on superseding present conditions by hijacking Soviet technology from a bygone era, Vega fathoms what could have been. He presents a roughhewn version of space art that not only meets the scientific standard set forth by the likes of Bonestell but also subverts its polished artifice, daring to dream of a future for a country where, because of war, US interventionism, and genocide, spacefaring is not possible.

Palm-3 World Station exemplifies this book's larger aims. It is a replica of Russian aerospace engineering in design and even positions Mir modules accurately. However, Vega's speculative imagination rehearses the fractious relations between global superpowers and Central America, a terrestrial stage from which ideological warfare and resource extraction play out a destructive endgame. Much in the same way as current private aerospace projects aim to colonize the cosmos, Vega posits a corresponding alternative for El Salvador. His sophisticated cyber hacked statement approaches the atrocities of Central American civil wars with transplanetary-relational practices of vision, scale, migration, and visual and material manifestation—an interconnective machinic tissue between nations, worlds, and even planets (as we shall see in chapter 3).[134] By literalizing the politically charged function of a high-tech copy in discarded materials, Vega makes transparent the punishing flow of first-world ideas and authorial power over Central America as a politically strategic and tactical security zone controlled to oversee US corporate interests, extractive capital, and military assets. To do this, he proposes a copy of a copy, a farcical facsimile that translates aerospace technology on behalf of and in keeping with a Latinx spirit of "making do," reversing first-world domination of the skies into something "Latin Americanized," technoculturally absurd, and yet possible.[135]

Armed with the improvisational tools to blast off, Vega echoes other visionaries discussed in this study who invest in, innovate, and sometimes work against aerospace machinery, mirroring the intent of space art and its goals of visual innovation as defined by Bonestell, McCall, Miller, and others. But as *Palm-3 World Station* demonstrates, the space program is not only theirs. It is also ours. By undercutting racist and colonial biases that abbreviate or omit Latinx creativity from the story of space-based art making, these artists rupture long-standing biases and brazenly traffic in the visual and material relics of a modern space program to accentuate ways of being and creating in ascension. The resulting tactical vocabularies and sensing attunements focusing this book align with vertical forces that yield strange shapes, weird things, and timescales that affront a Latinx art historical project preoccupied with terrestrial meanings, horizons, and procumbent planes. How to approach imagery and embodiments formed in response to this and other worlds? We must attend to modalities of aberrant seeing, elevated scales, inverted sight lines, and body politics redirected for the future of Latinx art historical study that creates, fields, mediates, and thinks with a transplanetary connectivity. More than the iconographic repertoire of astronauts, spacecrafts, or space suits, these artists' image statements channel the universe with a point of view beyond our perceptible capabilities of firsthand observation and thus invite ongoing, unclosed, and open ruminations about Latinx expression in the pacing of the universe, pulsating to the vast expanse of the cosmos. When displayed, these artworks reactivate institutions and cultural centers with a "range of geologic, racialized, gendered, and animal signifiers," transitioning "the life of the museum . . . fundamentally connect[ing it] to all forms of animate existence across spectrums of human experience and nonhuman sentience," as Jeannine Tang observes about the Museum of Transgender Hirstory and Art.[136]

By borrowing from transgender art theory it is possible to reimagine museums housing these artworks as endorsing a kind of trans-ing of the art historical present, even if temporarily. By literally cutting across, through, and beyond observational reality, as the Latin prefix *trans* suggests, these artworks frustrate nation-period rubrics that have long cohered to the familiar exhibition syntax of surveys, encyclopedic hangs, and chronological categorizations. Because Latinx art in transplanetary relation brings outer space home, the museum venue that once sheltered static objects predicated on an existential realism is suffused with other forms that rhyme to the universe's shapes, sounds, and vibrations and that may appear more lowbrow science fiction than highbrow fine art. But as Bob McCall suggests, if a Franz Kline painting could be an extraterrestrial landscape, why couldn't the terms of not only modern art but also art history writ large rethink its proximity to the cosmos? A transplanetary-relational turn for Latinx art and the exhibition environment housing it confronts the present terms of reality, subverts Westernized and progressive circuits of space-time, and mutates the educational objectives of museum space closer to scenes from this chapter in which Mexican publics thrill at the sight of a comet or are personally moved by stargazing as a liberatory act. Such affective displays of planetary sense nudge the museum closer to a sensational realm of the planetarium, fun house, cinema multiplex, and even spaceport where *energize* (*acciónar*) is a call-and-response to empower a Latinx collective being scaled to something greater and off-Earth.

Of course, the geopolitical consequences of xenophobia and anti-immigrant hostilities pervading the Americas are no *Star Trek* episode, and teleportation machines are hard to come by. Focusing a study on transplanetary relations *beyond* the normative land "sensing," as Gómez puts it, means that the ambiguous "Latinx art public" must be reassessed and reconfigured in an antinormative key.[137] As the next chapter argues, another definition of the Latinx audience is required as these visionaries prepare barrio residents' entrée to the future and make way for murals charged with all the creativity to fuel a rocket ship, readying it for take off.

2

Barrio Futurity

PUBLIC ART IN THE AGE OF APOLLO

Before he was dubbed the "Father of Chicano Science Fiction," writer Ernest Hogan was an art student.[1] Trained at Mount San Antonio College in Walnut, California, a community college and commuter paradise tucked away twenty-five miles east of downtown Los Angeles, this East LA transplant found opportunities in writing short stories, attending science fiction conventions, and illustrating ephemera for a staged production of *The Twilight Zone*.[2] He was also painting. His experience in the studio art classroom grew frustrating, however. Doing his best version of abstract expressionism, he explained that he "was having a good time playing Jackson Pollock, slinging and smearing paint, putting stuff like paint thinner to make it drip . . . and there was a problem with the drips. I liked them, but they had a tendency to flow in the same direction—down."[3] Hogan's efforts to do the reverse and "defy gravity" punctuate his 1990 debut novel, *Cortez on Jupiter*.[4] His story about Pablo Cortez, the son of neo-Aztec anthropologists, speculates on Chicanx art's futurity, offering a technologically sophisticated and gregarious direction for the field undisciplined by gravity, art institution, or formal education.

In a dystopian future California, Cortez squats at the art library, refusing the traditional classroom at California State University, Los Angeles. His chaotic run-in with Chicana artist Estela Villanueva causes armloads of books to fall to the floor. In the spill is a bricolage of art historical movements and eras. Surrealism lies alongside primitivism, and pre-Columbian art flops next to abstract expressionism. More important, recent publications from the Space Cultural Program, a corporate employer of space artists dubbed Spaceco, are tossed beside texts on Mexican muralism. Past and future intermingle in the textual jumble, literalizing what Hogan is implicitly doing in the novel: theorizing public art's future possibilities. Cortez and Villanueva join the Guerrilla Muralists of Los Angeles, a radical collective experimenting with rather outmoded art technology like painting walls to incite public art engagement irrespective of the dystopian surrounds. They set government buildings and transit infrastructure aglow, electrifying the built environment in ways that transform the look and innovate the reach of Chicanx muralism. Exploding the freeways not with bombs but with bursts of flamboyant color, Cortez is "putting art back into life where it belongs," as the guerrilleros' manifesto declares.[5] His insurgent action is short-lived, resulting in his apprehension by "LAPDers," which leads to his arrest and adjudication to work under Spaceco in deep space.[6]

There, he uses a "central freefall module" to paint on unprimed canvases suspended in air.[7] Hogan's novel posits a future for Chicanx creativity that does away with the physical properties of gravity that frustrated his art school experience of Pollock-inspired splatters and sloshes. It is worth noting that Pollock nurtured a practice exercised in the New York Experimental Workshop under his apprenticeship with David Alfaro Siqueiros in 1936. Hogan, in turn, forged a new course in ways that jumble, levitate, and fly. By discerning what Chicanx art could be in a way that eerily anticipates the 2015 parabolic flight experiments of the Mexican art collective La Gravedad de los Asuntos (Matters of Gravity), he redirects the tip of the artist's brush to the ends of an astronaut's weightless existence.[8] "Ever notice how the vapor trail of a spaceship looks like a feathered serpent?" Cortez observes.[9] His point metaphorically relates to a Mesoamerican past where the image of Quetzalcoatl, a mishmash of serpent and bird, traverses worlds like a jet engine that shape-shifts in the image of clouds.[10]

Unbeknownst to Hogan, the public art future he speculated about in 1990 would be actualized in the skies above Southern California and Central Texas thirty years later. In the summer of 2020, a multiethnic collective of eighty artists staged their own aerial insurgency by writing against a system of incarceration and immigrant criminalization directed under the first administration of Donald Trump. Drafting five pilots to sky-type messages of protest, political mobilization, and coordinates of carceral zones above detention centers throughout the United States, the project, dubbed *In Plain Sight*, "render[s] the range of stories behind such conditions of precarity—voicing a loud and expansive call to care" that activates "safe, healthy queer feminist worlds," according to scholar Jocelyn Marshall.[11] Though popularly used for commercial promotions and the occasional public marriage proposal, the aerial message or sky "tag" transgresses the airspace with abbreviated statements ranging from the politically charged to allusive wordplay. For instance, Beatriz Cortez declared "No Cages No Jaulas," a bilingual outcry above the LA Immigration Court. Gala Porras-Kim's more poetic flourish of "Mi Cielo T.Q.M." or "Mi Cielo, Te Quiero Mucho," a Spanish love note to "my heaven" that referenced both the sky and a term of endearment, appeared over a Rio Grande detention center in San Antonio, Texas (see plate 6).[12] These words dotted the stratosphere, turning it into a giant matrix printout. With texts that demanded carceral abolition, these creatives "cyber-hacked" an airfield with a fleet of airplanes that became the avionic technology of subversive poetry. But what *In Plain Sight* lost in the spurts and explosions of "cyberexaggerated color" found in *Cortez on Jupiter*, it made up for in gesticulation.[13]

Promotional materials for the event relied on the command "Look Up!" to forecast the impending action, which reimagined Independence Day by replacing Fourth of July fireworks with a textual cloud world to demand action on behalf of detainees. By reorienting a body politic to look up at renegade messages masked in the clouds, these creatives charged the passive onlooker as a receptor of social change. Migration was metaphorically rendered through Earth's outer extremities, a pattern of movement as sacred as the natural world. Whether compared to the terms of Chicanx science fiction literature like *Cortez on Jupiter* or a multiethnic art "grouping that performs a not-yet-answered call to assemble in response to shared yet distinct historical antagonisms," *In Plain Sight* unrooted viewers from the terrestrial plane with renewed urgency to act under a vision gleaned from vertical scale.[14]

Airspace is an aerial tableau redrawn and reinvested with a kind of political communication learned from the history of Mexican muralism where messages of protest are broadly scaled, magnified, and made urgent. With that, the divisions among aircraft pilot, muralist, and urban guerrilla reformulate and intensify the ways in which the solution for Earth's volatile security zones is propelled in an ascendant arc. Literature and public art are complementary media in this way, and under a transplanetary relational approach, aberrant visions and elevated scales intensify our questioning. As a result, we must wonder: How does one engage Chicanx public art activity when it refuses the present? What is the future of muralism when the terms of its engagement are nonlinear and ungrounded? To confront this quagmire, this chapter elucidates how art produced in service to the skies and outer worlds was no stranger to Chicanx mural practice and contested the brick-and-mortar confines of the urban landscape. With its transplanetary-relational trajectories in vision and scale, Chicanx muralism proves that since the 1970s this medium has been anything but pedestrian. Because the modern space program and Apollo activities attracted national media attention in popular science and entertainment venues, other visual registers electrified street artists by visualizing what spacecraft, astrophotography, and astronautic machines might mean for them.

This chapter begins by showing how a Latinx fluency in outer space dates to the Mexican muralists. This visual vocabulary is also traced by the concurrent activity of two artists regarded for their space art and scientific visualizations, Chesley Bonestell and Robert McCall. Although both creatives trafficked in an astronomical art discourse, making public artworks with sincere dedication to science and technology research, Latinx mural producers did as well. With a closer rumination on artists like Richard Haro, David Botello, Wayne Alaniz Healy, and Vargas-Suarez Universal (VSU), mural imagery, practices, and skill sets emerge that innovate the stucco and concrete facades of Southern California to enable a barrio mural futurity in ways that show that the "Latinx audience" was anything but monolithic. By expanding the scale and expanding the terms of public perception, this chapter elucidates how these artworks are transformative, transporting East LA residents (Haro), Department of Motor Vehicles (DMV) patrons (Botello and Healy), or beachside tourists (VSU) somewhere beyond observable reality. This vertical standpoint was made possible because of these creatives' enmeshments with LA's aerospace industries, science centers, and university histories. As a result, the cultural citations practiced in the Latinx mural repertoire were not preoccupied with past mythologies and present social ills alone. They forwarded a barrio mural futurity indebted to the science pillars and the principal agents representing the modern space age: the astronomer and astronaut.

This chapter investigates how Latinx artists since the zenith of the Chicanx art movement of the 1960s asked what muralism *could be*. This speculative question complicates a focus on political realities rehearsed in mural scholarship and instead forwards an important dimension in the history of

Latinx public art, elucidating its potential to reposition the barrio spectator away from existential knowns and the punishing forces of physical gravity. Though they are imaginative, these mural artists' true innovation is the way they unfasten urbanity from its gritty foundation and instead forge futures for residents where they didn't exist. Like a launch site promising to contact cosmic unknowns, barrio mural futurity equally makes a vertical play and brings the outer planets to everyday ethnic surrounds. To understand this transplanetary-relational formation, it is important to unfurl muralism's historic standing in the art of the Americas and its preoccupation with Earth.

Public Art's Outer Spaces

Starting in the 1960s, the mural activity of the New Left was a consequential artillery against the hegemonic and white supremacist powers of the US nation-state. Social protest movements, civil rights demonstrations, and calls from the third world galvanized insurgent forms of image making and publication countering yellow journalism and sensationalist headlines that privileged state authorities. In turn, Latinx creatives responded with a historical recovery project offering honorific portrayals of revolutionary icons like Emiliano Zapata and Augusto César Sandino and socialist philosophers like Vladimir Lenin and Mao Zedong. This political communication fostered a visual literacy in printmaking, frescoes, and murals. Because of its grand-scale address and monumental authority, muralism performed a crucial function for displaced and dispossessed Latinxs and Chicanxs in search of "the building blocks for the existence of a Chicana/o nation within the U.S. nation-state," according to art historian Guisela Latorre.[15] As a result, Latinx and Chicanx murals continued with a rebellious bent akin to the modern murals of postrevolutionary Mexico in the 1920s.

Artists like José Clemente Orozco, Diego Rivera, and David Alfaro Siqueiros developed a visual vocabulary "portray[ing] the ideology of a worker, peasant and middle class revolution against the former ruling class," according to Eva Sperling Cockcroft and Holly Barnet-Sánchez.[16] Their narrative style and representational language compromised wider recognition by art establishment types. While these vanguardists were stateside, their murals and prints offered expanded critiques about capital, colonial settler violence, and even the monstrosity of science. Plentiful examples of Mexican muralism's mixed reception in the United States range from mild protest (of Orozco's work) to downright destruction (of Rivera's and Siqueiros's works). Rivera's *Man at the Crossroads* (1933) fresco at Rockefeller Center in New

York City was particularly infamous for its lauded portrayal of Lenin. More germane to this discussion is Rivera's reproduction of the Plaskett Telescope, the likely prototype for his commentary about the future. At seventy-two inches, this astronomical instrument was once considered the largest of its kind, as Ronald Olowin observes.[17] Another important touchstone emanates from *The Epic of American Civilization* (1932–34), Orozco's ambitious mural in the basement reading room of the Baker-Berry Library at Dartmouth College. According to art historian Mary Coffey, when the school's president, Ernest Hopkins, invited the artist to Hanover, New Hampshire, in 1932, he was besieged by outraged alumni "decrying his decision to employ not only a modernist but also, and more disturbingly, a Mexican to desecrate the walls of their beloved New England institution."[18]

Despite the social consternation, muralism's support from the state modeled an infrastructural logic replicated in the New Deal era of the late 1930s when President Franklin D. Roosevelt greenlit the employ of muralists under the Works Progress Administration (WPA) and Treasury Department. At least 2,500 murals were created through government aid fostering a civic life with artworks installed at municipalities, recreational facilities, hospitals, and federal buildings.[19] Together, these historical antecedents were important factors in what would become the Latinx community mural movement three decades later. As Shifra Goldman notes, muralism "has been a vehicle of protest and demands addressed to the power structures for equitable solutions to problems facing those communities. It also signaled the pride, cultural values, hopes, and aspirations . . . especially among the young people who formed the 'troops' of the Chicano Movement in the 1960s."[20] Altering the facades of *mercados* (markets), *panaderías* (bakeries), *carnicerías* (butchers), housing projects, fences, alleyways, and vestibules in barrio neighborhoods, the "grassroots explosion" of Latinx murals was booming inside and outside.[21] The medium enticed an artistic gestalt "free from the trappings of colonized and co-opted aesthetics . . . that could accommodate itself to the unique social, cultural, and political position of Chicanas/os as a marginalized and disenfranchised community in the United States."[22] These resonant images manifested iconographic themes that congealed an identity and a culture with a nationalist and romantic zeal that showcased Catholicism, social struggle, and Mesoamerican referents.

Public art's cosmological motifs are little regarded. Certainly, these are no strangers to Latinx muralism: from Gilberto Ramírez's 1970 *Mural Tríptico* (*Triptypch Mural*) at San Diego State University, replete with the transition of Earth's rotation from dawn to dusk, to Mario Torero's *Colossus*, a mural painted beneath the Coronado Bridge in Barrio Logan circa 1975, setting off the mythic figure in a backdrop of starry light; from David Botello's *Dreams of Flight* from 1973, lauded for its depiction of childlike fantasies of the sky (as we will discuss momentarily), to Domingo Rivera's *Aztec Spaceship* from 1975, portraying the seventh-century Maya King K'inich Janaab' Pakal as an "ancient astronaut" boarding a Mesoamerican rocket ship anchored in San Francisco's Mission District (a topic I take up in the next chapter; see plate 26). These works hint at the modes with which contemporary Chicanx muralism kept pace in what Latorre calls "cosmic time," a "more dynamic and spiritual way to conceptualize history."[23] And while this cosmological recovery in Mesoamerican and even classical Greek mythological terms "permit[s] Chicanas/os to write themselves into a narrative of both historical and cosmic dimensions," it also substantiates how Latinx and Chicanx muralists fostered a public art culture by "looking up," an aberrant vision and a way to sense transplanetary relationality's communal key.[24] Though unlike the literal command that directed *In Plain Sight*, pointing viewers to the sky, the Chicanx murals here cover a wide expanse of aerial outlooks about ancient Aztec and Maya Indigenous cosmologies and even future homeboys in search of other worlds.

The transplanetary relations foregrounding these public art practices accentuate existing scholars' inexactitude or, for that matter, near disregard for the modern space program's powerful impact on Chicanx public art interventions. For instance, Goldman's groundbreaking study of Southern California's Chicanx mural movement entirely omits US space history and technology in its taxonomies of "early themes" despite evidence to the contrary. "Sun symbols" and the "moon" are included but are termed "nonreligious symbols" and disarticulated from their astronomical, technological, or speculative iconographies.[25] Also, Latorre's assessment of *Aztec Spaceship* prioritizes the seventh-century Maya stone relief over a closer discernment of its reimagining for interstellar travel. This retrofitting is simply seen as a "lure or hook."[26] As a result, Rivera's customized rocket upgrades are a gimmick as opposed to a serious Chicanx engagement with astronautic technology. Rather than asking what fuselages might mean for a Latinx painter producing art of this kind in a postwar context, the scholarly appraisal emphasizes a look toward the Maya archaeological record. Though an eye on the astronomical technologies of the ancient Americas is worth addressing (a topic I take up more completely in chapter 3), the "scientification" of Chicanx mural art—to borrow a term from Hugo Gernsback—is overshadowed by a more horizontally aligned Latinx art history in terrestrial terms.[27]

Certainly, Rivera's work is a stunning correlation between barrio muralism, narratives of Chicanx futurity, and dealings with space technology. This gregarious combination is equally evocative of a recognizable space art nomenclature. As discussed in the introduction, space art's origins as a promotional machine for NASA's Apollo program brought the space agency and the National Gallery of Art into the business of visualizing the future with scenes of spacefaring tomorrows. The plausibility of transforming science fiction into science fact bemused audiences as these artworks "act as windows," according to Ron Miller.[28] "They only provide glimpses of possibilities," he stresses.[29] This cultural activity resulted in a kind of precision "unlike [the work of] the landscape painter or portrait artist."[30] It visibilized the cosmos, enlivening "stars and planets" even for apathetic astronomers whose looking practices were often "reduced to tables and graphs."[31] Therefore, creative innovation meets empirical data in ways similar to what the paleontological or medical illustrator does and accentuates "the personality of landscapes" despite their extraterrestrial nature.[32] For someone like Miller, representational "believability" is a key objective of space art, a premise he forwards in an offhand remark about "panoramas" of astronomical artworks, which behave as metaphorical "emulsion" for the "strange places" astronomers investigate.[33] His choice of words mobilizes language closer to photography. In doing so, he encodes the panorama with the multisensory powers of an immersive setting where time and space are experienced differently, even suspended in frozen animation.

In this way, the exhibition technology of outer space display relies on some imagination, a willingness to traverse material circumstances and reside elsewhere. However, that process requires speculation and a capacity to transit into the unknown. That point of entry into how outer space is seen and felt contradicts astronomical art's founding predicated on scientific integrity. Ironically, this distortion between being *ni aquí o ni allá* (neither here nor there) is a pillar of Latinx transnational studies, which illuminates other discourses over racialization and the fractious regimes of legality/illegality in the Americas. Geopolitical borders activate majoritarian ideas about Chicanxs and Latinxs as perpetual foreigners, overlooking centuries of colonial occupation, militarized policing, and land dispossession. Certainly, this analogue is imperfect and not intended to conflate the wounding created through war and genocide with space art display but, rather, to think about these architectures under a similar speculative and specifically transplanetary-relational design. This quagmire is about how to see and thus experience the immensity of the universe through public art. Transporting spectators vertically is an explicit premise of the space science mural. No one captures this mode of address quite like Chesley Bonestell.

Bonestell was an amateur astronomer turned architect whose capacity to convey spacefaring with scientific detail and touches of anticipatory drama was indebted to his skillful draftsmanship. His renowned covers for historic issues of *Collier's* in 1957 and *Life* in 1944 and 1946 catapulted him into the mainstream. He excited a curious public reeling from postwar anxieties and Cold War fears with visually provocative depictions of space probes and lunar machines (see plate 23). "At a time when the public had not yet accepted space travel, Bonestell's images showed it to be something that humans could actually do," argues Howard McCurdy.[34] In fact, his artwork for the 1946 issue of *Life* took readers on a journey to the moon by depicting Earth's outer atmosphere and lunar landscapes in vivid aerial views. His imagery trailblazed public fascination with "a trip to the moon," an idea that had previously been stoked by Georges Méliès's landmark silent film *A Trip to the Moon* (1902).[35] This raucous comedy of rocket-riding astronomers encountering native Selenites on extravagant extraterrestrial worlds was consonant with other popular amusements at the time, including postcard keepsakes and popular fiction. The 1901 Pan-American Exposition exhibit at Buffalo, New York, was also titled *A Trip to the Moon*. The showcase invited audiences to an "immersive experience composed of theatrical sets, painted panoramas, projected images, sound effects, and live action," a multisensory event predicated on fantasy and plausible scientific objects.[36]

Bonestell's odyssey to Earth's satellite could not have happened without another skill set. As a special effects matte painter for Hollywood films, he produced large-scale backdrops on the set of the Academy Award–winning *Destination Moon* (1950), the Willy Ley and Robert Heinlein vehicle speculating on humanity's first lunar landing, decades before NASA's Apollo program achieved that task. Bonestell's accomplishments in magazine cover art, dioramas, and set design prepared him for the demands of art and science education in the museum environment.[37]

In 1956 he was commissioned to produce *Lunar Landscape* for the Hayden Planetarium at Boston's Museum of Science, a 10-by-40-foot wall painting "located seven degrees from the Moon's North Pole and five degrees to the left of the center of the lunar disc" (see figure 2.1).[38] According to space historian Tom Crouch, the mural is set at three o'clock in the afternoon on Eastern Standard Time with corresponding alignments of stars and planet synchronized for a June day.[39] These coordinates elevate the work's scientific precision, making Bonestell's details more empirical than speculative.

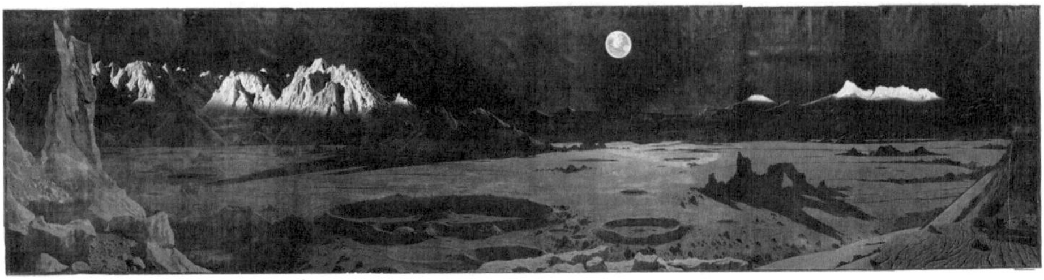

2.1 Chesley Bonestell, *Lunar Landscape*, 1957. Unframed mural (three sections), 10 × 40 ft. Gift of the Charles Hayden Planetarium of the Museum of Science, Collection of the Smithsonian National Museum of Air and Space.

His acumen was convincing to museum staff and audiences as he converted sculptural material for the mural study. He would pour Plasticine, photograph it, and apply that image to the mural, creating a convincing extraterrestrial surface. Despite his assertion of technical accuracy, Bonestell's effort was not infallible, as "the craggy peaks in his lunar landscapes are considerably more dramatic than our satellite's rounded, windswept hills."[40] Though Bonestell reached a level of national regard for his "equally realistic aerial views of the surface of the Moon" that "looked remarkably like the photographs NASA would produce with real spacecraft more than a decade later," according to McCurdy, his capacity to captivate museum audiences through the near accuracy of *Lunar Landscape* was ironically upended by the US space program.[41] After Apollo 11's dramatic touchdown, the television feed revealed not rocky peaks but smooth terrain, thus instantly making the Hayden Planetarium home to muralism's grandest science fiction achievement. "Chesley Bonestell gave us the Moon 'as it should have been,'" notes Crouch, quoting Ron Miller's retrospective account.[42]

The mural was removed in 1970 and eventually joined other wall-art depictions of epic aeronautical journeys and spacefaring adventures by Eric Sloan and Robert McCall at the Smithsonian National Air and Space Museum (NASM). While McCall's grandiose six-story *The Space Mural—A Cosmic View* was completed in 1976 in anticipation of another major commission, *Opening the Space Frontier—The Next Giant Step* (1979) for the Johnson Space Center in Houston, the impetus of these museum murals appeals to a mainstream public fascinated "with the possibilities of exploration, conquest, and settlement" in ways that mirror the settler colonial logics of US westward expansion, as religion historian Catherine Newell argues (see plate 7).[43] Whether placed among the clouds in Sloan's 75-by-58-foot painting overlooking a vacuous southwestern vista in *Earth Flight Environment* (1976) or planted on the lunar surface in *A Cosmic View*, publics are not only transported through a magnified visual address but educated through vertical sight lines where heads crane up and eyes strain upward. This gestural vocabulary teaches young people not only that meaning is encoded in the stars and skies but also that art-science education is attainable from the highest reaches of the NASM's walls. Unbeknownst to these air and space creatives, Latinx muralists were also punching their way up to the stars, but their transplanetary-relational trajectory was far from utopic. As *In Plain Sight* anticipated decades later, an aerial tableau is a profound site to contest the astronautical technologies aiding in racial and gender divisions.

Consider how on July 21, 1969, as Neil Armstrong descended on the moon, members of the National Welfare Rights Organization staged a sit-in at the Manned Spacecraft Center in Houston, Texas.[44] Italian photographer Mario De Biasi captured a multiethnic array of protesters enduring the muggy Houston heat with signs reading "Feed the Future Astronauts" and "Free Food Stamps for Texas Too!" (see figure 2.2).[45] However, one placard to the far left of the assembling crowd cuts through this anglophone textual field, reading "La Raza Tiene Hambre" (The People Are Starving). The Spanish signage juxtaposes the mock lunar lander with an audible retort that sounds its dissent in a language alienated in a Texas environment that assailed its Mexican American residents, practicing what Gloria Anzaldúa terms "linguistic terrorism."[46] De Biasi's camera reveals that this demonstration was a multilingual and multiracial coalition and, as a result, complicates historical appraisal of it. About the Houston protest, historian Neil Maher states that "seventy-five African American protestors wav[ed] signs demanding a halt to future moon missions until the federal government began cleaning up cities and providing for affordable and healthy urban housing."[47] His evaluation, though, underestimates the rich ethnoracial and Afro-Mexican *mestizaje* formed in coastal Texas, and thus another analysis is needed.

To this point, the public display at the foot of a space machine presents a jumble of languages. Perhaps like Villanueva's art books dropped by gravity in *Cortez on Jupiter*, this activist performance activates anglophone and hispanophone signage to empower the scientists of tomorrow. America's "future astronauts" must be fed. Even in this profound moment of dissent pitting the Apollo space program against economic and food insecurity, these women of color point to the space pilot to come in the image of them.[48] Through this outcry a Black and Brown future is called forward, hinting at the complicated

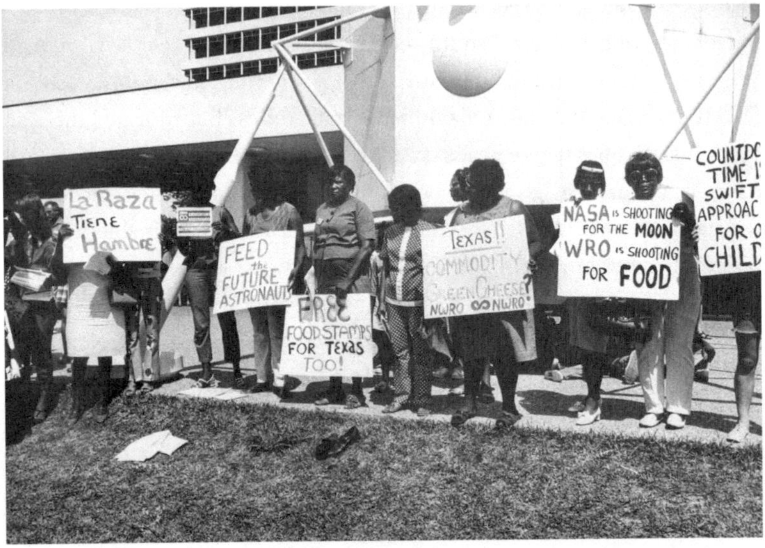

2.2 Mario De Biasi, National Welfare Rights Organization protest, Manned Spacecraft Center, Houston, Texas, 1969. © Archivio Mario De Biasi.

relationship among the civil rights movement, the US space race, the Apollo program, and, more important, the public artworks and demonstrations that such conflict would come to spawn. Whereas Gil Scott-Herron defined this conflict in his famed spoken-word poem "Whitey on the Moon" (1970), which illustrated Black social hardship in opposition to the excesses of US government spending and its underwriting of NASA space exploration, his criticism fits awkwardly around other minoritarian subjects who found means of cultural expression through the lens of Apollo missions.[49] Much like that future astronaut called out in the protest signage, people of color retained some representational stake in the aerospace industry, underscoring a larger and consistent transplanetary-relational dialogue in activism and cultural expression. The desire to go up catalyzed a Black and Latinx public art repertoire in a way deserving of closer attention. As this scene from the Johnson Space Center shows, counterpublics rallied, some spoke out in a different accent, and others pivoted from concerns of the present to those of the future, although without sacrificing the stakes of their communities. The potentiality of the US space program emboldened Black and brown outlooks on tomorrow in ways that shifted the discourse from a US ethnic minority perspective to a greater scaling and elevated vision. This chapter picks up on these transplanetary relations taking shape in the concrete surrounds of the built environment amid the Apollo program. Like Mexican muralists' composition of artworks resonant with their urban settings and everyday lives, these creatives resumed modes of address that also invited speculative lines of inquiry in keeping with the chief figures in this cosmic repertoire: the astronomer and astronaut.

Space Invading | Invading Space

According to Cockcroft and Barnet-Sánchez, the first significant cycle of Latinx mural art production occurred around 1969 to 1975.[50] Goldman argues that in California alone more than 1,500 murals "were made in the state during the first decade" of this artistic cycle, and Barnet-Sánchez and Tim Drescher further note that ninety-two murals were painted in Estrada Courts, a crucial hub of mural activity in East Los Angeles.[51] In 1973 Chicano activist and artist Charles "Cat" Félix spearheaded an effort to produce some of the most emblematic murals of the Chicanx art movement. Between 1970 and 1975, ample collaborative opportunities between the city's housing authority and regional organizations propagated public artworks that launched LA as a US public art capital "with the largest number of Chicano murals in the country."[52] Félix was an East LA resident who, tired of "looking at the gray, monotonous stucco walls . . . began to paint."[53] He faced an ambitious challenge when he was charged with the mural initiative at Estrada Courts, a planned housing community built during World War II. These murals established an important barrio public art lexicon and thus transformed what appeared to be an urban revitalization project with designs that ranged from cultural affirmation to naturalist outlooks and, even more, to a rebellious attitude.

Félix worked on behalf of Goez Art Studio and Gallery, an arts organization founded by brothers Johnny and José Luis Gonzalez with artist David Botello. This for-profit business fostered import sales of furnishings and creative activities in the city. According to Karen Mary Davalos, Goez was "a pioneer" because "the cofounders reframed their original emphasis on merchandise and fine art sales to include heritage tourism, community beautification through public art, graphic design, and a school for the visual arts."[54] Félix honed the energies of activist dissent, navigated gang turf wars, and maximized artist networks, resulting in "ninety painted surfaces."[55] These paintings were procured from an artistic pool already familiar to him. Though most creatives were self-taught, others were college educated or exposed to advanced studio art classes through the myriad of *talleres* (workshops) hosted by Goez and the comparable East LA cultural organization Mechicano Art Center. The creative stock circulating around Goez at that time was undeniable, and among the short-listed talents for Estrada Courts was painter Richard Haro.

Haro grew up in East LA and attended East LA College (ELAC), where he studied under famed Mexican American–generation artist Roberto Chavez. In 1969 Chavez joined the faculty of ELAC, where he developed curricular instruction on mural art making and techniques; by 1974, he chaired the Chicano Studies Department. Through a Los Angeles Community College District grant, he was awarded the opportunity to paint *The Path to Knowledge and the False University* (1974), a work proposed for the two-hundred-foot-long Ingalls Auditorium, greenlit by ELAC administrators.[56] Haro credited Chavez for teaching him how to be "realistic" in his practice, an ironic choice of words given Chavez's speculative art tendencies. "He kept me involved going to his studio, and he let me use the studio," Haro recalled.[57] The artist began painting in larger proportions under Chavez's tutelage, which built upon his creative foundations stemming from his youth. As a child, Haro often fell ill and was kept home from school. "My mom kept insisting that I draw, and when it was raining and when the people go by and [I would] paint them with an umbrella or shopping bags. So I started painting more and more, and then I got better and better."[58] A teacher in his junior high noticed that his creative activities were more than passing episodes. She alerted her colleagues, which affirmed something Haro intuitively understood. "She knew I had the talent."[59] Advice from Chavez "to keep painting" parlayed an important awareness of Goez-affiliated artists such as Félix, David Botello, David Lopez, Gil "Magu" Lujan, and Norma Montoya.[60] Chavez was painting murals at Estrada Courts, and Haro wouldn't be far behind, further confirming his self-awakening as a public art worker invested in higher, cosmic states of being.

In 1974 Haro completed *The Artist* with his sister Kate and son Daniel. It is a work that stands out among the Estrada Courts mural cluster for its portrayal of artistic imagination rendered in some speculative aesthetic of conjuration and creativity (see plate 8). Dulled in monochromatic hues and painted under "severe time limitations," the work has a pale specter that offsets a charcoal base adding ominous drama.[61] Splashes of color emulate light flashes, modernist paint splattering, or celestial explosions, a futurist and spiritual realization of not only Haro's recognizable signature but a look that eerily anticipates Hogan's abstract expressionist–inspired space art and even Chavez's auditorium mural with sacred actors, metaphysical ideas, and cosmic motifs.[62] Haro explains that due to the time constraints and Félix's flexibility, individual artists had more creative license, which served a bevy of ideas. The resulting phantasmagoric figure came "out of my mind. I had a picture of some of the guys that had painted like an artist [so Félix] called [the mural] 'The Artist.'"[63] He adds, "The lady that lived there said that her husband asked me to put this demon. I just did it because it came to my mind."[64] More in the transcendent mode in which biblical and interstellar themes converge, the piece stands out among a pantheon of iconic mural artworks lining Olympic Avenue with the gravitas of the "outside facing mural . . . for all to see."[65] Though this painting is no ordinary guerrilla mural akin to Hogan's, it resides in a prominent location in East LA, "mak[ing] a more public statement," one powerfully observed from a motoring car or cruising lowrider.[66] By no means is it Haro's only work at Estrada Courts, nor is it the only representation from his oeuvre to explore the connection between the unknown vestiges of barrio life. By contemplating what omniscient force is channeled through the artist's hand or palette, Haro's early mural prompts Estrada Courts onlookers to fathom ways of relating to Chicanx public art beyond the knowable and observable realm. Another Haro artwork expands on this proposition with possibilities derived from deep space.

In 1977 Haro added a second mural to the interior section of Estrada Courts, accenting the "nature walk," a famed section populated with an homage to regional flora and fauna. In *Outer Space*, Haro pivots on this ecocritical visual record by inserting a mural as an "important intra-cultural bridge," opening a deep-space rumination about other worlds (see plate 9).[67] Although Félix desired these innermost walls to circumvent "political trips and whatnot; we just wanted it nice and serene, nothing but Nature," in the aftermath of the moon mission and ensuing public exhaustion over spaceflight, Haro's enthusiasm for spacefaring fit awkwardly around Félix's pastoral outlook, a sharp contrast to the urban blight on the ground.[68] Certainly, his artistic statement might not have been agreeable to antipoverty activists' nearly antagonist response to the NASA space program almost a decade prior; it did hint, however, at a more nuanced thinking about the scope of barrio urbanism and cultural representation in light of post–Apollo 11 revelations.

Through its cool blue-hued backdrop, this 32-by-24-foot wall offers a viewpoint beyond the terrestrial confines of Earth. In the left foreground are two young men outfitted in urban streetwear on par with an East LA sartorial vernacular: white shirts, brown chinos, and slicked coifs. One teen faces the other. He seats himself on rocky terrain with his back turned to the viewer. We observe them mid-conversation. Positioned to the right of an iridescent rock formation radiating a teal glow are cholos appearing in the elsewhere. Their *charla* (talk) is unfinished, and thus this dialogue has yet to come. What they are about to say is not unlike the tactical efforts of those Johnson Space Center activists nearly a decade prior who understood that feeding socially impoverished Black and brown young people could reset the course for America's future astronauts and the space program, for that matter.

In Haro's articulation of an alien world with a clear view of Saturn, he conveys an East LA vignette located quite possibly on one of the planet's moons, like Titan. His mural is dialogic with a much-lauded Bonestell painting, *Saturn as Seen from Titan*, a work that Newell argues "launched a thousand careers" (see plate 10).[69] Bonestell's clean and contemplative vista conveys a picturesque environment quietly removed from the ethnic and genocidal violence engulfing the globe when he painted it during World War II, a predisposition that shaped his oeuvre (see chapter 3 for more). Perhaps intent on portraying "a utopian future free of political strife and full of hope," his "empty" land, vacuous planet, and unregulated airspace are a disingenuous meditation on the fraught and violent "alien" conditions that the multiethnic and immigrant publics of East LA found themselves in during the interwar years and at mid-century.[70] And so, with a point of view attentive to foreground and background in the composition, Haro accomplishes something that even Bonestell's exactitude does not. His painting lowers the terrain to the base of the wall at a life-size scale that blurs divisions between an extraterrestrial backdrop and Estrada Courts' green space. By creating a sight line that places these urban residents on the same landing as these barrio homeboys, he parlays new platforms for Chicanxs and Latinxs to relate to the cosmos, a transplanetary-relational shift that parallels the immersive and multisensory approaches that other speculation-driven and space art–inspired muralists were pursuing at that time in panoramic scenery and science museum interiors.[71]

Again, consider how McCall's *The Space Mural—A Cosmic View* at NASM towers over visitors in the building's lobby (see plate 7). Publics are presented with McCall's meditation on the big-bang creation myth, human spaceflight, and what he speculates as the impending discovery of new worlds christened by a brilliant cosmic light. McCall, an Anglo Protestant and army veteran who combined his interest in aeronautics with a holy charge over space exploration, boasts of national pride. The hierarchal ways of looking at the artwork command a nearly divine attention to the astronaut, a space techno-messiah whom museumgoers and, in particular, children are encouraged to look up to and strive to emulate. However, Haro's tactic adapts the Apollo program with subversive redirections, placing the barrio homeboys over the helmeted space pilot in space. By relocating Estrada Courts into higher orbit, rather than pontificating on the astronaut as the chief deliverer of the country's security, he deepens transplanetary relations—ways of connecting and communing with outer worlds—into the everyday urban surrounds.

By compelling the viewer to turn upward, Haro proves that a barrio future lies ahead beyond that earthly blue marble shrinking into the distance. Above the homeboys is an alien spacecraft, and its arrival stops the pair mid-action. Haro's composition conveys a feeling of wonder, echoing an affective register borrowed from the aesthetics of science fiction cinema. As film scholar Vivian Sobchack recounts, "Those images which awe us, stun us, do so not merely because they seem meticulously authentic but because they alienate us from our corporeal selves, from human notions of time and space. It is in this sense that they are truly alien visualizations although based on known scientific realities."[72] The pair are awed not only because a UFO descending on East LA would disrupt the banal happenings of Estrada Courts, but also because it would rupture the tenuous definitions of human and extraterrestrial. This shift, combined with the xenophobic discourse of Latinx illegality, intensifies what that spaceship might represent for these urban residents or even the casual spectator. As it levitates over the boys' heads, the flying saucer delivers a microcosmic city in its chamber, a passage to a miniaturized LA where future urban planning promises Chicanxs tomorrow. Here cholo life will undoubtedly endure.

Ironically, Haro's aerial habitat is not the work of some obscure science fiction B-movie that Sobchack touts but rather finds its origins in the "aerofuturism" of Hugo Gernsback. His dime-store digests fostered a subgenre of science fiction pulp serials in which stories like "The Empire in the Sky" and "Islands in the Air" were accompanied by illustrations of floating cities, microgravity modules, and suspended airport platforms.[73] These narratives dually reflect public fascination with aeronautical technological advancements and the United States' growing roster of island possessions stemming from the conqust of islands in the Antilles and Southeast Asia after the Spanish-American War in 1898 and the occupation of Hawaii in 1896.

This connection aside, Haro's mural is further indicative of the way aerofuturist aesthetics were quoted in artworks by artists in the Americas in direct and indirect ways. His bubbled world is immediately reminiscent of Argentine kinetic sculptor Gyula Kosice's *La Ciudad Hidroespacial* (*The Hydrospatial City*). Made of acrylic, Plexiglas, paint, and metal, his series of nineteen three-dimensional terrarium-inspired plastic domes contemplates human sustainability in flying contraptions powered by water (see plate 11). His proposal published in the *Madí Manifesto* (1946) discerns speculative architectural design with plausible scientific intent.[74] He apparently conferred with NASA aerospace engineers in a way that Bonestell would surely endorse.[75] The work amplifies a moment of Argentine progress and industrialization in the first half of the 1960s, where air, light, and volume supply all the sculptural materials for alternative forms of cohabitation.[76] His creative impetus for a future blueprint for Latin American society was completed in 1972, as a military coup sparked further humanitarian crises and state-led terror. It is worth reconsidering *La Ciudad Hidroespacial* (*The Hydrospatial City*) alongside Haro's outer-space mural. Certainly, Haro's wall art dates to 1977. The artists share a mutual attention to spacecraft and operating alternative habitats to shelter possible futures for their communities off-Earth and, in this way, they connect transplanetary-relational thinking from Buenos Aires to East Los Angeles. In their dual proposals for urban utopias escaping the strife of revolution and civil unrest by going up, they forward images of the Americas in an ascendant arc that cannot disarticulate space art and space exploration from the unstable political situations at that time. Consider how, for instance, McCall's oil painting *Desert Nocturne* (1977) depicts an airborne world extracting another module from an Arizona landscape (see plate 12). An Indigenous presence is emptied from this scene. Rick Guidice pondered inhabitable space colonies with NASA Ames Research Center scientists in the summers of 1975–77 with recognizable touches of a sanitized and mainly white suburbia.[77]

By theorizing what intervention hangs in the air, the intermingling of homeboys, the universe, and even space habitats in the Global South elucidates how Chicanx muralists were advanced and were thinking about what futures were possible in the mid-1970s. Although Chicanx muralism and Haro's work, in particular, were not a part of NASA's or NASM's curatorial prerogatives at this time, these creative repertoires were fielding transplanetary relational viewpoints that opened barrios, walls, and minds to meditate on what was possible for these homeboys over the Kármán line. By "comprehending the not-yet-here" that performance scholar José Esteban Muñoz calculates as "this temporal calculus [that] performed and utilized the past and future as armaments to combat the devastating logic of the world here and now," Haro suggests that despite the onslaught of economic hardship and state neglect on Southern California's Latinx demographic, another way is possible.[78] His pivot toward science fiction visuality, aerial viewpoints, and airborne sanctuaries points to other outcomes for Estrada Courts' "future astronauts." Though they are not uniformed in space suits or flight gear, these *vatos* are going places.

However, Estrada Courts as an artery to the future does not begin with Haro's trailblazing work. Daring to scale upward is also germane to the earliest East LA murals of his contemporaries, David Botello and Wayne Alaniz Healy. These muralists also scale upward, resetting barrio youth perceptions by redirecting their gazes from grounded reality to the liberating powers of the sky. In this next section, works like Botello's *Read Between the Lines* (1975) and *Dreams of Flight* (1973) foster other perspectives on Chicanx aeriality, technology, and the barrio of tomorrow. Healy with his accomplishments in aerospace engineering and mathematics nuances this medium further with an art-science conjunction unmatched in the city's civic art scene at that time.

As these renewed engagements with futurity and public art suggest, speculation complicates internal Chicanx art movement squabbles that falsely pit social realist representation against more experimental modes. These existential questions about being and belonging as "planetary creatures" undergird the political ideas and visions of the New Left.[79] As a result, barrio artists' outlooks on the solar system open the scale and address for the brick-and-mortar medium of wall art. More specifically, though Chicanx muralists conveyed cosmic meaning in their repertoires, as Latorre suggests, they also contemplated the consequences of space science and technology in ways gleaned by vanguard Mexican artists even in the 1930s. What Haro practices in the sun-saturated corners of public assisted housing is actually an advanced language about science fiction and science fact that was trailblazing and concurrent with other astronomical public art productions at that time. As we will see, that look toward scientific visualization, space history, and the aerospace industry formed the foundations of mural artworks by Botello and his later collaborations with Healy in 1975.

Cosmic *Familia*

Before realizing that Botello was the artist behind the mural heralding Chicanx flights of fancy on Olympic Boulevard, Healy admired the painting. Himself a self-proclaimed "math and science guy" from East LA, Healy graduated from Garfield High School in 1964.[80] Having completed trigonometry and math analysis before his final semester, he too ended up at East Los Angeles College, where he satisfied requirements in calculus. These foundations gained him admission to California State Polytechnic

University, Pomona (Cal Poly Pomona), where he double majored in math and aerospace engineering. At that time, he had not yet conceived of art as a career or trade. "I didn't know anybody that made a living as an artist. . . . I didn't know what an art gallery was, or an art museum. So art was something you did on your own," he reflected.[81] Without the requisite training, his artistic skill set was fostered mainly through family. He received informal tips from his brother-in-law and his uncle, Joe Alaniz, the latter of whom he called "my art educator."[82] In an interview with Roberto Tejada in 2007, he described Uncle Joe's prickly relationship with his father. "He actually worked with my dad. They were partners. I don't know if they really got along that well. . . . But I would see him draw or paint, and, you know, 'Oh, man, I want to do that,' you know. And he'd give me a tip or something like that. 'Do it that way.'"[83]

After graduating from Cal Poly, Healy spent four and a half years in Cincinnati, Ohio, where he worked on the CF-6 engine for General Electric. He made art in his spare time with a nostalgic recollection of "street scenes. Vatos hanging out, stuff like that."[84] He read about the Chicano Moratorium March on August 29, 1970, in the pages of the *Cincinnati Enquirer*. Stirred by the headlines that read "East LA Riots," he learned that this anti–Vietnam War demonstration attracted nearly thirty thousand protesters and ended in chaos.[85] When the smoke cleared, famed *Los Angeles Times* journalist Ruben Salazar was assassinated, representing the penultimate travesty for East LA Chicanx activists pursuing social equality. Healy knew that his time in the Midwest was coming to an end, and as he and his wife were expecting a baby, he returned to East LA in 1972 amid the tumult of these difficult times. Chicanx art movement activities grew, offering young upstarts like Healy new creative, organizational, and collaborative outlets that were not possible just years before. A chance encounter proved influential and transformed the once-incompatible realities Healy occupied, which compartmentalized art from science.

A show at Point Gallery in 1975 featured the East LA art collectives Los Four and Asco (meaning "nausea") and thus proved to be a historic moment in Latinx art history. This joint exhibition attracted the glitterati of East LA experimental, performance, and mixed-media arts to Santa Monica, a coastal setting on the city's west side. Botello, armed with posters detailing a map of East LA murals, a project he researched and coproduced through Goez, appeared on behalf of the nascent commercial venture. His conversation about muralism with another attendee, who cradled a child in his arms, proved fateful. "I rolled up and Wayne was there looking at the artwork. We finally recognized who we were after we were talking," Botello recollected.[86] The pair had attended grammar school together. "Crayon buddies from the beginning," as Healy retold it.[87] When the bulldozing of barrio neighborhoods to make room for the Long Beach Freeway (the 710) sent Botello to a different school district, these schoolboys lost touch. This chance encounter was a reunion of sorts. They realized they were simultaneously engaged in East LA mural production, with Botello at Estrada Courts and Healy at Ramona Gardens. The pair also shared an admiration for their respective unsigned works in the barrio. "When I found that David Botello painted [*Dreams of Flight*], I fell in love with him," Healy recalled. "As an aerospace engineer, [I remember] seeing this mural and saying, 'Wow! He's got it all covered.'"[88]

A collaboration between them was inevitable. To say that their mutual attention to Chicanx nationalist politics formed the basis for their creative camaraderie is an oversimplification. It overlooks the way a synergistic dialogue combined math, art, and public intervention, leading to a creative enterprise that made their colossal paintings standouts for the period. It also blunts how the astronomy, space technology, and post-Apollo image archives were frequent resources for new work. Translating these ideas was not unusual considering that Botello had some background in converting data into visual evidence. Like McCall before him, he had enlisted in the army, taught cartography to other servicemen, and made his Goez mural-mapping venture an extension of his military skill set.[89] Likewise, US national defense industries played a crucial role in Healy's creative repertoire. He was an aerospace engineer working on the North American F-86 Sabre jet fighter.[90] This intimate knowledge of aeronautical technology was yoked to a richly syncretic approach, allowing for an artistic technique that trailed the sky. Converting these ideas into something compatible with science-fictional ideas was not far-fetched. When the pair came together, their first piece was just as serendipitous as their initial run-in. The end product was a work that would come to be their most recognizable and visually defining.

Botello and Healy's principal collaboration was nearly fated. The piece was the result of a coin flip, and as the story goes, Healy was tasked with finding the pair's first wall. His search brought him to the corner of North Broadway and Daly Street in Lincoln Heights, where Crocker Bank stood. Healy supplied all the self-confidence that was needed that day. He spoke directly to the bank manager and pled his case for an 18-by-35-foot mural design not unlike his piece *Ghosts of the Barrio* (1974) at Ramona Gardens. However, his proposal did not account for the entirety of the building facade, which towered at ninety feet. Though the building manager approved the initial design, he tasked Healy with also completing four other panels lining Daly Street. In the rare position of having too much wall, the duo was energized by the expansive site. "This is easy!" Healy recollected about securing the commission, which drew on funds from the bank and the Citywide Mural Project under the direction of Judith Baca.[91] However, the difficult part required Botello and Healy to revise their proposal, taking the "Crocker Bank Mural Cartoon" study designed on November 24, 1975, and reimagining it for a five-part narrative structure.

Faced with the country's bicentennial celebration, the pair took exception to a patriotic discourse that traced American origins to the typical pantheon of "founding fathers," British colonies, Jamestown, and the New England corridor. "We were happening out here, too," Healy stressed.[92] Together, Healy and Botello channeled their frustration into multisectional panels. Each vignette not only countered a whitewashing of the past but also unveiled a pervasive Mexican presence in the United States, shifting a bicentennial focus westward. In the work, major synecdochical archetypes represented historical epochs replete with visual signposts of El Indígeno (The Indigenous), La Española (The Spanish), El Hacendado (The Farmer), and La Soldadera (The Soldier). For this bicentennial, the viewer would confront the atrocities of US empire beginning with scenes of Indigenous civilization, Spanish colonialization, Mexican revolution, contemporary farmworker struggles, and labor abuse. These images culminated in a political march toward *la familia*.[93]

It is not surprising that the newly formed Los Dos Streetscapers (more commonly known as the East Los Streetscapers, in tribute to the duo's nexus of artists and assistants) would debut a mural that captured a social movement fervor rhyming with vociferous outcries of "Brown Pride" and cultural nationalist ideologies. Latorre's response to Healy and Botello's mural argues it is "in keeping with the goals of *el movimiento*," as it perpetuates "the social unit of the family."[94] Despite "the old trope of equating family with the nation" being an important queer and feminist critique about early Chicana and Chicano art movement imagery, few acknowledge the kind of speculative work that this medium was also doing.[95]

Consider how the piece's title, *Chicano Time Trip*, proposes a "trip" in its spatiotemporal accords. The mural elicits a promenade across periods and social crises, beginning with the ancient Americas and progressing to the modern *la familia* (see plate 13). However, the paneling encourages counterreadings from right to left.[96] Healy and Botello propose a visual-verbal construction that reverses the horizontal logic of phonemic writing. Despite facing a largely English- and Spanish-language audience, this mural misapprehends a sinistrodextral system, disordering strings of modern language. In this "time trip," the roving motorist or passing pedestrian would find the graduated march toward the heteronormative Chicana and Chicano family unit possibly scrambled, akin to that spill of art historical texts in Hogan's novel, which catalyzed the formation of the Guerrilla Muralists. More than a recitation about the Chicanx family, the East Los Streetscapers introduce a writing system that indeed *trips up* more linear passages through a heteronormative righting of Mexican American history. That is, the speculative structures of *Chicano Time Trip* bend and fold periodization, capsizing life-cycle maturation and political destiny (see plate 14).

Such flexibility appears in a closer examination of the panel pieces, each presenting an anchoring thematic figure encompassed by hyperbolic shapes. The curvature of these lines unsettles flat and directional planes. In conic sections, the mirrored halves are perfunctory portals opening temporal encounters that add divergently thematic historical windows. This scrambled recovery of a vexed Chicanx political consciousness may have more in common with the sonic boom than with a unidirectional tromp toward heteronormative procreation. Sharing two fixed points from which these lines are constant, the hyperbolic shapes of *Chicano Time Trip* subdue any "straight" ordering of monumental mural narratives. This mishmash of timescales is further accentuated in Healy and Botello's unexpected pictorial overlays, finding themselves "painting over each other's strokes."[97] At edges, they come together, forging a collaborative language at curved rims and layers that bend space-time. Being geometric and technologically minded is an asset for these creatives who unfurl a barrio future for the mural form early on.

This heterochronic architecture, a cosmic trip through time, leapt from the built environment to the pages of *National Geographic* in 1979. A photographic detail of the piece was featured in the story "Los Angeles: City in Search of Itself" and thus epitomized the Chicanx mural movement that was giving the city its multiethnic flair.[98] Although the artists behind the piece were not named, the mural was instrumentalized by an editorial to punctuate a distinct urban visuality "priming the pride of the city's largest ethnic group."[99] The juxtaposition of the photo and text represented an arbitrary if not contradictory journalistic account of Latinx Los Angeles. The reporter's tone even bordered on caution, warning that "if present trends continue, the majority of Angelenos will bear Spanish surnames by century's end."[100] The two-page spread following *Chicano Time Trip*'s reproduction relied on a xenophobic rhetoric to alarm readers about foreign outsiders. "The city is plagued by an endless cycle of . . . illegal Mexican aliens that overtaxes U.S. immigration agents," the article reads, entangling undocumented laborers with insidious connotations about plagues, disease, or pollutants encroaching on Southern California with unyielding force.[101] And as the pages of *National Geographic* put it, this was no ordinary outbreak—it was *alien*—and given this paratextual connotation, this mural was indicative of this invasion.

Reading the East Los Streetscapers mural in this context suggests that its speculative dimensions are not bound to the transgressive paneling structure or reworkings of space and time. In its print reproduction, the mural is not about the triumph of the nuclear Mexican American family or a Chicanx history lesson. It is about "Mexican aliens" and disease, and although Healy is quick to argue, "I never got hung up on science fiction," it is difficult to disarticulate how this iconic example of Chicanx muralism is associated with the speculative genre.[102] Even if one reads the *National Geographic* coverage as the missteps of a photo editor or the calculated outcome of a propagandist, its image-text coarticulation exposes a tension between Chicanx muralism and traces of an outside foreign threat. By the late 1970s, this discursive crosscurrent brought someone like Healy, a painter and aerospace engineer, closer to not only barrio iconography but also science-fictional association. It is ironic that the same year this issue was published, he and Botello were growing more intensely focused on other transplanetary matters. Their Chicanx public address turned ascendant. Opportunity was to be had in outer space, and the East Los Streetscapers had bold plans for it.

In 1977 Botello and Healy proposed their next ambitious project, *Moonscapes*, through the California Arts Council and Office of the State Architect's grant program for art in public buildings. Culver City on the west side of LA was hardly a stronghold of Chicanx mural production. In fact, this neighborhood was better known for its film history, housing major studio backlots for MGM and Hal Roach Studios (among others), a cultural geography central to artist Vincent Ramos's aesthetic, as discussed in chapter 4. This part of the city was widely regarded as a "sundown town," a planned community founded by Harry Culver that catered specifically to white homeowners.[103] In fact, sociologist James Loewen observed that *Gone with the Wind* (1939) producer David O. Selnick was puzzled over Black protest about his film's antebellum romanticism despite operating shoots from a highly segregated part of Southern California.[104] More ironic still is the way West LA would become not only the epicenter of filmmaking but also the manufacturing site of another crucial technology industry: aircraft and aerospace. The racialization of city planning was germane to historian Josh Sides's study, in which he noted that lack of "residential proximity to [aircraft] production facilities . . . effectively eliminated blacks from the industry, even when the industry was not explicitly discriminatory."[105] Sides adds that a Mexican American generation fared better, with "housing opportunities for Mexicans and blacks in postwar Los Angeles . . . [being] a reflection of white attitudes toward each group," though working in this aeronautical belt of West LA was a different matter.[106] He points out that between the 1930s and 1960s, "employers and workers almost unanimously agreed that aircraft work was white men's work."[107]

What Botello and Healy were able to advance on the grounds of a government building at the close of the 1970s was radical for that time. The dimensions of the Department of Motor Vehicles (DMV) building totaled four thousand square feet, posing an irresistible opportunity for the pair. However, they were baffled by the building's facade, a saturated stain of dark black. Botello found the chroma off-putting at first, thinking it appeared more velvet painting than grand-scale Chicanx mural. "[It's] the color of space," Botello concluded.[108] His offhand remark stirred Healy, who realized that the DMV stood just four miles away from his current employer, Hughes Aircraft Company. "All the people around here are aerospace workers, and [Hughes is] one of the largest employers," Healy recalled, becoming more resolved that this mural would expand their reach to other multiethnic cultural geographies of LA.[109] Together, they could more boldly consider the cosmos by moving Chicanx public art to its outer limits. The pair was awarded the commission, which not only necessitated expanding their ranks (Botello's younger brother Paul took up a brush and assisted alongside George Yepes) but also required assembling an unusual image archive.

A photo documenting their studio in 1978 unveils the combination of print, photocopy, and photographic references informing the mural study (see plate 15). These images range from the empirical to the whimsical. A famed snapshot of Albert Einstein cycling around his home in 1933, taken by California Institute of Technology trustee Ben Meyer, augments the public perception of the famed physicist as no business and all play beneath Santa Barbara's sunlit skies. Ephemera are pinned at the bottom of a studio bulletin board: a photocopy of lunar surface craters is resourced for what will yield the mural's second section. Its smooth astrogeology contradicts the rocky canyons and ravines portrayed in Bonestell's much-lauded *Lunar Landscape* at the Hayden Planetarium, further inching this Chicanx public art piece and others like Haro's *Outer Space* among the giants in a space art mural repertoire. By mining an assortment of materials from magazines like *Scientific*

American and advertisements for the Pan Am airline, they take a nimbler approach where astronomical art is reimagined with a critical race outlook for this sundown town. Spacefaring is removed from the artistic direction of a NASA-appointed creative class. Instead, it becomes the property of starry-eyed barrio innovators. To make their mark, they equally recited icons familiar to space art imagery yet invested with a transplanetary-relational purpose.

AstroAmericas

In *Moonscapes*, Botello and Healy present a six-part mural where the visual archetypes occupying the public art repertoire of science museum aficionados like Bonestell, McCall, and Sloan are recalled. Otherworldly terrains, advanced flight technology, celestial objects, and the cosmos demonstrate how this public art piece at a DMV is consistent with an image economy that may appear to peddle NASA boosterism. However, from the outset, the pair make textual strides to question "our position in the universe" in a way that takes up the political questions raised not only by the National Welfare Rights Organization at the Manned Spacecraft Center nearly a decade earlier but also by photography scholar Allan Sekula, who in 1973 produced *Aerospace Folktales*, an assembly of 142 snapshots critically interrogating the grim aftermath of a Southern Californian aerospace industry in disarray. Layoffs at Lockheed-California Company, where his dad was employed in Burbank, are paired with factory workers filing out of a General Dynamics Convair Division plant in San Diego, dousing the state's aerial technology belt with cold water.[110] "How can we allow our society's overburden of advertising belligerence, 'labor-saving' electrical nonsense, and strategic arms overkill to take precedence over the care and maintainance [*sic*] of spaceship Earth as we hurtle through the cosmos?" the signage asks, suggesting that this mural is more than Cold War propaganda.[111] The East Los Streetscapers are mindful and transplanetary-relational in approach as they mobilize a vertical outlook that sees the public's custodial role as Earth's caretaker. In this way, they build on ideas first rehearsed in their early murals, from flights of fancy to time tripping. Combining Healy's aerospace expertise, Botello's science fiction acumen, and the antiracist furor fueling the Chicanx art movement and the xenophobic discourses perpetuated in mainstream media, this mural operation was no space opera. Instead, through the wall the artists discreetly explored communing with outer space. These reserves of cultural knowledge appear in the work from the multiethnic civilizations of the world, ancient and present.

The basis of *Moonscapes II: Cruising Through Space/Time* is discerned from the group's mural study (see plate 15). In the mural, to the right of the image of Einstein, is a conical grid superimposed with three sky watchers representing different epochs of interstellar research (see plate 16). An ancient Maya, ancient Chinese, and contemporary Puerto Rican radio astronomer look up, observing the metamorphosis of a star as it transitions from a red giant to a supernova, first recorded in China around AD 1054. The crab nebula, a remnant of a supernova explosion, is detected with advanced radar equipment nodding to Arecibo, which, at that time, was the largest stereoscopic observatory in the world. Built in Barrio Esperanza in Puerto Rico by the US National Science Foundation in 1964, it was later closed after sustaining substantial damage in the aftermaths of hurricanes Irma and Maria.[112] In this way, Healy and Botello held regard for this powerful cochlear apparatus hearing the universe's greater frequencies to show another way that the Americas, East Asia, and the solar system harmonize across space and time. By trans-ing sights and sounds, these figures transform tuning into a cosmic reverb more ancient and sacred than themselves.

In their reach toward the vertical expanse, they represent a counterimage to a traditional portrait lexicon that committed the decorated achievements of Western men of science in paint. Works like Marco Basaiti's *Portrait of an Astronomer* (1512), Gerrit Dou's *Astronomer by Candlelight* (1650s), Johannes Vermeer's *The Astronomer* (1668), and Jan Matejko's *Astronomer Copernicus, or Conversations with God* (1873) function as visual tributes to patriarchal forebears of astronomy. This aforementioned corpus in the broadest sense portrays embodied visualizations of skyward apprehension, modeling the proper decorum for visual literacy. In art historian Jonathan Crary's notes about Vermeer's painting, he elucidates a visual grammar reliant on "a solitary male figure absorbed in learned pursuits within the rectangular confines of a shadowy interior."[113] He adds, "In a rapt stillness, ponder[ing] that crucial feature of the world, its extension, so mysteriously unlike the unextended immediacy of their own thoughts yet rendered intelligible to mind by the clarity of these representations, by the magnitudinal relations," these portrayals of "great men" are circumscribed by Westernized props of scientific measure.[114] Whether we consider the celestial globes in Vermeer's and Dou's depictions or the heliocentric mappings recorded by Copernicus in Basaiti's and Matejko's figurations, colonial mastery, if not righteous control over Earth and the planetary system to which it belongs, is the authority of Europe. In this way, Matejko's depiction of Copernicus looking up into the night sky is not only a work of speculation (as the whereabouts of the late astronomer's observatory are unknown) but also a salient realization of early modern Europeans' "lust for universal knowledge, dreams of global enlightenment, and geopolitical imperatives of empire," as Denis Cosgrove argues.[115] These paintings perpetuate portraits of visual perception guided by the ideal colonial agent whose "solitary" work is, ironically, in service to extractive violence on land and sky.

That figuration is radically contradicted by the kinds of cross-ethnic and cross-racial unification centering the East Los Streetscapers' DMV mural. Astronomers of the Americas and East Asia come together in a Chicanx public art intervention shifting the sphere of humanity's intelligence about the universe into the cooperative tenets of cosmology, ethnoastronomy, and shared sky watching and even listening. Like the scramble of historical referents made in Hogan's spill of art books in *Cortez on Jupiter* or even the "supposing" work in Alfredo Véa's *Gods Go Begging* (see chapter 1), space knowledge is made visible not through familiar compositional tropes of the sixteenth and seventeenth centuries in European painting of drapery and candlelit interiors but through a crash course in "cruising through space/ time," as the title self-indicates. For the East Los Streetscapers, the future of "spaceship Earth" is predicated on a cosmic unity, a transplanetary-relational statement about alliances formed through a shared vertical kinship as they ambitiously truck through the vastness of deep space.

Such ascendant unification is the focus of a later yet comparable artwork, *Ganas, That Is All You Need* (1988) (see plate 17), which hung in the *Mathematica* exhibition at the California Museum of Science and Industry in Los Angeles following a successful commission by the Los Angeles Unified School District. Jaime Escalante, the famed math teacher from Healy's alma mater, Garfield High School, centers the composition. Portrayed against another darkened backdrop, Escalante is a suitable counterimage augmenting the "great men of science" traditionally found in portraits codifying scientific and technological achievement. Akin to their *Chicano Time Trip*, Healy and Botello organize a narrative in which different historical and speculative vignettes scale up and interconnect in a geometric congruity. Two hyperbola planes divide a two-dimensional canvas, adding perspectival depth to an otherwise flat surface. In the work's right quadrant, children play *fútbol* (soccer). A parabolic arc depicts the velocity with which the ball speeds, an equation best solved by the Mesoamerican glyphs to the right and the apple reaching out above them. Melding differential and integral calculus equations of the ancient Maya to the laws of gravity fathomed by Sir Isaac Newton above, these children are inheritors and practitioners of scientific knowledge even in the mundane activity of street ball. Healy and Botello's tack is simply didactic, showing how a history of math and science championed by Escalante and given cinematic meaning in the biopic *Stand and Deliver* (directed by Ramón Menéndez, 1988), discussed in chapter 1, demonstrates how the modern space program is indebted to the astronomers of the ancient Americas. Above Escalante's head, the cosmos opens. Here the NASA space shuttle meets El Caracol, the Mesoamerican observatory at Chichén Itzá in Mexico. The Pleaides—the closest star cluster to Earth, first observed by Galileo and used by sailors to navigate the sea—radiates in the upper left in a way that subtly contests a western European authority over the cosmos.

While these detail-oriented Chicanx muralists present faithful representations of aerospace technology and celestial bodies similar to other space artists mainly working on the East Coast, their intent is a speculative throwback to that bubbled space city in Haro's mural or that inquiry spoken by Véa's soldiers in Vietnam: "Do you suppose there will ever be Mexicanos in space?"[116] Healy and Botello's answer eschews the NASA astronautic program's privileging of Anglo-American pilots. Instead, they eye an alternative history for the Apollo program, seeming to ask, What would happen if Mesoamerican civilizations evaded Spanish colonization, allowing for modern space technologies to advance in the image of the Aztecs? That future visualized on a portable mural hanging in the California Museum of Science and Industry undermines the Adams-Onís Treaty of 1819, the Texas Revolution of 1835–36, and the Mexican-American War of 1846–48, parlaying a space science advancement in an ancient Indigenous key. In their hypothetical way, the space station would be carved from Aztec sunstone, a calendrical system keeping time with agricultural cultivation, day cycles, and meteorological change. By hacking NASA technology with pre-Columbian know-how, they reset the terms of international space cooperation in a way that reflects the collaborative ethos that the pair practiced in technique and visual content. With *ganas*, a Spanish term for gumption and grit, Escalante's portrait calls toward Latinx *higher* learning where, under the tutelage of this Bolivian immigrant, calculus, computer science, and astronautics are the suitable reward for hard work. Colonial discourses of scientific inferiority in the Americas are interrogated and contradicted. In this mural format, the gazes of children or even sky watchers of color (should we consider *Moonscapes II*?) seek starry pathways off-Earth. The future is plotted in ways divorced neither from the

NASA Apollo program nor from the speculative machinations that undergird Véa's humorous conjecture in *Gods Go Begging* as Mexicans piloted into space.

Fancy Flying | Flying Fancy

In *Ganas*, miniaturized moon men in vacuum-sealed space suits are uniformed in ways that make their racialization obscure and nonspecific. Though their racialized meaning is left open to interpretation, when compared to the pair's previous visual investigations, the Chicanx subtext is undeniable. For example, aeronautical motifs appear in Botello's 1973 *Dreams of Flight* (see plate 18). At the center of the wall in that mural is a young boy setting sail on a tire swing. Intermingling spheres rehearse a compositional structure found in other mural collaborations like *Chicano Time Trip*, consolidating a recognizable aesthetic language. In Botello's vignettes various scenes of flight portray a Chicanx courtship of the skies, which point toward ascendant possibilities. According to Barnet-Sánchez and Drescher, this mural is a work of dreaming where "Estrada [Courts'] children's aspirations for the possibility of a high-tech future [is] visualized in terms of history and Mesoamerican myth."[117] To fly is another means of Chicanx liberation, a way in which the simplicity of a tire swing or paper airplane is the platform from which aerial routes toward freedom are envisaged.

However, this Chicanx vertical climb cuts not only through the stratosphere but also through gender divides. In the artwork the child to the left of the tire-swinging dreamer winds the propeller of a World War II fighter biplane. A look of amusement precedes playtime, a countenance consistent between both iterations. And yet toying around opens new possibilities for Botello and, in turn, an opportunity for fresh interpretation. Between 1973 and 1996, the Latinx public perception of that youngster's gendering destabilizes and transforms from masculine to female presenting (see plate 19). Whereas Barnet-Sánchez and Drescher call this shift a matter of the artist's "increased awareness of gender discrimination," and thus an attempt to assuage the omission of girls among the hypermasculine and homosocial protagonists focusing East LA Chicanx muralism, trans-ing terms are rarely considered here. True, Botello's work is not the kind of tribute to transgender of color life, death, and activism seen in works like *Por Vida* (2015) at Galería de la Raza in San Francisco or *Pay It No Mind* (2019), a Stonewall commemoration in the Oaklawn neighborhood of Dallas, Texas.[118] However, any attempt to omit Botello's original iteration would be unfaithful to the artist's revisionist process, which began with a "self-supported restoration" and, as a result, shared transplanetary-relational implications.[119]

Gender is speculative in Botello's walled tableaux; masculinity and femininity manifest another kind of fantasy, a flight as natural as a star transitioning from red giant to supernova. Botello contemplates a mutable existence that reshapes in aerial terms. That is, if flight technology is a modernist symbol of societal progress, might the child's gender transformation be an equally innovative accomplishment of science? Botello's revisionist process unfixes art, space, and time in ways that look up only to revise gender as something to be modified and thus malleable. When manifested in the context of skyward fancy, might Chicanx gender fluidity be state of the art, akin to the supersonic jetliner in which the figure kneels?

According to Tobias Wofford, "Aviation technologies were often invoked in terms that echoed well-established justifications for the colonial project."[120] Certainly, aeronautics exalted in its airborne power, exerting oppressive force and symbolizing a "techno-dominance" hovering over racialized subjects and colonial possessions.[121] However, Botello's approach is more nuanced, suggesting that there is something galvanizing when East LA residents cast their gazes at scenes of flight. While this attitude is even more resonant with the *Moonscapes* project (as we shall see), his provocation is a transplanetary relation linking mural art with a racialized art project at a grander scale and with perceptual gravitas. Consider how the astronaut entry in the upper right sphere in Botello's mural expands Chicanx dreaming to the most advanced icon of human advancement. The moon man is monumentally inscribed for the barrio and, in turn, elicits a kind of cultural literacy borrowing from different visual registers: NASA boosterism, astrophotography, and US state defense imagery during the Cold War. An otherwise two-dimensional rendering of an "Apollonian gaze . . . a divine and mastering view from a single perspective," as Cosgrove states, has collective consequences here.[122] A scene positioned from a lunar standpoint, much like in Haro's piece, shifts the viewer's terrestrial location elsewhere. Earth becomes a distanced yet unifying blue marble, a delicate orb from which East LA residents shoulder its care and survival. To look up at this vignette activates a transplanetary relation that dually combines urban housing with the solar system, making these contexts coaxials in Chicanx public art making. Furthermore, by flanking the astronaut with an Aztec eagle knight, Botello proposes an aerial genealogy that enunciates a critical argument, demonstrating how verticality has played a profound role in reshaping and redirecting ethnoracial existence, whether pointing *el barrio* toward the moon or, in the case of his 1996 revision, at new chromosomal horizons. Indeed, Mexicans are in space, and they have long exercised their right to fly. The astronaut's racialization in this piece is a matter of compositional juxtaposition and image association akin to *Ganas, That Is All You Need*. However, Botello's partnership with Healy makes such representation an explicit connection in the DMV commission.

Because the DMV building's facade facing Washington Boulevard is on a heavily trafficked street in Culver City where commuting Hughes Aircraft Company employees were sure to take notice, a statement about civilization's future needed a hero on a grand scale. Again, the duo turned to the astronaut, who stands in a commanding frontal pose in *Moonscapes I: On the Tail of Healy's Comet* (1979) (see plate 20). The dominating posture makes the space pilot a chief agent overseeing an expedition and extravehicular activity (EVA) on this lunar terrain. The left arm stretches out, overlaying the fiery path of "Healy's Comet," a riff on the muralist's name as well as a simultaneous recollection of Halley's Comet, an omen of change and revolution, catalyzing that migratory force of star power in transplanetary relations, as discussed in this book's first chapter. The celestial object fires horizontally across the wall, intersecting with the astronaut's hand in a way that resembles the sword of a knight, the lightsaber of a Jedi, or the rod of an Olympian. This athletic comportment is perhaps another biographical reference to Healy, who belonged to the pole vault team in high school, a sport he shared with fellow track-and-fielder Buzz Aldrin. Although the life of an aerospace-engineer-turned-muralist scaling LA's built environment in the name of barrio futurity mirrors the fictional world of *Cortez on Jupiter* more than it does the biography of a famed Apollo 11 astronaut, his embedment in the work is most coherent in science-fictional terms. The visual plane of a comet crossing the moon man's body with a ferocious velocity invites a speculative game of "What if?" *What if* Healy's work at Hughes Aircraft Company had fostered opportunities to qualify him as a comparable "superman" in the US space program? *What if* his brownness was not a deterrent but a license for inclusivity in this ostensibly white and hypermasculine arm of this space science and defense industry? In this way, the muralists' open dialogue with LA's aircraft and aerospace industry is a Chicanx cultural rebuttal, a bid to imbue a figure like Aldrin within a pantheon of barrio urban figures. And as with the reimagining of astronomers in the *Moonscapes* mural as a whole, the duo strives to make the moon man a part of his East LA story. Looping Aldrin into the wall in this way was contingent on the visual record of Apollo 11 photography.

Reworking astronautic source material into Chicanx public art expression was not unlike the scientific visualization process that US artists "officially" registered with the NASA Artists Cooperative Program practiced that same decade. These activities in service to the public good were occurring simultaneously among these artists on opposite coasts. In their homage to Apollo 11, the East Los Streetscapers returned to a historic photograph from the moon landing where Neil Armstrong's reflection is cast on Aldrin's gold visor. In their iteration, however, it is not the moon that gleams on the bubbled surface but the opposite side of Washington Boulevard. In their reworking of the mirrored helmet, they join landscapes otherwise disjointed or rarely conceived in tandem under the auspices of Chicanx mural art. As a result, the cosmos came down to a sundown town where an icon found expression in a Chicanx and Latinx art lexicon thought unthinkable because that vocabulary traditionally belonged to other space art creatives, like astronaut-turned-painter Alan Bean.

Bean's *First Men* portrait series also takes creative license, replicating the gilded sight made possible by Aldrin's uniform.[123] In *First Men: Buzz Aldrin* (2007), Bean has cameraman Armstrong reflected in Aldrin's shielded visage. An accompanying piece, *First Men: Neil Armstrong* (2007), is more unapologetically speculative as the artist strives to imagine what the astrophotographer might have looked like taking the picture, since no visual record exists of this historic moment. With low-relief prints of moon boots and sprinklings of lunar dust in acrylic paint, Bean enshrines NASA and outer planetary matter in the artwork in a way reminiscent of Vargas-Suarez Universal (to be discussed momentarily). Thus, art historians find his "deep space and high tech" aesthetic akin to an eyewitness account from the fourth man to walk on the moon. These extraordinary paintings exert clout as cultural expressions but also preserve a perception of authenticity that even Bean champions, saying, "In the long view, I hope I come to be seen the way Charles Russell is viewed now—an artist who experienced the frontier that he painted."[124] Self-aggrandizement aside, Healy and Botello aspire less to manufacture American art's settler colonial paradigms as documentation of manifest destiny. Rather, they activate the astronaut figure as a border-breaking and boundary-defying transgressor. By showing not Armstrong but the image of Culver City in Aldrin's reflective shield, the artists portray Aldrin on a different scale and spatial platform, away from the contentious geopolitics of spacefaring, national security, and Cold War anxiety. The astronaut is a migratory symbol of a different kind. In his ascendancy he toggles between terrestrial and vertical borders, a transplanetary relation with consequences for the aerospace industry to which Healy belonged.

Linking other worlds is also a matter for the closet. The icon's uniform is overt in its meaning for urban barrio style. On the astronaut's left shoulder, viewers see the flag of Mexico branded on the space suit. By suggesting that this space pilot is no longer the fulfillment of a US defense industry intent on exerting technological authority on the world's stage, this figure is in service of a barrio futurity in which alternative versions of the Apollo space program unfold and tangle with another story about the Chicanx right to fly in ways that mirror those miniaturized EVA spacewalkers building an Aztec space station in *Ganas*. A story of US astronautic heroism in the image of white men reverses course. Apollo 11 is imaginatively remade into something that belongs to *el movimiento*. This speculative approach, whether rehearsed by Apollo 14's famed lunar module pilot (Bean) or by East LA's premier muralists (Botello and Healy), suggests manifold possibilities for the visual vocabularies of the modern space program and, as a result, stoked criticism and, in the latter's case, even mockery.

As Healy recalls, "We're cleaning our brushes at the end of the day when the cops come by [saying], 'Hey, you guys painting that?' 'Yeah.' [He] says, 'Hey, I didn't know Mexico had a space program.'"[125] The laughter is eerily premonitory of Véa's scene from *Gods Go Begging* where Cornelius snickers over another absurd vision of Mexican astronauts. The indignity that *Moonscapes I* and the East Los Streetscapers face from the moment of the mural's installation, in the form of humiliation by an agent of the police state, demonstrates its important political work linking not only the US space program to the Chicanx mural movement but also the racist attitudes safeguarding these missions from perceived artist-outsiders. As a result of making the Apollo program a matter of critical and creative import for the city's Chicanxs and Latinxs, these creatives boldly and tactically stir public reactions. Trafficking in transplanetary-relational tangents from space history, decolonial critique, and self-affirming cultural narration leads to other Latinx artistic addresses. These artworks nuance East Los Streetscapers' public appeals, indicating how visualizing lunar landings was a platform for several artists in the Americas to incite transformation.

Satire and overt political commentary guide more conceptual engagements with the moon landing archive, some that instigate and others that emote outlooks that rhyme to the universe's cosmic pulse. Consider the conceptual imagery of Nuyorican mixed-media artist ADÁL. Working with digitally enhanced photo documentation from NASA, he offers viewers sixteen photo prints on tiled metal, illuminating the colonial pretense of Apollo 11 with an alternative history led by an astro Boricua space crew called Coconauts. Sent on behalf of El Spirit Republic of Puerto Rico, they pilot Domino Uno, a space capsule that hails a Caribbean diaspora with its domino insignia. *Coconauts in Space* (1994–2016) is ADÁL's satirical take on the Cold War, exposing a government cover-up in ways that parallel conspiracy theories and thus uncover Puerto Rico's foundation in the Apollo program (see figure 2.3). By reversing the island as a passive receptacle of US colonial control, ADÁL asserts a refined and stealthy aerospace engineering program on behalf of the Antilles. To act in the name of this fictitious embassy, ADÁL unfastens US techno-dominance from the skies and cleverly rebuts Apollo 11's accomplishment. Adding text into his photography, like "Houston, We Have a Problem," a riff on the popular and often misquoted dialogue between Apollo 13 astronauts and mission control in 1970, he trolls NASA. Domino Uno is first in human spacefaring, and thus the settler colonial imperatives of the "new frontier" ideology are undermined by the scientific acumen of Caribbean coconauts. Despite its appearance, the installation's photo documentation is no longer authentic and exacting. Similar to how Bean's portraits of "first men" extrapolates from NASA history, *Coconauts in Space* meddles with viewer expectations, allowing for a photo narrative that is the stuff of political theater. Each plate retells a story about the modern space program from the perspective of the colonized in an experimentation with the boundaries of truth telling and speculation.

ADÁL's decolonial intervention is equally preoccupied with the astronaut's uniform, from gilded face shield to moon boot. Much like the East Los Streetscapers' emphasis on the urban landscape glimpsed in the space pilot's gilded visor, ADÁL casts a comparative reflection that is equal parts critique and comedy (see figure 2.4). A "found photo" proves a jibaro presence in outer space. By incorporating this symbol of struggle and technological ineptitude, ADÁL rearranges the timeline in which Puerto Rico's humble farmworker, romanticized in paintings by Ramón Frade and Francisco Oller, has been a spacefarer all along.[126] As a coconaut commander

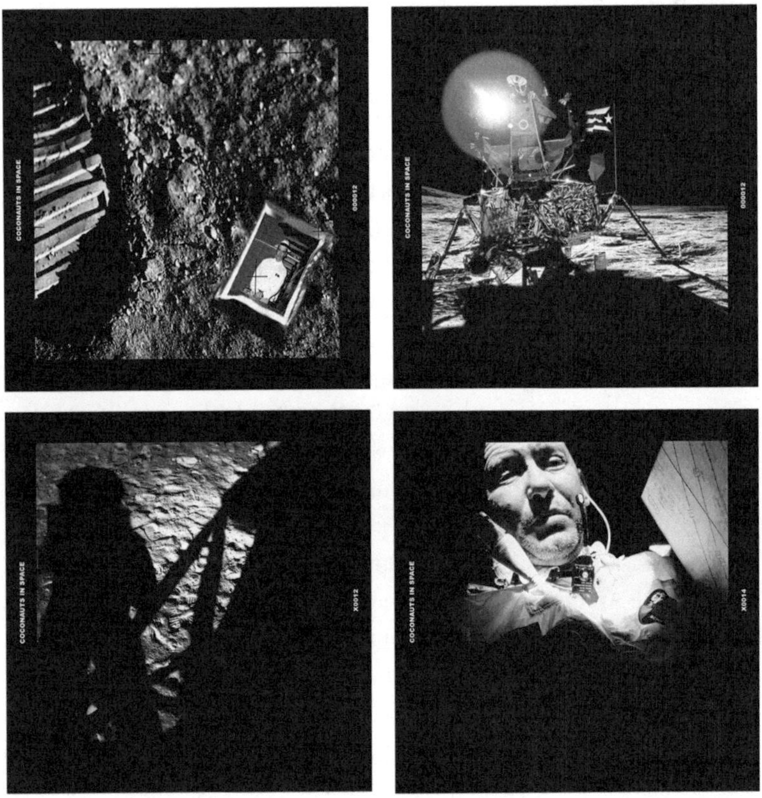

2.3 ADÁL, *Coconauts in Space* (details), 1994–2016. Four of twenty metal photo prints, 20 × 20 in. each. © Estate of Adál Maldonado and Masters Puerto Rico.

shuttles to the moon, ADÁL's jibaro astronautic industry wages a stunning rebuttal of the Apollo missions with an ethnoracial and decolonial vision. Ironically, *Coconauts in Space*'s wit is also reliant on NASA's image archive. The found photograph dusted by chalky lunar soil and juxtaposed with the imprint of a moon boot is an homage to the Apollo 16 mission in 1972 when astronaut Charlie Duke left his family's photograph on Earth's satellite.[127] Using a comparable plastic-wrapped remnant of humanity's existence, ADÁL invalidates a US space history archive that excludes the Caribbean and, in a transplanetary-relational turn, supplants the image of a white nuclear family with Puerto Rico's fondest agrarian hero. In this way, he places the jibaro outside terrestrial terms and forwards a future for the island off-Earth. Although ADÁL is cheeky in his social critique, Houston-based artist Dario

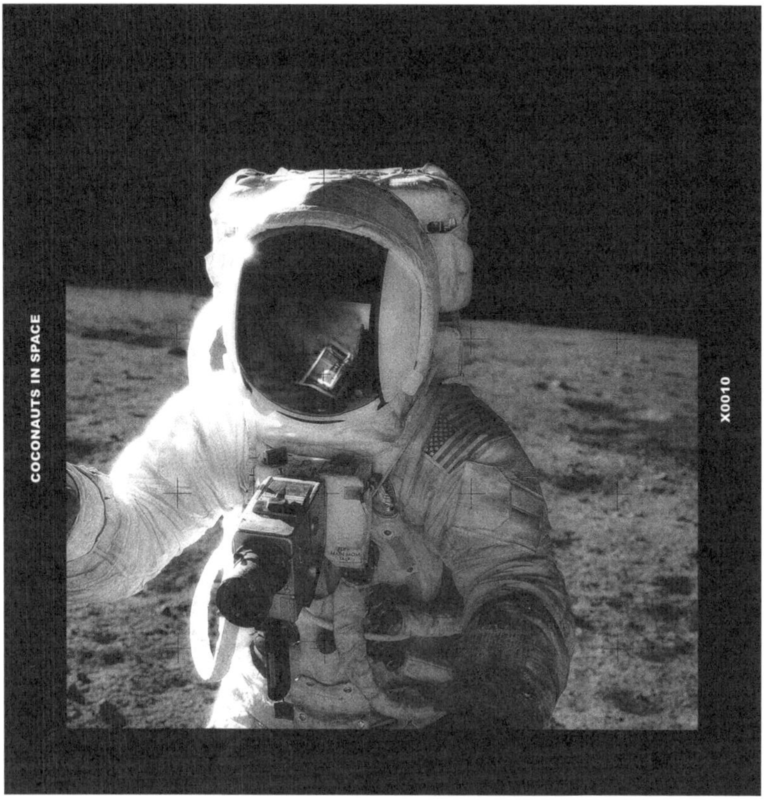

2.4 ADÁL, *Coconauts in Space* (detail), 1994–2016. One of twenty metal photo prints, 20 × 20 in. each. © Estate of Adál Maldonado and Masters Puerto Rico.

Robleto responds with more poetic elaborations. In his work, traces of the Duke family are not far behind.

In a microscaled installation environment, Robleto presents the look of a nineteenth-century botany display. In *Study for Moon Flowers* (2016), he uses acrylic glass casings, plastic domes, and a mirrored Plexiglas wall to house a fictitious lunar ecology drawn from a photographic seed (see plate 21). Inside the vitrine a horticultural specimen grows, scaling the heights of the nearly two-foot box. Stigma, stamen, and petals become the delicate life support system for a family portrait unveiled through the plant matter. A vaulted photograph grows triumphant with tendrils certain to resonate with the vernacular astronomer or popular science aficionado. The snapshot of the Duke family appears in this astrobotany experiment. Picturing Duke with his wife and young sons in their postwar nuclear family suburban glory, its flowering petals are a commentary on its power to visually camouflage and distract from the US State Department and Central Intelligence Agency (CIA) interventions throughout Latin America and Central America, specifically, that waged covert military operations in the name of national security. As authoritarian regimes were erected to protect US strategic locations and corporate investments in agrarian and mineral goods, the Duke picture places a more sentimental if not paternalistic spin on these military operations in the Americas. For NASA, the image warmed public reception of Apollo 16's costly if not anticlimactic mission by pinning the white heteronormative family unit's future on the technological security of outer space.

Unlike ADÁL's sardonic approach, Robleto theorizes the speculative capacity of the family photograph. Famously, Duke inscribed the back of the photo with the following: "This is the family of astronaut Charlie Duke from planet Earth who landed on the moon on April 20, 1972."[128] By inscribing a message for the future, the astronaut writes in an anticipatory measure, speaking to a recipient beyond Earth that may intercept his message. His foresight likely rhymed with Robleto's aesthetic, as he was equally moved by the universe's audiences yet to come. Such anticipatory expressions echo with more pronouncements in Robleto's investigation into a different NASA enterprise, the "Golden Record."[129] This phonographic album engraved with a sampling of the planet's audible remains was a creative endeavor of Carl Sagan and Ann Druyan for two twinned Voyager space probe missions in 1977.[130] That sonic compilation of encoded photographs, languages, and tunes represents what Robleto terms "the greatest work of art that art history has never accounted for," a gap that exists in studies of post-1960s art perhaps because it was incubated at a NASA laboratory rather than in an artist's workshop.[131] Robleto elevates this sound archive in an ascendant appeal that understands the album as a kind of DJ set for extraterrestrial life. As the Voyager spacecraft traffics into interstellar space, Robleto posits "border art" broadly as a transplanetary-relational trajectory for artworks like Hogan's free-fall module that roam the universe unfixed and unbounded. As the space probe journeys to cosmic unknowns, it follows a kind of beat that reverberates with nature's most ancient rhythms being guided by strange frequencies that may have also guided his father, who made his own vertical trek north, immigrating from Nicaragua.

Robleto's position about the golden record might be more deeply refined as it is not only "the greatest work of art that art history has never accounted for" but also "the greatest work of *immigrant* art that art history has never accounted for." By redirecting the Voyager project for the study of art, science, and transplanetary Latinx relations, scholars must confront how a space probe actualizes "artwork" disseminated through orbiting channels. Even now, a work of poetry by the first Mexican American poet laureate, Ada Limón, is engraved on the *Europa Clipper* in a 2024 NASA mission to study the ice crust on Jupiter's moon.[132]

In this vertical viewpoint, *Study for Moon Flowers* reimagines the astronaut's photographic discard as an immigrant artwork, a relic of extraterrestrial existence reworked and reinscribed by this lunar landscape in a way that even Bonestell couldn't have fathomed. As it births alien plant life in the vitrine, the grammar of the photo is no static plane. It accrues organic material, volumizing and encrusting a family picture in three-dimensional scale. Shells, urchins, butterfly wings, and feathers bud into another organism, trans-ing the photograph into a speculative ecosystem that combines the lunar, the aerial, and the root-bound into something else. Here, time, memory, and future clot in ways that evoke allusions to the roadside *descanso*, a temporary memorial that Robleto recalls seeing when he was growing up in San Antonio, or even to the *fotoescultura* (photo sculpture) tradition.[133] According to Karin Becker and Geska Helena Brečević, this border craftwork "emerged as an augmented form of portraiture, commissioned by family members who supplied photographs that artisans in Mexico City converted into framed sculptural portraits for display on family altars."[134] *Study for Moon Flowers* shelters and nurtures a biodiverse extraterrestrial environment that blossoms possibility for a keepsake that is migratory, like the Golden Record. The Duke family's lunar tendrils belong to Earth and its satellite, a transplanetary connection that is tethered to the cosmos like the family re-circuiting space-time in the East Los Streetscapers' *Chicano Time Trip* (1977). Together, they represent a kind of astro-kinship sharing in a cosmic progeny.

Because Duke's photo addresses the observer in rear and frontal views, the artist creates an object environment to see family through multifocal dimensions (see plate 22). For instance, a mirrored acrylic wall in Robleto's Plexiglas box allows for the vaulted snapshot to be seen in verso. But Duke's penned message on the reverse of the photo is replaced with Robleto's text, "Never Come to Terms with Time." The evolving physics of temporality confesses something about loss on the snapshot, a viewpoint perhaps aided by the artist's mother, who worked in hospice care in Texas. Humanity's feedback is unending, like that golden record set adrift in the vastness of space; family is that strange crackle sounding the cosmos, an unending sonic resource. By combining looks that are dually frontward and backward, Robleto's artwork encourages ways of seeing that are doubly sighted, that recast the gaze around an organic and inorganic jumble of horticultural forms, astrobotany, Apollo program references, and even epitaphic verse. Clearly, the astronaut is an image archive in which Latinx creatives are fluent and politically invested. Their visual indexing does not venerate this icon in space art propaganda but rather empowers barrio futurist thinking. These speculatively inclined approaches to the "Latinx public" deploy these moonwalkers to expand the platforms and substrates to an elsewhere where the future astronauts are multiethnic. By implicitly asking what could have been, these innovations and reformulations of Apollo program history face conflict over to whom outer space belongs. Again, an accomplished mural at the local DMV in West LA makes these fault lines transparent.

Arguably, the East Los Streetscapers' *Moonscapes* project stands apart from other public art initiatives in the city. It excels with its studied attention to aerospace engineering deriving from Botello and Healy's combined skill set, bringing nearly photorealist precision in combination with mathematical details. Installing the first of six sections in 1979, they monumentalized the Apollo missions within Chicanx mural art vocabulary, a fruition of expression that expanded on previous work that also interrogated aeriality and claims to the sky. However, in 2016 the piece was hit by vandals. Black spray paint defaced the Mexican flag adorning the space suit, thus eradicating any symbolic praise of the country.[135] A "Chicano-fied" first man on the moon was disturbingly "corrected" and disciplined within a master narrative about a space program predicated on profiles of heteromasculine white protagonists, US scientific mastery, and Cold War–era postering in the name of American patriotism. Clearly, this mural was no joking matter.

While it is difficult to demonstrate a causal effect between public art defacement and Donald Trump's election that same year, this assault predicted atrocities to come. Later, anti-immigrant violence grew, punctuated by mass shootings in El Paso and Uvalde, Texas, in 2019 and 2022, respectively. Because it brandished glimpses of multiethnic surrounds in the glare of a space helmet, this speculation about a hypothetical Mexican astronaut linked to the astronomical histories of ancient Maya and China and contemporary Puerto Rico proves threatening. The shield reflects a transplanetary-relational interchange linking the city's barrio urbanism with the universe. Likely, the offensiveness of the image comes in its bold speculative statement projecting a barrio future in ways that Hogan had only pondered in his prose. In their powerful retort to that cop who mocked, "I didn't know Mexico had a space program," the East Los Streetscapers dared to imagine a place for the city's liminal residents in Southern California's aeronautic space belt, an area where they were never supposed to be.[136] By looking up in this way, they directed viewers in a gesture that proved radical for what painting on a wall can do. This showing at the DMV, from the moment of installation to its defacement by vandals decades later, demonstrates how graphing multiethnic histories, ideas, and writing in the sky inverts racialized terrestrial bondage and, as a result, proves threatening to a US aerospace, defense, and military industrial complex. Sadly, it was triumph short-lived. In March 2025, nearly the entirety of the mural was whitewashed in a dismal coat of beige paint. Healy, Botello, and his brother Paul, an assistant on the project, were never contacted by DMV officials, a violation of the California Art Preservation Act.[137] The artwork's possible restoration remains a matter of negotiation between the artists and the California DMV at the time of this writing.

Nonetheless, what the East Los Streetscapers achieved here was merely a sign of things to come: namely, Vargas-Suarez Universal (VSU), an artist whose brashness and scientific literacy also innovated the medium for a barrio futurity that artists like the East Los Streetscapers and Haro couldn't have imagined.

Star People

No one advanced the suffusion of NASA imagery in public art practice in the past decade more than VSU. The son of parents working in the airline industry, a young Rafael Vargas-Suarez was raised against the backdrop of the Johnson Space Center in Clear Lake, a suburb of Houston, Texas. As a child, he pilfered a home library assembled from flight manuals, aviation information, and airspace charts. His imagination stirred in a suburban neighborhood populated by space program workers, aerospace engineers, and international diplomat families.[138] This upbringing combined with his later undergraduate training at the University of Texas at Austin, where he paired his fascination with astronomy and art history. This interdisciplinary study informed a passion for astrophysics in ways that author Ernest Hogan could appreciate.

In 1996 VSU served as the exhibition designer, juror, and participant in the inaugural *Young Latino Arts* exhibition organized by Mexic-Arte, a Mexican American art museum and institutional staple in Austin. He showed *Scientific Data Resurrection*, a collection of found material interventions on small canvases collaged from CD-ROM specimens, discarded science guides, world maps, and architectural records.[139] Using black backgrounds to convey infinite space, his depiction of metaphorical voids nods to past scientific "ideas that 'could have been'" but have otherwise been upended or gone dark.[140] "If we don't decide for ourselves, someone or something else will," VSU warns in a community arts forum about the possibilities and threats posed by technology circa 1996.[141] By entering this technocultural-science debate into an exhibition highlighting the work of over thirty Latinx artists under the age of thirty, VSU's "resurrection" revives planetary science and data collection as an unusual forum from which Mexican American audiences are provoked to see deep space in terms of cutting-edge creativity. Future forays into cultural knowledge are a matter of "what we learn about each other, ourselves, and our universe," he argues.[142]

The boldness of his approach from the mid-1990s demonstrates how a vertical perception guided him in other space science negotiations. Later, his work matured, with more explicit NASA visual materials. In 2007 he advanced a series of paintings entitled *Spacewalks-EVAS* based on improved access to the space agency's satellite footage and online streaming (see figure 2.5). True to his previous works for Mexic-Arte, these pieces also began in dense small-scale drawings. However, his drive to capture the monumental nature of spacewalks led to an expanded visual field with emphasis on the wall. His new drawings were produced on large polypropylene canvases using the same darkened material that aerospace designers use to wrap electrical cables in aircraft and spacecraft.[143] Projecting live video feeds from NASA television in his studio, VSU would trace movements and gestures performed in the International Space Station. With an aluminum oil enamel pen, this choreography of science, movement, and dance resolves in an abstract line drawing, innovating the representational vocabulary that Haro, Botello, and Healy proposed in the 1970s. Synchronizing his day with the scheduled activities of the astronauts, VSU made marks that create transplanetary-relational enmeshments, correlating himself and these space pilots in ways that are reminiscent of Healy, who paralleled the movement of Aldrin as a space pilot, moonwalker, and track-and-fielder.

Unlike Healy, VSU layers hand and body against the large-scale feed (see figure 2.6). As VSU's answer to Hogan's gravity-free space module, his bodily coordination moves in a way that enfolds Earth's low orbit with a studio space in Brooklyn. Finding ways to make spaceflight no longer the privileged sphere of US military defense and national security, this Mexican American creative improves on ideas introduced at Mexic-Arte decades before. Visual data information from outer space is to be felt, synchronized, and resurrected for audiences beyond the private controls of aerospace industries. By feeling a

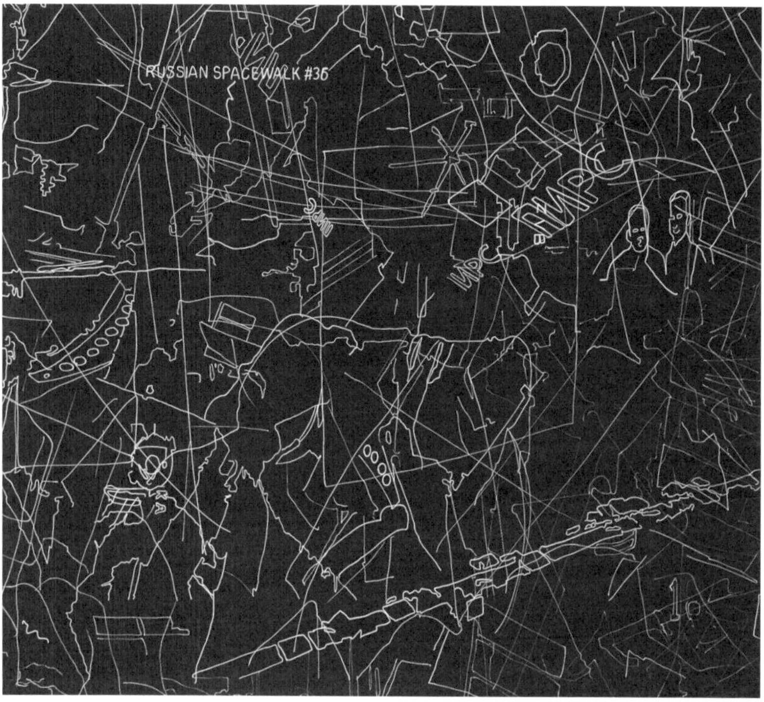

2.5 Vargas-Suarez Universal, *I.S.S. Expedition 37 Russian EVA 5 Hrs. 50 Mins.*, 2013. Aluminum oil enamel on polypropylene canvas, 54 × 47 in. Image courtesy of the artist.

spacewalk in the zero-gravity projections of live broadcast footage, his practice animates a transplanetary relation, being attuned to astronomical bodies beyond Earth's borders. Through a mere wall, VSU mimes an astronautic ballet and thus proposes higher plateaus for a "brown commons" where an "uncanny persistence in the face of distressed conditions of possibility" is felt, as José Esteban Muñoz argues.[144] In this coordinative dance, VSU feels brownness in "a movement, a flow, and an impulse" that elicit emotions on behalf of the universe on the International Space Station's televised stage.[145] In his mark making, he is working in unison with an aeronautical team. His collective intentions know no geopolitical allegiance as he materializes a visual language contingent on coordinated movements of spacewalking. The scale of his *Spacewalks-EVAS* project is rife with potential, expanding his mode of public address for something vaster and ascendant with consequences for civic life. The result placed him squarely back on the wall in ways indebted to the Mexican American muralists before him.

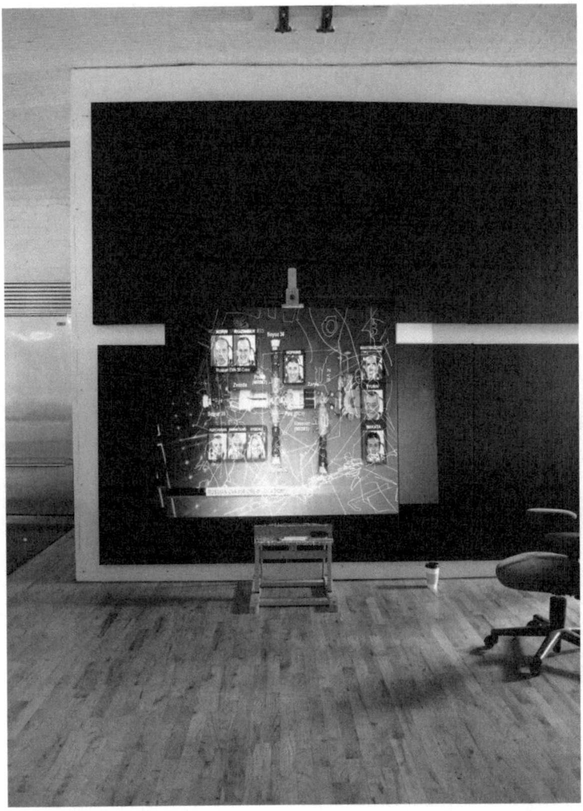

2.6 Vargas-Suarez Universal, *Spacewalks-EVAs* art practice documentation. Image courtesy of the artist.

In 2013 VSU was commissioned to produce *Starcycle*, a mural in conjunction with *The Vastness Is Bearable*, an exhibition curated by Miki Garcia for the Museum of Contemporary Art Santa Barbara (see figure 2.7).[146] The wall art was planned for the back facade of the historic Hotel Indigo, located in a heavily trafficked area of the city, which catered to tourists. The mural came with specific environmental obstacles, and thus it required the city council's involvement. His approval was conditional because local representatives worried about preserving the downtown's Spanish colonial image.[147] Specific paints and time restrictions were permitted, making the work a contrasting yet temporary addition to the city's cultural heritage. Despite these provisions, VSU's process was authentic to traditional approaches in neighborhood-based mural movement art making. He worked collaboratively with Youth Interactive Santa Barbara, an organization for

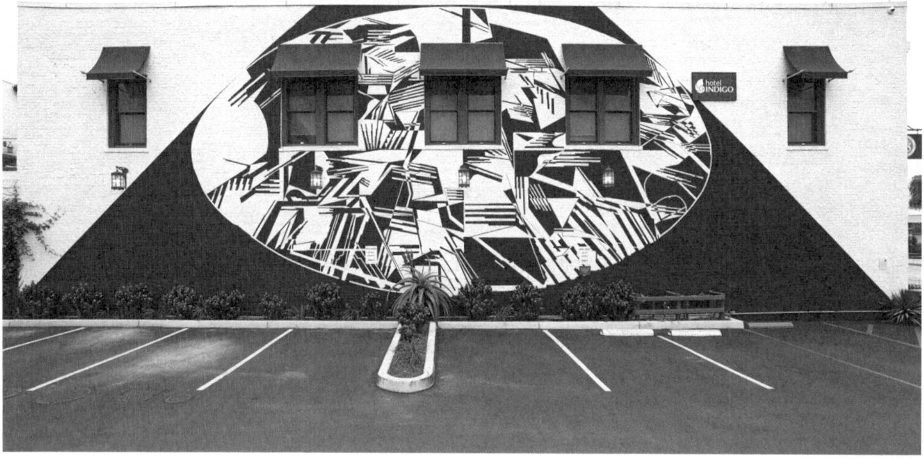

2.7 Vargas-Suarez Universal, *Starcycle*, 2014. In situ acrylic and enamel wall drawing, 27 × 81 ft. Museum of Contemporary Art Santa Barbara and Hotel Indigo, Santa Barbara, CA. Courtesy of MCA-Santa Barbara.

at-risk teens, many of whom were people of color or of unknown legal status. "They were great. . . . [N]ot only was it fun for them, but they said they were learning from it. I took it as not only them assisting, but there was a lot of dialogue. . . . [T]hey would bring their friends, and all of a sudden it became the place to hang out," he recalled.[148]

His activities not only are embedded in the Chicanx mural arts movement protocol of collective image production but also recalled a brief period of the medium in Santa Barbara spearheaded by Manuel Unzueta and Armando Vallejo at La Casa de la Raza in 1971. Artworks at Ortega Park once described in the pages of *Xalman* as ranging in topic from "Aztec era to cosmic unity" suggest how an otherworldly consciousness permeated civic art and culture in the city, a visual dialogue propagated by Latinx creatives there.[149] Likely this mural history was unknown to the city council and perhaps the Museum of Contemporary Art Santa Barbara at that time. It could be said that the artist's 27-by-81-foot trapezoidal design, rendered in abstract lines and achromatic finishes, is an inheritor of "cosmic unity" propagated by La Casa de la Raza. By returning the cosmos to Santa Barbara's built environment, VSU's black-and-white design was more restorative than offensive.

Staining the hotel in "the color of space," as Botello once termed the palette, VSU adapted an astronomical vision that visually reconciles the space science mural with Chicanx public art format.[150]

Abstract lines accentuate vectored shapes conveying a star's interstellar evolution on the hotel's facade. These forms demand that the public adjusts its vision to a different scale. The wide-angle view curves like a telescopic eye, inviting a magnified look at the unbearable vastness of the universe. However, this "vastness" is less foreboding and certainly closer in VSU's assessment. The hotel's back wall approximates a "technological vision," as Joan Saab puts it, where a star's life cycle changes, moves, and migrates.[151] By incorporating the windows into the design, VSU adjusts the exterior to meet a moment between stakeholders, youth apprentices, astronomy hobbyists, and even astrophysicists. As he opens the collective process of mural making to outlets in the solar system's beyond, VSU mimes an artwork on the verge of self-destruction. Like a supernova vaporizing into darkness, this mural would do the same, timed in synchronicity with the cosmos. It appears temporarily, shines brightly, and then disappears.

VSU's collaborative ethos and cosmic attentions make the painting trailblazing because of the way he brings those imperceptible celestial objects down from the sky and into the public eye. Whether the viewer perceives his design as a circuit board of intricate wiring or as a microscopic lens over a cellular organism, he nonetheless grants objects of otherworldly proportion a platform for earthly contemplation. Looking up in this way, viewers of *Starcycle* are challenged to interrogate observable reality, envision interstellar data of scientists, and engage the Chicanx mural anew through the transplanetary relations forged through his hands and those of young people of color.

By expanding the muralist lexicon to ruminate on astronomer portraits, space pilots, and star life cycles, the artists who are the focus of this chapter question the terms of Latinx public engagement for venues that are transplanetary relationally inclined and vertically aligned. What these creatives accomplished broadens and enfolds space histories, scientific data collection, and astrophotographic sources in ways that were, ironically enough, predicated on a US defense industry and space program that civil rights activists were critical of (and rightfully so). This fraught relationship aside, the profound impacts this image archive yielded for Latinx art making were ongoing, proving that the skies were not only the preoccupation of archetypical space artists in the science museums but also a register of Chicanx muralists in the streets. An artist like VSU stands as an heir apparent, but unlike his predecessors, he innovates the medium. His public art address suffuses data visualization and telescopic optics as pivotal outlets for Latinx representational politics, and thus he positions himself closer to the feathered plumes of Quetzalcoatl and the vapor trails of a spaceship that Hogan pontificated about in his science fiction writing about barrio futurity.

Taken as a whole, these mural activities negotiate a place for Latinx civic life shaped by transplanetary relational approaches. Whether transporting barrio residents to the lunar surface or recodifying the astronaut in aid of *la raza*, they imbue walls with the capacity to open windows onto other worlds and launch spacefaring adventures where they were never supposed to exist. Chief in this creative ingenuity are the astronomer and moonwalker, whose considerable presence has yet to be theorized in the Chicanx mural movement or Latinx visual culture studies broadly. Where there is space, there is room for speculative imaginings, and the artworks appraised here animate their surrounds to meditate on the beyond. Like those aerial tableaux dotting words of protest and hope over LA skies in 2020, the murals highlighted in this chapter were important precursors. This medium has long considered airspace in aid to the subjugated and racialized communities of Southern California and even Central Texas, functioning with the same urgency that modern muralists roused decades before in a postrevolution Mexico. And yet, as the *In Plain Sight* intervention suggests, for many Latinx creatives, the present built environment was not enough. Future spaces were needed where stone met brick and mud met virtual reality. As the next chapter shows, getting elsewhere meant extraterrestrial terrain had to be excavated and pathways laid.

3

Terraforming the Gallery

IN SEARCH OF CENTRAL AMERICA

Quite possibly, one of the most significant contributions to Latinx speculative art is not found in back issues of Buenos Aires's *Más Allá* (*Beyond*), that 1950s long-running serial servicing not only Argentina but also several Latin American countries, earning it "mythic status in [science fiction] circles."[1] Nor is it Cuban-born writer Luis Philip Senarens's tales of robotic steam man adventures in the Frank Reade Jr. dime magazine from the late nineteenth century.[2] Rather, the most profound contribution comes from a textbook, Jacqueline Barnitz's *Twentieth-Century Art of Latin America* (2001), an essential text in Latin American art history surveys. Its science-fictional content comes not from its apprehension of critical modernisms, movements, and debates in the field but from its back matter.

There, a map of Latin America highlights countries and cities central to novices unaware of their equatorial neighbors (see figure 3.1). However, notice what the map leaves off. Puerto Rico is missing. The Dominican Republic is erased. Paraguay is a negated landmass. Central America is a dark void.[3] Such nullification implies that this transcultural and transnational

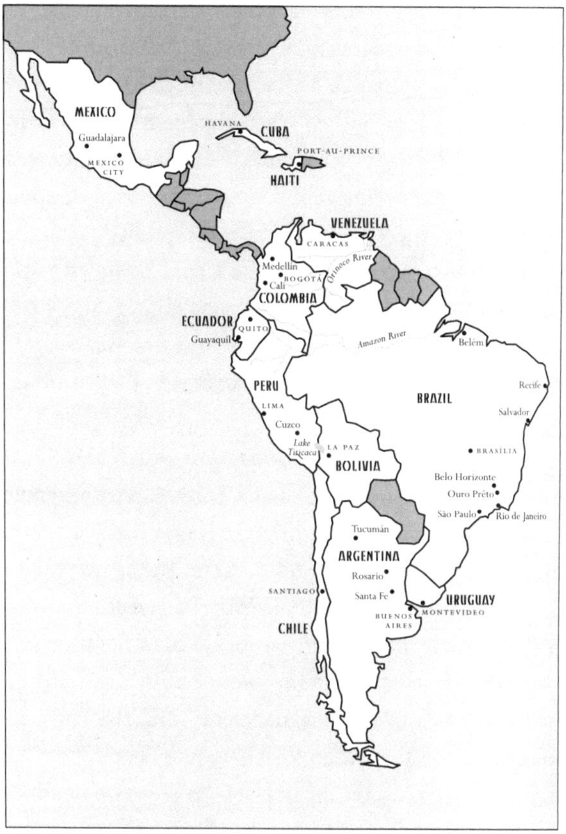

3.1 Map from *Twentieth-Century Art of Latin America*, by Jacqueline Barnitz (Austin: University of Texas Press, 2001).

isthmus, essential to "U.S. imperialistic projects—starting with the construction of nation-states, railroads, Pan-American highways, and canal zones to serve the commercial needs of U.S. companies," is empty of art historical significance and thus exists in a state of nullity, omission, and abjection.[4] Being illegible in the topographic definitions required for the pursuit of art geography and place-based knowledge reinforces something that literary scholar Arturo Arias ruminated about in 2007: "Despite this overwhelming presence . . . [Central Americans have] been nearly invisible within the imaginary confines of what constitutes the multicultural landscape of the United States."[5] Central America's undoing, an unmapping of this substrate, charges this region with a speculative power.

The region's extraordinary capacity reads like a fabulist tale. In a declassified report filed on November 25, 1952, at Coco Solo, the US Naval Air Force base in Cativá, Panama, a major reported seeing "a light moving across his line of vision from East to West. The light was yellow in color, giving a soft glow like a fog light or a candle."[6] This luminosity was disturbing, if only short-lived. According to the report, "The light disappeared in the West in about three (3) seconds time."[7] By "disappear[ing] in the West," this unconfirmed UFO sighting imbued the Canal Zone with an uncanny spatiality. This eyewitness account reaffirms something that Arias observed about the murky, unknowable opacity of Central America nearly half a century later. Whether by land or sky, when it comes to that isthmus, there is something otherworldly about it.

Although this hinge connecting North and South America escapes definition in the back pages of a Latin American art textbook, much like a mysterious aircraft evading US Naval Air Force apprehension in 1952, another sighting complicates matters. The same year a UFO was spotted in Panama, astronomical artist Chesley Bonestell aided journalist Connie Ryan in visually articulating the case for space exploration in the pages of *Collier's* magazine. In what Catherine Newell calls "the first time space exploration made the cover of a major magazine," this March 22, 1952, bestselling issue boldly declares that "Man Will Conquer Space *Soon*."[8] In a glossy page layout, Bonestell pictures the not-yet-realized and hypothetical techno-utopia of the future. In German émigré rocket scientist Wernher von Braun's feature article, "Crossing the Last Frontier," Bonestell illustrates details of aerospace engineering feats with his brand of precision. As a work of space program boosterism, Bonestell's piece heralds von Braun's double-V "spaceship," a model signaling the coming of aeronautics. His artwork proved strangely prophetic, depicting engineering marvels envisaged by scientists like von Braun, Willy Ley, and Fred Whipple. This issue would mark one of their many collaborations in print publications. Other partnerships include *The Conquest of the Moon* (1953), *The Exploration of Mars* (1956), *Beyond the Solar System* (1964), and *The Conquest of Space* (1949/55), the latter of which included a 1955 cinematic adaptation depicting a plausible mission to the Red Planet.[9]

Beyond portraying space traffic in the skies, Bonestell returns to Western landscape painting logics redolent of the Hudson River school, renowned for their pastoral appraisal of majestic vistas, as discussed in chapter 1. Of course, those ideologically charged settings portrayed a colonial settler viewpoint on territories emptied of Indigenous people, a dominion accomplished because landscape paintings locate "viewers at a height in the image from which they can survey a vast terrain spread out beneath them," argues art historian Martin Berger.[10] Placing the reader on a vacuous outer planet, Bonestell mimics the camera and mirrors those "photographs of Earth taken from the International Space Station," as Newell observes.[11] Relaying aesthetic vocabularies later perfected in the blue-marble picture captured by Apollo 17 in 1972, Bonestell invites *Collier's* postwar readers to look distantly at the planet's surface.[12]

However, the orbital machines constituting the so-called future frontier hover above no ordinary landmass. Beneath a spaceship, space station, and satellite telescope is Central America (see plate 23). In the distance is Earth's spherical horizon, unveiling the stretch of South Florida, the span of the Caribbean Sea, and the archipelagic curvature of Cuba. Becoming the planetary face from which von Braun promotes a crucial expedition to Mars, Central America, in particular, is positioned not as the abject geography of Latin American art but as the terrestrial passage from which a US readership imagines the future. This point was not lost on astronomical artist Robert McCall, who in 1988 painted an updated version replying to Bonestell's classic work. McCall's piece shows the latest NASA technological advancements, including the space shuttle, Hubble space telescope, and what would become the International Space Station.[13] McCall's piece differs from Bonestell's by focusing on the isthmus in the foreground and diminishing any visual attention to the Caribbean.

Together, these paintings hint at a visual irony that appears to correct the cloak of invisibility under which Central America is portrayed as something extraordinary. A sky once breached by a UFO in the Canal Zone also becomes the setting for a world to come where mainstream publics are enticed to imagine the future. Although Bonestell and McCall create work against the backdrop of the nuclear arms race during the Cold War, their attention to this fulcrum of the Americas is less a story about space science history and technological accomplishment. Instead, it pairs the United States' technological dominance with a terrestrial stage where revolutions are being fought and US interventions back authoritarian regimes with genocidal outcomes.

As a playground for US corporate capital and agricultural investment in valuable crops, minerals, and human labor, Central America has been a "security zone," a "scene of the United States flexing its military, economic, and political influence" since the nineteenth century.[14] Though the isthmus facing viewers in the pages of *Collier's* is a passive, empty, and idyllic landmass in the astronomical art imagination, the perspective of it is seated in the planet's low orbit. Bonestell and McCall reconstitute power relations in an aerial surveillance where "'looking down' was a vista afforded by technology," as Lisa Messeri argues.[15] Their artworks mutually portray aerospace machinery outside Central Americans' control. The isthmus becomes a literal terrestrial stage from which the story of the space race takes place. By looking down on it, Bonestell and McCall implicitly hint at the area's sociopolitical entanglements with national defense, the aerospace industry, and empire building. This downward vision seconds an earlier position peddled by famed scientist Percival Lowell, who argued that the telescope-armed astronomer looks only to rise "above human prejudice and limitation."[16] Of course, this position is deeply misguided when we consider Lowell's own debt to Native, Indigenous, and Mexican labor in the construction of his scientific campuses (a topic I discuss later in this chapter). Had Lowell looked more closely, he would have recognized that even in his career-defining investment to map the alleged "canals" engraved into Mars, another canal was being built.[17] African slave labor dredged to build a waterway through Panama, securing a US "satellite" for global capitalist expansion and strategic military positioning.[18]

The curious status of Central America, much like those Martian trenches or the UFO sighting in Panama in 1952, breaks down the divisions separating the region from outer space. That ambiguous relationship between Central America and spacefaring futures is implicit in the earliest art-science collaborations visualizing a modern space program for US audiences. That is, "if today everyone lives in a global modernity propelled by Western scientific technologies, then there are some who live in its darkest corner, its underside," Kency Cornejo relays about the isthmus in a near rebuttal of Barnitz's flawed map.[19] In response, this chapter asks: What speculative forms of spatial thinking emerge from Central American creatives in search of cultural definition amid negation? If astronomical artists like Bonestell and McCall flatten geography, reducing Central America to a prostrate playground of colonialism and expansionism, what are we to make of their turn seeing this region as the future face of US spacefaring?

This contradiction is not lost on Central American diasporic artists and their collaborators, who lean into the speculative geographies of the region with spatial knowledges rooted in ancient pasts, sacred passages, and lo-fi technologies of a decolonial "underside," as Cornejo puts it.[20] This chapter avoids emphasizing visionary blueprints that picture lifeworlds continuous with discussions of world building and utopia popularized in science fiction studies. Rather, it offers something more ambivalent and potentially nomadic by considering a spatial medium where artists like Beatriz Cortez, rafa esparza, and Jacqueline Arias build the platforms and pave the roads that crisscross space-time. "Making art as a nomad," Cortez argues, "means imagining other futures where those categories and ideas of nationalism and national identity are not so relevant and other worlds are possible."[21]

These artworks include sculptures, environments, and spatial designs drawn from planetary matter. With materials that reformulate, redefine, and resurface museum settings, Central American diasporic art is put *in place*, yielding countersites *out of place* and thus contesting sanitary gallery confines.[22] Making spatial interventions not dissimilar to the logics of exoplanet astronomers or the fantasies of science fiction writers, these creatives transmit transplanetary relations and cultivate radical ecologies to make museums more inhabitable for the abject and negated. By literally building refuge and creating habitats in molten steel and spills of mud, they upend "Central America" as a disciplining category in contemporary art. Inside these muddy incubators, geopolitical distances between borders, planets, and worlds collapse, intensifying how US colonial discourses about the future habitation of Mars have long garnered settler attentions to this region. In this way, terraforming the gallery is a call for spatial reclamation as these artists generate alternative architectures to house ancient pasts, shelter off-planet escape, and dwell in what Cortez calls "untimely conversations" (a point raised in the introduction).[23]

From the outset, this chapter widens the terms of Latinx placemaking and cultural geography by positing the uncredited yet consequential role that Latinx and Indigenous builders have played in constructing observatory science campuses. The astronomer's mountaintop habitation is indebted to and predicated on racialized labor. These hand-built surrounds mirror speculative practices as demonstrated in Cortez's time machines and otherworldly portals. More than sculpture, these works bear the imprint of immigrant labor, Indigenous design, and natural architecture in steely armatures, oxidized surfaces, and matured seedlings. The chapter foregrounds how Cortez nurtures ecologies and rooted networks that suffuse Maya archaeoastronomy with adobe overflows. The ultimate example of this aesthetic is visible in her collaborations with artist rafa esparza, whose transformations of Ballroom Marfa and the Whitney Museum in 2017 are studies in brown matter. Adobe mutates and shape-shifts, trans-ing the planet, and in esparza's other activations at the Getty Center and the Museum of Contemporary Art Tucson, *extra*terrestrial spills remold architectures. No one better exemplifies this practice than Costa Rican artist Jacqueline Arias, whose contribution to the Tucson show's companion exhibition, *Terra Forms*, uses sculptural scaffolds and virtual reality digital artwork to punch through the gallery, activate sensorial attachments to sediment, and transport viewers to the planet's core with Indigenous feminist knowledges. Layering hardened earth and softened fibers, she opens fissures and gateways, each reliant on cosmologies and even fashion design to engineer Central America's uncanny arrival.

Thinking transplanetary relations in the dirt, the artists discussed in this chapter forge extraordinary landings for an area castigated into art historical opacity and thus convert substances into openings about planetary origins. By tangling with spatial knowledges indebted to Earth's ancient, geological, and celestial epochs rather than linear and chronologically defined artwork, these creatives terraform the gallery. Land seeps into precious museum boxes, and alternative substrates rise up to give place to an isthmus otherwise obscured from the story of modern spacefaring and outer planetary study. In anticipation of a big brown world to come, these artists get down in the mud.

Space Ghosts

Land, space, and placemaking pervade transnational studies about art of the Americas. From the metaphorical reminders of homeland to the literal strife of border violence, the search for and disconnection from domiciliation is a contingent part of Latinx migration research. Dolores Hayden identifies "sense of place" as a distinguishable part of critical space theory where "sensory, aesthetic, and environmental components" accentuate the meaning of a cultural landscape.[24] Her emphasis shifts the terms of Henri Lefebvre's social reproduction of space and lessens the grip of neoliberal capital and state-sanctioned bureaucracies over spatiality, a perspective that Lefebvre aligns with power, domination, and control.[25] Hayden exposes experiences little recorded in more traditional architecture and planning histories. She notes, "Architecture, as a discipline, has not seriously considered social and political issues . . . yet it is the volatile combination of social issues with spatial design . . . that makes [both areas] so critical to the future of American cities."[26] By espousing cultural landscape approaches where space, egalitarianism, and sociality combine, she explicates how neighborhoods "nurture citizens' public memory, to encompass shared time in the form of shared territory."[27] However, it is worth rethinking how this approach might square with Richard Haro's *Outer Space* (1977) or the East Los Streetscapers' *Moonscapes I* (1979) murals, discussed in chapter 2. Clearly, the American city she foregrounds is predicated on state definitions of citizenry and legality and not the expansive scale or cosmic transactions in transplanetary relations centering this study (a point I return to momentarily). More complicated is documenting the undocumented in these "storehouses for . . . social memories" of "shared territory."[28] If cultural landscapes are entangled in everyday spatial practices—that is, the way citizens produce the character of space—how does the unmapped "underside," as Cornejo calls it, of Central Americanness reconcile with Hayden's power-of-place project? After all, being undocumented "creates a condition somewhere between the living and the dead, a spectral speech act that reveals the anxious feeling of *being* Latinx since the sixteenth century," scholar John-Michael Rivera argues.[29] This deathly underside deserves another look.

Speculative studies' approach to art-geography builds on Hayden's approach by enhancing the spectral dimensions of "new Latino urbanism" (also dubbed *barrio urbanism*). Consider how Latinx readaptive uses of urban and suburban mixed-use zones exteriorize what Raúl Villa calls the "geographical identity" of the barrio, or what Johana Londoño terms "place identity."[30] These spatial practices "enact environments," according to James Rojas, thus establishing how ethnoracial communities resist residential segregation and gentrification through public and semiprivate displays of cultural affirmation in aesthetic, aural, and perceptual markers.[31] Using careful negotiations of front-yard ornamentations and street-facing accoutrements, Rojas notes, "the identity of the place is created through the culturally related behavior patterns of the residents. It is not built; it is enacted."[32] Of course, Rojas's approach to East LA placemaking has been criticized for prescribing "spatial uses and cultural practices" and thus conflating the Latinx built environment with the "colorful facades and catchy signage," which Londoño also appraised, though with reservation.[33] How these design debates relate to Latinx speculative imagination in the built environment is widely excluded from scholarship about barrio spatiality. To earmark immigrant struggles outside these more conventional approaches in urban and architectural Latinx histories demands a channeling of apparitional presences, a kind of ghostly reckoning with those intangible haunts that trace the city's built environment.

Cornejo hints that the dense multinational and cross-generational Central American place in art-geography could be appraised for its nearly supernatural quality. As scholar Ester E. Hernández observes, "Alternative forms of memory [must] go beyond the transmission of culture and the learning of history to situate Central American experiences as lived experiences."[34] She explains, "This includes remembering the dead and the 'disappeared' in various public sites" because "the ghosts (of memory) left behind by violent repression reappear."[35] Hernández's correlation between US Central

American cultural geography and the precarity of immigrant lives hints at a place identity mired by spatialized erasures that leave some factions of Latinidades unseen. They linger in a spectral zone of being "somewhere between the living and the dead," as Rivera evinces.[36] Such nullification sharpens in Latin American art history, where, as Barnitz's map suggests, some art geographies are out of time and space, eradicated, or simply mapped as void. Articulating an entity more speculative if not spectral, Hernández troubles "shared" realities in Hayden's sense for a diasporic community that evades the time-space instruments of surveying, mapping, and planning. Simply, alternative terms for new Latino urbanism must also be explored because the more speculative vestiges of Latinidades frustrate spatial expressions grounded in the singular, tangible world. Where to place Central American diasporic art then is a difficult task for the "nearly invisible," as Arias espouses, suggesting a phantasmagorical articulation of the field. This nonpresence proves itself most noticeably under Latinx art curatorial appraisals in the United States.[37]

For instance, consider the 2017 exhibition *Home—So Different, So Appealing*, cocurated by Chon Noriega, Mari Carmen Ramírez, and Pilar Tompkins Rivas in a collaboration between the Los Angeles County Museum of Art and the Museum of Fine Arts, Houston. This exhibition presented seven decades of image making from artists across the Americas, who questioned "home [as] one of the most basic concepts for understanding an individual or group within a larger physical and social environment."[38] In thematic constellations, creatives were arranged like a "ghost story," according to Noriega, with "indexes of the fear that makes home a matrix of places that are 'social, geographical, even imaginary.'"[39] While this ambitious show mobilized the haunted relics of spaces, objects, and memories, some specters never materialized. Although Salvadorans represent the third-largest ethnoracial Latinx population in the United States and constitute the largest concentration of foreign-born persons in Los Angeles, none appears in the exhibition, reaffirming a trend in Latinx art surveys.[40] The broader curatorial objectives to look "at home as central to a complex social reality that is hemispheric and global, not strictly local and national . . . from the vantage point of what appears to be an absence," recommits another omission.[41] Central America is perpetually home*less* or, more boldly, beyond this world. One must wonder whether the institutional confines of a traditional gallery space are simply unaccommodating to art of this kind. If so, what are the alternatives? Solutions are taken up later in this chapter.

At the outer limits of Latinx art historical definition, Central American liminality is not unlike the science-fictional paradigms that Alicia Gaspar de Alba notes in her formative assessment of the *Chicano Art: Resistance and Affirmation* (CARA) exhibition from 1990 to 1993, the first major show of artists of Mexican cultural heritage on a national scale. Without conflating the ethnoracial specificity of Chicanxs with Central Americans, it is worth noting her observation that art galvanized by *el movimiento* (the Chicanx civil rights movement) resides awkwardly in cultural institutions, staging "close encounters of the Third World kind between dominant culture and 'aliens.'"[42] Her turn of phrase, riffing on Steven Spielberg's 1977 blockbuster film about a UFO encounter in Rust Belt Indiana (a film of influential weight, as I discuss in the next chapter), suggests the ways in which critical race inventions are unaccommodated if not otherworldly inside the "master's house." With this, Gaspar de Alba nods to Audre Lorde's famed comments of September 29, 1979, from the Second Sex Conference in New York City, where this Black feminist agent of social change remarked, "The master's tools will never dismantle the master's house."[43] Whether alien or specter, there is something simply uncanny about Central American diasporic art; or, as Cornejo observes, "the visual arts have perpetuated, by omission, such notions of 'non-place' with respect to the art of US Central Americans."[44]

Though they pertain to art history, Gaspar de Alba's words share a close corollary with the "planetary imagination" of space scientists in search of exoplanets and, by extension, extraterrestrial life.[45] According to Lisa Messeri, theorizing place is endemic to exoplanetary astronomy, "turn[ing] the infinite geography of the cosmos into a theater dotted with potentially meaningful places that are stages for imaginations and aspirations."[46] Scientists engage either in the virtual mapping of Mars or in the occupation of terrestrial facsimiles of the moon in Flagstaff, Arizona, or of Martian terrain at the Mars Desert Research Station in Hanksville, Utah. Here they formulate spatialized knowledges about alien landscapes based on earthly improvisations.[47] By playacting the unknown alongside telescopic data and aerological fieldwork, they fill in the blanks and create immersive possibility in a way that brings them into the fold of science fiction. Spatial understandings from haptic experiences that are improvised, imagined, or secondarily mediated through scientific instruments are part of the imaginative work of both artist and scientist. As Messeri comments, "Retreat[ing] even further from the Earth's surface . . . [and] from earthly locales" behind the lens of a telescope, the scientist leans into a romanticized "placelessness," a "purity afforded by newly established mountaintop observatories" in the twentieth-century United States.[48]

Despite "abandon[ing] cities and forego[ing] plains" in contemplative isolation with the cosmos, these astronomers' utopian pursuits assume a kind of habitation that literally rises above "human prejudice and limitation."[49] However, even in their fantasy worlds, their habitation is afforded by settler colonialism, exploitive labor, and extractive capital. Where would the field of astronomy be without a geographic dependency on US southwestern borderlands or on Latin America? Equatorial climate, scale, and elevation were germane to "a cultural consciousness of Martian life" in Lowell's work.[50] His discoveries were endemic to a US popular culture in the late nineteenth century "where the developing genre of science fiction incorporated some of Lowell's compelling notions."[51] His visions were accomplished because of racial capital and Indigenous laborers. Might colonialism and manifest destiny demand a rethinking of the science campus and its implication for Latinx placemaking theory, broadly defined? Allow this brief digression into the early years of the Lowell Observatory's founding.

Mexican Ghosting | Ghosting Mexicans

Lowell Observatory was established in 1894, not without incident. A graduate of Harvard University in mathematics, Lowell lobbied Edward Pickering, the director of the Harvard College Observatory, for a laboratory beyond the environmental distractions of an interfering modernity.[52] Lowell charged Andrew Ellicott Douglass, a former Harvard assistant who had recently completed a similar astronomical tour in Chile and Peru, to search for a suitable outpost. On March 7, 1894, Douglass arrived in Benson, Arizona, and scouted eleven stations, guided by his telescope to test the atmosphere.[53] Lowell approved the purchase of Douglass's last location, five acres in Flagstaff above the Arizona Lumber and Timber Company. A road up to the prospective observatory would need to be excavated to give access to the newly dubbed Mars Hill.[54] Though omitted from the official documentation of Lowell Observatory, with Hopi and Navajo workers in the vicinity, the campus may have relied on other forms of racialized labor for its construction.[55] However, this claim is speculative.

Lowell, Pickering, and Douglass sparked national attention with sensational research about Mars. Spirited by the work Giovanni Schiaparelli conducted around 1877 in Italy, this cohort affirmed that "an extensive system of canals arranged in an artificial manner, as if the work of intelligent beings," existed.[56] At Flagstaff they completed hundreds of drawings based on the use of an eighteen-inch refracting telescope borrowed from the Harvard College Observatory.[57] However, conditions during the winter of 1894–95 interfered with their mission. As Douglass explained in an 1896 editorial, "After two years' experience in Arizona we have found that the seeing at Flagstaff during the Winter is not very good, and we hope to get better results farther south."[58] Such encumbered vision impeded what he termed "good seeing," which "depends on the amount of apparent motion caused by our air, and has almost nothing to do with clouds, as most people suppose."[59] A resonant "better view of the starry heavens could be had through the incomparably pure atmosphere of Mexico valley."[60] Douglass therefore ventured to "pure . . . Mexico" in search of visual acuity and the impending apposition of Mars. On December 10, 1896, the Red Planet was expected to be positioned thirty-four million miles from Earth.

In the Mexican press, Lowell endorsed the latitudinal shift, calling the country "an especially fine field for astronomical work."[61] His decision had manifold reasons. In part, he sought crystal-clear horizons for "good seeing." He also demanded the best possible conditions for the new twenty-four-inch glass lens manufactured by Alvan Clark and Sons, the producers of the Lick telescope in California, which was considered the largest telescope in North America, boasting a thirty-six-inch lens. However, another area was growing critical. By 1884 the Mexican Central Railway was completed, connecting Mexico and the United States through mass transit. As Jason Ruiz notes, "Now, for the first time, Americans of middle-class means could board Pullman cars . . . and disembark thousands of miles later in the heart of Mexico City."[62] Though Lowell was no middle-class tourist, his renewed objective may have been aroused by the "profit from Mexico's tremendous potential."[63] It is no accident that by 1896 at least 80 percent of Mexican railroad stock was controlled by US investors.[64] This incentive of combining science and revenue exacerbated the colonial investment in the region's natural resources, which "became one of the dominant tropes found in American travel discourse associated with Porfirian Mexico."[65] Mines, agriculture, and food exports were part of the "prolific [visual and textual] field" from which "a profit could be drawn with very little effort," as Ruiz outlines.[66] I would add that the sky was equally valuable in this extractive field of colonial and economic control in a region considered the next stop in westward expansion and off-Earth futurity. "Mexico was the future of the United States," Ruiz concludes from his appraisal of late nineteenth-century travelogues; "it was 'the coming country.'"[67] Mexico's role at the forefront of a proto–space race dating to the late nineteenth century should not be minimized.[68]

Newspapers ran headlines such as "An Observatory Moving to Mexico . . . to Dodge Bad Conditions," "The Great Telescope . . . Work on the Lowell Observatory Pushed Rapidly in Order to Catch Mars Off His Guard," and "Flagstaff's Observatory Will Now Go to the City of Mexico . . . Three Noted Astronomers Owe Their Fame to Their Work in Arizona."[69] Amid this media spotlight, Douglass braved the train lines and was met with fanfare and public wonder. He was a carrier of US-based space science and became the chief delegate in Lowell Observatory's transfer from Arizonan to Mexican soil. Such physical movement broadened the terms of migration and the built environment. If the original site housing these US astronomers enabled breakthroughs in binary star studies and the mapping of strange new worlds, Mexico indeed represented the future. This transported dwelling would be on the cusp of unprecedented findings about Earth's interstellar neighbors. Douglass's move southward was guided not by cliché dime-novel stories of border exoticism but by the Red Planet. His transnational pursuit brought Arizonan scientific acumen to bear on Mexican skies. In search of "aliens," Mars, and the solar system, his charge was equal parts cutting-edge astronomy, engineering know-how, and political savvy. To get up there, workers' hands were needed.

On November 7, 1896, Douglass arrived in Mexico City, as anticipated by the administration of Mexican President Porfirio Díaz. Lowell had initiated conversations with Díaz that summer. His previous experience likely had prepared him for these talks. Before picking up telescopic mappings of Mars, he had served as a foreign secretary during a decades-long career in Japan and Korea after earning his undergraduate degree.[70] His request must have resonated with the ambitious Mexican president, who sought US capital investment and advanced technologies in the pursuit of modernizing the nation-state. If the impossible feat of railroad engineering propagated newfound tourist profits, perhaps something similar could happen through another untapped resource, the sky. It is no surprise that on the heels of Douglass's visit, newspapers reported that Díaz "has been most active [on] behalf of these American astronomers and has not only welcomed them to Mexico but has instructed the Mexican national observatory to furnish every possible aid to them in their work. Scientific men look upon this enterprise as the most important of the nineteenth century."[71] The transfer of Lowell Observatory was a symbolic win for Díaz and confirmed a political optic of him as a champion of science for a global stage. His win, however, would affirm later critiques that he "ceded the sovereignty of his nation in order to modernize it," as Ruiz puts it.[72] With the Lowell Observatory in place, Díaz stood to be recognized among these "scientific men," reaffirming Douglass's sentiment that Díaz was "not only a very eminent statesman, but a man who fully appreciates the value of scientific work."[73] Díaz advised the Department of Encouragement to waive customs duties to make the transfer of the dome, telescope, and personal belongings possible.[74]

What remained unclear was a viable new home for the advanced Clark telescope. During his visit Douglass scouted four possible locations. He paid principal attention to Cerro de Guadalupe, a summit hosting a shrine to La Virgen de Guadalupe and overlooking the lakes of Texcoco and Xochimilco. However, the lingering wet season made "good seeing" impossible.[75] In response, he resorted to studies of elevation. Though Cerro de Guadalupe stood at 150 feet above Mexico City, nearby Tacubaya was 100 feet higher. The area also housed the National Observatory, a mere three-quarters of a mile south.[76] The location stood to foster closer collaborations with Mexican astronomers such as Felipe Valle, who guided Douglass and other associates through the site-selection process, even "allow[ing] them to spend nights at the observatory."[77]

Such professional courtesies underscore another spatial practice crucial to astronomers: nightly inhabitance. More than their compatriots in biology or medicine, space scientists have a kind of spatial knowledge that is deftly sensorial—aware of environmental conditions, climate, and body orientation as they inhabit surrounds, living with and alongside their telescopic instruments. An 1898 newspaper report about Lowell scientists gleaned the kind of closeness made possible on campus: "Through the coldest of nights, without a fire—for artificial warmth would disturb the 'seeing' qualities of the instrument—Dr. See and Mr. Cogshall, his assistant, lay side by side, swathed in overcoats and Navajo blankets, watching for 'sights,' which were immediately recorded."[78] Slumbering intimately under the stars conveyed a kind of emotional work for those dedicated to the field who succumbed to these demands and experienced their fraternity under close quarters and nocturnal conditions. Messeri expands on this haptic investment, adding that "ways of inhabiting the observatory are changing, yet astronomers still assert a need (or perhaps, more accurately, a desire) to be there."[79] This desire "to be there" heightens the sensorial lessons to be gained through the science campus's architectural authority. Astronomer self-definition aside, the case study of Lowell Observatory demonstrates other spatial dimensions of the building that are equally crucial.

In addition to considering altitude, Douglass weighed proximity to transportation. "Tacubaya was chosen some 250 feet north of the stage road which passes over the mountains to Toluca and an equal distance west of the new Cuernavaca Railroad."[80] Because the entire campus weighed thirteen tons, including a forty-foot dome and heavy weights, customized train cars were built for the journey.[81] The 150-pound Clark lens traveled in a separate trip, under Lowell's supervision. Coordination between the Santa Fe Railroad and its subsidiary, the Mexican Central Railroad, expedited the move and included permission to delay the cars for seven hours "on [the] road nearest the Observatory."[82] Transit development, from roads reaching mountainous summits to railway thoroughfares, was more than commuter planning policy. Evidence of Native, Indigenous, and Mexican labor was engraved into the land for the purposes of science, modernity, and capitalist collusions.

The installation of the Lowell Observatory was emblematic of networks built by Mexican workers, alive and dead. According to Douglass in a report for readers of *Popular Astronomy*, "a gang of fifteen Mexican laborers" worked to unload "nearly seventeen tons of material exceedingly difficult to handle."[83] He added that carting an iron casting for the dome resulted in one fatality. "An ignorant driver . . . was undoubtedly intoxicated. At noon he proceeded to do more drinking and almost first thing in the afternoon fell from his wagon and was killed."[84] More than perpetuating the violent representational discourse of the intoxicated *borracho* popularized in racist US media depictions of an unruly and lawless Mexico, Douglass's depiction of the "ignorant" laborer evades any liability for dispensing pulque, "passed to the native workmen in order to keep their energies alive" (see figure 4.3).[85]

While it is unclear whether the circulation of this fermented nectar was recreational or ceremonial in practice (a topic I take up in the next chapter), its symbolic use to enliven workers constructing the observatory had the opposite effect. Douglass's account received another assist from the press: "In the brief space of eight days, with the help only of native Mexican laborers, wholly inexperienced in work of so difficult a nature, . . . the construction of the largest wooden dome ever built, will be a matter of wonder to those who know how delicate and arduous a task."[86] Portraying worksite death as predictable because these "native Mexican laborers" are "wholly inexperienced" and thus unskilled, the newspaper depicts the driver as merely another drunk, someone who dies in anonymity. "No one seemed to know where the man lived," Douglass added.[87] His dismissal of Mexican life echoes the desensitization to ethnoracial death and dying, a necropolitical viewpoint in accord with colonialism, hinting at how specters nonetheless remain, haunting the settler colonial archive.[88] Thus, the workman's lapse into the void is not the consequence of overindulgent barbarism but much in line with the kinds of nefarious negations that render the isthmus as the "underside" of art geography, an unseen void. Nonetheless, this campesino's death brings Mars closer to Earth, a sacrifice that haunts "landscape representation [that] serves the purposes of modern capitalism: erasing the essential contributions of labor to capital accumulation," as Michelle Arevalos Franco argues.[89] For late nineteenth-century readers of *Popular Astronomy*, gone is the way "[workers'] lives are burdened by precarity and injustice through the systemic flaws of a labor regime profiting from their vulnerability."[90]

Lowell Observatory's remaking in Tacubaya is an accomplishment of science and architecture, the largest wooden structure of its kind at that time. Its status as a structural feat, however, raises questions about "the processes of division and devaluation of labor inform[ing] a social understanding of whose work 'counts' and whose work is worth documenting."[91] If the architectural surrounds of the observatory depend so much on astronomer self-definition, one linked to intimately communing with the stars, might laborers "fundamental to the construction and maintenance of landscape architecture projects" enshrine it as a Mexican place?[92] Photography of the observatory's construction is printed in *Popular Astronomy* and documents the dominant labor relations among scientist, designer, engineer, and worker. Arranged as a "photo album," this printed souvenir records this important south-of-the-border endeavor, drawing a visual distinction between astronomer and worker. Some imagery replicates the solitary "man on the mountain" archetype with Lowell and Douglass commanding the instrument with the means to invade Mexican skies and control the terms of ocular power scrutinizing Mars. Their bodies lean onto rungs of the observatory ladder, scavenging the skies for extraterrestrial life.

Occupying the outsides of the scientists' domain are campesino laborers. They reside at the periphery of some photos, where they level terrain and install tracks to transport heavy materials. Inside, they erect rafters and build mounts, balancing themselves on towered wooden scaffolding in vaulted, dangerous conditions. This visual documentation perpetuates divisions of labor and minimizes the worker through a media optic that champions the architectural majesty of the Clark telescope. Unseen are the ways that these "inexperienced" laborers "were caught in a brutal system of debt peonage that closely resembled slavery."[93] Under the Porfiriato, this exploitive servitude worsened after the nation's economic debt crisis in 1907.[94] The figures captured during the observatory's building implicitly reference the political and material divides taking place behind the hands fabricating the means to sight Mars, as well as the geopolitical entanglements between nations underwriting this construction zone.

After the observatory opened, Lowell courted the country's elite, aligning US capitalist investments with science's modernizing technology and extractive designs on "pure . . . Mexico." An open-house reception attracted Mexican city councilmen and "ladies of the city," who mingled with teachers and scientists anxious to view astronomical bodies with a state-of-the-art instrument like the Clark telescope.[95] A *Mexican Herald* story from February 12, 1897, discusses this occasion, adding that "a much larger number of English-speaking people would have been present . . . but all through the afternoon and into the night the grey clouds flapped back and forth, only occasionally allowing a glimpse of Mexico's matchless heavens."[96] Not to be outdone, President Díaz and members of his cabinet and staff toured the facility in March 1897 before the United States regained possession of the telescope. His presence confirmed the Lowell Observatory as "one of the most finely situated on the continent," and through his cooperation the Porfiriato was assured greatness.[97]

A postconstruction snapshot captioned "Lowell Observatory in Mexico" affirms this binational accomplishment in architecture (see figure 3.2). However, rather than removing the human actors or natural elements, the composition is a study of architectural design and, better, a rumination about the campus's landscape through social and environmental signifiers. The traditional pastoral attentions to the countryside accentuate a sense of place through transcultural differences. Maguey plants and cacti ornament the grounds. A minor wooden shelter accents the observatory's bucket design, broadening the kinds of architectural languages at work on this science campus nearly five miles outside Mexico City. Vernacular improvisation and precise Western engineering appear to equalize in this visual rendering.

Leaning against the doorway, a campesino in peasant attire takes a pause from arduous and unsafe work. He is not yet in and not yet out, and his relaxed comportment and crossed sight lines with another man nearby hint at a social exchange extending from the threshold to the foot of the building. Further left is another figure brandishing a sombrero. He faces forward, perhaps attentive to the photographer. His hand retreats into his pocket in a gesture conveying confidence and certainty. His feet are level with the base of the observatory, and his hat aligns with the telescopic aperture as both point up. He stands at the intersection of grounded Mexican land and sky. Entangled with the spatial logics and visual rendering of this transnational observatory, he animates the ways in which campesinos are the hinge between

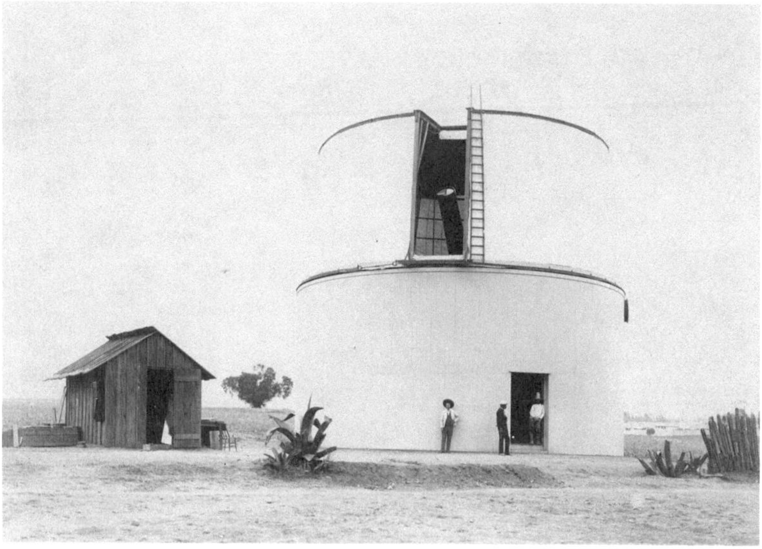

3.2 Lowell Observatory in Mexico, ca. 1897. Photograph. Box 21a, Andrew Ellicott Douglass Papers, 1867–1962, Special Collections, University of Arizona.

planets and worlds. Whether laboring or stuck in pockets, campesino hands are an irrefutable part of the construction and even extend to the building surrounds and lands, and they even reach into the vastness of the universe. The campesinos' work in life and death allows for transplanetary-relational trajectories to be forged even after the telescope's eventual deinstallation.

By the time the Lowell Observatory returned to Flagstaff in 1897, the US press touted this national triumph with flattering reviews of scientific advancement. A story titled "An Arizona Telescope" from an 1898 issue of the *Paterson Evening News* sheds a spotlight on the scientist's mapping of Martian channels.[98] The accompanying visual detail is no ordinary image, however. An etching of the photograph of the observatory is reprinted in the newspaper (see figure 3.3). The inked version diminishes the details. The Clark telescope is less monumental. Its telescopic shaft recedes, swallowed into the shadow of the open dome. The campesino in the doorway abates in cultural specificity. His garb appears less socially specific and more narratively cast for the purposes of engaging the other ambiguous figure lingering at the door. Despite this dampened acuity, the man brandishing his sombrero is prominent and clearly conveyed, making this image evidence of Mexican astronomy, surely an unusual sight for late nineteenth-century US readers.

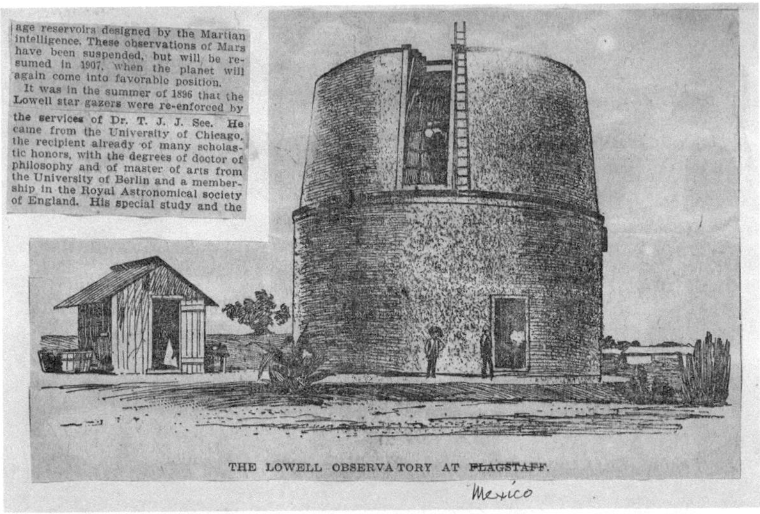

3.3 Engraving (after photograph of Lowell Observatory in Mexico, figure 3.2) from "An Arizona Telescope" in *Paterson (NJ) Evening News*, 1898. Scrapbook, box 21a, Andrew Ellicott Douglass Papers, 1867–1962, Special Collections, University of Arizona.

For these reasons it is surprising that the image is captioned "The Lowell Observatory at Flagstaff." With its clear illustration of maguey and a sombrero-wearing hombre, this article surrogates Tacubaya for Flagstaff. By visually substituting Mexico for Arizona, the editors of the *Paterson Evening News* incidentally comment on a former Mexican territory occupied by the United States after the Mexican-American War of 1846–48. In their misattribution, a landscape populated with sombrero-adorned men is mistakenly Arizonan. In his scrapbook Douglass intervenes and scribbles "Mexico" to correct the printed record. Despite his effort to fix this image-text imprecision, his privileging of geopolitics over Mexican workmen falters under this observatory's illustrated portrait. From road to building, these workers were consequential to the transplanetary-relational pathways on both sides of the US-Mexico border, opening vertical guideposts to look up. The newsprint seals campesinos into the built environment, pinning them to the grounds and walled foundations that transgress terrestrial planes with a verticality that stretches US-Mexico border cooperation into something Martian. In this way, Douglass's editorial intervention cannot undo what these diminutive figures make possible as they symbolically subvert a labor regime that would rather cross them out. Despite this misattribution these campesinos refuse to be disarticulated from the telescope's architectural history. As a spectral presence, they trace Lowell Observatory like a ghost story about debt peonage, dislocation, necropolitical violence, and US empire. Though their reappearance occurs like a haunting, they represent something that Douglass may have wanted to scribble away. His scrawl is indicative of the kinds of erasures that leave the Americas and Central America, in particular, as a site of negation.

These uncredited markings of Latinx builders spanning the architectural history of science campuses from the late nineteenth century onward in the US-Mexico borderlands suggest that the uncanny and supernatural are perhaps better epistemes to understand what Latinx new urbanism is and what Latinx placemaking was and continues to be: speculative. Although Central American diasporic artists and their collaborators in this chapter confront these elisions more than a century later, their "untimely conversations" intuitively rebuild these connections, returning to the earth, where dirt, plants, and soiled hands elicit something extraordinary.

Drawn in Stone

As a symbol of late nineteenth-century Western scientific modernity, the Lowell Observatory plots the American Southwest and US-Mexico borderlands with operations indebted to the optical advancement from lens manufacturers in Cambridgeport, Massachusetts, and Pittsburgh, Pennsylvania. However, mixed-media artist and sculptor Beatriz Cortez refuses to relinquish the observatory to a space history beholden to settler colonialism and titans of the industrial age. Rather than separating labor from an epicenter of astronomy research in the built environment, she rejoins the hands of immigrant worker through a kind of radical collectivity honed by the technological and scientific toolkits of modernization and the ancient Americas. In doing so, she invites a haunting that neither draws from the past to activate the present nor profiles the honorific character of individual struggle in labor history. Instead, Cortez dares to fathom the future in the present with sight lines and guideposts derived from ancient epochs and cosmology. With a cosmic optic that sidesteps a post-Enlightenment field of astronomy driven by linear directions and progressive counts of time, her take on contemporary art overlaps now with layers of then.

Even as her sleek sculptures and mirror-encrusted time-traveling machines present cool facades in a palette resonant with science fiction spacecraft, her shiny exteriors are a false front. Behind them are Indigenous lifeways and ancient origin stories that take the viewer beyond empirical reality, time, and space. Spores like those in her collaborative work with rafa esparza, *Nomad 13* (2017), grow in a broadly conceived "space garden," and like that sacred tree of life connecting the underworld with the outer world, "plants are survivors of repression, prohibition, colonialization, slavery, capitalism, imperialism, eugenics, and genetic experimentation."[99] Her seedlings sprout biodiverse artworks in the name of speculative machinery.

Such viewpoints focus a work like *Nomad 13*, demonstrating how a hexagonal sculpture born of Earth's resources, steel and mud, can provoke coexistences that are simultaneously grounded and aerial.[100] Art making is practiced in a collective approach that links marginalized worker and migrant with celestial entities of the universe. Trans-ing the planet in this way, her space garden is a shape-shifting formation of cosignatories. Touches of air, water, and sunlight reset a gallery ecology with leafy sprouts and tendrils that alter institutional relationships with fine art sculpture. Categorizing *Nomad 13* as "land art" is likely to miss a kind of art collaboration that refuses the presentist and human-centered interventions popularized by Leslie Labowitz-Starus's sprouts, Richard Long's rock slabs, Charles Ross's tunneled apertures, and Robert Smithson's crystallized Salt Lake design. Rather than exert an anthropogenic supremacy over the natural environment, Cortez cultivates a nomadic, transgenerational, and even transplanetary relation where migrant and seed commingle in a creative choreography nourished from something elemental. Different epochs and eras feed into an art making that nods to a future garden detached from a progressive march. Instead, an organic time capsule regrows the past to unfurl new beginnings in stretches of root and plant matter.

These temporal tangles were the focus of Cortez's 2022 solo exhibition at Pitzer College Art Galleries, *Cosmic Portals*. Her intentions contemplate abstraction broadly. Her view announces a transient and transplanetary resiliency that speculates on celestial objects, meteorological aberrations, and divine signs as resplendent guideposts. By pontificating on abstraction as the ancient Indigenous Maya apprehended meaning from the stars, Cortez recalibrates the terms of sculpture under epic or "hyperobject" scales. By "hyper" I am referring to Timothy Morton's definition, an episteme germane to Cortez's thinking, as they mutually ponder relations "to some other entity, whether they are directly manufactured by humans or not."[101] The magnitude of Cortez's extrapolating outlook invites collective art making in vast terms. In this way, archaeoastronomy's guesswork about the stone records of ancient astronomers finds new purpose in her practice. As they mutually look up, they also link up through alignments gleaned in the East Los Streetscapers' *Moonscapes* mural depicting primordial holders of the universe's knowledge (see chapter 2). In this show Cortez's speculative discernment takes her to the ruins of El Caracol, one of two surviving circular structures of Mesoamerican architecture believed to have been an observatory. On this landing at Chichén Itzá in the Yucatán of southern Mexico, El Caracol housed scientific and ritualistic insights. The tower's three extant windows spurred debate among astroarchaeologists, Maya studies experts, and historians of the ancient world, who asserted directional meaning for these apertures to the stars and Venus, in particular.[102] This spiraling staircase points in the cardinal directions as a much-hypothesized astronomical tool of measure, a landing of worship, and a counter of time. What calendrical, solstitial, and equinoctial insights could be abstracted from this stone platform were not lost on Cortez. As in *Nomad 13*, she resumed the hands of scientist and builder to construct openings of immense proportion across time.

Her rendition, aptly titled *El Caracol*, restaged the Pitzer gallery with a ten-foot steel spiral staircase (see plate 24). The vacuous white cube is reoriented and rebuilt in a likeness of Indigenous stone technology and a Maya clockwork. As viewers walk the thirteen stairs, each step curves, reanimating footwork in the sacred day count of agricultural cycles. At the top, viewers rise up and look out in a transplanetary-relational comportment, attaining a sense of place among the stars. Through a steel facsimile of stone that gave ancient Maya observational gateways to Venus, the moon, and the sun, Cortez literalizes this isthmus's connection between worlds. For gallerygoers, each passing step and window is a passage to the magnetic reverb of the planet. Her work is an architectural homage to the "possible astronomical sighting scheme" through the interdoorway designs at Caracol, which maximize heliacal rising and setting, as Anthony Aveni and colleagues observe.[103] More important, Cortez's steely intervention is a site of science, history, and speculation in which an ancient apparatus to the stars is reimagined against the progressive order of time-space.

Despite the decayed, crumbled walls and disrepair evident in El Caracol, its ruin is an opportunity for supposition. Though the famed archaeologist Oliver Ricketson reported disappointment because "the upper terminus of the stair way cannot be ascertained, for, a little more than halfway to the top, the whole northern section of the building has completely fallen," his team believed at least a total of four windows existed, "completing the pattern of alignment to the cosmic regions," as Gerardo Aldana y Villalobos espouses.[104] Because Cortez's sculpture is no ordinary replica, her upper landing revives the platform from which Central American futures are certain to come. At this ascendant point, looking up is a collaborative performance where traces of the ancient Maya are abstracted from this helix structure. Like in a nautilus shell, nature's mathematical patterning spirals and coils at various distances and in various directions. Once aligned with the most elevated point, viewers see other ways to speculate on reality, a kind of Central American space knowledge belonging to other temporal circularities, planetary perceptions, and magnetic pulses electrifying the cosmos. The experience of Latinx contemporary art is snaked in ancient ways and organic matter, which demands other definitions for work that transgresses Westernized organizations of space-time. A visual past of a flattened Central America is more decumbent for Cortez with stairwells climbing up. As her metallic armatures mirror Mesoamerican portals to celestial bodies, she entices experiences that are inextricably crafted by the hands of laborers whose art histories are little detected in the "official" mappings of *Twentieth-Century Art of Latin America*. Cortez's emphasis on the collective power of art making further meshes with collaborators of an unexpected cosmic source.

Outside the gallery are eleven steel boulders on the Pitzer College green (see plate 25). In various hues of oxidation, these sculptural pieces are covertly disguised, perhaps miming the campus's desert gardens, a sophisticated display of succulents nested among arid beds, granite slabs, and river rocks which Pitzer charged Huntington Botanical Gardens arboriculturist Joe Clements to add to.[105] Lounging among the students on the lawn, these recessed stones anticipate a vertical guidepost. Soldered veining and puckered ends where welder meets steel hint that these are no ordinary rock formations. These boulders are metal casts with oxidized facades transmitting ecological exchange and ascendant arcs. Their configuration is a microcosmic environment that hinges on interstellar pathways.

Each boulder approximates a star, forming the constellation of what European astronomers call Orion after the huntsman from Greco-Roman mythology. No astrological homage, however, this starry arrangement is biographically significant for the artist. Cortez recalls seeing the constellation when she was a child growing up in El Salvador. The constellation tethers land, time, and cosmos—a transplanetary relation from her Southern Californian standpoint. Cortez argues, "I can turn my head, my feet, I can be in El Salvador if I just rotate. . . . I can look at that constellation, and I can be over Palenque in ancient times."[106] Like a time machine corporeally activated with a twist of a neck, she charts a migratory portal lined with stars. The simultaneity of being in coexistence between worlds, temporalities, and cosmologies attunes to a frequency known to the ancient Maya. In collective unity, they hum with the universe in a reverberation echoed in the mythos of Maya King K'inich Janaab' Pakal of Palenque.

Ruler of this ancient city in southern Mexico, the Maya king has become the subject of some debate since his tomb was discovered by Mexican archaeologist Alberto Ruz Lhuillier in 1952 (see figure 3.4).[107] Archaeoastronomers place Scorpius on the lid, an image closely linked to Orion, "marking the portal to the underworld in the rift of the Milky Way."[108] For science fiction aficionados, he is proof of ancient astronauts in the pre-Hispanic world, a topic given some merit in Chicanx mural art. As mentioned in chapter 2, artist Domingo Rivera painted *Aztec Spaceship* (1975) in San Francisco's Mission District, "twisting" the Maya king's sarcophagus ninety degrees and launching him in an ancient rocket fit for space (see plate 26).[109] As Cortez, too, "turns," she doubles the bodily rotations of a tomb and rocket ship, performing a movement not unlike her *El Caracol* artwork, where ancient and contemporary measures of time layer body and land. An indication of her transcended reality and speculative expression is inlaid not in a science-fictional time machinery but in the puckered ends of metal boulders. Though this reverence for stonework and earthly material may seem contrary to the sophisticated aerospace and defense technology of NASA, her movement on behalf of multiple geographies and celestial entities says otherwise.

Cortez eyes the worldview of the ancient Indigenous Incans. In Quechua, the huaca is a revered stone body, a rock or mountain in the landscape meant for "both extraordinary and sacred things."[110] According to art historian Carolyn Dean, these sites were "the preserved bodies of ancestors and natural formations in the Andean landscape" to the mystification of a Spanish settler colonial religious order.[111] Huacas, with their "transmutability . . . contrary to traditional Western thinking," were "often perceived *as* inhabitants of settlements; in fact, they were believed to be the original owners of certain territories, and they were often the most important residents of particular places" in their most rudimentary and untouched forms.[112] In her appeal to natural architectures of Earth and the cosmos, Cortez imbued the college green with a rock formation in contact with worlds missed by the human eye. By apprehending planes that extend upward and downward, she asks not what we see in the cosmos but what the cosmos sees in us. In this trans-ing enmeshment of stone tethering the bodies of human and celestial scale, Salvadoran sculpture knots and folds contemporary art in on itself. This collective artwork serves as the foundation of ancient cosmology and an

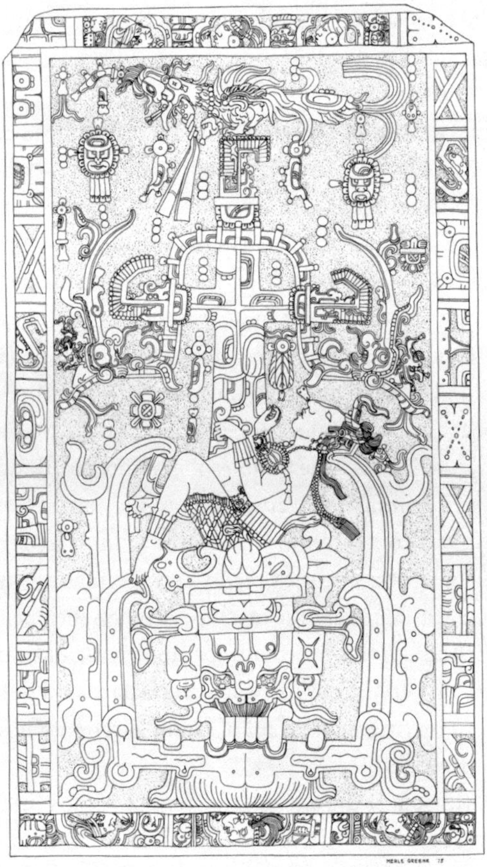

3.4 Line drawing of carved art on the cover of K'inich Janaab' Pakal's sarcophagus (AD 683/1970s), Chiapas, Mexico. From Collection 133, Merle Greene Robertson Collection, the Latin American Library at Tulane University.

entry to the universe. Although Cortez's transplanetary-relational approach was an unexpected yet significant contribution to the *Cosmic Portals* exhibition, its reception was particularly violating.

Two rocks vanished from the outdoor grounds of the Pitzer galleries, causing alarm for the artist and gallery staff. The theft had dire consequences not only for the show but also for Cortez's statement to redefine the terms of art abstraction in the designs and cosmic visions of ancient Indigenous lifeways in the Americas. In particular, the vandalism of *Cosmic Mirror (Sky over Los Angeles)* defiles a reflection that brings the cosmos down for a conversation with celestial entities dating to twenty-nine thousand years ago. This theft sabotaged the pathways traced by Andean divine stones and the ruins of a landmark observatory in the ancient Americas, abruptly halting an "untimely conversation" and refusing this mirror to the sky. A setting on the green that joins Salvadoran art with stars, isthmus, and abstract aesthetics is undone, foreclosing its meditation on migrations across space-time. In their confiscation, these abducted stones eerily echo the unmapping of Central American art history, making omission tantamount to the out-of-place disjunctions that leave this diaspora in an art historical "underside," as Cornejo observes. After several public appeals online and via social media, the artworks reappeared by unknown means.[113] Either they were returned by a misguided culprit, or they reemerged to complete their untimely journey compliments of King Pakal. No matter the circumstance, the act of erasure that *Cosmic Mirror (Sky over Los Angeles)* endured on the grounds of this campus speaks not only to the vulnerabilities of ancient ways in present times but also to the dislocation that these artists face in the struggle to visualize a Central American future on their own terms. Such discordance was not limited to this specific incident at Pitzer College. A struggle over transplanetary and transgenerational dwelling resonated with Cortez's first collaborative work with LA-based artist rafa esparza.

Brown Queer Suns

Hints of a brown world to come appear courtesy of *Tierra. Sangre. Oro.* (Land. Blood. Gold.), a 2017 group show staged at Ballroom Marfa, an art and performance space in Marfa, Texas. A cultural destination in a West Texas epicenter galvanized by Donald Judd's minimalist monuments and expansive network of art-world investors, this rural town in the Chihuahuan Desert has become a cultural tourist destination for the Lone Star State. Spoken of in the same breath as Art Basel and the Venice Biennale, it is also a hub for extraterrestrial enthusiasts drawn to the Marfa Lights, those mysterious celestial orbs captured in Joel Salcido's science-fictional photo essay *Los Marfianos* (2014). esparza collaborated with a broader collective of nine Latinx creatives and performers during his residency, but Cortez contributed the final touches to the exhibit. Here esparza erected his "brown laboratory," reformulated to fit the architectural impressions of a former dance hall that once played host to the transnational rhythms of norteño danzón and banda music.[114] Esparza, Cortez, and their collaborators confronted the chic branding of this

West Texas setting with something unapologetically brown. Like those late nineteenth-century specters pictured in the dusty surrounds of Tacubaya, Mexico, brown bodies, histories, and laborers rise up and haunt this scene. Their presences linger in the beat of a clave or stomp of footwork; their inhabitance is recorded in the desert grounds. They remain in what José Esteban Muñoz terms "shared flourishing," renewing a brown sense of the earth.[115]

What the terra firma may record in its amorphous and mineral deposits is central to *Portal Sur, After Copán* (South Portal, after Copán). The geographic callout references the classic Maya city of Copán, the ruins of which are found in present-day western Honduras just outside Guatemala (see figure 3.5). With its corbeled brick arch, *Portal Sur* recites ancient Maya structures that "consist of a *spatial* translation of a *temporal* idea, a clever and highly visible, unwritten way of expressing the manner in which the counting of time and the directions of space go together."[116] Installed before Ballroom Marfa, this gateway not only augments the cream-colored art deco facade with a Mesoamerican Indigenous design; it anticipates "the white-turned-brown cube" inside it. By presenting visitors with another portal, esparza and his collaborators reimagine the built environment attuned to other circuitries of space-time (see plate 27).[117]

Crossing the threshold, viewers realign with a north-south axis. This directionality points them in step with the ancient Maya orienting "architectural-calendric principles devised in the south [and] . . . carried forward in time and northward in space."[118] Esparza and collaborators retrace the path of Copán's ritual promenade, a path guiding sacred followers to other planes of existence. As Aveni posits, this spatialization is "mutually complementary functional dualism for construction and space at north and south ends of that axis, in which north stands for the celestial supernatural sphere, and south, for the underworld or worldly."[119] Placing the ancient Maya architectural record and sacred expression in an outpost of contemporary art tourism, Cortez, esparza, and collaborators transfigure planes of existence outside colonial settler organizations of reality. Instead, other routes reveal themselves, traced by the unseen presence of West Texas's toilers of the land, laborers who beat their feet as they beat the earth. If Emiliano Zapata's saying remains true that "la tierra es de quien la trabaja con sus manos" (land belongs to those who work it with their hands), then Cortez and esparza materialize that revolutionary gestalt with the planet's brown matter.[120]

In this, adobe forms the foundation of their collective effort, a turn toward the region's organic and plentiful resource: mud. This vernacular building material is observed throughout West Texas, spanning generations

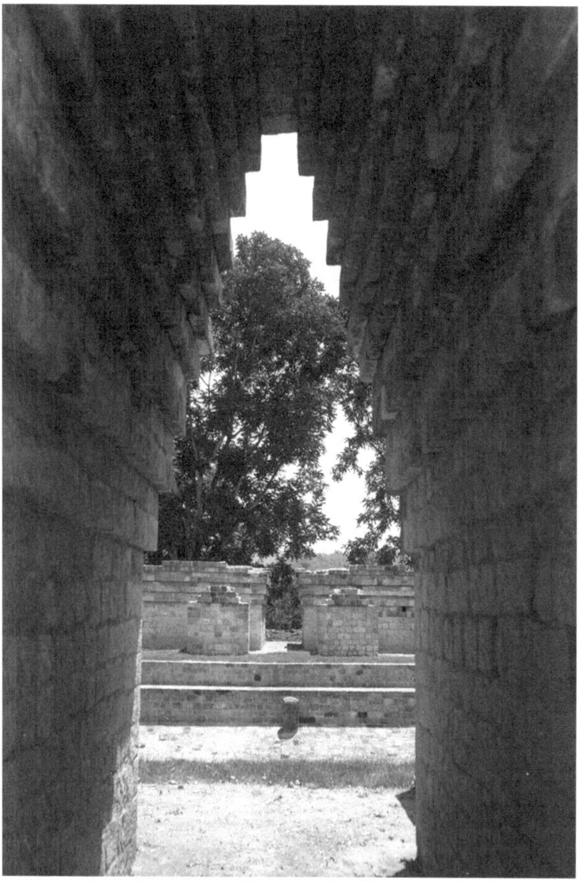

3.5 *Looking Through the Center Passage Towards West Structure, Ball Court, Copán Ruinas, Honduras*, ca. AD 738. Gift of the Carnegie Institution of Washington, 1958. © President and Fellows of Harvard College, Peabody Museum of Archaeology and Ethnology, 58-34-20/38174.

and homesteads in a way that reaffirms a Latinx "land sense," as discussed in chapter 1. Whereas "adobe itself tells stories through the particular definitions of space it implies," those stories are derived from a formative architectural record in the Americas and Spanish colonial Southwest.[121] Adobe is formed from clay, animal dung, water, and straw, and its use by builders of the pre-Hispanic world is also a brown outlet for transplanetary relations. In adobe's combination of soil and animal, the animate and inanimate worlds combine and reconfigure in entanglements of temporal accords and spatial redefinitions (as we shall see). As a building material, adobe connects progeny in a cultural exchange of skill sets and craftsmanship—a suitable twist on the way "the churning and baking of the bricks" are equally nourished by suns of the starry and queer kind.[122] Esparza's spatial aesthetic is a statement about his transgressive desires, which failed to uphold Mexican patrilineal order and heteromasculine expectations. His interest in working with masonry required a transfer of learned knowledge from his father, a trained *adobero* from Jalisco, Mexico. After the artist disclosed his sexual orientation, a wedge grew between them. Adobe remedied this chasm, and through charitable acts of collaboration and intimacy—digging into the earth and turning soil—they closed this divide. In this way, *Portal Sur, After Copán* conveys a queer, feminist, and transplanetary sense of group art making derived from the Chihuahua landscape, fed by the air, and baked by the sun. Bricks also bear the imprint of transgenerational hands, as esparza guided students from Marfa High School, many of whom were Tejanx, immigrant, and/or first-generation American, forging pavers between worlds. As they compacted the soil and worked the mud, they partook in an exchange with the building materials of ancient Indigenous knowledge systems and queer parental love. In their joyful exchange, new bridges were built and portals crossed.

Although these new bricks were molded from the West Texas landscape, more were needed. Esparza and Cortez trekked down to Ojinaga, a township in the Mexican state of Chihuahua. Here *adobero* Don Manuel Rodríguez awaited with materials needed to stage their landing with material references bearing transnational and transplanetary meaning. Gathering contributions to the project from the aged bricklayer, esparza and Cortez transported these items formed from border earth, dried by the Mexican air, and crafted by the elder's skilled hands. Trucking adobe bricks from south to north, they circumvented US border customs banning the import of certain Mexican goods. In this promenade they performed a kind of migration in the path of the sun; caring for earthen remains constitutional to forming another gateway to this brown world. Although adobe may not appear to be the material of choice for Silicon Valley venture capitalists or aerospace defense contractors, it plays an unexpected role in the history of space science, speculative aesthetics, and the future of spacefaring.

For architect Nader Khalili, adobe building material is not only the stuff of historic buildings in the Southwest; it is guiding aerospace scientists to ponder plausible future alien habitats. His proposal uses SuperAdobe, a building material he practiced to create emergency shelters in his native Iran and, later, to house Iraqi refugees after the first Gulf War (see plate 28). His emphasis on low-cost supplies like sacks of sand, which spiral into low-relief walls, not only strove to resolve humanitarian crises with sustainable solutions but also contemplated the future of space travel. In 1984 he presented a ceramic module structure based on SuperAdobe systems to NASA scientists at a symposium called Lunar Bases and Space Activities of the 21st Century. He argued that in his planned blueprint for human habitation, by maximizing the "larger spans of corbelling and leaning-arch earth-structure systems" on the moon, "timeless materials and timeless principles can also help achieve humanity's quest beyond this planet. . . . [T]raditional earthen forms can be generated on other celestial bodies, such as the Moon and Mars, in the form of magma structure, ceramic structure and fused adobe structure."[123] For Khalili, "indigenous lunar architecture" filled with outer planetary soil would give NASA the best and most practical means to house space colonies.[124] He did not live long enough to see the fruition of his vision of lunar colonization.[125] He did, however, model these extraterrestrial shelters outside the Mojave Desert in 2001, speculating on outer space living (see plate 29).

His experimentation echoes other aerospace scientists' theorization of how the mass production of Martian regolith bricks might support Mars settlement.[126] Future colonists' survival is surprisingly predicated on skill sets, manufacturing materials, and architectures advanced by the Indigenous people of the Americas, who labored and built up the present US southwestern borderlands with mud, stone, and rock. In this way, the divides between pre-Hispanic adobe brick and NASA-sponsored Martian habitats narrow, showing how an ordinary ballroom in West Texas is also an extraordinary bridge that conjoins scales and worlds. *Portal Sur, After Copán* made no effort to be a "digestible" barrio aesthetic in a chic art capital like Marfa, as Londoño might argue.[127] Instead, this opening linked nations, crossed borders, aligned planes of existence, and, better yet, brokered transplanetary relations in a way anticipated by those Mexican laborers at Tacubaya in 1896.

By installing a gateway that nimbly navigated the cosmos with mud, *Portal Sur, After Copán* seemed to ask, "Does brownness belong in the white cube?" Answers appear in the form of brick floors that layered the interior of Ballroom Marfa, a picture as striking as another esparza collaboration with Cortez at the 2017 Whitney Biennial in New York. Here esparza fabricated *Figure Ground: Beyond the White Field*, an adobe-ready environment prepared from the soil and water around the Los Angeles River, a major tributary in the city that was reengineered in concrete, a resurfacing of a natural channel that snakes its way throughout the county (see plate 30). Traces of this environmental ruin are baked into bricks that were crated and shipped to New York to supply the foundation for a walled rotunda. Other pieces found their way into a variety of projects, including *Nomad 13*, a space garden collaboration with Cortez featured in the Pacific Standard Time: LA/LA exhibition *Mundos Alternos: Art and Science Fiction in the Americas* (2017–19), as mentioned earlier in this chapter. The large-scale environment at the Whitney became "the first time [the artist thought] about really being immersed in a space made of adobe."[128] The installation, however, proved to discomfort Whitney preparators and administrators, a lesson in curator anxiety that esparza likely learned from a previous performance at the Getty Center, which I will discuss momentarily.

Figure Ground was sequestered to a space that would reduce its environmental threat to the Whitney Collection. The pungent earthy notes aside, the physical restriction of his vast adobe dwelling bolstered the artist's sentiment about building with ancient materials as having a "history of conflict with art history."[129] The response of the Whitney Museum in its object care protocols underscored esparza's suspicions about institutions' difficulty with work that confronts the brick-and-mortar armatures of museal architectural authority. esparza and members of his artisan collective, like Cortez, contest spatial disciplining and thus disturb sanitary surrounds with a kind of brownness otherwise resigned to the void in Barnitz's art geography or flattened in Bonestell's topographical landmass. Much in the same way that Gaspar de Alba once referred to the unaccommodating reception for Chicanx art inside the "master's house" as something akin to "close encounters of the Third World kind" circa 1990, esparza's collaborative insurgency at the Whitney was alien in the broadest sense.[130] Adobe was invasive, diseased, and *alien*ated from the clinical nature of the museum environment, and its racialized connotations as brown matter are worth considering. His literal browning of the precious white cube quoted José Esteban Muñoz's oft-cited "brown commons," which argued for Latinidades' antinormative defiance of the "official national affect, a mode of being in the world primarily associated with white middle-class subjectivity, [that] reads most ethnic affect as inappropriate."[131] If the "brown commons . . . is about the swerve of matter, organic and otherwise, about the moment of contact, and the encounter and all that it can generate," might adobe's standing as antinormative museum material elicit a kind of Latinx collective knowing that comes into being in the unruly, laborious, and literally *extra*terrestrial foreign presence of mud?[132] Muñoz further expands on how "affective performances that reject the protocols of (white) normativity help map out cultural spectacles . . . [which] to borrow a phrase from one of Cherríe Moraga's poems [evokes] 'dreaming of other planets.'"[133] That kind of dreamwork invites antinormative and unruly speculations for esparza and his collaborators. By showing what muddy surrounds can do, esparza lays out other landings that announce to the art commercial establishment pathways through which to move forward in unsanitary and queerer ways.

Hints of this adobe-laden world to come were evidenced in esparza's 2015 Getty Center Museum performance, entitled *The Mexika Eagle, Space Navigation No. 0: XIMAMPA* (see plate 31).[134] Embodying his cultural and institutional alienation, he appeared on the palatial grounds with adobe bricks in hand. Outfitted in a space suit and polyurethane bubbled helmet, he was no ordinary astronaut. His suit was embellished with a vintage Saltillo serape fabric and belted with a stepped fret–style sash. His bare feet were collared with *chachayotes*, rattled instruments consistent with the Danza Azteca ceremony in Indigenous Aztec tradition. Each step was cautiously made, making viewers wonder whether this moon man was a voyager arriving onto a strange land or born of this planet. Refusing to set foot on the gleaming marble floors financed by the Getty family trust, esparza carefully avoided physical contact with this unknown and even hostile territory with adobe tiles paving his way. Through performance, he forged an isthmus materializing for onlookers how Indigenous and Latin American laborers excavated the land, carving passages to observatories that house optical technology to tarry about the galaxy. With tile, he moved with extraneous motion. Each step was a brick-by-brick procession. His "earthy" action stirred the museum administration's anxieties in a way that anticipated the Whitney's reaction two years later. According to esparza, Getty's risk-averse programmers requested that felt be added to the bricks' undersides (to protect the travertine floor), that pavers not be left behind (a tripping hazard), and that adobe be dyed a vibrant hue to help identify physical residue (to enhance the vision of museumgoers).[135] Adobe, esparza countered, came in one color: brown.

Undeterred, esparza marched toward a brown tomorrow. His perspiration in the space suit and the punishing summer heat of the Getty Center's courtyard wet the dirt (see plate 32). As he lugged bricks weighing around forty-five pounds each, his travail confronted the pristine architectural facade and inevitably stained it, echoing what Muñoz terms "brown worlding," a performance practice "described as an opening to other worlds, a passage to alternative realities, as a way to build worlds that are contestatory, oppositional, or merely alternative."[136] More so, this "path," as Muñoz notes, is also attuned "to see what is here but is concealed . . . a sustained practice of seeking, finding and, again, touching an aspect of being with and in the world."[137] As the bricks were laid, esparza dragged time in smears of brown matter, human plasma, and exhalation. Sweat smudged the plastic shield of his bubbled helmet, reflecting his arduous trek, fogging the surface, and blinding him. His knees bled as he carried bricks, climbed, and crawled along his adobe isthmus, needing the full three-hour duration to reach his endpoint. He arrived exhausted at a pseudo–space station nestled in a water feature, emptied because of LA County's restrictive guidelines caused by a debilitating drought.[138] Across a threshold of velvet ropes appeared a Mesoamerican version of the *Millennium Falcon* designed by printmaker Dewey Tafoya. Framed and inset in a metal frame, it signaled the appropriate end to this space opera performance. Esparza tied plaster casts of his feet, face, and hands to the ends of fifty brown helium balloons, wishing to release the pain and trauma he endured on the grounds of this planet into the universe.[139] His vertical intentions exacted transplanetary relations, proposing an alternative version of aerial futurism subsisting of antiquated if not speculative technology once lauded in that literary exemplar, Jules Verne's *Around the World in Eighty Days* (1872).[140] In a lo-fi spaceship, he released queer of color injury and wounds into the ether going beyond the Getty Center, an ascendant reversal of the campus which rests at the edge of the Santa Monica mountains. Like Cortez's steely observatory, he advanced a kind of pathway, a portal, made possible through hand-packed earth, communion with celestial entities, and balloon guideposts directing the viewer to look up.

Ironically, in this environment, adobe is dangerous, toxic, unstable: in short, alien. It did not belong at the Getty Center, at least not without some adjustments to protect the precious travertine, sixteen thousand tons of which was imported from a quarry east of Rome.[141] Esparza's moon man was not an astronaut colonizing another planet in a conventional sense of terraforming; rather, he returned land there and accentuated its undeniable brown stain. In astronautic drag, the performance showed brown matter's injurious unbelonging in a fine art palace on the west side of LA in which "legitimate" art histories are hung, displayed, and protected. With bricks composed of collective labor and queer kinship, he offered an earthen substrate that strove to connect otherwise unmapped and unaccommodating art geographies beyond the void. Such nullification was something that esparza and Cortez knew all too well. By terraforming the gallery as a transformative process of reclamation and transplanetary relations, esparza and his cohort cultivated a radical ecology to recast sanitized environments. Brown matter breaks down into gases, organisms, and animal discharge, sculpting the atmosphere, making it breathable and believable for a great brown world to come. Standing on his land bridge, this astronaut invited other departures and trajectories to remake the museum into an image closer to the star-destined outlets that Indigenous, Black, Asian, and brown bodies built. However, esparza's practice expanded and found political potency in scales beyond the earthen slab.

Virtual Adobe

Mutable and muddy terrains coagulated under another esparza partnership set in the arid landscape of Arizona and in the Sonoran Desert. During a three-month residency at the Museum of Contemporary Art Tucson, esparza collaborated with artist Timo Fahler and reunited with curator-at-large Laura Copelin, who had managed his work at Ballroom Marfa. Guiding the two artists was the exhibition concept of *were-:Nenetech Forms*. *Nenetech*, which means "close together" and "twinning" in the Mexica Nahuatl language, acknowledges transition where two organic and inorganic forms double. Through the artists' use of the Sonoran Desert, soil shape-shifts, fusing a trans-ing biomimicry to nature.[142] Guiding their participatory process is the kind of impressions made in the dirt as border dwellers are pushed further into the desert, endangering their survival. As immigrants negotiate harm by gun and sun, their survival requires physical transformation to camouflage in the environment and to pair with solar radiation. Because the curatorial premise forwards *were* in the project's title, meaning "to be" or "to grow into," esparza and Fahler court the horror genre, affixing *were-* to *Nenetech*, a fusion of languages with which to ponder humanity's bestial nature. Like the "transcorporeal ontology" in the borderlands philosophy and prose of Gloria Anzaldúa, this duo's work reveals something trans-ing about adobe's porous and moldable shape.[143] Though this muck indexes queer reconciliatory intimacies between father and son, as previously discussed, the *were-* prefix alludes to a transspecies symbiosis for Latinidades in which mud and immigrant twin with land, air, and sun to become something abhorrent and potentially monstrous to contemporary art history broadly. In *were-:Nenetech Forms*, we breathe and immerse ourselves in transmutations of soil and beast, flesh and planet. In this way, esparza and Fahler reoccupy the hyphen in the exhibition's title not in the familiar linguistic violence that separates—for instance, "Mexican" from "American" in Mexican-American—but rather to insist on trans-ing reflections of worlds, nations, and even biological classifications. To be "were" is a distorted yet natural provocation that mixed-media artist Jacqueline Arias intuitively knew.

As a University of Arizona MFA candidate at the time of the *were-:Nenetech Forms* exhibition, Arias was already accomplished in the art of the dig. In her thesis project, *Imbrication*, she contemplated the physical properties of earthen material as it decays, degrades, and potentially births new life. Because dirt incubates a complex biosystem, it chronicles a planet's story, health, and disease. Elements of climate, land use, and human presence also link the geological record to immigrant narratives. Immigration and Customs Enforcement (ICE) agents, for example, arm their border patrol vehicles with boards that drag along empty roads to erase evidence of their tire tracks and, as a result, create temporal mechanisms to clock human use and even disguise police activity in the Sonoran Desert.[144] These techniques weaponize the planet's surface, enhancing dirt's capacity to surveil and track immigrant biodata. Arid surrounds become a climatic collaborator aiding an ICE panoptic machine to better see covert means of immigrant border crossing.

However, the environment is equally calculating. Being missed by border patrol is the way that dirt is also a keeper of ancient knowledge.[145] This sense of time in biorhythmic pacing is central to Arias's endurance exercise, *Plants* (2007) (see plate 33). Also featured in the *Imbrication* series, *Plants* shows Arias *planted* in the broadest sense. Her arms grow into the earth, searching deeply for the secrets kept inside soil. She grabs for a past unknown to her, as a home country is stripped from her, uprooting her national sense of belonging. In the video she is also *transplanted*, trying to establish new roots like a tree. Hers is no immigrant story about the Northern Triangle. She twins with different timescales, mirroring the way seeds have been scattered and moved around geological and ecological epochs. Posed in quiet stillness, she focuses her concentration in a motionless squat. Her limbs dig down into the underworld like a trunk unfurling its roots. Certainly, aspects of her endurance exercise are shared in other Latina feminist installations and performances with natural materials. Works by Laura Aguilar, Teresita Fernández, and Ana Mendieta are the most relevant here. Arias's transplantation takes strange forms and unifies with land and atmosphere as wind sweeps her hair and the sun moves about her body.

Her performance adds another confession to dirt's recordings. As a four-year-old adoptee from Alajuela, Costa Rica, Arias lived temporarily with an American military family stationed in the Canal Zone of Panama.[146] According to the artist, her biological mother had entrusted her and her brother to this household. She would often make the long trek from San José to visit her children in temporary custody. One day she discovered they had been moved and claimed as adoptees in the United States. For Arias and her brother, the experience was akin to abduction, a story that reads more like science fiction than US patrimony. Her experience echoes a history of US interventionism and collusion with the Catholic Church in Latin America with Operación Pedro Pan in Cuba being one of the more notorious episodes. Likewise, Arias's family separation is eerily haunted by Afrofuturism discourse allegorizing the transatlantic slave trade as alien invasion and kidnapping.[147]

The wounds inflicted by US military occupancy in Central America and, on a biographical note, a desire to be planted highlight another facet of her transplanetary-relational approach. Arias's take on dirt in *Plants* elucidated a transspecies affinity to detaching and reattaching. With gesture, she surrenders a conflictual relationship to territory and dwelling by burrowing into the dirt. Her hands are no longer hers, hybridizing a body to the natural environment in search of truths, sacred voices, and reunification with something deeper known to the planet and, potentially, the universe. In her trans-ing performance, Arias's body plunges, becoming part of a geological and cosmological stratum layered in ancient Indigenous knowledge, communion with other realities, and meditation on worlds that span up and down. Her impassioned efforts to rectify national fissures, familial traumas, and migratory narratives in ways set forth by the likes of Cortez and esparza set the foundations for another mixed-media address that surpassed the quiet cavity of this woodland in New York. What digging remained unfinished in *Plants* was completed under esparza's and Fahler's theoretical charge in spills of mud.

Arias and seven other MFA students assisted in *were-:Nenetech Forms*, working as art practice and collaboration interns.[148] Together, they produced adobe from natural materials sourced from the Sonoran Desert. Esparza drew on a familiar architectural lexicon by adding an outdoor adobe rotunda; though it was smaller than his Whitney Biennial installation, his cylindrical portal was scaled with grander intentions. He pointed *Earth Eye—Mira Sol/R/Ojo/Negro* toward the sun like a solar observatory (see plate 34). Cortez was not far behind. The tarp draped over it as a roof was a welding curtain, an industrial material used to deflect UV rays and harmful flashes. In this way, her labor was a ghostly trace recited in the crimson radiance enmeshed between the onlooker and the sun. The red-and-black palette accented the chromatic details of ancient codices, an aesthetic homage to Maya temples and solar observatories. The transplanetary-relational foundations between artists esparza and Cortez and apprentice Arias extended beyond the Museum of Contemporary Art Tucson to another countersite with designs on the desert.

Nearby, the University of Arizona's Joseph Gross Gallery was an extension of *were-:Nenetech Forms*. Similar to the way in which the curation at the

Museum of Contemporary Art Tucson twinned the organic and inorganic worlds, this satellite site was a comparable double. Revisiting the masonry flooring for site-specific activations such as *Figure Ground: Beyond the White Field* (2017), Carmen Argote's *Hunting and Gathering* (2017), and esparza and Cortez's *Nomad 13* (2017), esparza and his collaborators chose not to tile these bricks. At Gross Gallery, a showcase of MFA student work broke new ground in *Terra Forms* (see figure 3.6). Pouring enough brown matter to resurface the entirety of the white box, the participants sculpted soft earth with their feet, doing away with square molds to usher in an extraordinary terrain in the image of esparza's brown world. With each step, they choreographed counterfootwork in ways that would ostensibly subvert the border forces pulling boards across the Sonoran Desert and instead pound alternative pathways and passages, in Muñoz's sense, to enshrine physical impressions of racialized subjects otherwise nullified, erased, or antinormative to gallery environments. Arias and her compatriots motion toward a brown futurity once felt by those migrant workers dancing *rancheras* in the building now called Ballroom Marfa. They move and mold transplanetary relations that return to those primordial builders of the ancient Americas, to the adobe settlements that dot the US Southwest, and to the building blocks of future Martian architecture. In this way, Latinx placemaking is *extra*terrestrial—undisciplined, mutable, and transgressive—alien to realms that discipline the arts in temporal and national categorizations.

In this way, *Terra Forms* in name alone trafficked in art, science, and speculation. The poured floor is doubly about the builders of Latinx placemaking and the discourses of geoplanetary engineers who contemplated cloning Earth on Venus or Mars. In their thematic callout, they draw parallels to aesthetic ideas more on par with science fiction than land art.

Before Carl Sagan theorized the reproduction of Earth's atmosphere on Venus in the pages of *Science* in 1961, other antecedents abounded in literature.[149] Most regarded was Kim Stanley Robinson's 1990s trilogy about a terraformed Mars.[150] However, writer Ross Rocklynne had pondered such planetary projects in *Astounding Stories* since 1937 (see figure 3.7).[151] According to Howard McCurdy, Rocklynne "described a successful attempt to move fifty-two million cubic miles of frozen water from the asteroid belt to Mars."[152] Rather than flood the gallery, the *Terra Forms* group imagined Rocklynne's pulpy text with an adobe reenvisioning. Sonoran Desert mud, water, and dung filled the Gross Gallery. "Inside the white cube," as Brian O'Doherty classically extolled, they transformed and transfigured the art object environment in the image of extraterrestrial liberation.[153] A brown

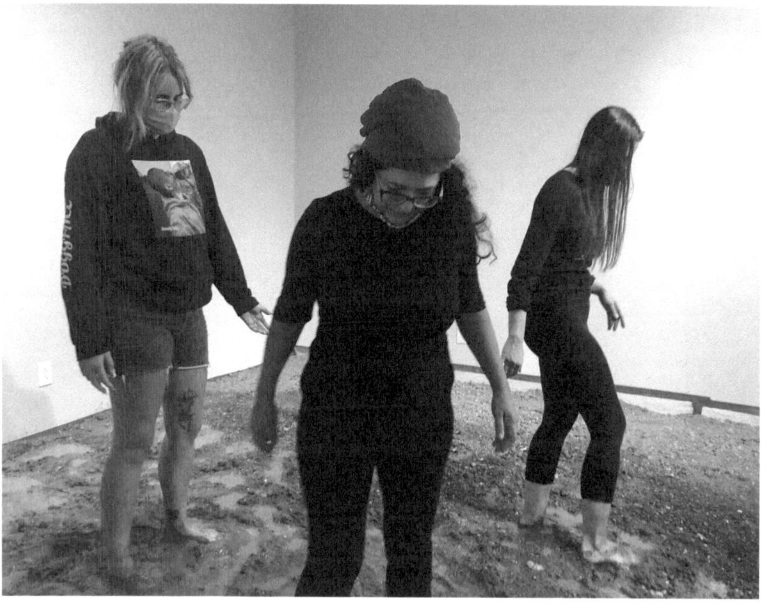

3.6 Jacqueline Arias, *Terra Forms*, 2021. Adobe floor installation documentation photograph with the artist (*center*). Joseph Gross Gallery, University of Arizona School of Art. Image courtesy of Jacqueline Arias.

world to come activates in another kind of landing rendered through the building material from another epoch. Together, these creatives build the platform for a collective and browner art existence in ways first pondered in front of Ballroom Marfa and on the palatial floor of the Getty Center. This material transgression was not the first of its kind, however.

Such conjunctions appear in the practice of Houston-born artist Vargas-Suarez Universal (VSU), discussed in chapter 2. His site-specific installation *Search for Life: Aliens, Water, and Surveillance* was generated from twenty-five gallons of silt from the Rio Grande (see plate 35). Under the advisement of English earthwork artist Richard Long, VSU timed his painting to take ninety minutes, the duration necessary to support mud application without the possibility of cracks destroying the artwork (see plate 36).[154] It was drawn on a large-scale projection of a Martian landscape, and the earthen hue and organic texture deceived viewers at the Rubin Center for Visual Arts in El Paso, Texas, who believed they were looking at an idyllic rumination on the Chihuahuan Desert. Not only did VSU punctuate the historic astronomical relationships between Mexico and Mars as portended by the

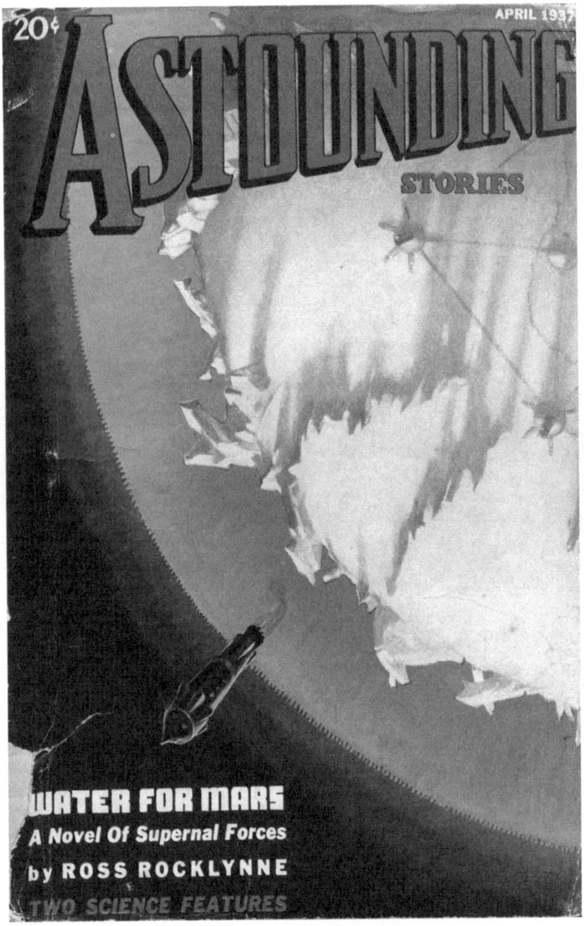

3.7 Howard V. Brown, cover art for pulp digest *Astounding Stories* illustrating *Water for Mars*, by Ross Rocklynne (1937).

Lowell Observatory over a century prior, but he also underscored the techno-dominating power of downward views, where the same technological tools used to surveil immigrants from Mexico and the Northern Triangle were also used to detect aliens on other planets. In his piece ICE and NASA entangled, distorting the terms of border policing on vaster scales.

As VSU pondered "aliens" on and off Earth, he roused irrational fears about the unforeseen and unknown, playing off post-9/11 paranoia.[155] A terrain geographically "alien" to the public formed a sociopolitical mirror performing the doubled reflection of the Chihuahua border region. Mud functions in an antinormative register in ways later negotiated by Cortez, esparza, Fahler, and Arias. Though VSU's work uses mud differently, he shares in an *extra*terrestrial transgression of museum space, resurfacing interior architecture to geoengineer another kind of environment sculpted by Rio Grande water and grainy silt. More to this point, a shovel was added to the mural installation like a grammarian's punctuation mark. His statement with political gusto was underwritten with gilded thermal blankets, the same kind of wrapping that warmed immigrant children separated from their families under the first Trump administration, as we discuss in chapter 5. By juxtaposing a mud-caked wall with an agricultural worker's tool, VSU reminds his viewers about the laborer who haunts stretches of border space on the ground and points toward the sky. The shovel is a spectral signpost pointing to the digs and trenches that bridge worlds, and as Arias's contribution to *Terra Forms* proves, the virtual realm is an equally consequential platform.

Pivoting on her foundational practice in *Imbrication*, Arias's artwork for *Terra Forms* rests on an adobe block. Entitled *del Andamio (From the Scaffold)*, her sculpture was a hybrid of laborer's tools (see plate 37). At one end, adobe bricks stacked to form stair steps to another platform, akin to the ritualistic ascent of Cortez's *El Caracol* sculpture. The top stair then is joined to commercial-grade steel. A scaffold shape-shifts into a form that melds its physical properties. Bridging the material divides of ancient and contemporary matter, Arias conjures memories of her brother, a construction laborer who erected vast buildings and yet existed outside the legitimating terms of urban planning, landscape design, and "official" architectural histories. The work's strange shape is a biographical homage to those unseen campesinos drudging to build the roads, pipelines, and gateways to US astronomical study across the Americas. Somewhere between memory, steel, and earth, her hands meet his. Together, they share in the void and in the "non-place[ment]" as US Central American artist and worker, dislocated from the officiating discourses of the state, art establishment, and national belonging—a vexing that intensified under their statuses as Costa Rican adoptees uprooted from the isthmus by US military intervention.[156] Her mutant artwork asks: If a scaffold is an instrument to support not only a building but also a worker, on what other structural forms of support can Central American creatives and builders rely?

Akin to the way two dichotomous organic materials fuse, becoming at once hard and soft, *del Andamio* allegorizes the structural supports to be improvised amid immigration, social hostility, and alienation. Sometimes this scaffold is the creative work of science fiction: a counterfactual ask about what could have been. To again root her search for protection in the mud, she exposes how Earth's terra firma has the capacity to create new foundations from which to retool and rebuild. By reciting aesthetic negotiations that Cortez and esparza performed before her, she mutated the contemporary and ancient, altering her brother's futurity and giving him something to hold on to. *del Andamio* was a gesture of love and recognition of alternative kinships and extensions of family that found "support" between worlds, timelines, and the transplanetary traffic about the isthmus. Of course, not all scaffolds in the work were visually discernible. Others were made virtually possible.

In addition to her sculptural installation, Arias composed an augmented reality project. This technology invited viewers to wear Oculus headsets and extend their sense of the world through a cyber-adobe environment. Through the visor, users realize that the gallery is a cavernous temple. Ambient sounds of water droplets echo in the brick surrounds. Videographic windows open portals to profiles of immigrant workers based on Arias's video footage from active construction sites at the university (see plate 38). Like apparitions, their faces recast the built environment. Behind the visor, Arias portrays these laboring avatars as racialized abjection, as laborious haunt, as Central American erasure. Her digital adobe builds from something like Cortez and esparza's *Portal Sur*, digitally hacking openings that traverse Western colonial organizations of space-time for workers besieged under the passage of SB 1070 in 2010, which allowed law enforcement to freely detain someone based on suspicion of their residency status.[157] By inviting ghostly interactions in a bid to reclaim a more complex "landscape representation" that lies outside empirical reality, Arias provokes viewers to confront the ghost and apprehend the elusive hauntings of workers that appear in glitchy software.[158] These laborers evade the trappings of faceless banality, and like an escape hatch, this virtual adobe opens another kind of interface pointing down to an underworld.

Punching through the mud-caked surrounds, the virtual reality moves the viewer into the orbit of Indigenous Guna women of Panama. Their Molas, handsewn textile craftworks, are intricate patterned overlays. Layered in geometric spirals and "labyrinth" designs, these blouses "developed around the turn of the twentieth century" in the San Blas Island region at the epicenter of the Panama Canal and Caribbean Sea. The woven garments mediate planetary and environmental references, ecology, and animal life.[159] Protecting Indigenous Guna women from harm, according to the artist, the appliqué stitching is not only divine but, with Arias's computerized rendering, also speculative. Guna digital fibers weave around an aerial map of Panama, contesting with vibrant threads the art historical void that pervaded Barnitz's map (see plate 39). Emerging from modernity's underside, as Cornejo suggests, these electrifying stitches are profound as they regraft geological crusts, cracks, and crevices. Behind the Oculus, Panamanian craftwork usurps hardened adobe, reimagining brown matter in a trans-ing stitch of earth and embroidery. In these virtual depths, Indigenous women in the Canal Zone recode these aerial patterns, which twist and turn into doorways of the planet's origins. For Arias, virtual reality remakes the Gross Gallery's terraforming into a trapdoor that hinges on the phantom labor of workers, tethers Indigenous women's cosmic knowledge and unravels a universe that holds secrets guarded in the planet's core and Guna craftwork.

Just as Arias's performance piece had her plunging her arms into the darkness of soil, she persuades *del Andamio* viewers to dig down for answers because, as Cortez contends, "plants are survivors of repression."[160] The impact of Arias's work challenges how Central America appears as the terrestrial passage to a colonial and aerospace-defined future for so-called first-world technocultural regimes. By looking up and looking down, she transforms ocular relations, constructs new supports, and shuttles the viewer through the uncanny trapdoors of the Canal Zone, where negation and abduction are not satisfactory endpoints for art historical mapping but rather loci from which Indigenous knowledges tangle, knot, and root.

From these terraforming interventions, something else emerges beyond a land-art taxonomy. Artists like Cortez, esparza, and Arias design the platforms where the dislocated Latinx visual artist and displaced laborer find harbor in the sand of the desert, the rocks of the green, the molten steel of the earth, and the agronomic archive of the ground. Through brown matter, hard and soft materiality concretizes the isthmus, remaking the museum and gallery environment into a radical ecology that foments what Cortez dubs "untimely conversations."[161] As "contemporary art" confronts its ancient ligatures, these artists show that the art geography of Central America is timed differently. Temporality encrusts and entangles. In muddy scaffolds, the hands of the builder join with the artisan, planet, and sky. A community of laborers and artistic collaborators incubate across epochs, dimensions, and collectivities, challenging the place of Latinx art; it is not resigned but punches its way into the sky and worms down to the planet's crust. This chapter shows how these creatives arrive at the ways in which racialized labor has long constituted space history's architectural past, forging the centers of astronomic observation and building the substrates from which the Americas connect to celestial bodies, constellations, stars, and, in particular, Mars.

These haunting vicissitudes have yet to be rectified in the astronomical, art historical, or urban landscape in Latinx cultural studies in any meaningful way, as described earlier in this chapter. And yet the ways in which Central American spatial intervention remains unplaced ironically shares in a science-fictional elsewhere even echoed by exoplanet scientists' "planetary imagination," as they mutually find ways to extrapolate a place beyond Earth.[162] This parallelism, while not symmetrical, demonstrates how astronomer and creative in the Americas occupy and commune with the universe in a manner unsuited for the "official" mappings of Latin America in twentieth-century art history. Although the artists who are the focus of this chapter are more skillful and accomplished in Mesoamerican cosmologies and Indigenous worldviews than their Westernized astronomer counterparts, they are mutually fluent in a visual language about existences that vex firsthand perceptibility and trouble the physical investigation of objects, whether of the celestial or alien kind. Approaching transplanetary relationality in this way expands the terms of Central American diasporic art and enhances its spatial stakes, allowing ordinary building materials to geoengineer the museum in the image of a muddier and browner world.

This imaginary work opens windows into alternative existences and ways of being that may appear better suited for late-night cable TV than for architectural studies of the adobe record or stone ruins. However, the persistent attachment of art, science, and speculation to Latinx creativity suggests how being rooted somewhere is also a search for elsewhere. As the artists discussed in the next chapter prove, cheap flicks and drive-in gimmicks offer a profound education in liberation, from how to recognize the real/reel to unmasking monsters lurking behind the scenes.

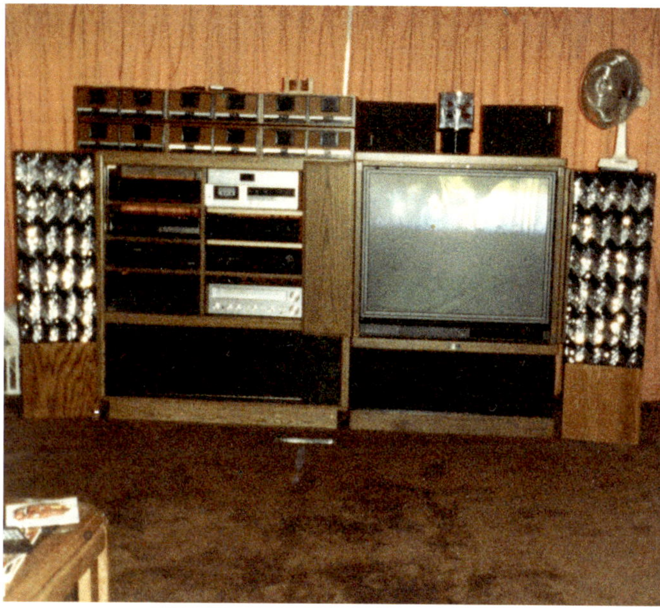

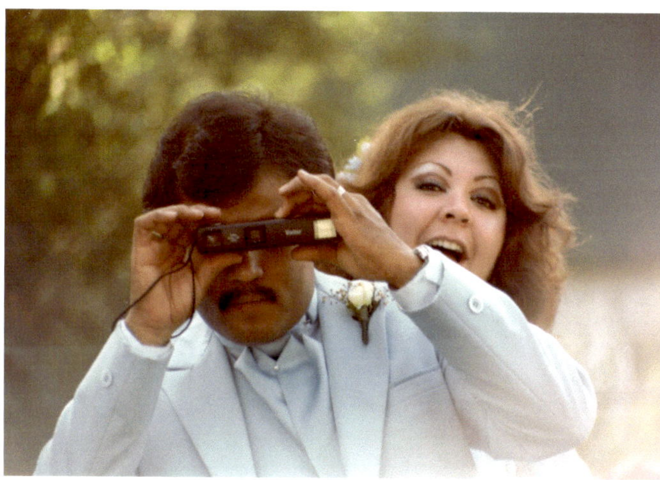

1 Dad's "System," composed of VCR player, surround-sound subwoofers, amplifier, equalizer, cassette tape decks, and video library, ca. mid-1980s, Boulder, Colorado.

2 My father, Robert Hernández (1951–2020), with my mother, Debra Hernández (née Madrigal), at a family wedding, August 1982, Boulder, Colorado.

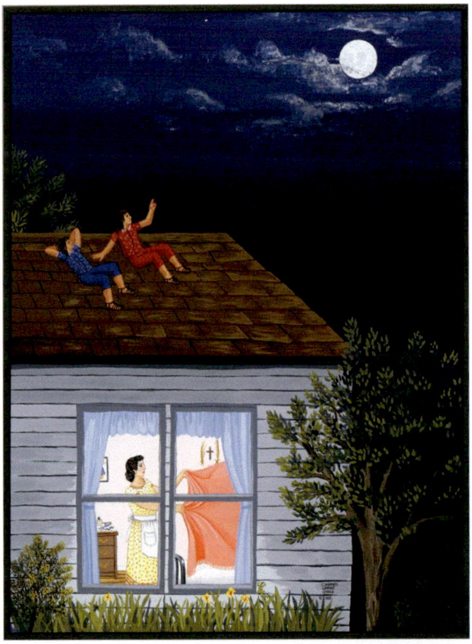

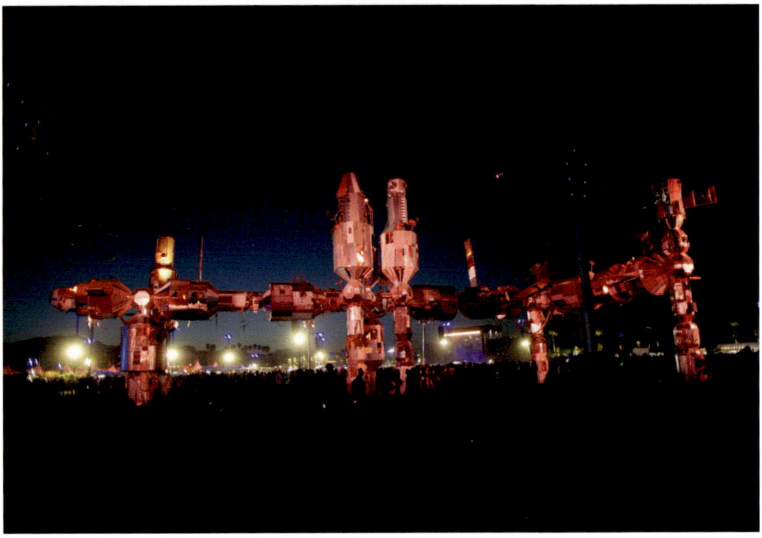

3 Carmen Lomas Garza, *Camas para Sueños* (*Beds for Dreams*), 1985. Gouache on paper, 28⅛ × 20½ in. Smithsonian American Art Museum permanent collection.

4 Simón Vega, *Palm-3 World Station*, 2018. Assorted materials, 150 × 80 × 50 ft. Photograph by Heinz Köbernik. Image courtesy of Goldenvoice/Coachella 2018.

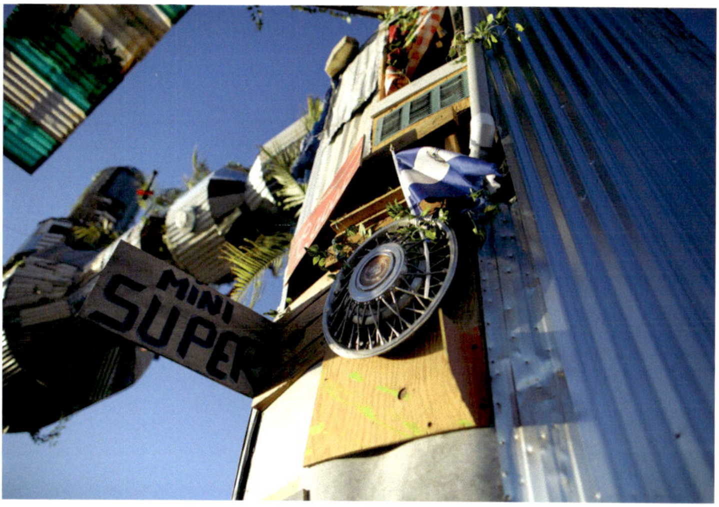

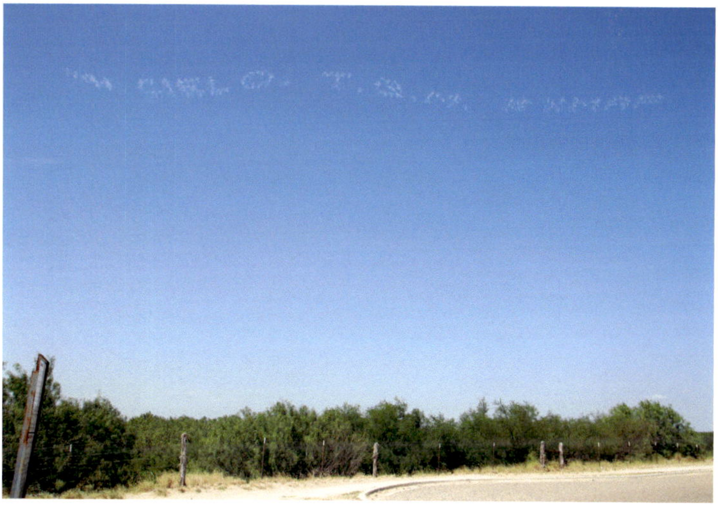

5 Simón Vega, *Palm-3 World Station* (detail), 2018. 150 × 80 × 50 ft. Photograph by Heinz Köbernik. Image courtesy of Goldenvoice/Coachella 2018.

6 Gala Porras-Kim, *Mi Cielo, T.Q.M., #XMAP*, 2020. Performance still no. 5, San Antonio, Texas. Part of the In Plain Sight coalition of eighty artists fighting immigrant detention and the culture of incarceration conceived of by Cassils and rafa esparza. In Plain Sight acknowledges the support of Canada Council for the Arts. Courtesy of the artist. Photography by Sandra Chapa (PBS).

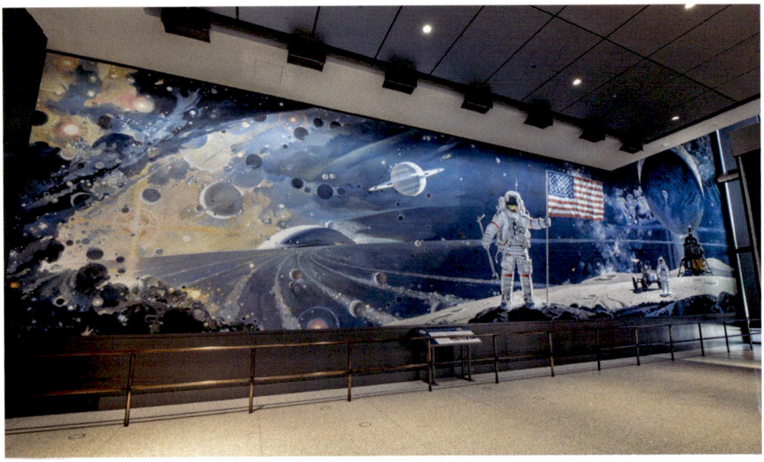

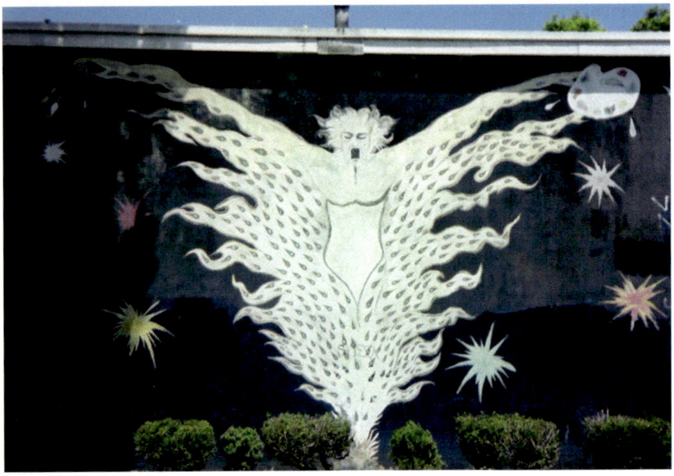

7 Robert McCall, *The Space Mural—A Cosmic View*, 1976. Acrylic painted canvas bonded to wall surface, 146 × 46 ft. Smithsonian National Air and Space Museum.

8 Richard Haro (with Kate and Daniel Haro), *The Artist*, 1974. Paint on concrete, 18 × 23 ft. Estrada Courts, East LA. University Archives and Special Collections, California State University, Fullerton. Photograph by Rich Puchalsky.

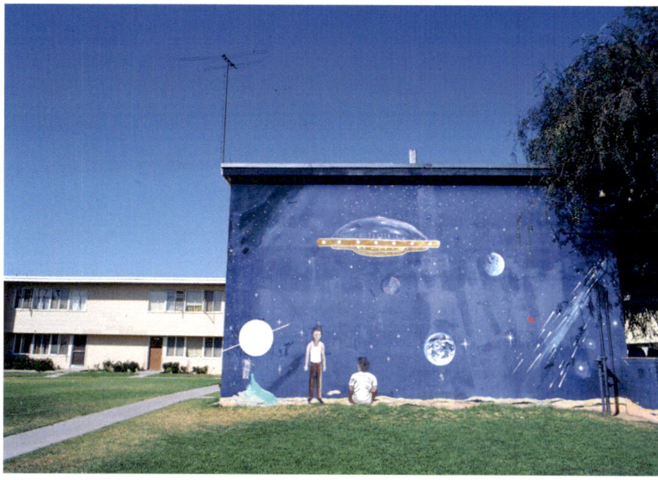

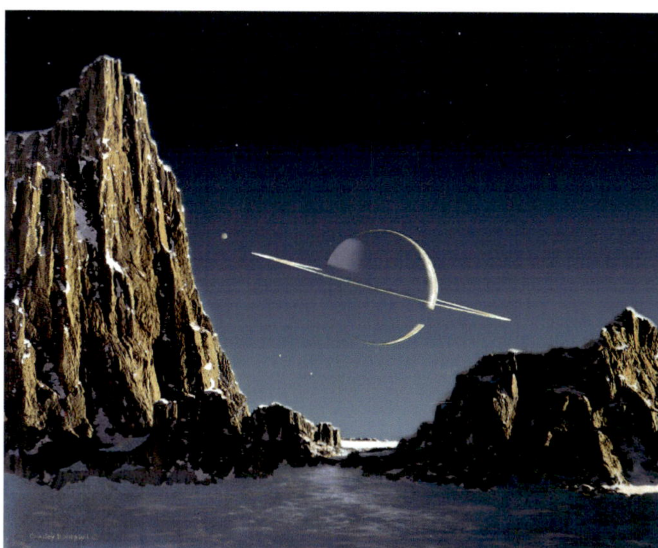

9 Richard Haro, *Outer Space*, 1977. Paint on concrete, 18 × 23 ft. Estrada Courts, East LA. Photograph © Elisa Leonelli.

10 Chesley Bonestell, *Saturn as Seen from Titan*, 1943. Oil on board, 18½ × 23 in. © Bonestell, LLC.

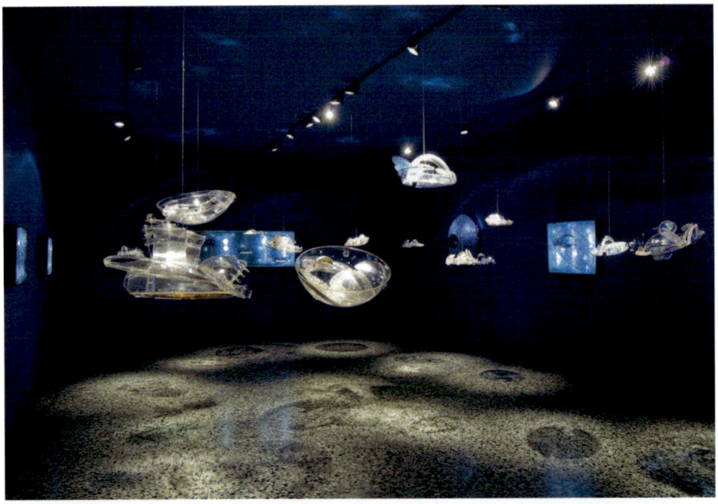

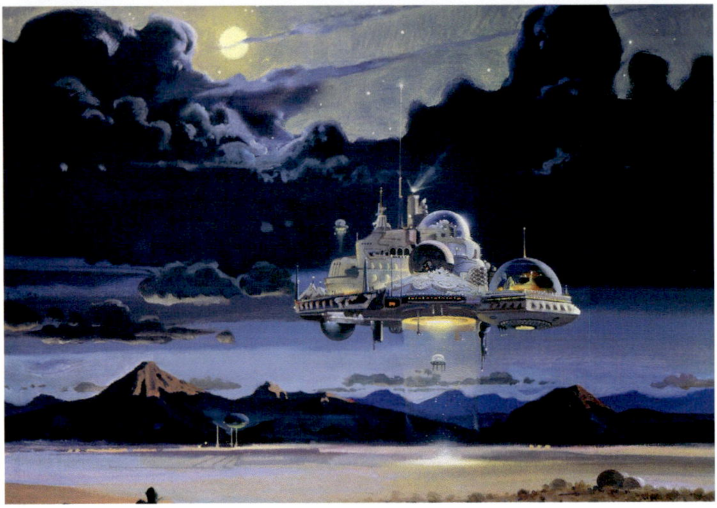

11 Gyula Kosice, *La ciudad hidroespacial* (*The Hydrospatial City*), 1946–72. Acrylic, Plexiglas, paint, metal, and light; dimensions vary. Museum of Fine Arts, Houston. Museum purchase funded by the Caroline Wiess Law Accessions Endowment, 2009.29.1-.26 © Fundación Kosice—Museo Kosice, Buenos Aires. Photograph © Museum of Fine Arts, Houston; Photographer Thomas R. DuBrock.

12 Robert McCall, *Desert Nocturne*, 1977. Oil on Masonite panel, 25½ × 31½ in. (in frame). Gift of Mr. Nick Maggos. Smithsonian National Air and Space Museum.

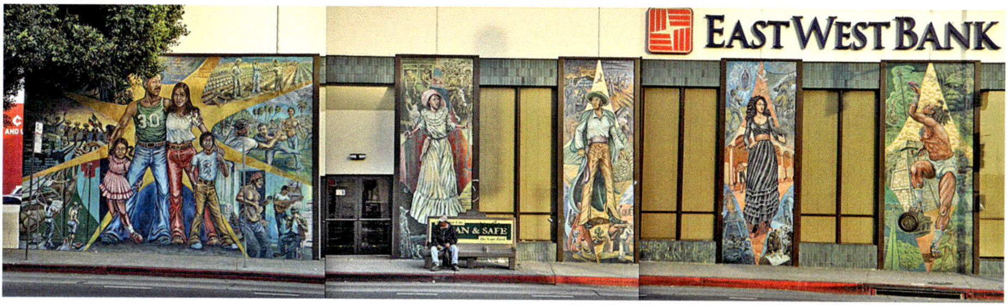

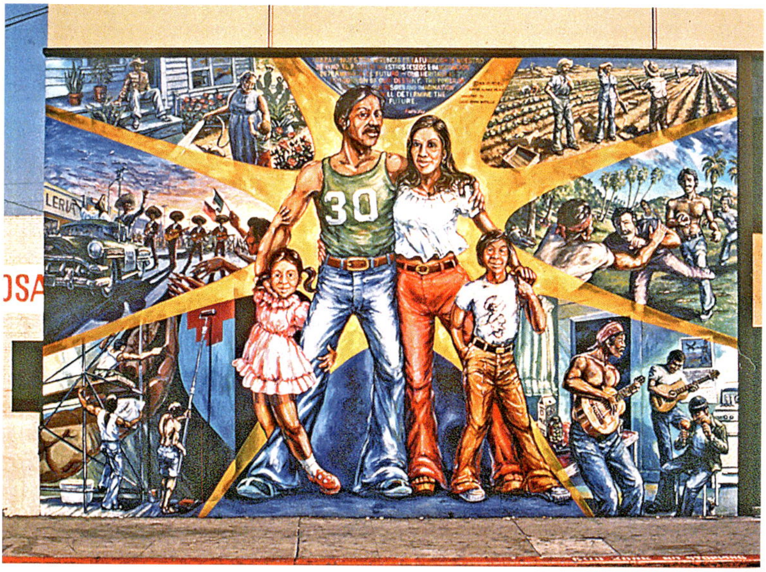

13 East Los Streetscapers, *Chicano Time Trip*, 1977. Acrylic on concrete, 20 × 90 ft. Photograph by David Botello.

14 East Los Streetscapers, *Chicano Time Trip* (detail), 1977. Acrylic on concrete. Photograph by David Botello.

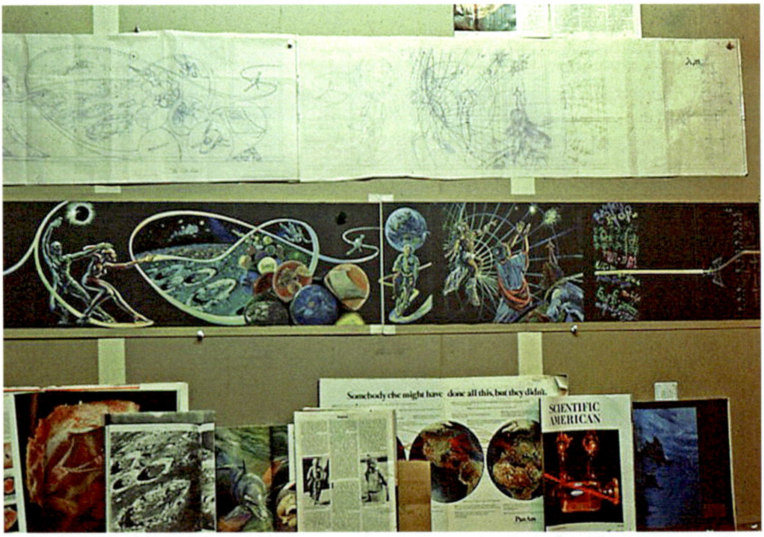

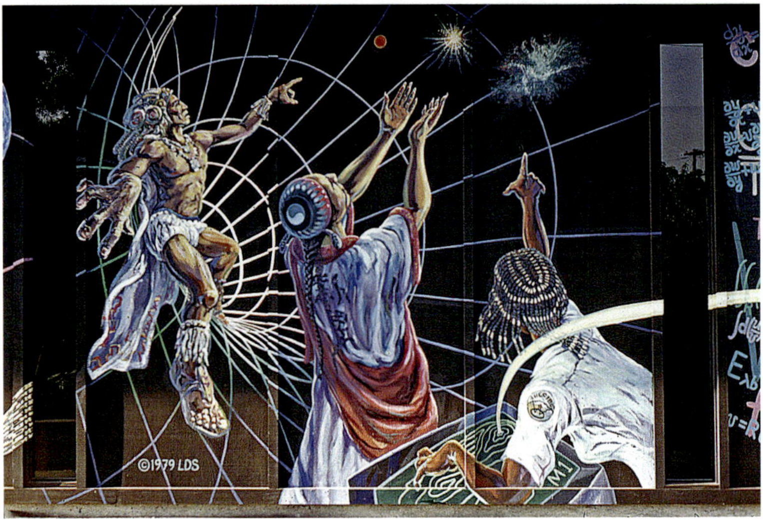

15 East Los Streetscapers, *Mural Study for Moonscapes II: Cruising Through Space/Time*, 1978. Paper assemblage. Photograph by David Botello.

16 East Los Streetscapers, *Moonscapes II: Cruising Through Space/Time* (detail), 1979. Painted wall mural, 4,000 sq. ft. Photography by David Botello.

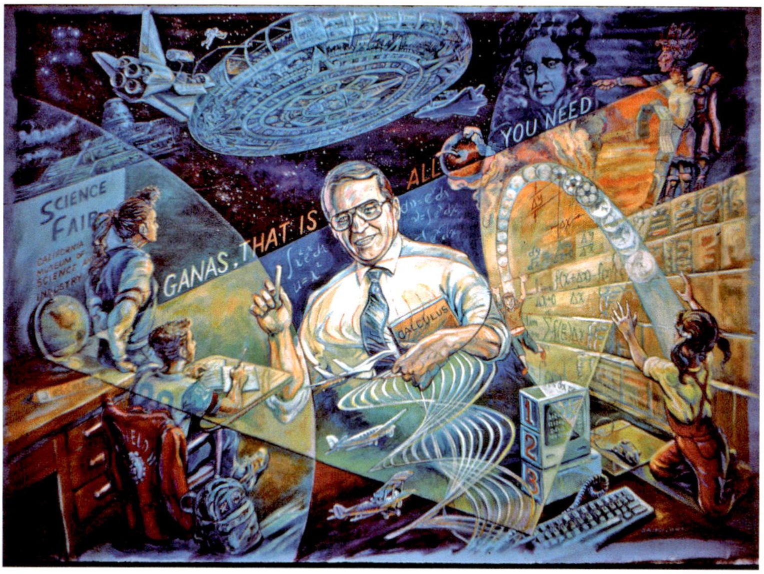

17 East Los Streetscapers, *Ganas, That Is All You Need*, 1988. Portable mural, acrylic on canvas, 6½ × 9 ft. Private collection of Wayne Alaniz Healy and David Botello. Photograph by David Botello.

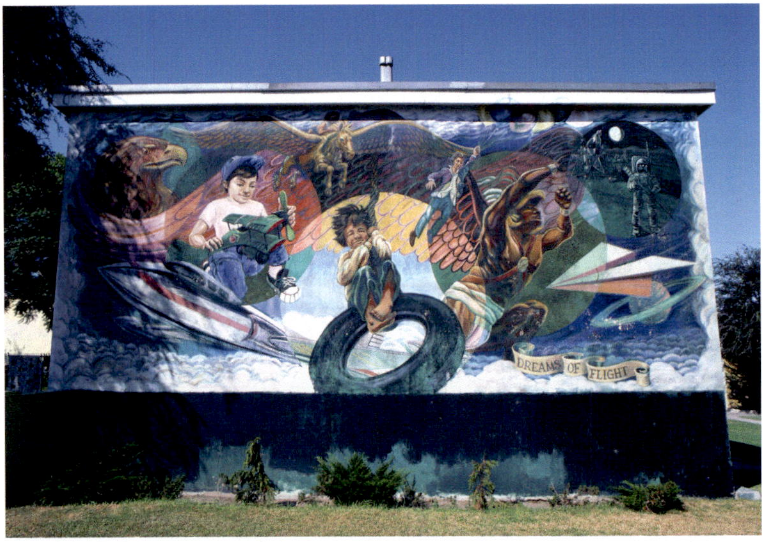

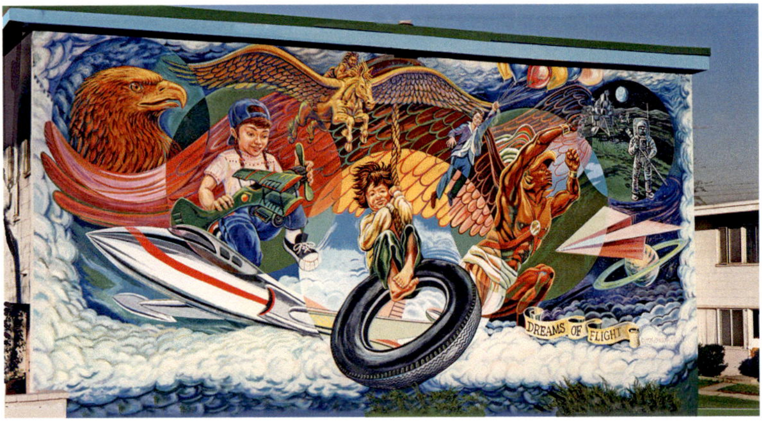

18 David Botello, *Dreams of Flight*, 1973. Paint on stucco, 32 × 24 ft. Estrada Courts, East LA. Photograph © Elisa Leonelli.

19 David Botello, *Dreams of Flight*, 1996, revised. Estrada Courts, East LA. Paint on stucco, 32 × 24 ft. Image courtesy of the artist.

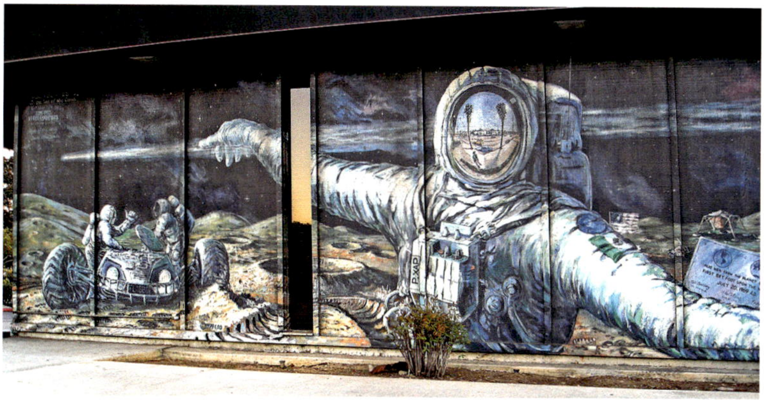

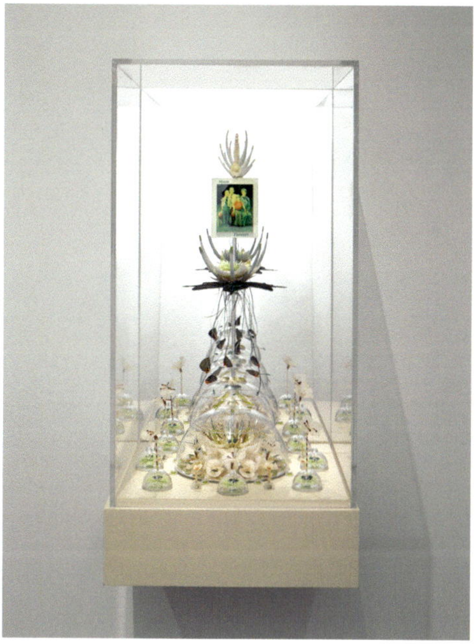

20 East Los Streetscapers, *Moonscapes I: On the Tail of Healy's Comet*, 1979. Painted wall mural, 4,000 sq. ft.

21 Dario Robleto, *Study for Moon Flowers*, 2016. Cut and polished seashells, urchin spines, butterfly wings, feathers, plastic beads, plastic domes, glue, print on paper, painted wood, and mirrored Plexiglas vitrine, $23\frac{1}{2} \times 12 \times 12$ in. Image courtesy of the artist.

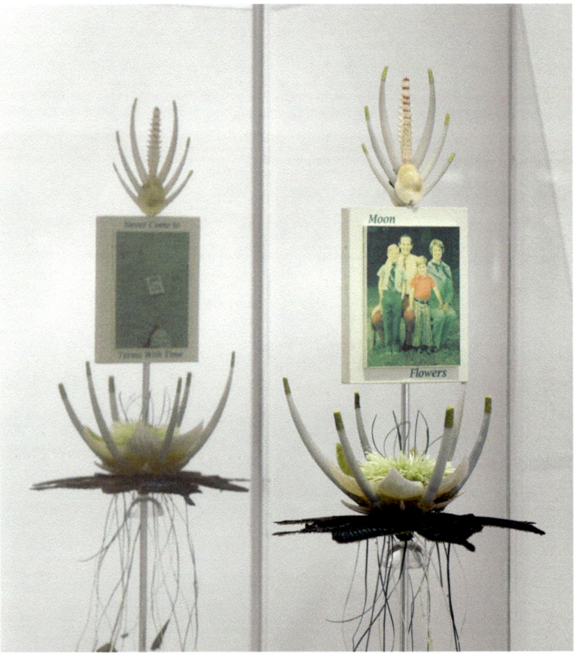

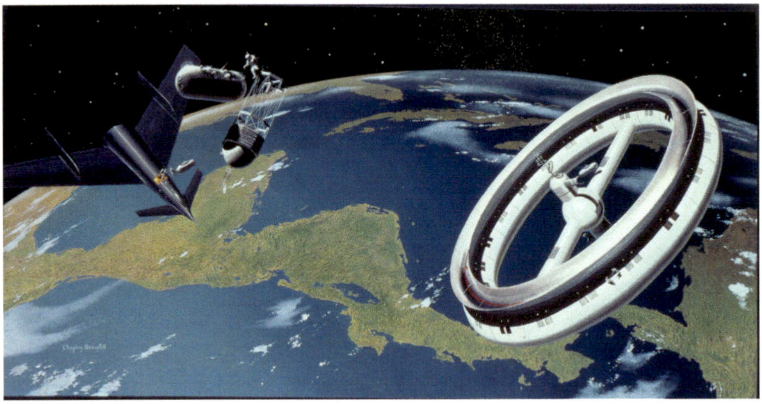

22 Dario Robleto, *Study for Moon Flowers* (in verso; detail), 2016. Image courtesy of the artist.

23 Chesley Bonestell, *Space Station, Ferry Rocket, and Space Telescope 1,075 Miles Above Central America*, 1952. Illustration from "Crossing the Last Frontier," *Collier's*, March 22, 1952.

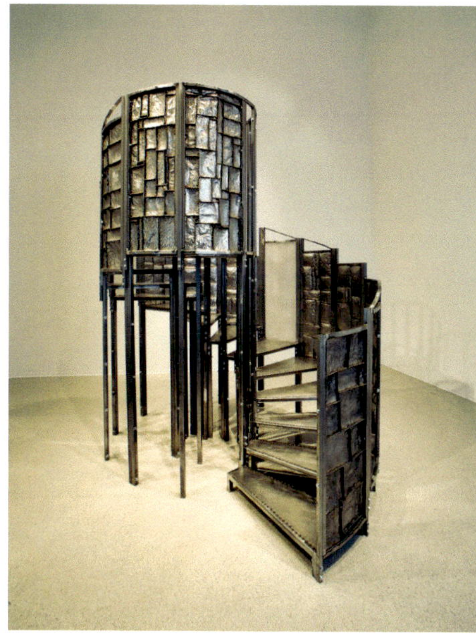

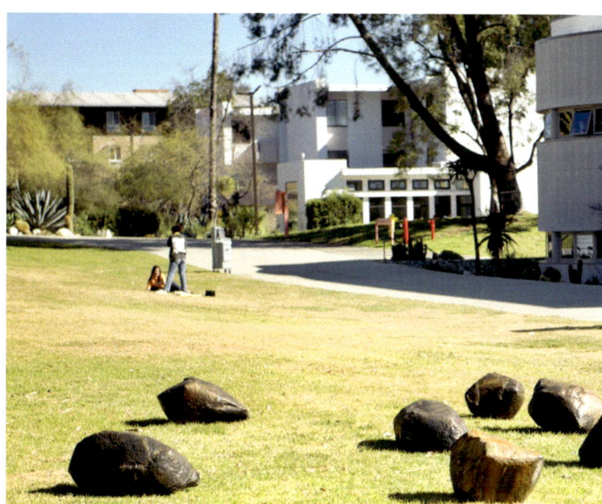

24 Beatriz Cortez, *El Caracol*, 2022. Steel sculpture, $10 \times 7\frac{1}{2} \times 9\frac{3}{4}$ ft. Installation view from *Beatriz Cortez: Cosmic Portals*, Pitzer College Art Galleries, February 5–April 12, 2022. Photograph by Ramak Fazel. Image courtesy of the artist.

25 Beatriz Cortez, *Cosmic Mirror (Sky over Los Angeles)*, 2022. Oxidized steel sculpture; dimensions vary. Installation view from *Beatriz Cortez: Cosmic Portals*, Pitzer College Art Galleries, February 5–April 12, 2022. Photograph by Ramak Fazel. Image courtesy of the artist.

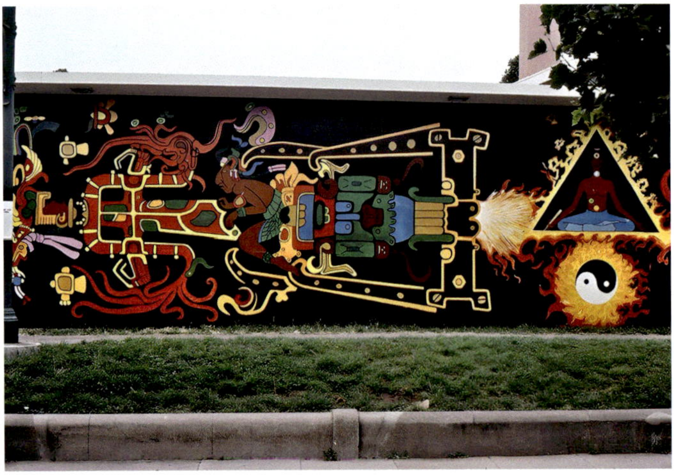

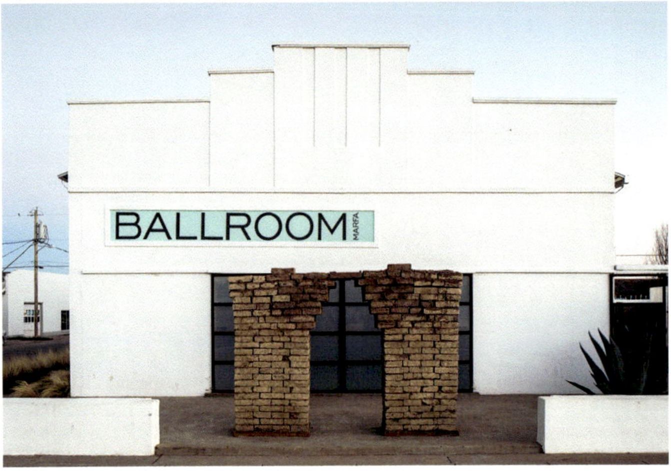

26 Domingo Rivera, *Aztec Spaceship*, 1975. Politec acrylic on stucco, approx. 12 × 36 ft. Photograph by Tim Drescher. Image courtesy of Lincoln Cushing.

27 Beatriz Cortez and rafa esparza, *Portal Sur, After Copán*, 2017. Steel and adobe made with soil from the Americas south of the US border; dimensions vary. Courtesy of the artists, adobero Don Manuel Rodriguez, and Ballroom Marfa. Photograph by Alex Marks.

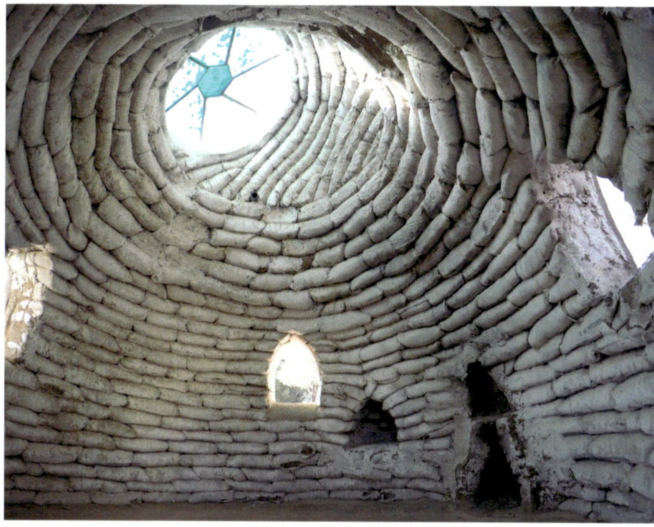

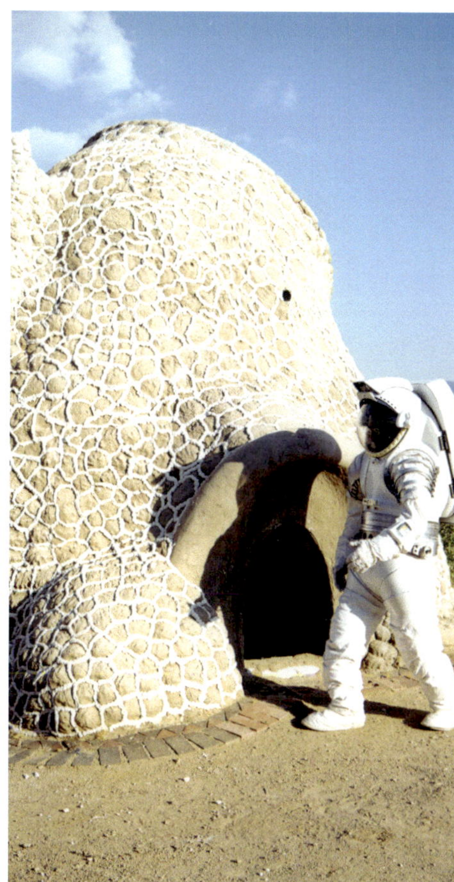

28 Nader Khalili, Super-Adobe bag coil interior of Mars One, 1994. Courtesy of CalEarth Institute.

29 Nader Khalili, prototype of SuperAdobe exterior of Mars One, 1994. Photograph courtesy of CalEarth Institute.

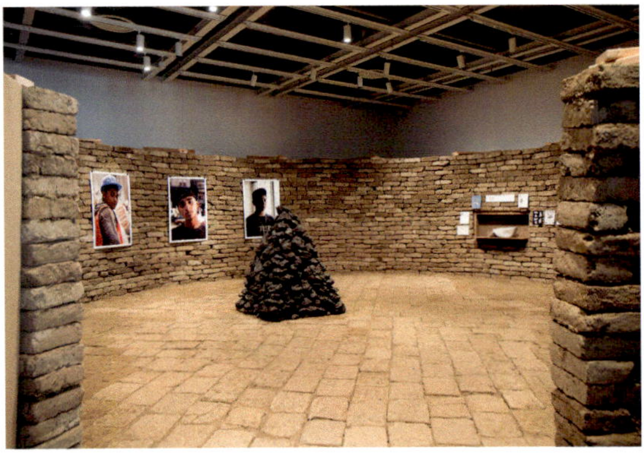

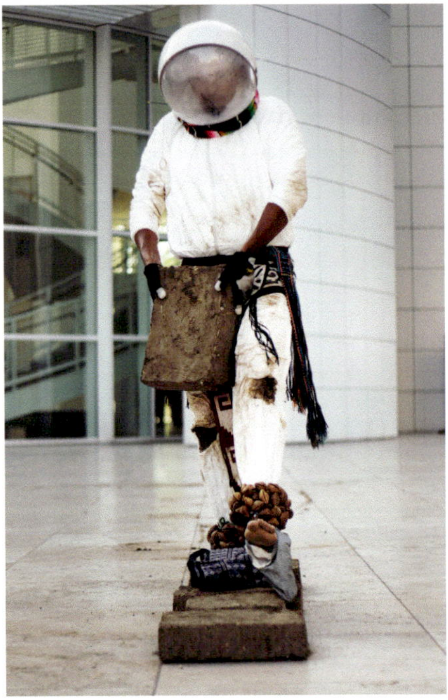

30 Installation view of the Adobe rotunda, Whitney Biennial 2017 (Whitney Museum of American Art, New York, March 17, 2017–June 11, 2017). Visible works are (*center*) rafa esparza, *Figure Ground: Beyond the White Field*, 2017; (*left background*) Beatriz Cortez, *Carin*, 2016; (*right background*) Dorian Ulises López Macías, *Untitled*, 2013–15; (*right*) Gala Porras-Kim, *Reconstructed Southwest Artifact* (ca. 900/2017), 2017. Photograph by Bill Orcutt. Courtesy of Whitney Museum of American Art, New York.

31 rafa esparza, *The Mexika Eagle, Space Navigation No. 0:* XIMAMPA, 2015. Performance documentation, Getty Center, Los Angeles, CA. Photograph by Julie Pham Vu. © 2015 J. Paul Getty Trust.

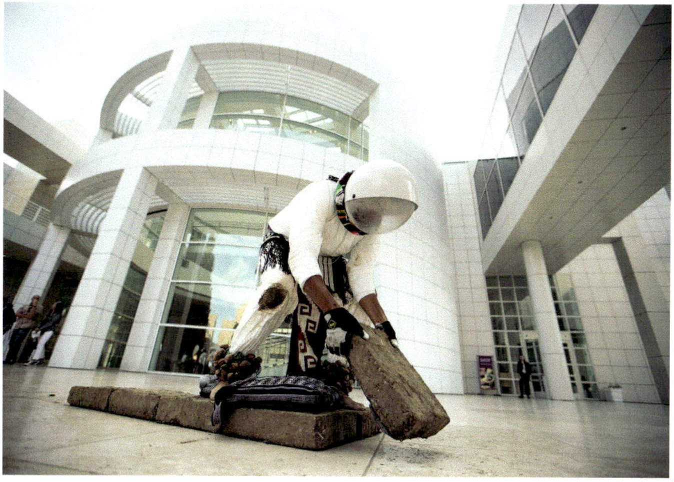

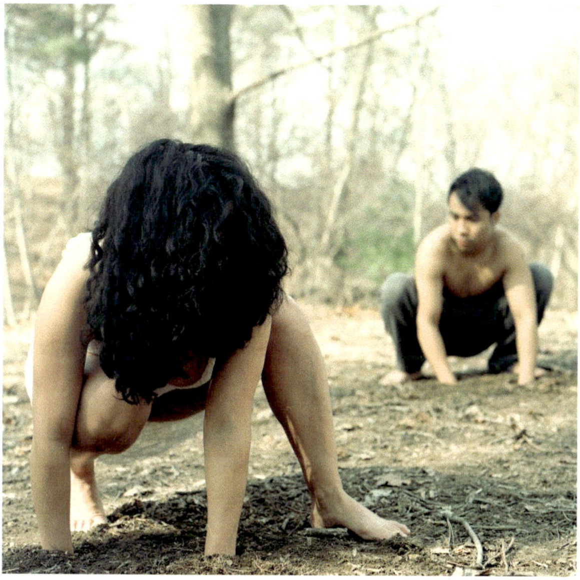

32 rafa esparza, *The Mexika Eagle, Space Navigation No. 0: XIMAMPA*, 2015. Performance documentation, Getty Center, Los Angeles, CA. Photograph by Julie Pham Vu. © 2015 J. Paul Getty Trust.

33 Jacqueline Arias (with Toney Chem), *Plants*, 2007. Video performance from the *Imbrication* series. Brooklyn, New York.

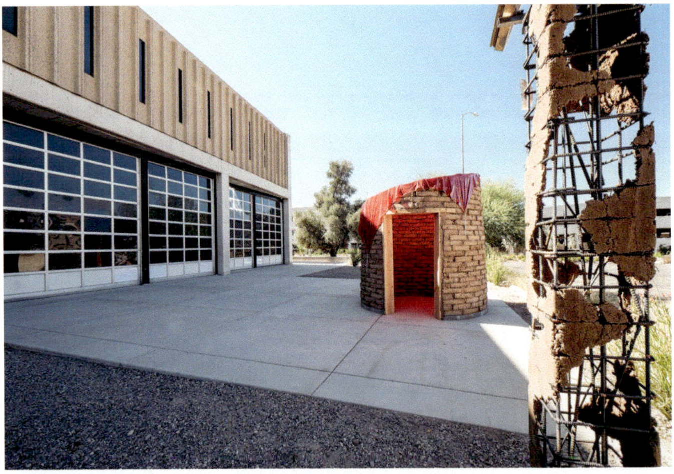

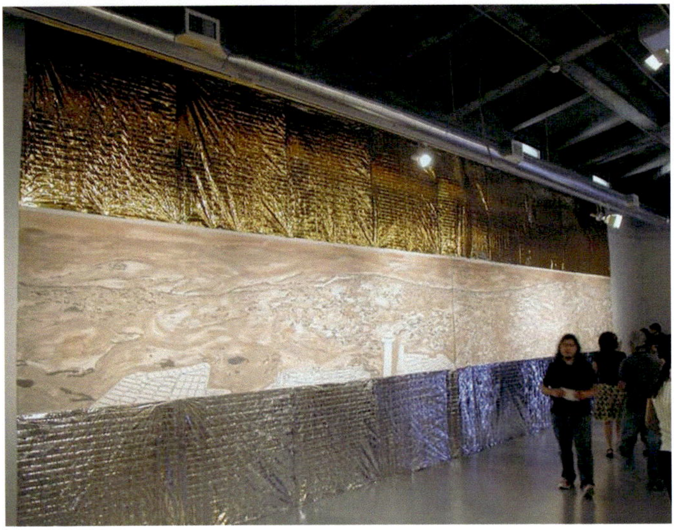

34 rafa esparza (with Timo Fahler), *Earth Eye—Mira Sol/R/Ojo/Negro*, 2021. Adobe; dimensions vary. Photograph by the Museum of Contemporary Art Tucson. Image courtesy of rafa esparza.

35 Vargas-Suarez Universal, *Search for Life: Aliens, Water, and Surveillance*, 2008. Rio Grande mud, iron oxide, oil enamel, vacuumized aluminum thermal blankets, shovel, and wall, 14 × 40 ft. Image courtesy of the artist.

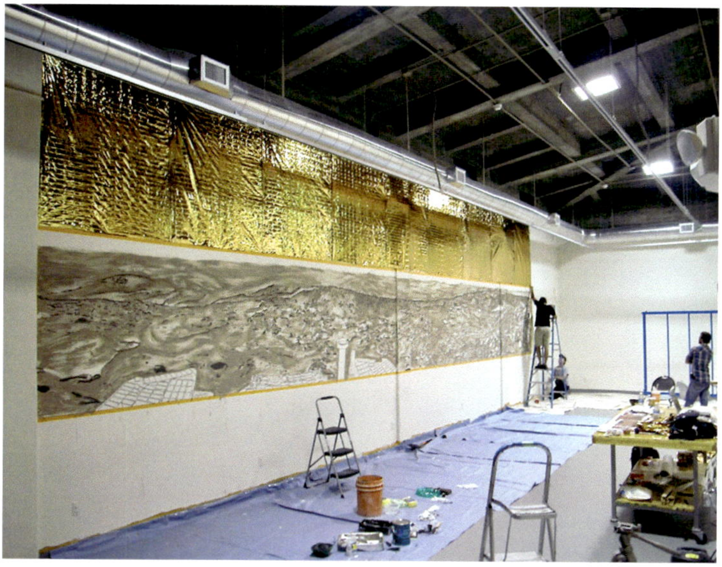

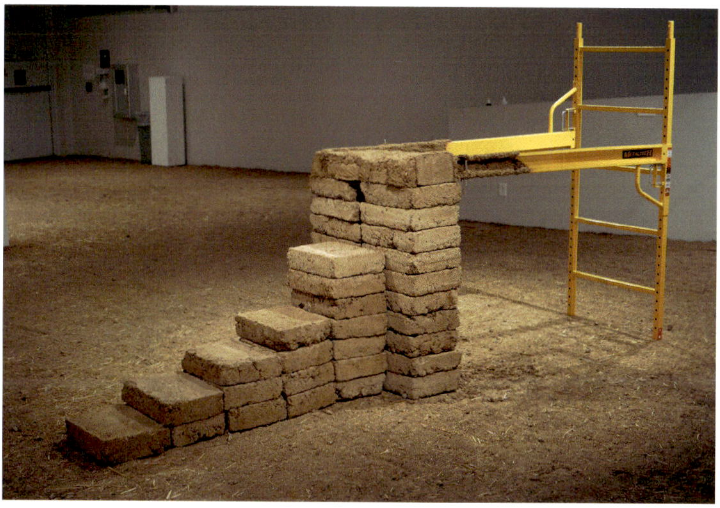

36 Vargas-Suarez Universal, *Search for Life: Aliens, Water, and Surveillance*, 2008. Installation documentation. Image courtesy of the artist.

37 Jacqueline Arias, *del Andamio* (*From the Scaffold*), 2021. Steel scaffold and adobe mixed-media sculpture; dimensions vary. In *Terra Forms* at Joseph Gross Gallery, University of Arizona School of Art.

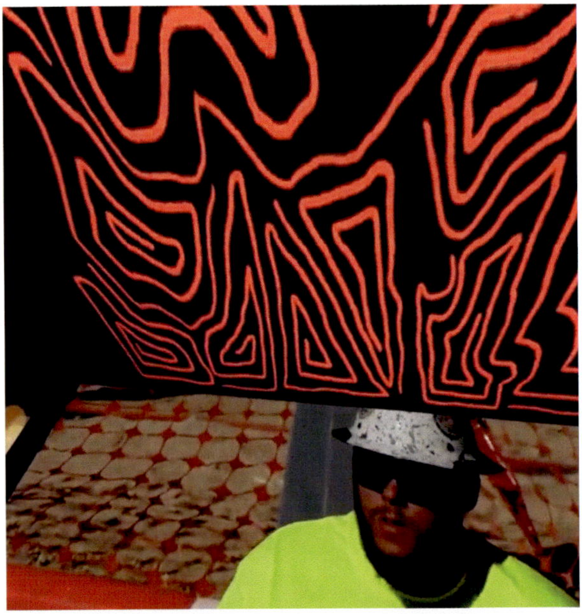

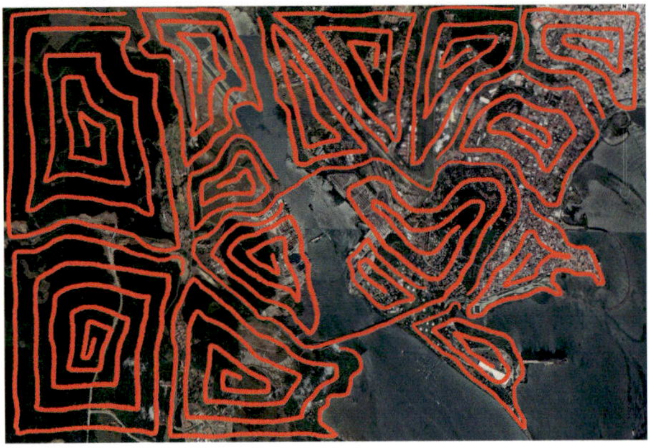

38 Jacqueline Arias, *del Andamio (From the Scaffold)*, 2021. Virtual reality detail. Image courtesy of the artist.

39 Jacqueline Arias, source material for *del Andamio (From the Scaffold)*, 2021. Virtual reality detail. Image courtesy of the artist.

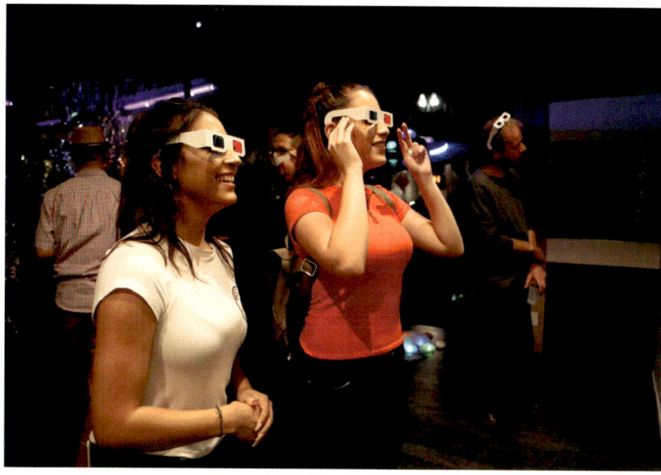

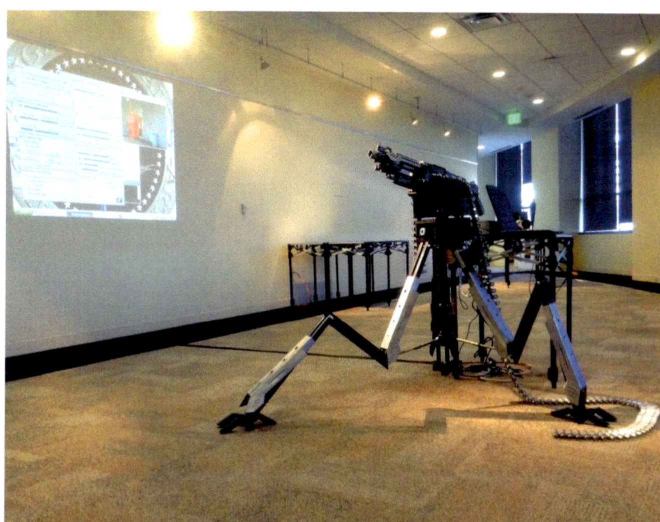

40 *It Came from Beyond the Border*, 2016. Purple Gallery, El Paso, Texas. Installation photography by Gaby Velasquez for *The Prospector*.

41 Angel Cabrales, *Turn of the Sentry*, 2014. Mixed-media sculpture; dimensions vary. Trinity River Campus, Tarrant County College, East Fork Gallery, Fort Worth, Texas. Photograph courtesy of the artist.

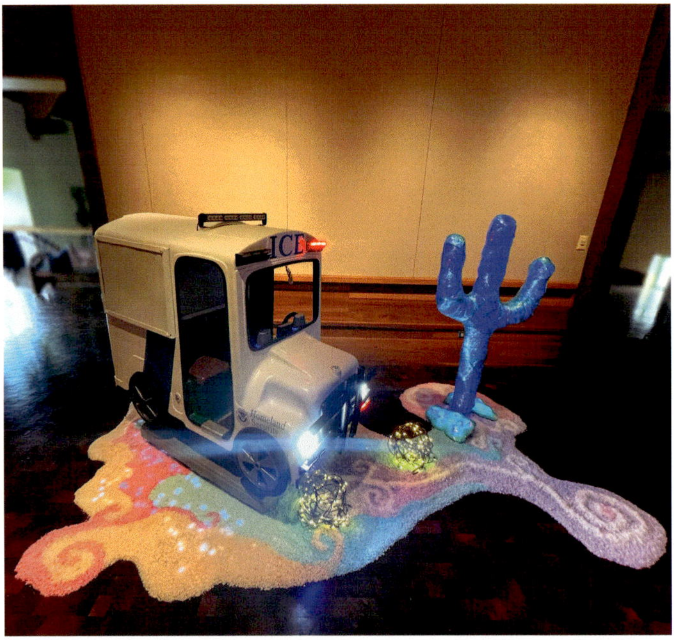

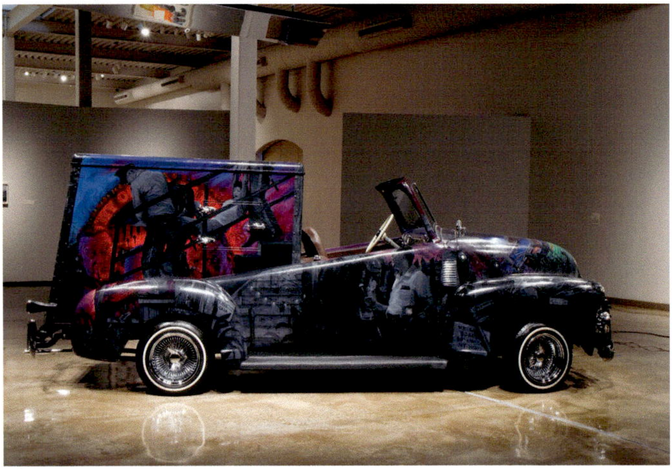

42 Angel Cabrales, ***DREAM** a Little **DREAM***, 2018. Mixed-media sculpture; dimensions vary. Photograph courtesy of the artist.

43 Vincent Valdez, *El Chavez Ravine*, 2005–7. Mixed-media sculpture; dimensions vary. San Antonio Museum of Art. Courtesy of San Antonio Museum of Art.

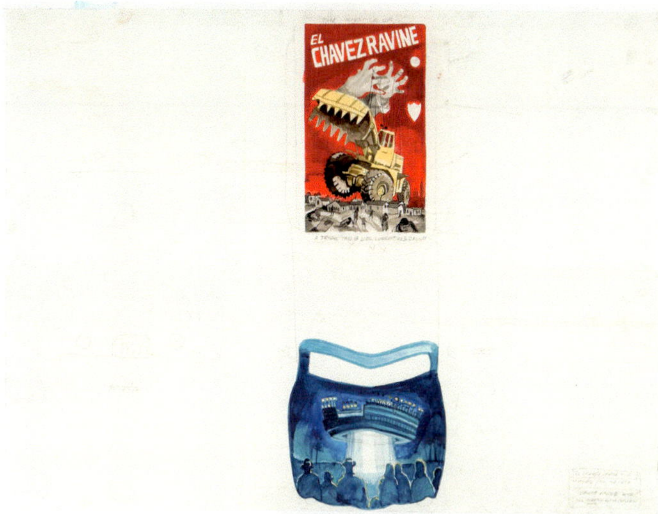

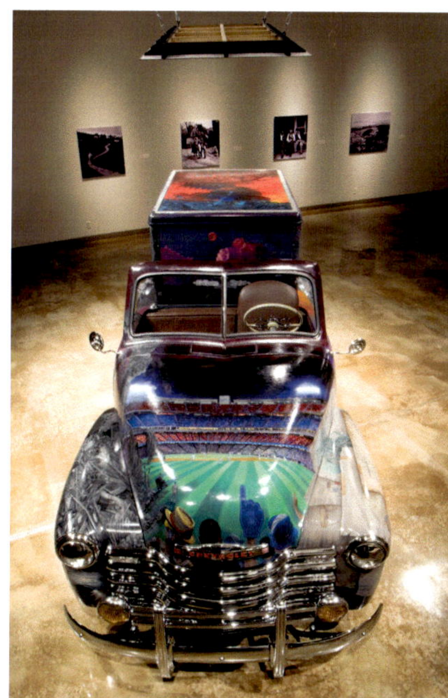

44 Vincent Valdez, preparatory study for *El Chavez Ravine*, 2005–7. Courtesy of San Antonio Museum of Art.

45 Vincent Valdez, *El Chavez Ravine* (aerial view), 2005–7. Courtesy of San Antonio Museum of Art.

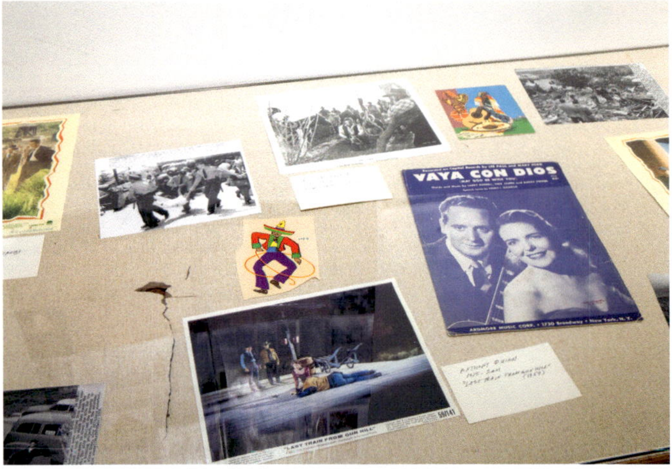

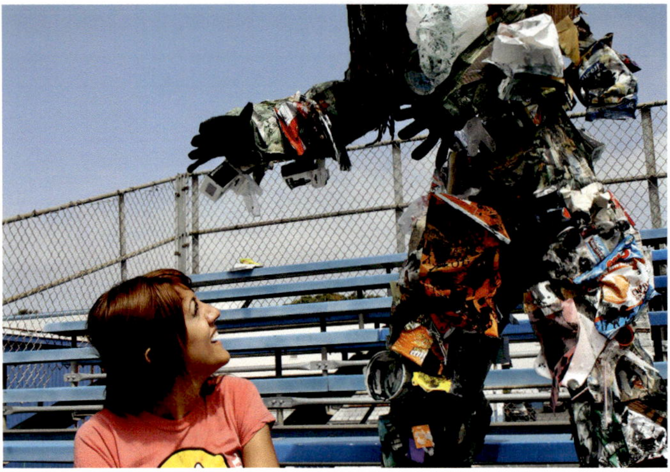

46 Vincent Ramos, *Wolf Songs for the Dead*, 2020. Paramount Studios backlot, photographic detail of memorabilia and records from Chavez Ravine demolition, for Frieze Los Angeles 2020. Mixed-media installation; dimensions vary. Photograph by Isabel Avila. Image courtesy of the artist.

47 Vincent Ramos, *Planets Beyond Jupiter, 1959, 2009, 2019*, 2009. Performance documentation, 18th Street Arts Center, Venice, CA. Photograph by Charchi Stinson. Image courtesy of the artist.

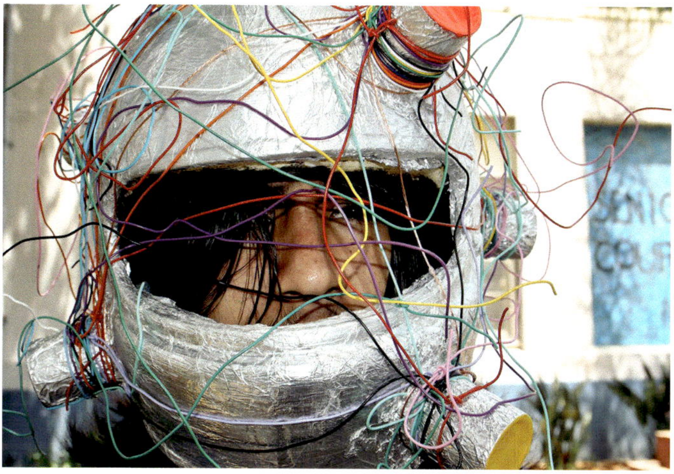

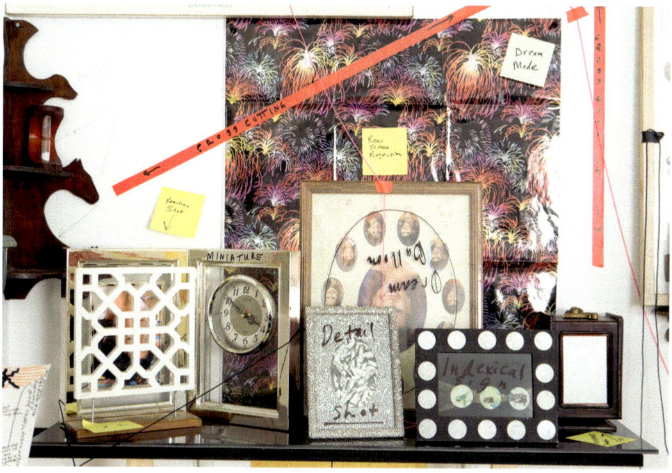

48 Vincent Ramos, *Planets Beyond Jupiter, 1959, 2009, 2019,* 2009. Performance documentation, 18th Street Arts Center, Venice, CA. Photograph by Charchi Stinson. Image courtesy of the artist.

49 Vincent Ramos, *Planets Beyond Jupiter, 1959, 2009, 2019* (detail), 2009. Mixed-media installation; dimensions vary. Photograph by Charchi Stinson. Image courtesy of the artist.

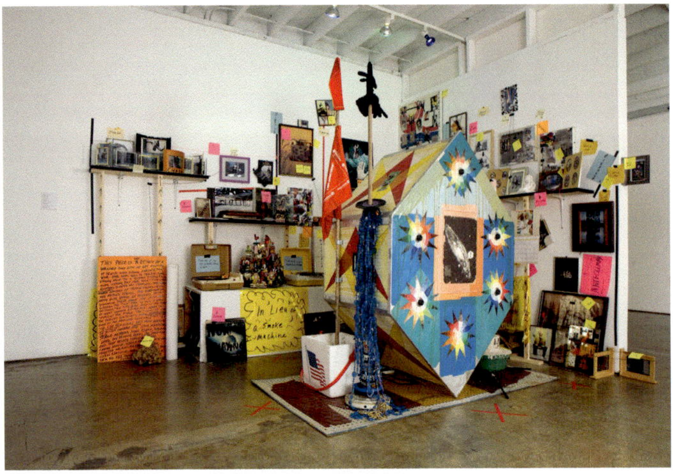

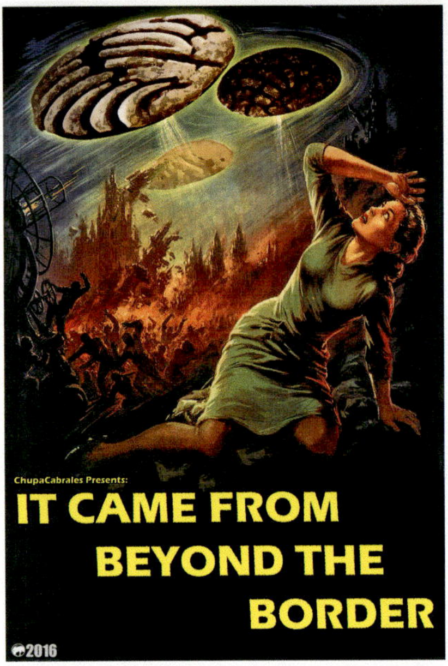

50 Vincent Ramos, *Planets Beyond Jupiter, 1959, 2009, 2019*, 2009. Mixed-media installation; dimensions vary. Photograph by Charchi Stinson. Image courtesy of the artist.

51 Angel Cabrales, *It Came from Beyond the Border*, 2016, from the *Tequila Science Fiction* series. Digital image on paper, 40 × 27 in. Photograph by the artist.

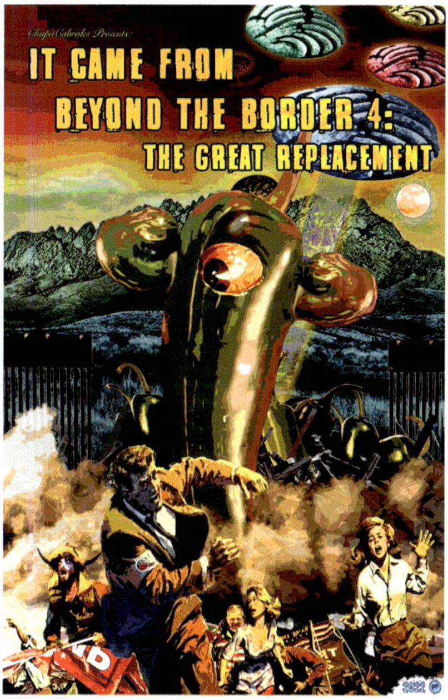

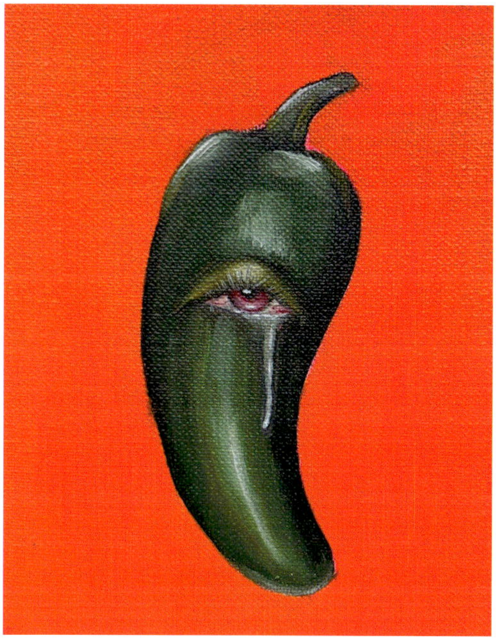

52 Angel Cabrales, *It Came from Beyond the Border 4: The Great Replacement*, 2022, from the *Tequila Science Fiction* series. Digital image on paper, 40 × 27 in. Photograph by the artist.

53 Sam Rawls, *El Chillito*, 2022, from *Las Frutas Lloronas*, still life. Oil on canvas, 5 × 7 in. Photograph by the artist.

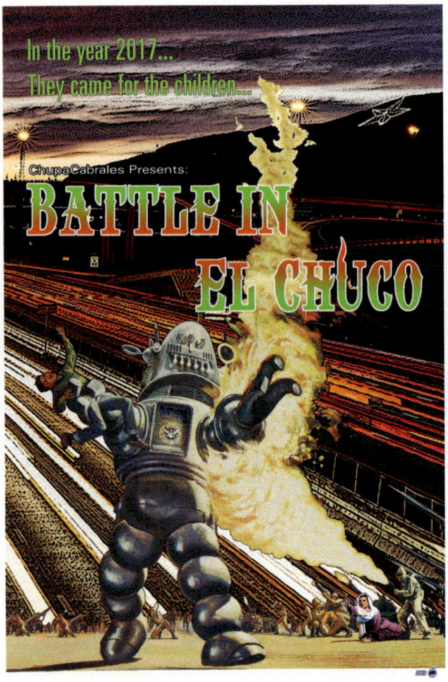

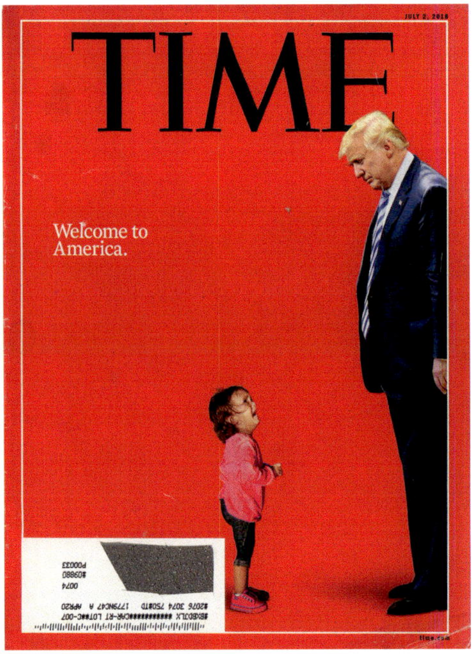

54 Angel Cabrales, *Battle in El Chuco*, 2017, from the *Tequila Science Fiction* series. Digital image on paper, 40 × 27 in.

55 *Welcome to America*. Photo illustration based on a photograph by John Moore, *Time*, July 2, 2018.

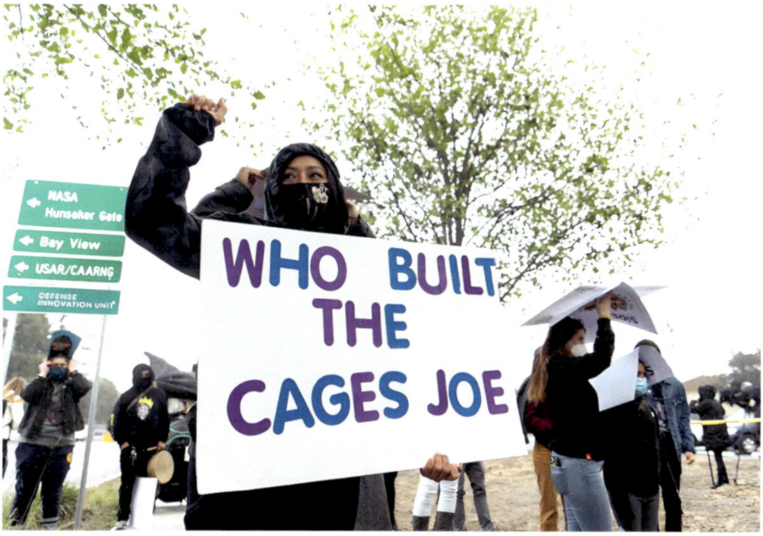

56 Magali Gauthier, *WHO BUILT THE CAGES JOE*, photograph of Brenda Zendeja protesting the possible incarceration of unaccompanied minors at the NASA Ames facility, Mountain View, California, on March 15, 2021.

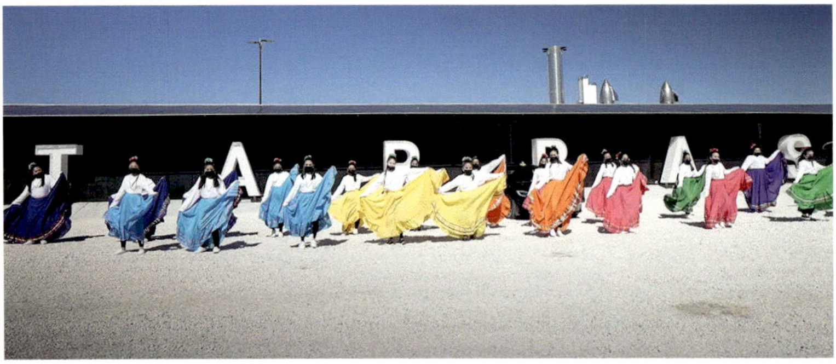

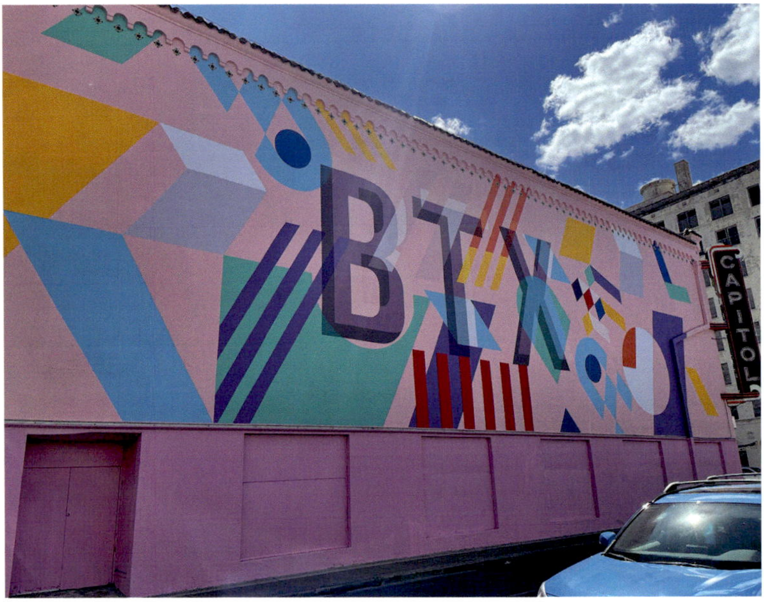

57 Student *ballet folklórico* dancers at the 85th Annual Charro Days festival in Brownsville, Texas, which Elon Musk attended as an invited guest, February 9, 2022. Screenshot from YouTube. https://www.youtube.com/watch?v=xdbBOOYn9_Q&t=199s.

58 Teddy Kelly, *BTX Mural*, 2021. Paint on concrete. Corner of Levee and Market Street, Brownsville, Texas. Photograph by Dan Solomon for *Texas Monthly*. https://www.texasmonthly.com/news-politics/is-brownsville-becoming-btx/.

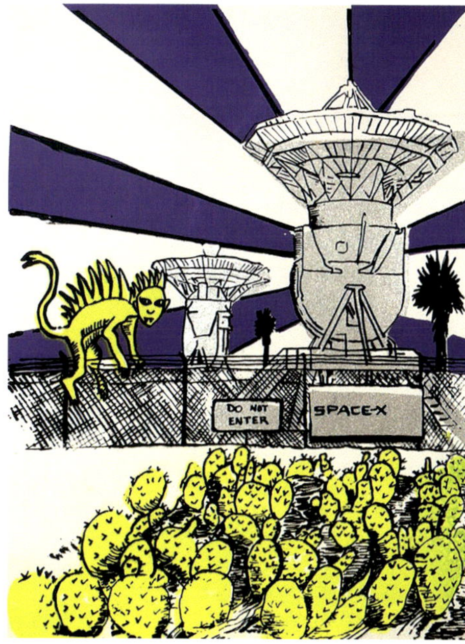

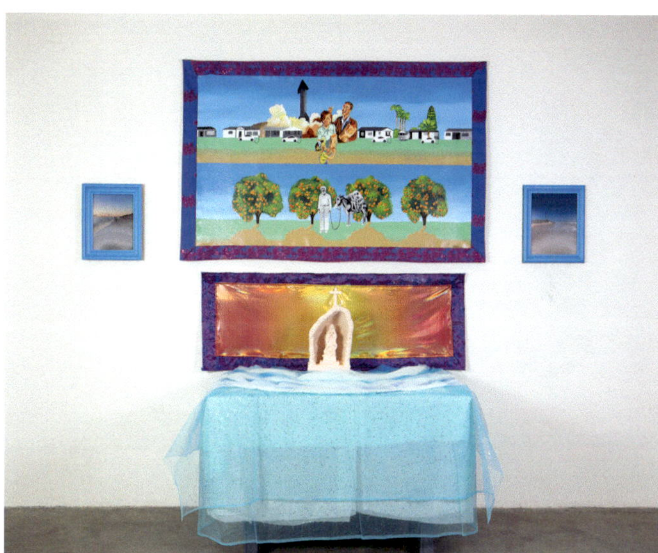

59 Celeste De Luna, *Fugitive Alien Break In*, 2019. Serigraph on paper, 9½ × 13 in. Image courtesy of the artist.

60 Nansi Guevara, *Colonization of la Boca del Rio*, 2022. Acrylic painting; dimensions vary. Photograph courtesy of the artist.

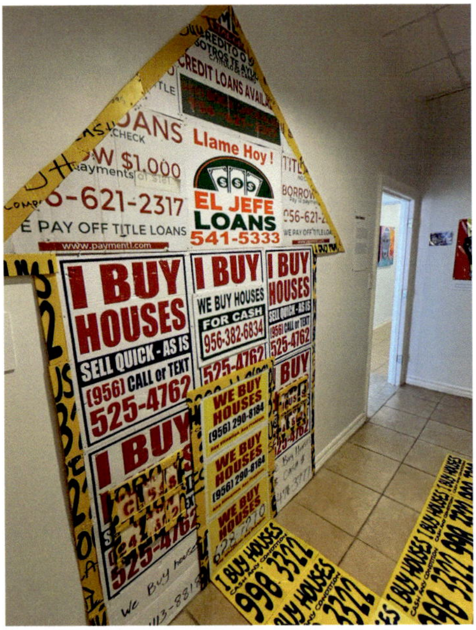

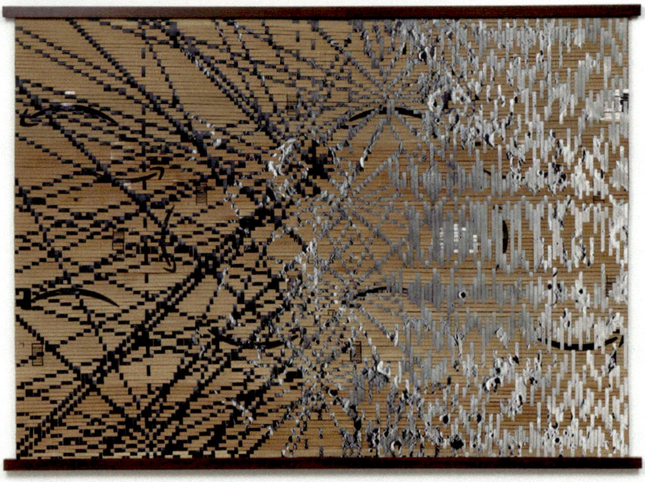

61 Josué Rawmírez, *House Not Home*, 2023. Found objects, assemblage; dimensions vary. Photograph by the author.

62 Clarissa Tossin, *Future Geography: Shackleton Crater, Moon*, 2021. Used Amazon.com delivery boxes, archival inkjet print with matte lamination, wood, 60 × 84 × 1½ in. Courtesy of the artist and Commonwealth and Council, Los Angeles. Photograph by Paul Salveson.

4

It Came from Beyond the Border

TEQUILA SCIENCE FICTION AND THE LATINF/X SENSIBILITY

With their hairy lettering, ominous orchestral score, and alarming voice-over to "Run! Don't walk" (¡Corre! No camines), the B-movie trailers of science fiction's golden age are crucial vehicles exciting audiences with forecasts of the shock and awe to come. From flying saucers hanging on strings to players in monstrous rubber suits, this visual vocabulary sets the tone for fantastic and wondrous possibilities about to unfold. These visions are achieved through the best of bad practical effects. Such strange allusions are not just bound to the movie set, however. A 1912 portrait from Wickenburg, Arizona, makes these weird happenings bizarrely tangible.

Teresa Grijalva de Orosco and Francisca Ocampo Quesada pose in a formal studio photograph called *Comadres* (1912) (see figure 4.1).[1] They sit on a draped platform, and the darkness of the scrim and bench intentionally obscures interior furnishings and sitting-room conventions in the early twentieth century. The opaque surrounds trick the eye, making the parlor more Mexican American magic show than traditional portrait salon. Their

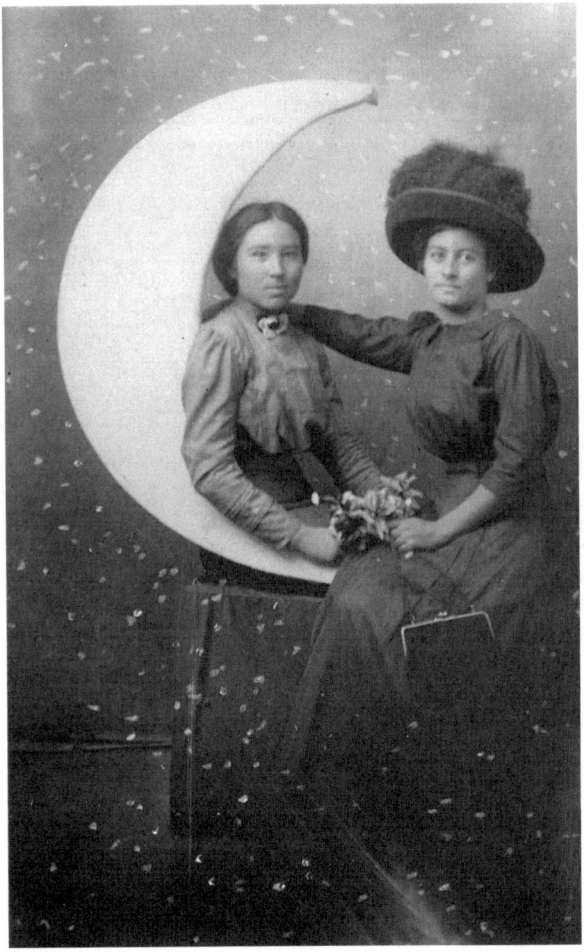

4.1 *Comadres*, ca. 1912. Photographic portrait of Teresa Grijalva de Orosco and Francisca Ocampo Quesada, Wickenburg, Arizona. Teodoro Ocampo and Mariana Rodriguez Ocampo Family Photograph Collection, MP SPC 173, Arizona State University Library: Chicano/a Research Collection.

seated bodies appear to levitate in midair, an appropriate comportment considering that this photo is being taken in a major corridor of geopolitical and, more important, otherworldly change. As the previous chapter details, Arizona's Lowell Observatory had already shifted operations from Flagstaff to Tacubaya in search of Mars and extraterrestrial life. Less transnational and more transplanetary-relational, *Comadres* is a curious meditation about altered realities and intimate bonds that women of color fostered through cheap props, self-expression, and outer space settings.

In *Comadres*, kinship yields a kind of intimacy not only between the women but also between the women and the moon. Teresa's arm weighs on Francisca's shoulder. Conversely, Francisca's hand mutually grips the flowery bouquet in Teresa's lap, indicating that this is no ordinary flight. The close posture conveys a familiar if not affectionate comportment, one set for lunar orbit. They are attired in their best finery to ride the moon, adornment that is evocative of Francisca's status as a scion of Wickenburg, Arizona's founding Mexican family in 1863.[2] Although the multitude of white brushstrokes on dark paper creates impressions of a starry night, its poor production quality is an imperfect yet charming accent, an improvisational backdrop akin to cheap B-movie set design. Though the women are suspended in midair, their launch is an appropriate metaphor for the alternative reality they are facing.

At the time of this photograph, Arizona had entered US statehood. In turn, a Sonoran Desert home to Indigenous people and Mexican nationals became a new possession of the US government. As an afterimage of settler colonial violence combined with the civil unrest and armed conflict engulfing Mexico during the revolution of 1910, this photograph elucidates a conflictual relationship with time, space, and even Earth. If "the ubiquitous snapshot can become a site of resistance and reorientation," what meaning can we make of Latinas who stake their visibility and thus US citizenry on the illusionary optics of elevated scale?[3] If "one will exist, for the future, in someone else's archive," as Shawn Michelle Smith espouses about photography, how might the "sentimental register" of this photo *feel* alternative relationships to space-time in a fantastic portrait of women relating to each other and the cosmos?[4] As art historian Christopher Steiner argues about postcard portraits, "most novelty or fantasy photos were forward looking, as they celebrated new technologies and new modes of transportation."[5] This photo survives as an advertisement for a Latina future to come, an arrival of national boundaries and a flight of citizenship improvised before the camera like a gestural ad-lib enabled because of these cheap practical effects. Together, Teresa and Francisca perform a kind of feminist intimacy made possible in this torrent of change, a kind of lunar affection enunciated in the vertical transit of transplanetary relationality.

Whether they were playacting or witnessing history, these Latinas' search for self-definition is enshrined in a science-fictional aesthetics of bad taste. Their "moon landing" is consistent with the popularity of Georges Méliès's silent film *A Trip to the Moon* (1902), where stop-motion photography transformed film aesthetics and rocketed humanity to Earth's satellite. As a trailblazer of cinematic practical effects, Méliès impacted the popular zeitgeist, with carnival rides, postcard souvenirs, and fairground amusements emerging as well (see chapter 2). He was a lauded magician of film illusion, and his reach is evident even in the arid corridors of the Sonoran Desert, making *Comadres* consonant with the pursuit of Mexican American women's representational politics and social criticism accented by science-fictional aesthetics. Thus, the portrait made in a small photo studio in rural Arizona is a refuge for an image world made up of special effects, optical trickery, and lowbrow marvel. This picture imparts a working-class "rasquachismo," as Tomás Ybarra-Frausto classically dubs it, though with a "resourcefulness and adaptability" that improvises being off-Earth.[6] However, what are we to do with adaptive creativity when the terms are otherworldly? Expressing what I call a *Latinf/x sensibility* (a substrate of Ybarra-Frausto's term) adjacent to the media blender of "cultural detritus," according to Jeffrey Sconce, this chapter invites another consideration for images like *Comadres* that rise up and stand out like an illusion from a 3D rag.[7]

As this chapter serves as a showcase for Latinx schlock, shock, and awe—a suitable tent show for the best of the bad movies that enamored my dad in his final days (see the introduction)—this plunge into the bizarre begins with the theatrical machinations of mixed-media sculptor Angel Cabrales, who dubbed this artistic cycle "Tequila Sci Fi." His case study creeps along like a fun house of altered realities where each tableau mesmerizes onlookers with special effects about political depravity and social hardships. Much like *Comadres*' ascent to the moon, visions drive upward to find Latinx collective meaning in the strings anchoring illusory spectacles that borrow from a film language of cheap gags and movie magic. The chapter's opening zooms along like a loungy space-age pop overture where stereophonic sound is the appropriate ambience to weigh the art historical merit of "uninhibited extraterrestrial adventure stories" illustrated on "cheap" pulp paper.[8] Though the artists showcased here may appear more conversant with the cineplex than with the blue-chip art gallery, these practices are an undeniable facet of Latinx expressivity deserving of merit, and when they are placed in a transplanetary-relational framework, other cosmic connections come to the fore. Allow this grind house reel to play. A creature feature is unleashed on Latinx art history with a suite of stunts, feats, and death-defying jump scares. Tequila science fiction harbors those with a penchant for big fun and bad taste. To begin, a showman like Angel Cabrales shocks the audience with automated weaponry, Immigration and Customs Enforcement (ICE) kiddie rides, and light gels dousing El Pasoan art consumers in iridescent hues. His sensationalist bent lays the groundwork for other cinematic magicians, like Vincent Ramos from Los Angeles, an accomplished Chicano contemporary artist and a B-movie aficionado.

Ramos's revelations about a science-fictional Venice, California, reveal alignments with Ray Bradbury among other "unmade" creature features staged at a local high school. In a Hollywood studio backlot, he mishmashes memorabilia with true-to-life horrors of Latinx Los Angeles like the Zoot Suit Riots and Chavez Ravine, which confront atrocities with the skill set of a special effects technician. Ramos's work, similar to a comparative artwork by Vincent Valdez, startles and surprises viewers with his activist intentions. As the final act spools on the projector, tequila science fiction crescendos in a gustatory play over taste and foodways.

Shot straight (no chaser), the chapter returns to artists like Cabrales and Sam Rawls, who invite flavorings that refuse to go down easily. Whether through the reappropriation of pulp poster iconography from the first half of the twentieth century or the peppery sting of mutant chili, they dish out sharp political critiques to elevate not only eyes but mouths. By way of a tail leader on the last film reel, the chapter muddles through the surprising entanglements of speculation, tequila, and extraterrestrial life. Tequila, a distilled product of the agave plant, elicits ancient ideas and cosmic outlooks in ways consonant with transplanetary relations and, as a result, becomes a suitable pairing for Latinx expressions indebted to the academy of fine arts and late-night TV. Although that fusion may sound contrived or distracting from a different argument justifying Latinx art's aesthetic sophistication, it is these artists' overlooked yet refined chicanery that points to a missed creative register. With Latinf/x-sensible guile, these artists prove that somewhere in this trash bin of refuse and movie magic are ways to awaken the sleepy giant, dance on the strings of puppeteering, and topple disenfranchisement like a movie monster obliterating all that stands in its wake. Change is possible with a generous pour, a dash of salt, and a twist of lime.

"Run, Don't Walk" | "Corre, No Camines"

If anything, theorizing science fiction visual aesthetics begins with pulp magazine cover artists from the 1920s and the "shabbily made" charm of low-budget films from the 1950s.[9] According to Vivian Sobchack, "The major visual impulse of all SF films is to pictorialize the unfamiliar, the nonexistent, the strange and the totally alien."[10] However, little considered is the way this imagery elicits a "definite and sustained *visual style* arising from its subversion of the familiar."[11] Despite science fiction's capacity to distort empirical reality and verifiable truth, "many film critics have seen not a style, but rather a lack of style" in the genre.[12] When science fiction is deemed bereft of aesthetic quality, its art historical legitimacy recedes. Though Sobchack's observations principally focus on postwar US film history, her perspective is applicable to art of the Americas. Herein lies the catch. As major culture industries like motion pictures attempted to profit from big pedigreed film dramas, they often turned to the sensational and exploitative nature of science fiction and horror genres to stay afloat. This "pulp paradox," as Bradley Schauer puts it, underscores how "the majors tried to have it both ways."[13]

As a result of this ironic arrangement, B-movies were resourceful, profitable, and culturally worthy of studio investment. Being a paradoxical image archive absent of good taste yet rich in box office returns yielded an extrapolative visual language that, in part, presents what Gary Wolfe terms a "feeling of endless possibility, like standing at the edge of a vast abyss that is close enough to us to be real, yet great enough to be unfathomable."[14] This fascination with possibilities beyond sentient reality also promoted wondrous visual trappings in the shoddy practical effects and schlocky aesthetics of creature features. These prominent horror genre motion pictures from the 1950s make very effective cinematic use of the visual image of a monster. Referring to *Creature from the Black Lagoon*, Wolfe applauds "the raw visual appearance of the beast" committed to celluloid, whereas "in fiction, this immediate visual impact is lost."[15] So even in "their worst made mediocrity," according to Sobchack, "low-budget [science fiction] film has style enough to spare."[16]

If art history of the Americas could reconcile its relationship with the "too fantastic and silly . . . stigma of pulp," as Patrick Lucanio and Gary Coville describe the look of the genre, it might also triumph over the science-fictional inflections of modern and contemporary US artists. Doing so would press the field to better attend to the meteorological aberrations of Georgia O'Keeffe's New Mexican landscapes, the crude world machines of Alice Aycock, the boxed celestial microcosms of Joseph Cornell, or the way that the spiral jetty of Robert Smithson plays with the bizarro realm of *The Twilight Zone*.[17] Might art history not also shoulder its own "pulp paradox"?

Consider how, since the 1920s, high modernists distanced "machine-like lives and machinic thinking" from "traditional art, the natural world, and even the real."[18] Despite this remove, avant-garde creatives from the United States and Europe like Salvador Dalí, Marcel Duchamp, or Man Ray would dredge new terrain, showing how the "cinematic imagination" and the "[science fiction] imagination" were interconnected, mutually "respond[ing] to the new world of science and technology and the changes they were rapidly bringing to modern culture."[19] Their accomplishments in fantastical dreamscapes, Rotoreliefs, and surrealist rayographs are oddly resonant with both experimental aesthetics and the birth of cinema itself.

According to Tom Gunning, the origin of film never privileged narrative storytelling but rather favored a "cinema of attractions."[20] His argument that "viewing experiences relate more to the attractions of the fairground than to the traditions of the legitimate theater" demonstrates how film's "exhibitionist quality" underscored avant-garde enthusiasm for the medium.[21] From trick films to optical illusions, an "esthetics of astonishment and stimulation" focused the screen, having more to do with the entertainment of a roller coaster than with dramaturgy.[22] Commanding all to "See!" in the spirit of the ringmaster, showman, or magician, early film "root[ed] in stimulus and carnival rides" transformed spectatorship into a more flexible "cinema of effects" that resonated more with the genre films of horror or science fiction than with the fine art exhibition.[23] However, this appeal to the popular "attraction" borrows from an early avant-garde practice that eyes other realities less concerned with "creating a self-sufficient narrative world upon the screen" or on the canvas, for that matter.[24] As Kevin Heffernan observes, "This earlier regime of attractions pulses under the surface of the later cinema of narrative integration."[25] The "astonishing spectacle" of this image archive presents Latinx artists with copious opportunities to be more experimental and speculative in approach, like the early modernist avant-gardes before them.[26] If Latinxs are the "orphans of modernism," as Chicano photographer Harry Gamboa Jr. once claimed, how do we rectify their fluency in speculation when optical trickery, amusement, and even cultural depravity are legitimately modern in their own right?[27]

Given such proficiency in the gregarious intersections of art, science, and speculative imagination, what is to be done with a coming attraction translated for Spanish audiences? As a B-movie trailer warns "Run, don't walk," could "Corre, no camines" signify differently for a Latinx media consumer? Take artist Armando Norte, who grew up in East LA in the 1950s. Cheap film exhibitions at drive-in theaters were pseudo language schools predicated on science-fictional exchange. He remembers, "My dad liked [the drive-in] because English was his second language so when he would see something *visual*, he didn't really have to understand every bit of dialogue being thrown [at him]. He just knew there was a giant monster, there were flying saucers flying around. As children, my sister [Marisela Norte] and I would be in the backseat watching that movie so all of *that* became our . . . visual library."[28] Vocabularies of shock and awe trained creatives like the Nortes, for example, in social and cultural critique and ideas about technology, futurity, and the sky—an affective alignment posed by the "giant monster." Such conversance among East LA creatives like the Nortes at mid-century closes art historical distances between the extraterrestrial idioms in modernist works by Willem de Kooning, Franz Kline, and Jackson Pollock (see chapter 2). Rather than critique the creature feature as a metaphorical stand-in for the alien Other in ways that have been effectively interpreted by numerous critical media and race scholars, we should ask what other kinds of creative solutions that visual library offered for Latinx creativity and political expression. To understand this translation, an understanding of a Latinf/x sensibility provides clues.

The creatives discussed in this chapter rework the castoffs of popular culture, relishing the diverse abundance of a media wasteland. As an ordinary East LA drive-in theater suggests, Latinx media consumers are skilled readers in what Sconce calls *paracinema*, which he explains as "a counter-aesthetic turned subcultural sensibility devoted to all manner of cultural detritus."[29] Sconce champions the aficionados of sleaze, who treasure "disreputable movies and suspect cinema" in "excess of, or opposed to, those [films] valued by official, legitimate culture."[30] Though Sconce maintains a presumptive focus on "Hollywood cinema and the mainstream US culture," his approach precludes the more transnational, transcultural, and transplanetary-relational connections factoring into a Latinf/x sensibility, which savors "viewing experience[s] [that] can be both baffling and frustrating, as challenging as any deliberately difficult 'art film,'" as Doyle Greene surmises about Mexploitation cinema.[31] Being proficient in media reputed to be lowbrow means that the Nortes, for instance, nuance Sconce's manifesto with artistic machinations created by and in spite of barriers imposed by language and citizenry. Practical effects like flying saucers on strings or performers in rubber suits are profoundly important to a liberation project that surmounts racialized, national, and linguistic divides. B-movies are critical apparatuses for discerning self-meaning, fantasizing possibility, and making community in the "worst made mediocrity" of low-budget cinema, as Sobchack suggests.[32] Indeed, Latinxs' courtship of genre motion pictures was reinscribed by a 2015 story from National Public Radio, which reports that Latinxs compose half of the box office when it comes to horror films.[33]

That resourceful skill set drawing on bargain bins and media throwaways is inherent to the making-do sensibilities of *rasquachismo* because, as Ybarra-Frausto argues, it "projects an alternative aesthetic—a sort of good taste of bad taste."[34] Further, to borrow from Anna Indych-López on her related citation of Puerto Rican kitsch, "the boundaries of high/low or fine art/mass reproduction do not only become slippery, but irrelevant."[35] The creatives emphasized here navigate that slippage. Pivoting on *rasquachismo* in its techno-cinematic intersection, Latinx consumers nod to the spirit of the cyberpunk hacker, media activist guerrillero, and cable hijacker. Though Ybarra-Frausto claims that "*rasquachismo* is a sensibility that is not elevated," Latinf/x-sensible creatives scale up like those Mexican American women dangling in midair in suspension of reality, intercepting the signals of a strange world to come.[36] In their image making they awaken to the illusion, comfort the weird, and court the practical effect. As Sara Ahmed puts it, "Possibility means grasping terror as well as joy."[37] The critical joy residing in a UFO pulled across the screen empowers an accomplished media acumen in the embarrassingly exaggerated, absurdly lit, and poorly contrived. To have a taste for the distastefully bad is a thirst for something else, something that tequila science fiction can quench.

Those partaking in a Latinf/x sensibility share in a community forged by those who can stomach the crude, like the spice, and yet are mindful of a formative avant-garde hinged to the entertaining excesses of early cinema. Like the Mexican American women's lunar portrait, these image makers launch upward, in search of answers elsewhere. The "pulp paradox" described here crystallizes how much of Latinx representational language and search for visibility is predicated on lowbrow amusement. Though one might fairly question, "What political potential is found behind a jerry-rigged paper moon dangling on strings circa 1912?" a Latinf/x sensibility asks, "Why not?" To understand its import for the study of Latinx art, an adjustment of vision is needed.[38] To see what lifts off the screen, 3D glasses must be donned. At this time in the program, buckle in and get seated. We have arrived at the gates of tequila science fiction, and the show is about to begin.

All Strings Attached

When the Purple Gallery opened its doors to sculptor Angel Cabrales on October 27, 2016, this art space in a gentrifying downtown El Paso was unprepared for the light show awaiting it.[39] Audiences were encouraged to don 3D glasses while balls of LED lights and a flying saucer were suspended from the ceiling in a model of the cosmos (see plate 40). The exhibition, *It Came from Beyond the Border*, was a satirical homage to obscure B-movies like

Universal Studios' first foray into 3D technology, *It Came from Outer Space* (1953), or Columbia Pictures' *It Came from Beneath the Sea* (1955)—with geopolitical commentary. While the show's purple ambience attracted busy foot traffic in this trendy art district and drove viewers' gazes upward, the glowing spheres illuminated Cabrales's art ideology in a flamboyant hue. He conceived of the cosmos's origins as "la piñata cosmica [that] cracked open and . . . spilled forth its candied galaxies into the universe."[40] Juxtaposing a staple at Mexican American birthday parties and quinceañeras with another source of human creation, his ordinary papier-mâché is a gateway to the galaxy littered with sugary Pulparindos and other sweets. Border craftwork is an appropriate stand-in for a NASA space probe as *chisme* (gossip) transmits into the universe.

Cabrales's dedication to both astronomy and immigration underscored an exhibition courting film aesthetics from an earlier era of exploitation and space-age imagery at mid-century. This mélange shaped an art encounter sculpted by a B-movie prop room and costume shop. Cabrales appeared in a metallic sports coat paired with neon eyewear and his signature purple coif. For attendees, the open-ended title was a predictor of coming attractions, a polychrome future foretold in the artist's electrifying adornment. However, Cabrales's unapologetic romance with science fiction pulp began not with low-budget B-movies but with the unlikely surrounds of a missile base in White Sands, New Mexico.

Three boys crowd the armature of a rocket platform in a display of US military and scientific power (see figure 4.2). They hang on the missile's sleek aerodynamic casing. Their relaxed posture and playful mugging suggests that this family snapshot is ordinary for the Cabrales family despite a weapon of mass destruction centering their play. A young Angel Cabrales's confident pose forms the center of the visual field. His self-assurance exudes a familiarity with rocketry, hinting at how this nefarious scene is an ironic playground for young boys' fantasy and recreation. At the time of this photograph in 1981, his father was an engineer at White Sands Missile Range with classified details on the Patriot missile, a state-of-the-art intercepting ballistic weapon. Because of his father's high security clearance, grade school was anything but ordinary for Angel. For one assignment, he interviewed his father about his occupation. The noticeable brevity of the account frustrated Angel's teacher due to its apparent lack of sincerity. "My mom had to explain what my dad did. He worked on missiles and could not tell me. And the teacher was like, 'Oh, OK. How about he interviews you instead?'"[41] Cabrales quickly realized that not all children had family picnics

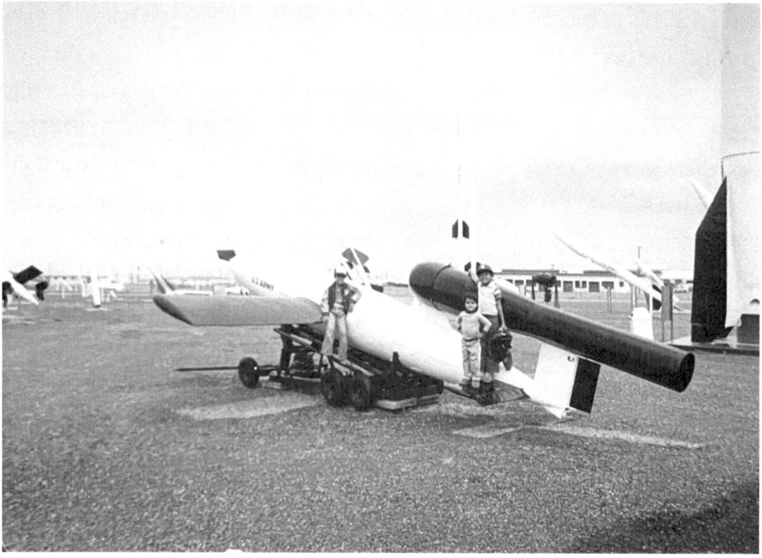

4.2 Angel Cabrales (*right*) with brothers Joel (*left*) and Joshua (*center*) at White Sands Missile Range, New Mexico, 1981. Photograph courtesy of the artist.

"eating sandwiches under missile fuselage" or had unprecedented access to a space shuttle, like he did when bad weather in Southern California redirected *Columbia* to land at White Sands Space Harbor on March 30, 1982.[42] This snapshot is a predictor of a life and creative journey that inspired the child to dream of a place in a universe far, far away, like the distant worlds captured in George Lucas's *Star Wars: A New Hope* (1977), a film that gave the Cabrales boys endless entertainment. However, there was something about his science fiction consumption that always augmented his sense of reality beyond his grounded border surrounds. Growing up on the outskirts of Anthony, New Mexico, he knew that somewhere between watching the moon through his father's telescope and crisscrossing a canyon that stretched between New Mexico, Texas, and the Sonoran Desert, there was something fantastic about his backyard borderlands.

His capacity to think and express himself in artistic and scientific terms would wait until his undergraduate studies at Arizona State University (ASU), a turn more circuitous than direct. At first, he matriculated at the New Mexico Institute of Mining and Technology, separating from the geochemistry program after two years. "I bought a sketchbook and started drawing again, and I realized as much as I loved science, I really loved art, and I didn't know how I could become an artist, but that's what I wanted to do. I would give up my scholarship in science to find a way to become an artist, and that did cause some arguments with my parents."[43] After a year at the College of Santa Fe, where he majored in drawing and painting, a course with sculptor Rick Fisher awakened a deeper interest in building large-scale metalwork capable of light casting. Recognizing the limitations of the sculpture program, Fisher directed him to ASU in Tempe, where facilities and interdisciplinary training in woodwork, foundry, neon, and steel could more fully guide him as he drew on that missile base, where empty rocket data books and stacks of computer punch cards had formed the basis for his self-taught illustrations and draftsmanship since grade school.

At ASU, a fortuitous course with Lewis Alquist showed him how to reformulate his practice closer to the "deadpan conceptual gags" for which his mentor was known.[44] Alquist's confrontational practice extended to vintage Fiesta tableware, where orange uranium glazes crackled nervously around a Geiger counter, and kinetic sculptures were reformulated in the shape of rifle mounts and sniper optics.[45] Teetering between madness and the aesthetics of a nuclear age, Alquist's deadly contraptions provoked his audiences with ruses that thrilled the body in ways consistent with exploitative film genres like horror and science fiction. Something about Alquist's shock sculpture resonated with Cabrales's own desire to leave 2D work behind, "to reach through this window and pull it out into this reality." Because, he further reflects, "I want people to be completely incorporated in the artwork."[46]

Their conversations empowered a new mission closer to the missiles Cabrales's dad engineered and the feelings of dread triggered either from automated defense artillery or from the threat of human annihilation by a radioactive mushroom cloud. From Alquist, Cabrales learned that "not everything is sculpture, but everything is sculpture materials," a mantra that became a through line in his practice, emboldening an ethos of confrontation in his graduate studies in the MFA program at the University of North Texas, near Dallas–Fort Worth.[47] His MFA show, *Disaster Capitalism: A Tradeshow for the Future Present* (2009), drew on the George W. Bush administration's shock doctrine for the Iraq War, which legitimated waterboarding despite its being a human rights violation. His commentary on this absurd logic resulted in a mixed-media artwork parodying a future security state commercializing this form of torture for at-home use. His humorous yet disturbing take on the US defense industry's justification baited the viewer, making a reactive chuckle complicit.

In 2014 Cabrales braved another work that reframed troubling reactions in the aftermath of the Sandy Hook tragedy, in which twenty schoolchildren in Connecticut were slain by a gun. Second Amendment advocates diluted outcries for sensible gun reform with a call to arm schoolteachers. Cabrales's pessimistic sculptural retort resulted in *Turn of the Sentry* (2014), installed at Tarrant County College's East Fork Gallery in Fort Worth (see plate 41). In it, Cabrales rigged a sentry gun out of Nerf toy parts. This weapon, otherwise outlawed in Texas, was duplicated for a gallery setting in homage to Alquist. In another twisted entry in his playland of weaponry, Cabrales adapted a childhood favorite into a marauding surveillant with harmful intent. By solving gun violence with more gun violence, his satirical artwork rattled school officials when a reported gun scare put the administration on edge. Rather than arbitrarily shooting attendees with Nerf balls, the kinetic sculpture was reimagined to silently track viewers wearing purple. Like Alquist before him, Cabrales energized sculptural environments with anxiety-inspiring if not menacing affect, thus making viewership a sensorial experience as bodies dodge, squirm, and pace cautiously. For some, his sculptural munition teeters on novelty, but others may regard it as being in bad taste. Despite these mixed reactions, Cabrales was conducting an artistic exercise in finding ways to materially respond to failed state protections, contradictory messaging, and flaccid legislation. A complementary artwork would prove that some provocations were better aimed at the stomach.

The distasteful undertones of the East Fork Gallery show are made overt with miniature assault rifles made from pan dulce. By asking audiences to literally eat their guns, his doughy hors d'oeuvres covertly decry a national culture of gun violence and armed conflict along the US-Mexico border, where cravings for human sustenance are interchangeable with firearms. His metaphor toys with the inherent conflict between seemingly innocent childhood memories and unseen xenophobia. Cabrales recalled sharing cross-border adventures with his abuela, moving from her home in Sunland Park, New Mexico, to border towns and sister cities in Mexico as a kid. In 2008 he returned to the mountain range that she traversed daily and discovered that a border wall obstructed the path. "That canyon was actually on the Mexican side. I didn't realize as a kid [that] my grandma was walking us into Mexico, and we were playing with these kids from Anapra and coming back. It really hurt to see that part of my life could never really be revisited."[48] The irony surrounding a childhood undone by a growing militarization of the border landscape brought Cabrales, a visiting instructor at the University of Texas at El Paso at that time, to another project, which arose from a serendipitous incident.

Taking his fine arts students to ASU for a neon workshop, he stumbled across discarded playland rides gathered by the owner of a nearby gallery. These defunct coin-operated amusements transformed through his renovations to become the kiddie version of US Immigration and Customs Enforcement (ICE) vehicles. In *DREAM a Little DREAM* (2018), a child-size ice cream truck is retrofitted as a Homeland Security vehicle (see plate 42). In *DREAM Catcher* (2019), a miniature helicopter is customized with emergency lights, enfolding a whimsical fantasy about aviation into the horrors of police custody. Cabrales's titles for his pieces satirically riff on the *dreamer*: referring to both the subconscious state of surrealism and the acronym for immigrant youth in the United States who qualify for permanent protection under the Development, Relief, and Education for Alien Minors (DREAM) Act.

Both amusement park sculptures were showcased in the 2018 Transborder Biennial at the El Paso Museum of Art and portrayed twisted playgrounds of injury, detention, and separation.[49] On the floor of this perverse amusement park are spills of candy in abstract designs, light strands balled and loosely gathered, and arrays of cacti in Day-Glo teal and purple. Creating something like a dystopian window onto Willy Wonka's chocolate *maquila* (or factory) after NAFTA (the North American Free Trade Alliance), Cabrales proposes a sweet life that can never be. Though these radiant accents read as part rave and part set decoration, they are also a paracinematic interlude, a radioactive stage for a fantastic desert dusted in nuclear fallout. The nostalgia provoked in these relics of children's playlands are bait for a grimmer reality that quantifiably worsened under Donald Trump's first and second administrations as his draconian immigration policies ripped children away from their families and jailed them (more on this topic in chapter 5). Cabrales's installation plays like a campy plot in a B-movie creature feature, in which an ICE (s)cream truck is the latest flamboyant villain. Branded with a Homeland Security insignia, this kiddie ride may appear to be a carnival amusement gone bad, but as in all good monster movie franchises, the end is just the beginning.

Frankenstein Low and Slow

Cabrales's sculptures navigate land and sky in ways that recall dormant Cold War paranoia about spy technologies and alien invaders, which reset the terms of racialized segregation and homeownership. According to Eric Avila, "The rise of Hollywood science fiction paralleled the acceleration of white flight in postwar America . . . record[ing] popular anxieties about political and sexual deviants."[50] Other artists working with a Latinf/x sensibility make the symmetry between speculative imagery and neighborhood conflict clearer. The mixed-media sculpture entitled *El Chavez Ravine* (see plate 43), by San Antonio–based artist Vincent Valdez, completes this corollary. In 2005 Valdez started a nineteen-month residency in Los Angeles. Working from a former taxi service station in Boyle Heights, a historic multiethnic and multiracial enclave on the east side of the city, the artist rendered the story of Chavez Ravine in his most ambitious artwork to date. His diverse source material included references to archive, sound, and scrapyard. Photography from Don Normark's book *Chavez Ravine, 1949: A Los Angeles Story* and films documenting housing evictions circa 1959 enhanced Valdez's outlook and crisp replications, including the infamous ejection of Aurora Vargas. Ry Cooder's album *Chávez Ravine* encouraged a change of medium for the young artist, who applied his aesthetic to a three-dimensional mural that *moves*. Rebuilt from parts pieced together by the Ruelas family, lowrider aficionados, a 1953 Chevy truck is more Frankenstein creation than auto collectible. The carcass of a Good Humor ice cream truck was found, retooled, and revived. The Chicano car customization crew broke time's fatal choke hold on the abandoned relic. Raised from the dead ends of a junkyard, this automotive art piece is an exceptional specimen, an appropriate East LA retort to the cruising DeLorean time machine popularized in Robert Zemeckis's *Back to the Future* franchise. In its return, this motorized mural resurfaces atrocities on its shell, shuttling the horrors of vile dislocation from the city's racist past.

In 1949 a public housing project and new freeway were planned as part of "a coordinated citywide redevelopment program."[51] This move, in turn, displaced more than 1,100 families in an area home to mostly Mexican suburbanites since the early twentieth century.[52] The land grab by the city of Los Angeles weaponized eminent domain and evicted a multigenerational and postwar barrio public. According to historian Ronald López, residents "did not receive adequate compensation for their homes and land, and found that segregation and high prices excluded them from many areas."[53] Instead of a new housing project, the Los Angeles Dodgers Stadium replaced this Mexican suburbia, making this seizure of land a site of ethnoracial trauma, eviction, residential displacement, and generational haunting. Valdez's response half a century later revisited that tragedy with a Good Humor vehicle that time-traveled with a muscular rebuilt body and refinished exterior. Even though the artwork reaches back to postwar LA, bearing witness to the attacks by city developers, politicos, and police, it also tells a narrative of an extraterrestrial kind. The truck's shell reproduces vignettes based on Valdez's nineteen-month study of photography, testimony, and imagery. His steel canvas reflects the character of lowrider car clubs with shiny enamel paint and chrome finishes, though with a Latinf/x improvisational outlook. His portrayal of LA history is a blend of pulp illustration and airbrushing technique that recites a B-movie memorabilia aesthetic. By leaning into the "darker side of urban life," as Eric Avila argues, Valdez's mobile artwork is part car and part canvas, with a cinematic twist.[54] As preparatory studies indicate, Valdez's approach was indebted to low-budget movie monsters, otherworldly dimensions, and UFOs on strings.

Consider an early concept study in 2004 for Valdez's car design. In a rough graphite sketch, the artist outlined a nine-step narrative proposal about "mysterious floating disks over city." Valdez suggested that the story of Chavez Ravine be told from a "force" of fear, a UFO that invades, hovers above, menaces, and abducts the Mexican American residents of the neighborhood because, as he writes in a typeface loosely derived from science fiction postwar film graphics, "IT WAS always home." By unfurling this violent episode of LA history like a drive-in exploitation flick, Valdez presents a version of events with an invader that dots the LA skyline. A proposal for *El Chavez Ravine* (2005) demonstrates how this speculative approach matured with ink-on-paper vignettes referencing a pulpy visual style. The lid of the cab portrays Dodger Stadium in the air. It hovers over Mexican American residents. A powerful light beam cast from the undercarriage amazes onlookers, stunned by astonishment if not fear (see plate 44). More Steven Spielberg's *Close Encounters of the Third Kind* (1977) than Jack Arnold's *It Came from Outer Space* (1953), this mothership is reminiscent of an advanced spacecraft in the style of sophisticated special effects. The dark bluish hues and light fields accentuate the astronautical spectacle dazzling the crowd.[55]

His study recites lyrics to "El U.F.O. cayó" (The UFO fell) from Cooder's album. The song describes a fallen UFO, a fellow alien dislocated from home; akin to the dispossessed residents of Chavez Ravine, it seeks to escape. Seconding Richard Haro's *Outer Space* mural from 1977, as discussed in chapter 2, Valdez's artwork reverses a traditional alien invasion narrative, showing that the real monster is not what is in the sky but what terrorizes Latinxs on the ground. For these reasons, it is surprising that a more overt UFO narrative for the Good Humor truck was ultimately toned down but not entirely eradicated. What made the cut was a nighttime engagement at Dodger Stadium in which Valdez appears to ruminate on what is an unresolved situation for many Latinx residents. Though they formed a baseball fandom dubbed "Los Dodgers," some team fanatics remain awkwardly aligned with the injury caused by this demolition in the name of sports entertainment.

Another proposed section for the truck retained Valdez's Latinf/x outlook in a style that appeared to be lifted from the pages of *Astounding Stories*. Ultimately, the Spielberg-inspired flying stadium was omitted. "The narrative that I was trying to tell . . . it was more important for me to leave it an open-ended chapter rather than a conclusion. And I think that's why I decided to scratch the stadium as landing invader, UFO, foreign entity, something that was leading to distortion or hysteria," Valdez recalled.[56]

His final rendition of the truck's hood is a plainly sociohistorical representation taken from the stadium's interior, channeling the emotion and pandemonium from arena spectators. The UFO iconography is no more. This portion of the ice cream truck is flanked with the black-and-white details of uprooted residents to the left side of the cab and a muted palette of city redevelopment plans on the right. Turning muted film into Technicolor celluloid adds practical effects flair akin to Dorothy's dreamland from the famed MGM motion picture *The Wizard of Oz* (1939). Clearly, this is no Oz. Valdez's vignettes read like a "movie poster," as curator David Rubin suggests, a jump cut of Mexican American history in the city modeled through car customization with consequences for the present and future.[57] Overall, Valdez's elision of the alien spacecraft may dampen the profound influence of postwar science fiction as a visual resource and narrative structure. However, as with the Technicolor turn in the painted enamel, reality was charged with a speculative transformation. Referencing his talks with Cooder, Valdez recalls, "It really was one of our first conversations. . . . Just the influence of American sci-fi not only as visual but in terms of its subtle or subconscious symbols and metaphors, whether it be culturally or politically . . . that was the thing that drew me to not only the genre but also the project itself."[58] In short, science fiction was foundational for this project as he and Cooder communed through generic images and texts. Their exchange found expression in other parts of the cab.

On the truck's lid, a fright show is unveiled. In Valdez's preparatory sketch from 2005, a propaganda poster titled "The Injustice of El Chavez Ravine" portrays the atrocity of developers and government corruption that animated this "tragic tale of lies, corruption, and racism," as the studio's promotional art indicates. The palette of hues of crimson was likely the byproduct of Valdez and Cooder's earliest correspondence. In a 2004 letter, the musician lauds the work of Dell Publishing Company illustrator Gerald Gregg, whose surrealist-inspired cover art "utilized a simple concept . . . where the human figures were usually dwarfed by outsized symbols of their fears."[59] He expands that "maybe [a] hand emerges from red cloud, hovering overhead?" to set a "very creepy, ominous" tone allegorizing the Red Scare and Cold War panic.[60] What resulted in Valdez's study is a monster that is dual parts machine and capital. A yellow tractor with snarling and jagged teeth in its bucket towers over a gloomy Chavez Ravine washed in gray hues. A nondescript public scrambles as omnipotent hands reach from the clouds, pulling the strings of the bulldozing tractor. The terror incited by the unseen puppet master suggests that wronged Mexican American residents on the ground need not worry about UFOs when the horrors of land dispossession rain down. In the far-left corner of the composition, a hand in the foreground points skyward, suggesting that the structure of the sight line and monstrosity ordering this science fiction narrative is aerial.

This vertical ordering of vision and scale is clearly defined in Valdez's final iteration for the top of the truck's cab (see plate 45). A backdrop of sinister clouds forecasts the horrors to come. A mechanized monster topples barrio residences as flocks of birds are seen in the periphery, escaping the metal jaws of the tractor's bucket. The panicked occupants scramble. Their confusion and outcry draw their heads upward in reaction to the devastation and the clawed hands reaching out toward them. Valdez's play with scale and perspective is resonant of pulp art strategies in the first half of the twentieth century. Whether the figures are pointing aloft or looking skyward, his different iterations underscore the settler colonial domination over airspace but also the vulnerabilities of local Mexican American residents' experience under it. However, what is powerful is the way his racialized public dares to see the monsters and puppet masters. This return stare stands to identify the sources of collective pain, injury, and displacement. By hewing to a pulpy aesthetic, Valdez conveys a Latinf/x outlook and, moreover, a transplanetary relation that activates Latinx ocular relationships and thus pleads with his audience to also look up.

Above the ice cream truck is a mirror suspended by cables from the gallery's ceiling. Valdez borrows a display technique from the realm of auto showrooms and lowrider car clubs.[61] As publics pause to contemplate the image, they perform a movement modeled by figures in the composition as they mutually gaze up to see the strings of the monster hovering above them. Akin to the way that transplanetary relationality transmits and transfigures location, vision, and scale, the museumgoer attunes to the horrors found above them. However, the deceptions revealed there are more than B-movie clichés. Unveiled are the unseen entities of racial capitalism, urban gentrification, and police surveillance. By maximizing a Latinf/x sense of Mexican American history, he proves how a gimmick can connect the LA of now with an LA of then.

Valdez's work of gesture and reception is closely evocative of the kinetic sculptural playland of Cabrales. Although these artworks of cheap thrills and bad taste may appear better fitted for an amusement park than a gallery setting, they demonstrate how ideas and graphic stylings derived from the pulp archive resonate with Latinx artists. Despite Avila's argument that "special effects alone . . . do not explain the immense popularity of science fiction thrillers," this cultural repertoire is an undeniable register of Latinx expressivity.[62] Together, Cabrales and Valdez insist on seeing the strings and thus invest in cheaply made creature features as forums in which a politics of resistance and social justice stands out like a 3D illusion from flat and polarizing texts. If a tragedy like the bulldozing of Chavez Ravine or the threat of child separations arrives by way of refurbished ice cream trucks, surely the strings of tyranny can be spotted, parodied, and resisted. Even if they cannot be cut physically, they can be inverted. These artists' skillful designs and accomplished studies of B-movie iconography and shoddy production values suggest how returning to the first half of the twentieth century establishes an experimental language for Latinx creatives fluent in the potentiality of discarded media. In this "pulp paradox," a Latinf/x outlook on immigrant history, transnationalism, and even transplanetary relations empowers both gimmick and improvisation to litigate racialized historical and present atrocities once more. Beyond metaphors, these artists' callbacks not only are nostalgic but also perform socially critical work with an audience's turn toward overhead terror on strings. Other practices, too, are aided by not only pulp imagery but also the lo-fi technologies of novelty and forgotten B-movie gems.

Attack of the Trash Monster

For mixed-media artist Vincent Ramos, Chavez Ravine is also a matter that appeals to his Latinf/x sensibility, a connoisseurship that grew out of movie memorabilia and Hollywood studio souvenirs. Dubbed a "collector-artist" by curator Rita Gonzalez, Ramos works in assemblage and ephemeral art installations that "repurpose[ ] cast-off materials of visual culture and, through the act of revival, ask[ ] the current generation to give the imagery new life."[63] His treasured discards from LA's postwar film history, celebrity memorabilia, and music culture are prompts generating his archivally focused artwork. He was raised in the coastal neighborhood of Venice on the west side of LA in the 1970s, and his memories are excited by the sounds of 45 LP records, Roger Corman creature feature reruns on late-night television, and family *charla* (chitchat) "as they relate to the Chicano experience, as they relate to the familial, as they relate to Southern California . . . [representing] all those little seeds of information."[64] One seed in particular made an impression on young Ramos's racial consciousness. When the Los Angeles Dodgers beat the New York Yankees in the 1981 World Series, his grandmother's crass response resonated with him. "The first time that I ever heard ANYTHING about the injustices towards Mexican-Americans/Chicanos was when my grandmother talked about Chavez Ravine. . . . She despised the Dodgers."[65] Her retort tainted the triumph of LA's baseball team by reminding young Ramos that the stadium was a project of urban gentrification and racial violence. As this championship was the third of the Dodgers' victories over the Yankees—they had also won in 1955 and 1963—these games coincided with Ramos's "collecting impulse" to salvage materials from his youth, items connected to his parents' nostalgia, and records that document a history of Latinx LA, especially at mid-century.[66]

Unfolding a familial footprint on the west side was important to Ramos because the city as he knew it was overlooked for its contributions to Mexican American urban history. This local context honed Ramos's creative practice, which suffused thrifting with theoretical investigations about evidence of timescale and timeline. His search for Latinx pop cultural remains led him into the storerooms and wastelands of media discards. Garage sales, garbage bins, flea markets, and estate sales were the dig sites from which the disposed relics of Latinx representation were excavated. Pieces of Chavez Ravine informed another media archaeology project. His assorted findings were reassembled in a glass case for Frieze Los Angeles 2020 that was entitled *Wolf Songs for the Dead* (2020).[67] Named in tribute to the Paramount Pictures' silent western *Wolf Song* (1929), starring Gary Cooper as a fur trapper and Lupe Vélez as an elegant señorita and set in the adventure-filled Mountain West, Ramos's collection was unique if not tactically played. It appeared in the backlot of Paramount Pictures, tucked away in a project space behind New York–style brownstone facades. The experience of that artwork was mediated by fantasy and artifice where impressions of another city linger somewhere between movie magic and simulacra. The search for the real by the reel was a connection long undergirding Chicanx conceptualism from the 1970s, from which the LA-based group of artists called Asco (meaning "nausea" in Spanish) was a touchstone for Ramos.

His inclusion in a world-renowned art fair that even attracted celebrities like Jennifer Lopez and Alex Rodriguez was compliments of guest curators Rita Gonzalez and Pilar Tompkins Rivas. Ramos's project was summarized as "working around issues of representation for Latinx people in media, museums, cultural contexts, merging with historical timelines in LA," but it was also deftly aware of racial stratification and generational trauma like his grandmother's.[68] In *Wolf Songs for the Dead*, photojournalist documentation of Chavez Ravine showing residents dragged from their homes by the Los Angeles police is combined with materials showcasing Latina Hollywood stardom. His juxtaposition demonstrates how two distinct pictures of racist operations police or commodify the brown body (see plate 46). Exhuming a film like *Wolf Song* for contemporary consideration nearly a hundred years after its release in US movie theaters proves how the artist effectively occupies the paradoxical spaces of Latinas on the fringes of LA film and urbanism.

His installation juxtaposes media marketing and the entertainment industry against the material realities of an anti-Mexican carceral system. His work for Frieze LA was supported by a brief residency in the archives of Paramount Studios. Framed headshots from little-known actors of Latin American descent were mined from this investigation. Ramos's own collection of memorabilia and fanfare was on view, suggesting that even in this microinstallation he treated with care found media that film preservationists might disregard as unexceptional relics of long-forgotten cheap movie productions. Ramos displays a triumphant make-do attitude, a Latinf/x-sensible custodianship for media remains on the margins of Paramount's prized film catalog. In a Latinx art historical context, his practice is indebted to *domesticana* aesthetics, especially in his use of "material memory" of Mexican American performers from the Hollywood studio system's golden age.[69] The most exemplary model of this archivally directed articulation is Amalia Mesa-Bains, whose altars not only venerate feminist icons from the Americas (see chapter 1 for more) but also, like Ramos's works, display a devotion to the movie icons of the past. Mesa-Bains's much-lauded *Ofrenda for Dolores del Río* (1984) is replete with film stills, headshots, souvenirs, and film canisters, making the artwork a forerunner to Ramos's media excavations. However, more than just a network of artifacts, tchotchkes, and divine relics, Ramos's artwork is a media mapping of geography and politics to subordinate what Leo Rosten classically dubbed "the movie colony" with his ethnoracial memories of these film factories.[70] Ramos grew up in the shadow of MGM Studios and Twentieth Century Fox, and his racial formation in Southern California coalesced around these sound stages' manufacturing realities, augmenting his own sense of belonging and, in sum, his alienation on the city's west side. It is only appropriate that his installation at Frieze LA 2020 was presented on a staged set, an experience of Chicanx art and racist atrocity mediated by a decoy Manhattan.

Reality was fiction for this Chicano who matured with a heightened awareness of the ways in which these industry pillars cosmetically engineered representations of LA. As a result, a refined understanding of media production culture grew, an awareness that coalesced after his older brother shared his Polaroid pictures from the set of *Grease* (1978). Shot on location at Venice High School, where the elder Ramos brother was a student, the John Travolta and Olivia Newton-John vehicle catapulted the pair to the A-list, inspiring a generation to hand-jive. Those photos of Hollywood luminaries instilled an inherent awareness in Vincent that a school long chronicled in the family's history was no ordinary place. Detached from the 1970s, the set design unfurled a nostalgic look back at the 1950s, when juvenile delinquent pictures ushered the greaser archetype into the national spotlight. The school functioned for young Ramos as a time machine, refusing chronological closure and embarking on a quantum mechanics that vibes to what, as Frankie Valli sang, "is the time, is the place, is the motion."[71]

That space-time portability, more physics than lyricism, catalyzed Ramos's first major installation, for a group exhibition entitled *Post-America L.A.* (2009), curated by Pilar Tompkins for the 18th Street Arts Center. Her curatorial premise organized a show that forecast world powers and global authority ten years into the future.[72] Artists were invited to contemplate a city futurity in which "Los Angeles [was] projected to increase by several million inhabitants (projections vary, yet they are mostly slated to be immigrants from Latin America and Asia)."[73] Ramos's contribution, in the tradition of Chicanx public artists before him, focused on youth. He returned to Venice High School, his alma mater, at the invitation of two retiring schoolteachers from the art department, Joanna Carrabbio and Marco Elliott. Not only was Ramos trained under Elliott's instruction, but so was another famed Latinx contemporary artist, Juan Capistrán.[74] At the school Ramos worked with twenty-five students of color; his collaborative art practice introduced a younger generation of west-side millennials to contemplate the near future by looking back to Venice through a 1950s lens. Guiding his art education curriculum was the speculative literature of longtime LA resident Ray Bradbury.

Bradbury, born in Waukegan, Illinois, arrived in Southern California at the age of fourteen. Early on, he "became a creature of books and imagination," rifling the public library in search of publications and serials peppered with stories of unusual and weird happenings.[75] The Bradbury family had a brief stay in Tucson before moving to LA. Allegedly, he saw a performance of sideshow magician Mr. Electrico, which stirred his creativity and potential to "feed from the power of suggestion."[76] The lessons he learned from that shock man carried over with him to other amusements, like an exhibit at the Santa Monica boardwalk, where cases of fetuses in glass jars modeled prenatal growth for the young man and further stoked his desire for immortality. This display staged something "strange, like I was on another planet," recalled Bradbury.[77] Between the sideshow and the amusement park, the author lost himself in adventure narratives about Ozar the Aztec from Street and Smith's *Top-Notch Magazine*, a colonial narrative about an Anglo newborn found and raised by a lost Aztec civilization in Mexico.[78] He was also captivated by astronomer Percival Lowell's scientific discovery of canals on the surface of Mars. At ten years of age, a young Bradbury read Lowell's *Mars as the Abode of Life* (1910) with enthusiasm, a book that bolstered his fixation on the Red Planet.[79] Ironically, that book was published the same year that the Porfirio Díaz administration went to war with Mexican revolutionary insurgents, hinting at the bizarre synchronicities between Bradbury and greater Mexico.

Bradbury's Mexican machinations are found in his debut short-story collection, *Dark Carnival* (1947), which marked his entry into short-fiction fantasy and horror years before his famed novels *The Martian Chronicles* (1950) and *Fahrenheit 451* (1953) sealed him within the speculative literature canon.[80] George Burrows's cover art for the dust jacket echoes the nightmarish visions Bradbury experienced during a road trip south of the US border in 1945.[81] His encounter with Señor Cerda in Uruapan, Michoacán, introduced him to the wood craftwork of the Purépecha Indigenous people. Exaggerated faces and caricatured visages of beasts and mythological creatures fascinated Bradbury, who not only collected but reproduced exceptional examples of masks for the book's cover, adding monstrous tones through ritualistic costume. Other experiences from his Mexican road trip, ranging from mummy catacombs in Guanajuato to Day of the Dead festivities in Pátzcuaro, brought death closer to him in a way reminiscent of that day on the Santa Monica boardwalk around 1934.[82] The terror that both thrilled and haunted him from those events would carry through in his writing, proving that Mexican frights were never far away. This disturbing reality even echoed in bloody squabbles when stateside US servicemen and police assailed young Chicanas and Chicanos adorned in zoot suits in 1943.[83] He observed this unrest against the backdrop of the Bradbury home in Venice, the setting where he completed a draft of *The Martian Chronicles*, picturing another kind of alien conflict from the standpoint of this sleepy coastal city.[84]

Perhaps for these reasons, Bradbury's texts, like *Death Is a Lonely Business* (1985) and *The Illustrated Man* (1951), became textbooks for Ramos and his high school students. These readings were supplemented with another

Paramount Pictures drive-in favorite, *The Blob* (1958), in which a meteorite carrying an amoebic predator crash-lands in a small Pennsylvania town. Encouraging students to think with and about the B-movie was an appropriate choice, especially considering Bradbury's irrefutable mark on the genre and his noted regard for local Mexican American publics, an intersection that Ramos's preparatory work for the art project made clear.

Before starting his residency at the 18th Street Arts Center, Ramos intuitively knew that getting the author's approval would authenticate his project with a kind of favor that science fiction aficionados might acknowledge with high regard. Ramos blindly sent a letter to the home address of the writer, who responded with a handwritten note. According to the artist, the envelope bore Edgar Allan Poe stamps encircled with a handwritten scribble reading "Ray's grandchild," an epistolary nod to a genealogy of speculative inheritance.[85] Bradbury invited Ramos to attend a play based on his short story in North Hollywood, where they briefly met. Here, Ramos discussed his vision and intention for the Venice High School collaboration. "I essentially wanted his permission, you know, to do this, so at least I told him about the project," Ramos recalled.[86] Bradbury was receptive. His consent was particularly meaningful given his declining health. Soon after, in 2012, this literary goliath passed away. His consent was symbolic as well as personally significant for the artist. Ramos's 18th Street Arts Center project is a continuation of Bradbury, who trailblazed science fiction storytelling with tethers to Venice, LA urbanism, Mexico, and sideshow theatrics.

Ramos's piece entitled *Planets Beyond Jupiter, 1959, 2009, 2019* (2009) answered Tompkins's charge, "speculating about the future [by] also looking to the past to talk about the future."[87] By reciting those Polaroids from his brother's camera, Ramos returned his twenty-first-century Chicanx teens to all things 1950s. In his archivally directed artwork, he immersed these youth in a time capsule of golden age imagery. Postwar pulp publications, creature features, beat literary culture, and racist atrocities like the forced removal of Mexican residents at the Chavez Ravine and the militarized deportation of millions of immigrants during Operation Wetback in 1954 made the case that Venice was no ordinary landscape. The city was a supernatural apex and creative epicenter for a bohemian aesthetic typified by the likes of Wallace Berman, whose underground image-text prose circulated in *Semina*, a self-published compendium of metaphysical thought, occult beliefs, poetics, and handmade printing that defined West Coast avant-garde literature.[88] Ramos's pupils were equally improvisational, though linking an experimental Venice to a narrative of exceeding personal importance:

future environmental disaster. As with any good homage to Bradbury, low-budget scares were needed.

Ramos's approach made use of the photography methods of the "No Movie," a regarded register of the Asco group that interrogated the representational negation of the racialized Other through an expanded sense of cinema predicated on the singular 35 mm film still.[89] As a photographic syntax for the performance work of his students, Ramos composed a series of pictured tableaux featuring five students playacting scenes of the future. One scene depicted how an ordinary day at Venice High School could become the stuff of nightmares (see plate 47). A young Chicana feigned terror. Her gaze turned upward in this attack of the trash monster; like Janet Leigh before her, she is not the clichéd "final girl," and so the conservative tenets of ecohorror must transform. Behind the mask was the student's sister, subverting the "imperiled woman" trope typical of the postwar pulp art tradition.[90] Reversing the sexist dyad constituting victim and victimizer in science fiction and horror genres, the Chicana unmasked from the monstrous costume performed a kind of revenge, adding one more plot twist undoing the racialized gender tropes of the genre. In this updated scenario, these bleachers were no longer the setting from which T-Birds and Pink Ladies broke into song but rather the stage of another kind of scare where Venice's only protection from impending ecological ruin was a barrio homeboy adorned in an innovative yet crudely made space suit (see plate 48).

Though this scenario may reproduce the familiar archetype of the macho astronaut as the chief protagonist of B-movie narratives, it is the semblance of visual experimentation, improvisation, and performance combined with a Latinf/x attitude that empowered a group of young Latinxs armed with all things Bradbury. In this way, it is worth reconsidering the assailed teen's upward-turned look at the trash monster. Though laughter breaks the moment, she confronts this jump scare with boundless brown joy. Her noncommittal comportment is not an outright rejection of Ramos's project but rather an awareness of the mechanics of the scene. By confronting the stunt, she refuses to succumb to the attack of the trash monster because she sees the person behind the mask. Her Latinf/x attitudinal knowledge arrests the antic and dismantles the horror. Ramos's decision to include this photographic outtake codes the work in the unserious ends of the No Movie milieu and reinvents it for a generation of time-traveling Latinx teens better versed in the absurdity of pulp narrative logics than contemporary performance art. With this, Ramos portrays a future Venice with critical Chicanx social satire of today borrowing from a narrative structure of yesterday. This temporal dexterity is apropos to the art piece's timely attribution. Ramos's title, *Planets Beyond Jupiter, 1959, 2009, 2019*, pays tribute to his mother. She had graduated from the school in 1959. Together, he and his student cohort re-created a cultural terrain most hospitable if not recognizable to his mother circa 1959 for a 2009 art project about a 2019 in the future. His approach knotted Venice in a simultaneity of time-space that required an equally complex exploration of media caught in the tangles.

Ramos's installation in *Post-America L.A.* portrayed an unmade science fiction motion picture in a deconstructed form. He invited viewers to contemplate a B-movie lexicon by turning its visual, editorial, and technological elements into a fragmented celluloid environment. Props, camera directions, editing techniques, and special effects were presented like storyboard mappings converting 2D concept designs for 3D viewing. The site transformed Chicanx cinematic negation into a paracinematic experience. Using nearly thirty-five years' worth of art projects scavenged from the trash cans of art teacher retirees, Ramos salvaged orphaned slides, lesson plans, tutorial models, and exceptional specimens of art pedagogy. These discards accrued and clustered on adjoining walls, manifesting an experimental form of cinematic engagement. The remnants of Venice High School creatives were interspersed with found objects, curios, and photo transparency transfers, giving impressions of motion for static film stills. Self-adhesive notes were stuck to walls. Camera directions were written on paper slips standing in for this deconstructed screenplay. The texts were markers that replaced the language of a mechanized Bolex with analog guidelines. Callouts for a "close-up," "jump cut," "reaction shot," and "cut away" embellished props, using crude handwritten notes to command an audience to see directorial cues in unfinished forms (see plate 49). In the installation a mountain of balled-up tape parodied a meteor, patriotic wrapping paper improvised a lo-fi dream sequence, and a cartoonish cloud doodle served as a pictographic substitute, reading "in lieu of a smoke machine."

Centering the gallery space is a two-hundred-pound steel table salvaged from the school's garbage (see plate 50). Turned on its side, the hexagonal shape references the film leader countdown sequence of a motion picture reel. Brandishing star-shaped color wheels and astrophotography reproductions, this science lab table is part film launch and part rocket launch. Its celestial facade retrofits an ordinary piece of classroom furniture into something functionally customized for spacefaring. As Ramos's answer to the *Millennium Falcon*, this contraption cruised to the orchestral sounds of Gustav Holst's early twentieth-century suite *The Planets* and Frank Zappa's *Chunga's Revenge*, which played on dueling turntables. All this visual and textual density is presented snarled in strings of yarn, which added a dizzying pathway for trash-can finds. His presentation gives "low-budget" Chicanx filmmaking new meaning. This unmade science fiction film literalizes a paracinematic regard for media even in its crude state. In this way, the strings that web the walls are not the cautionary tales of puppetry and capitalism in Valdez's work or the villainy of amusement park castoffs in Cabrales's sculptures. Instead, they represent the timely entanglements of nostalgia, place memory, and search for home in Ramos's reflections on the pulp archive at mid-century.

This Latinf/x reception for the discarded and forgotten relics of genre motion pictures led Ramos to recall one of his mother's earliest memories from growing up in Southern California. She remembered watching Howard Hawks's *The Thing* around 1951.[91] Her story of cinemagoing suggested something pivotal for Ramos's practice, as he realized how his family's history was as much tied to LA's west side as it was to science fiction horror. Akin to the "creature feature" connoisseurship nurtured before the Nortes at a drive-in in distant East LA, she too found ways to belong in the city and the vastness of beyond. His corresponding installation at the 18th Street Arts Center was reverential toward what exploitation movies gave to his Mexican American family: his mother's media consumption in postwar LA and even his brother's castoff Polaroids. For Ramos, that kind of visual literacy sparked a participatory art making that speculates on a future with young people, better preparing them to confront America's monsters with a pedigree in Bradbury and a cultural patrimony in the speculative arts.

Now in Chicanovision 3D

Although Ramos's unmade movie of jump scares and lo-fi camera directions need not be paired with 3D glasses to enhance its scares, its antics were source materials for creatives like Cabrales, who also found his way to the Bradbury corpus. Consider how Bradbury's narrative "The Meteor" was the basis for Universal-International's first major 3D venture, *It Came from Outer Space*, about a UFO that crash-lands in the Arizona desert. It was a top grosser in Los Angeles when it opened on Memorial Day weekend in 1953. Later it was paired with another 3D spectacle from the studio, *Creature from the Black Lagoon*, about a gill man discovered in the Amazon.[92] This Universal Studios double feature was rhetorically quoted in Cabrales's similarly titled *It*

Came from Beyond the Border, an exhibition that turned a flying saucer on a string into ready-made art at El Paso's Purple Gallery. If that theatrical display wasn't enough, 3D technology was essential to the viewing experience there (see plate 40).

Cabrales's layered resin dyes in low-relief wall sculptures animate a more sensorial experience, a Latinf/x translation of "exploitation-type shock effects" for El Paso audiences.[93] By augmenting visual apprehension in space, time, and color, he nostalgically reflects on moviegoing reception in a manner reminiscent of Ramos. Having grown up in the 1980s, Cabrales too fondly remembered seeing science fiction and horror motion pictures in Anthony, New Mexico, consuming such fine fare as *Jaws 3-D* (1983). "I used to love going to the movie—for a 3-D movie—and just running around ruining my eyes for the rest of the week [wearing the glasses]. . . . The way you looked at colors is all messed up," he recalled.[94] Knowing how the combination of red and green light could turn a MAGA hat brown, he acquired an education in the visual perception of luminosity and eye trickery, ocular gags that were germane in not only the 3D revival of beloved horror flicks like *Friday the 13th Part III* (1982) and *Amityville 3-D* (1983) but also a dormant cycle of science fiction film history dating to 1952–55. His reanimation of this novelty for Chicanx art in the purple-hued corners of a West Texas gallery allowed for another fantasy world to stand up and stand out against the flat dimension of art display. Unbeknownst to the viewer is that this intervention was manifested on behalf of the Chupacabrales, the artist's alter ego, which riffs on his last name and the mythical bloodsucking monster the Chupacabra.

The pseudonym is an appropriate maturation of an art practice that boldly and even haphazardly transgresses a material existence in this world. As he moves the Chupacabrales moniker into the realm of contemporary art, Chicanx art is experienced in an illusory space, provoking alternative ways to perceive work that flirts with the lowbrow and dares to jump out against a static environment. For Cabrales, practical effects and the orchestration of production design are profound apertures to decode the world around El Paso and Ciudad Juarez, if only temporarily. *It Came from Beyond the Border* toys with the senses, enticing the audience to see immigration with different eyes and in different dimensions. Cabrales's residual shock effect was not dissimilar to the lo-fi technology undergirding Ramos's creature feature, a project more "unmade" than No Movie.[95] In both cases the artists' fluency in the pulp image archive returns to the meaning and function of cult cinema memorabilia, an aesthetic register stoked even by Valdez's mobile mural.

Ephemera are germane for Ramos, whose castoffs from Hollywood studio publicity centered his installation work at Frieze Los Angeles. In *Wolf Songs for the Dead*, his mixed-media workspace is accented with "movie posters" on the surrounding walls. These posters were sized to the exact dimensions of the traditional materials distributed by the studios in magazines or press kits, and the creased folds added texture to collages of ephemera, newsprint, and print advertisements. These thematic works on paper connected archival and popular cultural images, juxtaposing them into a bricolage of a palatable Mexico. Reworked on drab builder's paper, his conceptual reimagining of this keepsake was produced close to the "movie colony's" unseen workers. By reusing this salvaged material of manual labor, he turned Hollywood studio industry relations with LA's urban landscape brown.

A similar interrogation of movie memorabilia and vintage pulp artwork is the focus of Cabrales's poster corpus. At the *It Came from Beyond the Border* exhibition, a print of the same name appears on a short wall. Signed by "Chupacabrales," the B-movie satire foregrounds a cowering woman on a mountainous hillside (see plate 51). Having collapsed onto the uneven terrain, she grips the ground. Her gaze moves away from the darkened surrounds and turns upward. Her vision of the night sky is interrupted not by any ordinary UFO but by pan dulce spacecraft. These Mexican sweet breads beam their intrusive lights downward, assuming a powerful position in the skies. As invaders and symbols of future otherworldly technology, pan dulce produces a covert if not racially charged threat to white female fragility, the family, and the modern space program's right to occupy the sky.

By reclaiming the upper atmosphere with aeronautical technology of the tasty kind, Cabrales interrogates Cold War anxieties over aerial invasion, shifting the racialized terms of surveillance and airspace to food politics. As the imperiled woman's enmeshments in a browner world dawn upon her, looking up echoes a transplanetary-relational approach discussed in this book thus far. Her skyward-facing terror is a rumination not only about outer space but also on interior space. Science fiction is a consumptive experience in ways that underscore other facets of pulp movie exhibition, where snack foods, refreshments, and sweet indulgences shape media watching. Coming-attractions trailers are paired with concession stand advertisements. By working within a promotional repertoire of unforeseen horrors that "invariably *anticipate* motion, as [these images] usually seem to freeze an ongoing or forecast a soon-to-occur action," according to J. P. Telotte, Cabrales finds meaning in B-movie anxieties about eating and, reciprocally, being eaten.[96] Although postwar exploitation pictures at that time depicted a world falling prey to giant ants or marauding spiders in the aftermath of atomic testing, none of these films quite compared to the terrifying food wars that Cabrales foresaw: a fight happening over the *pansa* (or belly).

Pansa Wars: When Jalapeños Strike Back

Although the print *It Came from Beyond the Border* captures how studio publicists at that time sought "a sense of wonder, often through a similar emphasis on a character's gaze" to stimulate imaginations, Cabrales's consumptive politics combines a vertical spectacle with baser instincts.[97] Toeing the border between good and bad taste, his take on the pulp visual archive is inherently linked to the gustatory politics of Latinx speculation. The appearance of a concha invasion is another painfully palatable sampling from his oeuvre where flan bombs and sweet-bread guns question the United States' tolerance for digesting a variety of social ills in the name of constitutional freedoms. Furthermore, by dehumanizing and even diminishing immigrants' human rights in terms of family separation, militarized border policing, or mass shootings at an El Paso Walmart in 2019 and Robb Elementary School in Uvalde in 2022, the mainstream media ingest and spit out sensationalizing tidbits of border violence in ways that prompt an artistic redress.[98]

Cabrales's retort is delivered with a fiery pop. *It Came from Beyond the Border 4: The Great Replacement* (2022) is a digital print portraying a towering one-eyed jalapeño tearing down the border wall, causing a crowd of January 6 insurgents to scatter in terror (see plate 52). Riffing on other horror B-movie greats born in the grocer's produce aisle, like *Attack of the Killer Tomatoes* (1974) or *Soylent Green* (1973), this pepper is no passive seasoning. This green creature *feels* its appropriation and commercialization in Santa Fe interior design trends or in a growing US culinary industry absorbing Mexican foodways into high-end dining experiences and designer gastropubs. Like a sleepy giant awakened, this border-crossing monster is another unexplained aberration appearing nowhere and yet everywhere.

Cabrales's regard for the unyielding and omnipresent jalapeño is shared in *Las Frutas Lloronas* (Weeping fruits), a series of still lifes by South Texas artist Sam Rawls. These oil paintings reimagine the legend of La Llorona, a weeping woman who drowns her children. She represents a wild and unruly monster with "dangerous feminine desires that threaten familial structures."[99] Rawls's reproach recasts the violent histories of agriculture and US interventionism on behalf of corporate interests in Latin America and the

Caribbean. Her jalapeño portrait depicts a singular bloodshot eye straining to open (see plate 53). Rather than going berserk, the pepper cries. Though the cause of such outpouring is left ambiguous in Rawls's composition, the artwork subtly contemplates what the synthesizing of the Llorona tale may mean for racial capitalism, corrupt systems of agricultural labor, worker abuses, and post-NAFTA trade and supply chain shortfalls. Does this "fruta llorona" wail about the children she drowns, the atrocities committed on the broken bodies of farmworkers picking crops for corporate growers, or the horrors that the monstrosity of femininity enacts on the cisheteropatriarchal order? Together, she and Cabrales recite a Chicanx cyclopic eye, perhaps quoting the classic alien physiognomic form in *It Came from Outer Space*. By reimagining a peppery monster closer to the Bradbury-based B-movie, they give the snack gallery a Latinf/x attitude. In this way, they are certain that this flavoring will refuse to go down easily.

The gustatory politics invoked in work by Cabrales and Rawls recalls "eating the other," a way that "the commodification of Otherness has been . . . successful, because it is offered as a new delight. . . . [It] can liven up the dull dish that is mainstream white culture," according to bell hooks.[100] In this still life, Rawls's spicy if not fantastic invader (at least in Cabrales's case) is anything but obedient. It will hit you. The pepper's profile is a counteraesthetic to the restrained or muted definition of good taste and corresponding "high art," which "tequila sci-fi" mocks. Cabrales builds on his 2016 coinage with digital prints in pulp art style that reimagines the Chicano political graphic through a paracinematic blender. These print works entertain with an unapologetic embrace of special effects antics, a sensibility appreciated by the Latinf/x aficionado. Sometimes presented together in the film exhibition venue of a movie palace like the Magnolia Theatre in the Oak Lawn neighborhood of Dallas in 2019, Cabrales's movie posters evince how despite postwar anti-Mexican and Mexican American atrocities like Chavez Ravine and Operation Wetback, bad media discards from that time were valuable as they elicited visual vocabularies from which to confront and reconcile generational trauma. Despite his astute visual reading of this B-movie aesthetic, Cabrales proves that none of the classic science-fictional tropes is sacred. In *Battle in El Chuco*, Cabrales's sensationalist purview portrays the horrors of child separation as embodied by an ICE-branded Gort abducting a Mexican child from his home in West Texas, making the pulp archive a covertly palatable art statement for audiences on both sides of the US-Mexico border (see plate 54).

Like Ramos, Cabrales is in the business of making fine art from B-movie trash. More than condemn the racist limitations of the genre, he seconds the pulpy visual register with a subversive jolt to the eye and stomach. Alongside Valdez, Ramos, and Rawls, Cabrales practices an aesthetic language of lo-fi and low-budget genre pictures that triumphs in the rough-hewn and parades the novelty. This pulpy realignment for Chicanx art forwards image making dubbed tequila science fiction, a cycle of cultural production that hangs ethnoracial liberation behind 3D polarized lens and dangles revolution on strings. Together, he and other Latinf/x directed creatives sort through the media wasteland to refine a platform and mode of cultural transmission that, like Mexploitation cinema, traffic in diffuse transnational readerships and reset the terms of taste for art history in the Americas.

Tequila science fiction subdues discourses of discriminating judgment in artistic appraisals because the crude aftertaste of this spirit is paradoxically smooth *and* distasteful. Its applicability to this artistic showcase is necessary. After all, tequila makes no apologies, whether lingering on the lips of exhausted *vaqueros* (cowboys), fueling the fantasies of *cantantes* (singers), or breaking out into dive bar crowds chanting its name, made famous by the Mexican American rock band the Champs. This liquor shares in a transcultural exchange of entrepreneurs and celebrity ventures, with everyone from Eva Longoria to Kendall Jenner hawking the latest top-shelf version of their alcoholic wares. Rather, by returning to this drink's beginning as a "symbol of Mexican identity . . . that eventually embodied certain attributes associated with masculinity and the working classes," Latinf/x-minded creatives are perhaps the most appropriate messengers for the genre. If the origins of mainstream science fiction are pulp, then the origins of tequila science fiction are its crude, frothy forebear: pulque.[101] By moving closer to the life source of tequila in tequila science fiction, this sap offers the Latinx consumer a more cosmic finish. To get there, a return to the agave plant as a vestige of Indigenous knowledge takes this conversation back to where it started—a vertical axis driven toward the stars. This transplanetary-relational connectivity is an implicit yet unexplored dimension in what artists in this chapter reveal, and as such, its tethers to the US-Mexico borderlands and outer space must be reconsidered.

Cosmic Cantina

By means of a flashback, another late nineteenth-century vignette from the previous chapter is worth another look. On December 8, 1896, astronomer Andrew Ellicott Douglass oversaw the reinstallation of Lowell Observatory, which migrated from Flagstaff, Arizona, to Tacubaya, Mexico, for an impending study of Mars. In a photo, Douglass is shown providing "pulque for men" (see figure 4.3). It is not apparent that he imbibed it, but rather he observed the campesino worker consuming "a fermented, mildly alcoholic drink" drawn from the same blue agave plant that when distilled produces mezcal and tequila.[102] Ingested by Indigenous people for the purpose of ceremony, pulque "was a sacred mixture in Aztec culture that only the elderly, nursing mothers, and the ruling class were allowed to drink during religious festivals."[103] At the time of this photograph, a Mesoamerican past tangled with a modernizing late nineteenth-century Mexico and an expanding science industry grounded in the US Southwest. A railway connecting the two countries represented the future, anticipating new horizons for westward expansionists.[104] US visionaries excited by colonial travelogues eyed the south and the resources to be extracted there, from agriculture on the ground to the acuity of the sky. Pulque or its distilled pairing, tequila, was an "exotic curiosity," another curio in the nation's pursuit of manifest destiny and an expanding empire.[105]

By 1896 tequila was already circulating in US-Mexico border cities such as Rey de Copas in South Texas and Salon Palacio in West Texas.[106] Cantinas not only quenched a US thirst for this Mexican good but also provided a covert way to skirt Prohibition laws like the 1919 Volstead Act, according to Marie Sarita Gaytán in her groundbreaking study on tequila.[107] It is ironic that a drink so closely constitutive of "Mexican backwardness," because nourishment was derived from crude plant sap, as recited in *The Free Lance* in 1896, would later be a part of a nation's future trajectory.[108] Here US-Mexico scientific cooperation parlayed important astronomical data about Mars and thus provided greater insight into visual evidence of extraterrestrial life. Although this photograph from Douglass's camera is merely a record of leisure or exotic fodder over the drink satiating the tastes of vaqueros, campesinos, and tourists alike, it demonstrates how this nectar is potentially a transplanetary-relational outlet.

Because the cantina spatially mediated tequila consumption in the late nineteenth-century US-Mexico borderlands, its setting is rife with speculative potentialities. This overlap is not unusual in the history of science fiction motion pictures: The Mos Eisley from George Lucas's *Star Wars* (1977)—a film that was incidentally a Cabrales family staple—immediately comes to mind. In this classic scene, Luke Skywalker and Obi-Wan Kenobi go in search of pilots Han Solo and Chewbacca for safe passage through the Alderaan system. Whereas the rowdy bunch of liquor-swilling aliens provides

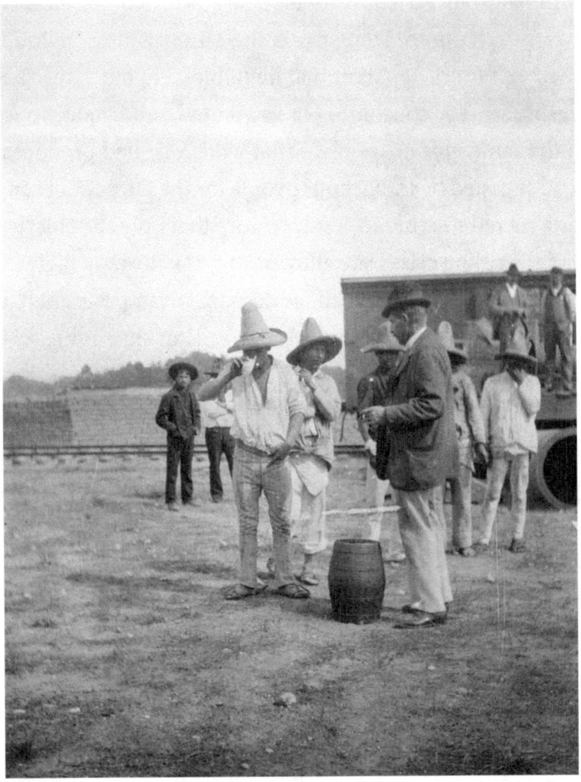

4.3 *Pulque for Men*, 1896. Photographic documentation of Lowell Observatory reinstallation in Tacubaya, Mexico. From the Andrew Ellicott Douglass Papers, Special Collections, University of Arizona.

a standout moment in the film, it is difficult to deny how US perceptions of Mexico underlie Lucas's portrayal. Here lawless aliens, downtrodden space adventurers, and crafty smugglers intermingle in the smoky underbelly of this spaceport, a proverbial border town. Though it is unclear whether tequila is served in the cinematic rendition, comedian Richard Pryor's homage to the classic scene in his short-lived NBC variety show from 1977 is less opaque.[109] Featuring performers festooned in original extraterrestrial costumes borrowed from Lucasfilm, the opening sequence of the scene is an homage to the Lucas blockbuster set on a small soundstage in Burbank, California. The camera slowly pans from the red neon sign announcing "Star Wars Bar" to the drunken pandemonium within it. In a cameo, Doikk Na'ts, one of the cantina's musicians, drunkenly gestures. The camera lingers

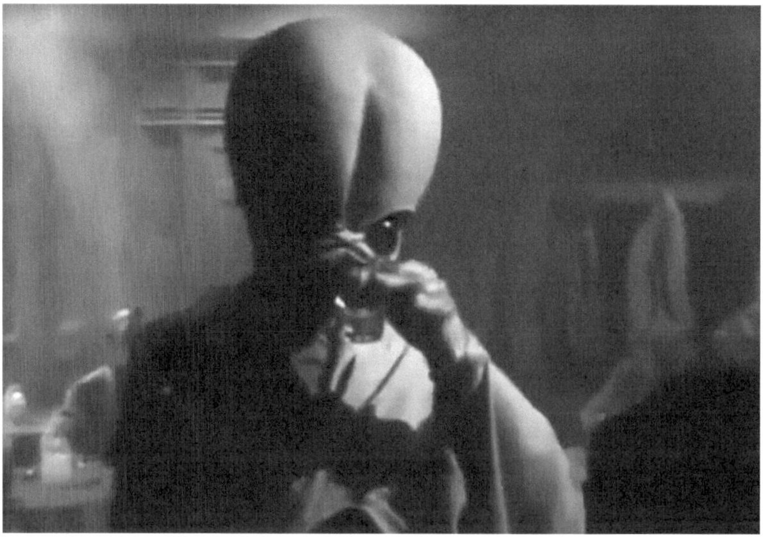

4.4 *Star Wars* sketch from *The Richard Pryor Show*, 1977, featuring original costumes from the motion picture, including a tequila-shooting Doikk Na'ts. Image courtesy of NBC-TV and YouTube.com.

as he swills tequila from a shot glass (see figure 4.4). The alien performance is comical even as the racialized tones intensify. Pryor, the barkeep, is the straight man in this cosmic cantina mash-up, playing it up for laughs. His performance further suggests that even in the 1970s, Afrofuturist parody is a clever foil to these alien antics.

Latinx visual idioms are recited, encoding the Mexican border bar into Pryor's bit. The funnyman, in turn, makes tequila an explicit drink of choice for aliens, though he resists any allusions to human illegality. Instead, what this *Star Wars* satire makes clear is that cinema's defining science fiction blockbuster was always in the presence of Mexico. Though it appears as a future libation, it was one clearly linked to the past. Thirsting for the Other, as hooks says, makes "pulque for men" a transplanetary relational matter.[110] Not only does that powerful nectar wet the tongues of aliens in a galaxy far, far away, but it also guides Douglass's transborder installation of the Lowell telescope. The astronomer and colonial settler, to the right in the frame, assumes a powerful position as observer, surveillant, and science industry capitalist controlling the terms of labor and taste. To his left, the campesino drinks. In the subtlety of his gesticulation, the worker resists the physical toll of heat exhaustion. His recuperation relies on an ancient communion with land and even sky, a performance of belonging attuned to the cosmos rather than to national identity. As he is nourished from the agave plant, his backward orientation around modernity, time, and advanced space science technology invites enmeshments with outer planets. He stands to rebuild Lowell Observatory, where the universe is brought closer to Tacubaya, to America, to Earth.

Tequila lingers on his lips as Mexican backwardness and forwardness, a drink of communing with cosmic deities and ancient ways. Whether agave is imbibed by a worker or an alien, its metaphysical and sacred power is key to unlocking the cosmos. The worker's presence in the photograph is about transforming how to belong to a planet and universe greater than the extractive logics of the Westernized colonial science enterprise. At once, he is a picture of technological inferiority and a relic of a modernizing Mexican state, yet gifted in knowledge about nineteenth-century astronomy. He represents an important envoy for tequila science fiction, as he is not only a symbol of exploitative labor around scientific study of the solar system but also a tastemaker who traverses borders on land and across sky with an unfiltered preference for that enchanting musk.

For artists in this chapter, tequila and science fiction go together like lime and salt. They join a transplanetary relationality doused in the firewater from the agave plant that deceptively goes down and hits hard. This tangy rush of flavor correlates with a Latinf/x predisposition for titillation, amazement, and excess where the sideshow, amusement park, concession stand, and cantina are a multimodal part of the art-making experience. By advancing visual vocabularies indebted to the lowbrow, low-budget, and lo-fi media, these artists see the strings, stand up to flat oppressive reality, and embrace the colors of 3D alterity. Such acumen is possible because the treasured gems of B-movie discards are lessons in both liberation and libation. Creatives rehearsing a Latinf/x attitude grasp the foundational amusements of avant-garde experimentation and early filmmaking and thus galvanize expressions that stress the pulp archive's consequences for *rasquache* and *domesticana* feminist aesthetics. By way of a postcredit scene, it is time to more carefully consider this repertoire's gender politics.

As with any B-movie, roles can be reversed, casting can be against type, and narrative closures can be retconned. Whether one reconsiders the vision of *comadres* on the moon or a young Chicana laughing off an attack of a trash monster, femme-presenting and cisgender women have been key to the fruits of agave nectar's symbolic meaning, consumptive pleasures, and speculative meaning. According to Gaytán, pulque was brewed under Spanish rule in the seventeenth century by Indigenous women licensed to serve one hundred customers. In turn, they "sold pulque from the doorways of their homes," thus evading regulation by authorities and subverting Spanish codes of law with a resistant activation of domesticity.[111] They were consequential to the gustatory politics of pulque, and in the present context, Latinas are undeniable fixtures of the fermented sap's distilled kin, tequila. Though unseen in the scientific endeavors at Tacubaya, their handiwork is perhaps present in that cup of nectar aiding these workers' construction of the armatures granting a grander search for intelligent life on Mars. The distasteful flavor that Latinf/x sensibilities favor (and that tequila science fiction profiles) is also a story about women's labor, history, and culture making. Simply, women of color have been critical to the decolonial and physical contestations magnifying how capitalism, space science, and technology tangle. In response, they produce creative outlets against oppressive controls over land, sky, and home.

As the next chapter shows, these stakes intensify around an all-too-familiar battleground being fought that takes Latina art, activism, and speculation to the front lines as the billionaire space race grows, reshaping the terms of the US-Mexico border from the home front to the aerial front.

5

Rage Against the Machine

THE ART OF LATINA SPACE FEMINISM AND PROTEST

Throughout this book we have contemplated the power of ocular relations: the way the machinic eye extends what our naked vision sees, the way "looking up" accesses a manner of transitioning in transplanetary relations on a vast scale. Thus, the terms *borders*, *geopolitics*, and *(il)legality* realign for a Latinidades reimagined in stranger forms and vertical ascension. Whether we consider two young women moongazing on the rooftop of their South Texas casita in Carmen Lomas Garza's *Camas para Sueños* (1985) (see plate 3) or the refractions of Orion interconnecting Southern California with Central America in Beatriz Cortez's *Cosmic Mirror (Sky over Los Angeles)* (2022) (see plate 25), turning skyward is a resource of fantasy, simultaneity, speculation, and liberation.

However, looking up at infinite skies is not always about endless possibility. Beyond what Garza and Cortez can see is the space detritus enveloping Earth.[1] These are the remains of a privatized orbital tourism industry gone wild, a boom in satellite broadband exploration, and a nascent lunar marketplace where astrogeology meets the extractive push for extraterrestrial mining and US outposts on the moon. The uptick in expanding private and for-profit aerospace tech companies demands another turn of the neck in Cortez's gestural sense. Although looking up may provoke existential wonder as it did for a young Alexander Maldonado spotting Halley's Comet from a horse-drawn carriage in 1910 (see figure 1.7), it also has the capacity to confront and face oppressive forces towering above us, some visible and others not.

This conflict intensified on an infamous cover of *Time* magazine, which digitally altered the Pulitzer Prize–winning photojournalist John Moore's picture of a Honduran child detained on the US-Mexico border (see plate 55).[2] The vacuous bloodstained backdrop sets the stage for her terror as she faces the stern if not indifferent downward gaze of Donald Trump. The digital cover art unapologetically represents Trump as the draconian embodiment of the zero-tolerance immigration policy, like a pillar of oppression. His superimposition on the photo stokes the child's fear and dread. The headline, "Welcome to America," comments on a paradox of American values, democracy, and ideology with a shamed chagrin.

The child's decontextualization and literal extraction from the border region are not without precedent as the post-1960s civil rights movement deployed children in national press coverage with the idea "that depictions of the weakest and most submissive victims facing the most brutal and active aggressors would be the most effective images to catalyze white interest," as Martin Berger argues.[3] He continues, "Such scenes . . . produced profound discomfort, given the racial identification that whites felt with the perpetrators of violence."[4] Showing scenes of anger and intimidation toward Black children did not necessarily result in mainstream social change, as "images of their physical abuse in the visual record of mid-twentieth-century America" were omitted by white editors.[5] The July 2, 2018, issue of *Time* is equally truncated, flattening the complexities of anti-immigrant and anti-Latinx hostilities that were further stoked under Trump's presidencies. Unlike post-1960s civil rights coverage, journalists would ease into emotive registers eliciting white neoliberal feelings about a failed immigration system and a nation in crisis over its jailing of children. The child's depiction visually personifies border violence, or what the front matter of the issue describes as a "symbol of the human cost of the Trump Administration's immigration-policy crackdown."[6] The magazine labeled her as a "2-year old Honduran girl crying"; she is unnamed, and her identity is just as elusive as her legal status. Reduced to an affectual identifier ("girl crying"), she is instrumentalized for *Time* readers through a familiar pathos reminiscent of the way civil rights photo documentation circulated in popular journalism with a uncomplicated reading of ethnoracial conflict.

In Moore's source photography found in the periodical's interior, the child looks up at a US border patrol agent apprehending her mother in McAllen, Texas, a location just opposite Reynosa, Mexico. Her direct stare is subtle but empowering as her vision confronts the imposing forces that grow above her. To capture this snapshot, Moore likely crouched in the field. His camera lowers in a way masked by the crimson magazine cover, which denies any depth or additional dimension. The Honduran girl, later identified as Yanela Sanchez, stands her ground and brings Moore's camera to her level, showing how her terrified gaze also conveys a command over public opinion, camera technology, and even digital photo editing.[7] A closer look shows how her teary stare reacts to dual pillars of oppression in the pages of *Time*, one visible (President Trump) and the other invisible (the border protection officer). Through the digital photo-collage format, the image reveals itself to be a double exposure, presenting twinned symbols of cruelty and xenophobia in the name of border security. As this periodical points to a nation's identity crisis over freedom and rule of law, links to the space industry and the history of civil rights protest hide behind the sensational headline.

In the aftermath of the first Trump presidency, dozens of people descended on the NASA Ames Research Facility in Mountain View, California, on March 15, 2021.[8] Renowned for its contributions to the Pioneer missions in the 1960s and the *Lunar Prospector* program through which lunar polar water was detected on the moon's south pole, Ames took on another alien mission. It was set to detain overflow from the nearly 8,100 unaccompanied minors arrested on the US-Mexico border.[9] Protesters working in collaboration with the San Jose–based activist organization SIREN (Service, Immigration Rights, and Education Network) decried this directive from the US Department of Health and Human Services (HHS). The administration under President Joe Biden sought to use facilities left vacant at Moffett Field, an availability created by the decline of NASA space missions. An official statement from the NASA Ames facility affirmed HHS personnel's intentions to tour the site as a possible location to "shelter" immigrant children at a place that was home to Hangar One, one of the largest freestanding airship enclosures. This moment captures NASA's entanglement with US Immigration and Customs Enforcement (ICE) in a maneuver that eerily mirrors alien capture plots in science fiction. However, this situation is more nuanced than that.

Carrying signs reading "Kids don't belong in cages" and "Who built the cages, Joe?," demonstrators appear to contest the cruelty of child detention and its continuation under the Biden administration (see plate 56).[10] Little addressed is NASA's role in treating these Mexican and Central American children as surplus, storing them like munitions among other military and aircraft defense technologies. This comparison is not entirely out of the question when one considers how multilayer insulation used to control heat and temperature exposure in spacecraft, satellites, and launch vehicles is repurposed to blanket these children while they slumber. Their bodies find warmth literally wrapped in high-tech materials adapted for high-orbit space missions in search of exoplanets, celestial objects, and even extraterrestrials. Such coverings make them more closely identifiable with Ames, the same facility that developed C-PICA, a state-of-the-art heat shield to protect high-orbit space assets in collaboration with Elon Musk's SpaceX company (a topic I return to momentarily).[11] By remaking the image of these children through the stuff of aerospace technology, NASA contradicts a first-world colonial supposition that Latinxs have little to do with space science and history. As this book demonstrates, in the Americas, labor, land, and even airspace have been hardwired into the modern space program. These intersections range from the transborder exchanges of Lowell Observatory in the late nineteenth century (as discussed in chapter 3) to the current establishment of mission control centers and launch sites dotting the US Southwest by a privatized space industry, with which this chapter is concerned. As this episode of immigrant strife, public protest, and militarized security details, NASA and HHS colluded. Mutually complicit, the two agencies have supported bidirectional trajectories for immigrant children's futures, one pointing toward downward expulsion and the other pointing toward the sky. As a result of these government conflations, it is possible to discern how these young detainees remake aerospace technology's visual imprint into something recognizable to their border existence in between horizontal and vertical directions. It is no longer the sole province of a US military industrial complex or space science enterprise; it is also theirs.

The subtleties of this truth can also be deduced from the issue of *Time* already discussed. Peggy Whitson's retirement from NASA is announced mere pages after Yanela's upward-turned cry is pictured.[12] Her mark in history as the first woman astronaut to command the International Space Station is commended, suggesting how NASA, immigration, border conflict, and even feminism commingle in the periodical's visual and textual fields. Taken as a whole, these corollaries nuance trite and oversimplified news bites that pit antigovernment protester against NASA, immigrant detainee against archconservative. This image archive even relates to past photo documentation of demonstrations waged by the Poor People's Campaign at Kennedy Space Center in Cape Canaveral, Florida, and by the National Welfare Rights Organization at the Manned Spacecraft Center in Houston, Texas, in July 1969, as discussed in chapter 2 (see figure 2.2). These clashes over the disproportionate investment of government dollars in defense spending in the 1960s, rather than "feed[ing] the future astronaut," must contend with a changing space industry.[13] Investments by NASA in private spaceflight companies like Blue Origin, Northrop Grumman, SpaceX, United Launch Alliance, and Virgin Galactic have increased competition, yielding unprecedented growth in the private and manufacturing sectors.[14] Ethnoracial publics and border communities directly impacted by global capitalism, relaxed trade regulations, and renewed urgency to dominate human spaceflight on a world stage are facing devastating ecological consequences to fulfill billionaires' visions of dragging humanity into "becom[ing] multiplanetary," as Elon Musk resolves.[15]

This chapter takes a page from those immigrant children shrouded in silvery space blankets to demonstrate how Latinx artists and activists find themselves plugged into the connective tissue of space barons and Silicon Valley tech entrepreneurs in ways inconceivable to Apollo-era minoritarian activists in 1969. If anything is for certain, it is that the future belongs to women of color, and specifically to a Latinx visual politics of femininities and gender expressions. These femmes remain on the front lines, developing their own visual vocabularies and tactical interventions in defense of children, climate, and the planet more broadly. These responses are not always captured in the "oppositional consciousness" framework of third-wave US feminism centering Chela Sandoval's polemic methodology of the oppressed.[16] They pivot on the "'science' of oppositional ideology," as she proposes borrowing from Louis Althusser, and intensify human-environment-technology conjunctions informing another kind of activist art about aerospace industrial threats in the sky.[17]

This chapter first details Latinx affinities for and the Latinx romance with NASA. I discern how women's domestic work and creative expression imported a Latina space feminism, the basis of which belongs to a visual field founded on the representational politics and mythos of space knowledges beginning with the Apollo missions and political activities surrounding the administration of President John F. Kennedy. With this imagery in the foreground, I outline how the prominence of two major private aerospace companies, SpaceX and Blue Origin, reactivated the US-Mexico border region, inciting new fictions and frictions about a future that betrays what Kennedy's Camelot once symbolized for a Cold War–era Mexican American generation.

As a result, Latinidades tangle and inflect differently with a deepening attention to a revitalizing and expanding space economy. Activating transplanetary relations with urgency, these creatives foster art and activism with unprecedented access to and intensifying awareness of these space science epicenters, billionaire tech giants, and creative community partnerships underwritten by a philanthropic pretense. Their corresponding artworks yield powerful and sometimes contradictory replies about a privatized aerospace industry intent on futures nearing certain disaster: residential dislocation, resource extraction, and other ecological and psychological harms.

By focusing on Latina space feminist and queer of color reactions to SpaceX and Blue Origin, I present the creative incubators formed to defend the Rio Grande Valley (RGV) from Musk's devastating thumbprint. Though artworks and curations by Celeste De Luna, Nansi Guevara, and Josué Rawmírez foreground this chapter, works by other feminist and transgender Latinx cultural workers who traffic in these circles and, in Texas, show an intimate awareness of the techno-dominance assailing home, land, and even the moon.[18] I turn my attention to mixed-media artist Clarissa Tossin, whose weavings based on Indigenous Brazilian craftwork examine how Amazon founder Jeff Bezos is complicit in astrogeological prospects in lunar mining. The chapter closes as transplanetary-relational approaches grow more urgent in light of the "second space race's" threat to aerial, spatial, and communal sovereignty over the skies. Because the space industry looks different at present, Latina space feminists' incipient knowledge reacts with a corresponding oppositional gaze guided by a vertical arc. Occupying the front lines, they foster fields of cultural exchange at art, science, and speculative intersections that defend Indigenous lands and precious ecologies for a Latinx future in jeopardy.

Dead Kennedys

A black-and-white gelatin silver print captures Gregorita Aguilar in the private sanctuary of her home (see figure 5.1). Aguilar was photographed by Morrie Camhi in 1977; her half-rounded eyes look to the right of the frame. Her visage is partially lit by the New Mexican sun. Aguilar's home is in Los Ojos, a small and mainly Indigenous and Latinx community in the northern part of the state flanked by the Jicarilla Apache reservation and the Southern Colorado borderlands. It is difficult to know what ignites the sparkle in her face. What does she see out that window? Her hands gather around the tapered ends of fabric. Hers is a critical joyousness, a recoiling break from impending domestic work signaled by the sewing machine. The modern technology's power grows at the foreground of the composition. With the waves of cloth gathered at the right of the frame, Camhi's lens captures her labor and creativity as a garment worker. Aguilar pinches the folds of fabric, proving that she is *digital* in a handed sense of the term. Her skill set shifts from the woven textures of textile to the machinic interventions of home sewing. The equipment's presence is a modern symbol complicating a scene of unhampered needlecraft.

The textile accenting her workspace appears to recall Spanish colonial loom practices from the sixteenth century. As Churro sheep were introduced as livestock for food and wool in the New Mexican countryside, yarn-spun wares (including blankets and carpets produced by Indigenous and mestiza women in northern New Mexico) helped to fortify a Spanish settler colonial system of commodity and trade. The varied bands in the style of Rio Grande weavings come from a fiber technology predicated on Hispanic lifeways since the sixteenth century.[19] Perhaps unbeknownst to Camhi is the way this is not another "classically constructed, intimate portrait" of Mexican Americans, as Hal Fischer recounts about the series, but a planetary-minded Hispana sewing accoutrements from the wool of livestock to gift warmth. Though a blanket is hardly the chief equipment of human spaceflight, other transplanetary-relational outlets enliven her domestic interior.[20]

A portrait of President John F. Kennedy hangs prominently in Aguilar's home space. Rendered in plushy black velvet, it is an honorific homage to the slain US president, a sign of devotion further punctuated by the crucifix adorning the hanging's upper right edge. Similar to the way Catholic paraphernalia attaches spiritual meaning, her ornaments traverse the ordinary and the divine. Her cross implores the heavens and thus demarcates an interior stage for faith, loss, and, in particular, patriotism. Aguilar's portrait is a refraction of twin Kennedys, one that occupies her day-to-day reality and the other a mirrored projection. By demonstrating how even the most sacred of altars can come in the tackiest of forms, her home harbors the armatures of self-presentation and a performance of national grief. Here, her appearance before Camhi's camera is a study in becoming American as she portrays respectability through dual reflections of Kennedy, one conceived in a kitschy collectible and another in the representational logics of national mourning.

Camhi's portrait of Gregorita Aguilar unveils the manifold ways grieving Hispanic publics in the US Southwest memorialize the late president. While Camhi completed his *Los Ojos* series in 1977, Mexican American photographer Louis Carlos Bernal was also producing pictures about rural

5.1 Morrie Camhi, *Gregorita Aguilar at Home, Los Ojos, New Mexico, 1977*, 1977. Gelatin silver print photograph, 12 × 14⅜ in. Gift of the Mexican American Legal Defense and Education Fund, Center for Creative Photography, University of Arizona. Copyright Sharon Camhi.

barrio subjects in his native Arizona. Though born in Douglas, a border town proximate to Sonora, Mexico, he grew up in Phoenix. Later he served on the art faculty at Pima Community College, teaching photography. His appetite for the quotidian pacing and banal tics of barrio everyday life, or what David William Foster calls "idyllic familiness," unveiled the discreet and intimate corridors in diverse locales like Douglas, Arizona; Silver City, New Mexico; El Paso, Texas; and Lubbock, Texas (among others).[21] Women's domestic interiors are a recurrent theme in his corpus. His *Dos Mujeres, Douglas, Arizona* (1978) remains a standout among his chromogenic prints, inspiring curatorial and art historical attention. In it, a young woman is depicted with needle in hand mending a dress in a portrait couplet with her sister, who occupies the recessed bedroom. However, the camera's shifting depth intensifies the *calendario* above her head with the gravitas of Roland Barthes, making it a punctum demanding closer attention.[22] The print keepsake hung on the green-hued wall, emblazoned "Cia Harinera Estrella," was likely secured from a local proprietor in Agua Prieta, a border town opposite Douglas in Sonora. With a bold typographical emphasis on *Harinera Estrella*, the merchant brands itself as offering top-tier, high-quality milled flour, which had supported foodways spanning the Americas since ancient times. Its textual association further imagines consumption with *Estrella*, or star. Activating the mundane corridors of this Arizona home, this literal citation implies something greater, something cosmic about this border region and, conversely, the women belonging to it.[23]

The seamstresses in Camhi's and Bernal's photography elevate domestic work, proving that handicraft is spacecraft. Though these connections may appear far-fetched in terms of the art, science, and speculative conjunctions surveyed in this book thus far, women of color have stitched alternative forays into the cosmos. After all, Playtex garment workers were crucial to the production of the modern pressurized NASA space suit.[24] Their accomplished practices in precision sewing and textile manufacturing made women like Hazel Fellows a crucial contributor to the Apollo program space missions (see figure 5.2). This "digital" expressivity is a kind of homemaking hacktivism recoding domesticity and handicraft into otherworldly coordinates. Garment work practiced in this way appeals to the transplanetary-relational possibilities of Amalia Mesa-Bains's "domesticana sensibility," in which homely needlepoint is a cosmic matter that can compel activist attentions.[25]

Consider another Bernal photograph, *Rosie Siqueiros, Barrio Anita, Tucson, Arizona* (see figure 5.3). We see a young woman at ease as she leans into the plushy crimson embrace of her couch. Her home furnishing centers Bernal's frame, crowded by stacks of folded laundry. An ironing board sits upright in a state of rest. It also reclines like Siqueiros, perforating a living environment with the symbols of leisure. Her frontal stare is sensitive and careful, sharing a visage that is cosmetically adorned and thus labored. Her hands are clasped, tense, hinting at an anxious if not uncertain commitment to Bernal's camera. Just above her line of sight is a nearly parallel portrait of President Kennedy. As in Camhi's depiction of Aguilar from one year prior,

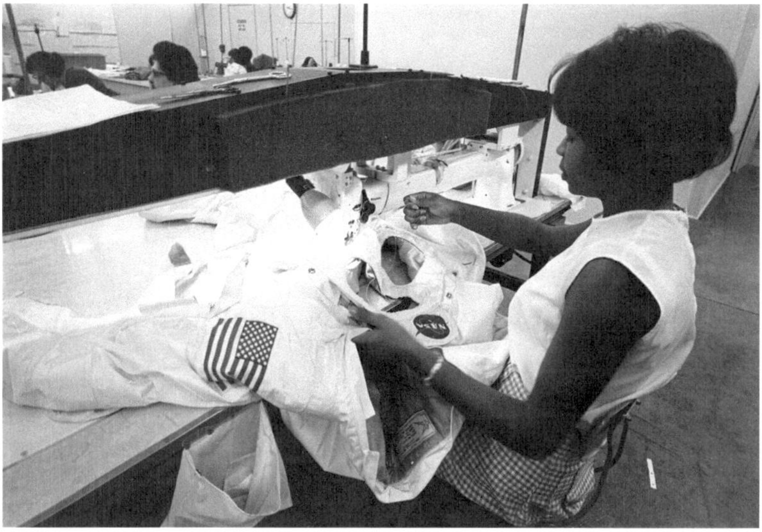

5.2 Precision seamstress Hazel Fellows adds final touches to the Apollo A7L space suit at the International Latex Corporation in Dover, Delaware, on August 9, 1968. Photograph courtesy of the Smithsonian National Air and Space Museum (NASM NASA-68-H-457).

Hispana self-definition is a pursuit lined with velvety pathways and affordable fabrics. Siqueiros's physical comportment nearly shares a vertical axis with the twinned Kennedy images, suggesting a symmetry with the slain president. Her visibility relies on a kind of commingling with Kennedy, and like Aguilar, she arranges a self-presentation in a metonymic shorthand of US citizenship and motifs of democratic ideology. As Jennifer Wingate notes, "The red accents in JFK's tie and in the US flag beside him also visually link him with the sofa on which Siqueiros sits and the pillow on her lap."[26] In this chromatic schema, the material culture occupying Siqueiros's personal domain nuances the "devotional icons" recited in Mesa-Bains's *domesticana* ruminations about "the day-to-day experience of working-class Chicanas."[27] In this quiet corner of Tucson, veneration is not limited to Catholic iconography or the frills of the divine. Included, too, are the relics of Camelot and a president gone too soon. What that national narrative meant for these Mexican Americans' stakes in the modern space race requires a different but related pursuit of Kennedy, whose image leapt off walls of black velvet and onto the brick-and-mortar surrounds of the everyday.

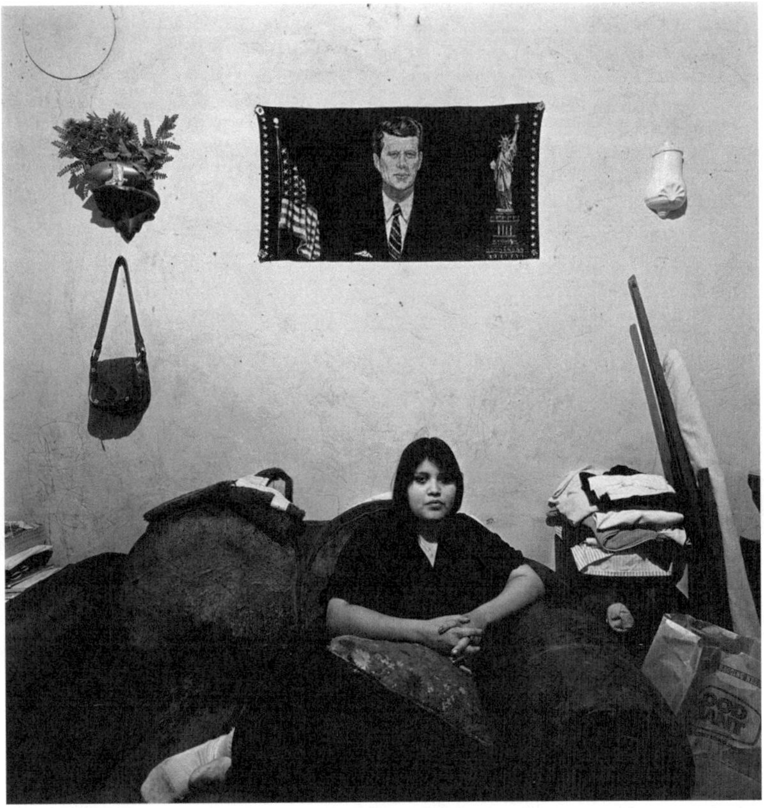

5.3 Louis Carlos Bernal, *Rosie Siqueiros, Barrio Anita, Tucson, Arizona*, 1978. Chromogenic print, 9¹⁄₁₆ × 9¹⁄₁₆ in. Gift of the Mexican American Legal Defense and Educational Fund, Center for Creative Photography, University of Arizona. Copyright Lisa Bernal Brethour and Katrina Ann Bernal.

A mural found just one block north of Whittier Boulevard, that legendary LA thoroughfare of Chicanx activism, cultural production, and civil rights struggle, brought Kennedy—and, by extension, the Apollo missions—to bear on transplanetary relations. Roger Minick's black-and-white photograph *Community Center Building, East Los Angeles, 1978*, taken the same year that Bernal was also contemplating the place of women, labor, and homemaking, unfurls an unusual yet cosmic crossroad (see figure 5.4). Most distinctive is the way that this Chicanx mural defines wall painting with political urgency in the present. The piece reimagines

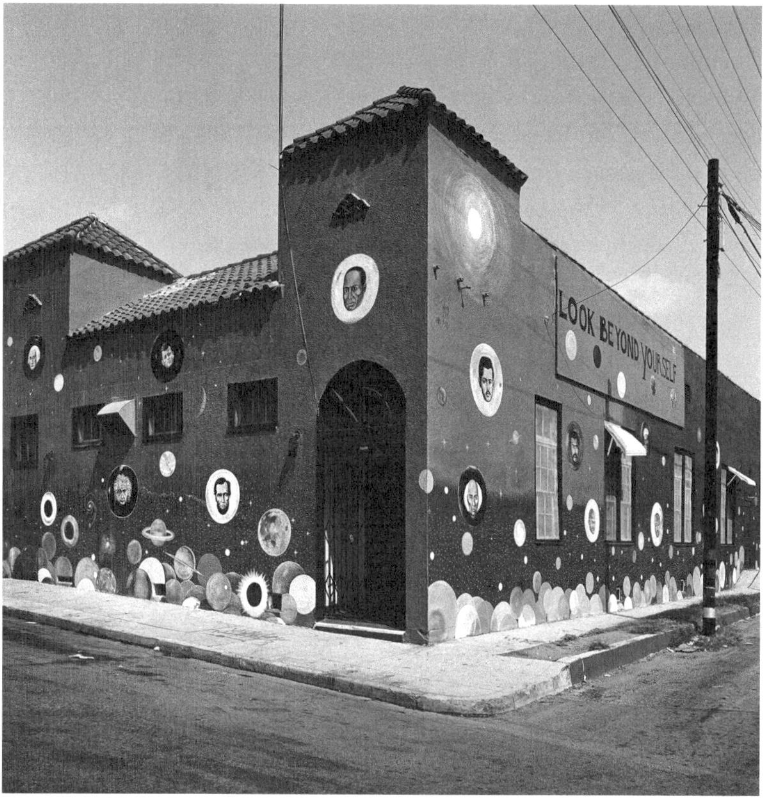

5.4 Roger Minick, *Community Center Building, East Los Angeles, 1978*, 1978. Black-and-white photograph, 10⅝ × 10⁷⁄₁₆ in. Courtesy of the artist.

the "unraveling [of] the persistent territoriality of hegemonic systems and architectural normalcy," as Jennifer González argues.[28] Nonnormative in its speculative provocations of Chicanx muralism, this artwork reiterates how creatives at that time adapted to cosmic modifiers and forwarded a visual library of astronomical references. Minick's photograph continues to affirm how territorial definitions of barrio urbanism demand refinement because Latinx artists sought modes of public address in vertical ascension (see chapter 2).

Minick's photo record captures a work that scales skyward and negotiates optical tensions for the viewer. Telescopic views and starry distances operate like a stand-in for a science and technology education afforded the more affluent residents of the city. Like a counterobservatory, the artwork is no passive exercise in urban beautification. A barrio demographic is confronted and called out in street-facing signage that reads "Look Beyond Yourself." The textual declaration in thickly laden lettering is a command and a declaration. To look *beyond* is not only a beckoning to the viewer but also a transplanetary-relational directive. Hailing the public to gaze upward and outward, the textual address is a callout of both the stars and public history. Consider how the site, built in 1927, hosted the insurgent activities of the National Synarchist Union's Southern California chapter.[29] Emerging in the turbulent aftermath of the Mexican Revolution, which resulted in Mexico's New Left (Partido Revolucionario Institucional) controlling the nation's governance until 2000, this right-wing movement sought a return to the country's prerevolution grand design.[30] The union praised moral values and lauded Catholic principles in a way that promoted fascist sympathies, according to some scholars, which alarmed many during the US interwar period. In that building, Synarchist chapter members gathered around a vision of a Mexico that went against the clock and thus imagined a national politics of what could have been. Meetings at 830 Hicks Avenue were guided by a transnational urgency and a retrospective eye.

A decade later, the building would continue its patriotic tradition. In the postwar era, it became a Veterans of Foreign Wars headquarters, Post 1013. The organization hosted Pearl Harbor Remembrance Day and a film screening of *Survival Under Atomic Attack* in 1953 and a breakfast coordinated by the women's auxiliary with the aim of "sewing for the Veterans and Pacific State Hospitals" in service to the greater Lincoln Heights area in 1964.[31] To say the building was a purveyor of science fiction activity is perhaps a stretch. It was, nevertheless, an arbiter of various political factions forming in LA during the first half of the twentieth century, simply hinting at how Mexican nationalism, the threat of atomic annihilation, and wartime service members were strangely interconnected like patchwork stitched together in an unassuming Spanish colonial structure in East LA. Home to machinations about a world to come or a world to end, these assemblies were fitting time stamps for what Chicanx muralist Richard Haro would articulate on the building's outsides.

Having produced *The Artist* and, most especially, *Outer Space* at Estrada Courts in 1974 and 1977 (see plates 8 and 9), Haro continued his speculative expression and attention to astrophotography visualization for eastside residents in LA. The building's mural aesthetic is a continuation of his repertoire, a barrio futurity rendered in images of eclipses, spiral galaxies, and other nebulae. His aesthetic language benefited from NASA satellite imagery reproduced in the popular media and science magazines. But by positioning the viewer in a skyward direction, Haro ensures that barrio residents, too, can envisage the *beyond*, extending their reach outside this ethnic enclave. The celestial bodies and uncanny cosmic occurrences portrayed streetside illuminate the transplanetary-relational way Haro redirects geopolitical stakes from turf wars to star wars. Thinking *beyond* is another artist appealing to an urban demographic circa 1978, urging it to confront the meaning of the Apollo missions for *el movimiento*. Haro's mural, installed one block from Ruben Salazar Park, a green space where the *Los Angeles Times* reporter by that name was assassinated, elevates muralism to the vicissitudes of space art, reminiscent of large-scale works by Chesley Bonestell, Robert McCall, and Eric Sloan. While I will not rehearse here an earlier argument from chapter 2 about these corollaries, his piece invites another consideration of the astronomical tendencies of Chicanx public art iconography and the heroic pantheons included within them. Haro's motifs resonate with referential signifiers about US democracy, science, and the import of technology in ways previously found in Mexican American women's domestic interiors.

This nimble aesthetic crystallizes in another Minick photograph titled *Four Young Boys with Lincoln, Kennedy, and Einstein, East Los Angeles, 1978* (see figure 5.5). In this visual document, we are presented with a more detailed view of the mural, which forms a cosmic backdrop for a quartet of adolescent boys. The young men's tough exteriors, impenetrable glares, and streetwear adornment offset a celestial gestalt about deep space. This association between homeboy and solar system stands out within the photo lexicon typical of Oscar Castillo's, Luis Garza's, and John Valadez's cameras preoccupied with barrio urbanism.[32] A pantheon of historical icons rises around the youth, profiling the faces of science, technology, and democracy's future. Orbs appear honoring Albert Einstein and Abraham Lincoln in radiant portraits. They glimmer amid the blanket of stars. With knees bent and faces doused by the LA sun, the quartet of boys leans into the stucco facade and appears visually ascendant. Their coordinated postures make a collective statement, a *carnalismo* (cholo brotherhood) physicalized in the ether of elevated scale. They pose before Saturn. The planet's signature ring peeks out, encircling them in its orbit.[33]

By aligning them with a major planetary finding of Galileo's astronomical study, Minick captures these young people leaning their bodies into the wall painting, anchoring themselves to this opening of the cosmos and technology of tomorrow. Eerily, his photograph is an echo of Haro's other mural, *Outer Space* at Estrada Courts. But unlike those depicted in

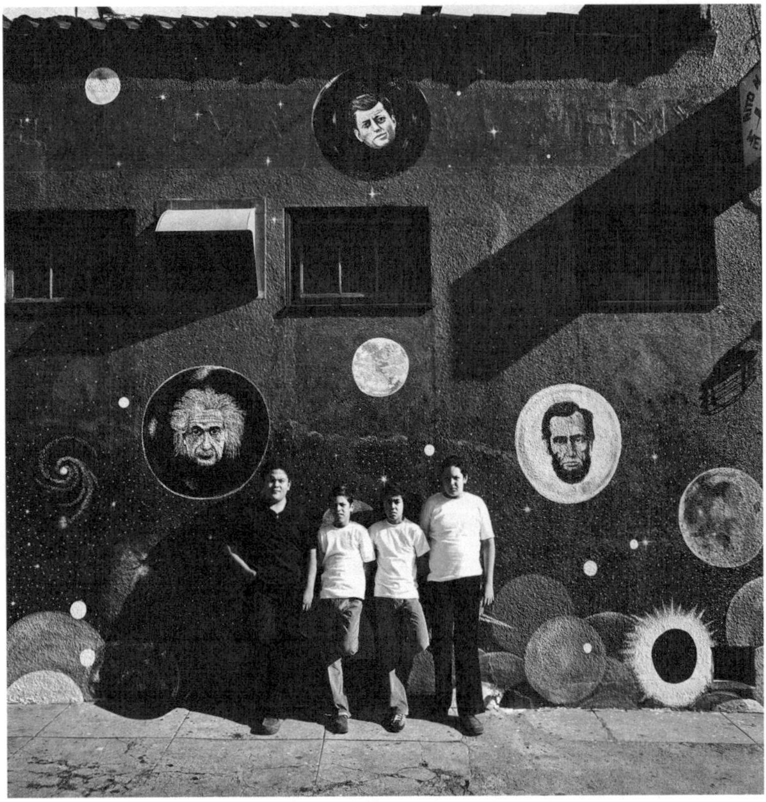

5.5 Roger Minick, *Four Young Boys with Lincoln, Kennedy, and Einstein, East Los Angeles, 1978*, 1978. Gelatin silver print photograph, $10\frac{5}{8} \times 10\frac{7}{16}$ in. Courtesy of the artist.

Haro's precursory piece, these youths are no flattened representation of future homeboys; they *are* future homeboys. With bodies weighted and brows furrowed, they convey an urban existence that belongs to another world, another timeline. By appearing someplace *beyond*, they navigate the rings of Saturn and rest somewhere between the figurative pillars of general relativity (Einstein) and abolition (Lincoln). Freedom of thought, freedom from gravity, and freedom from enslavement are interlinked, and liberatory outcomes are answered by outer space. In this way, *la raza*'s forward progress is as indebted to the discovery of quantum mechanics as to archaeology of the ancient Americas. After all, at the time this photo was taken, modern Mexico was shaken by the accidental discovery of the Templo Mayor, where the stone of Coyolxauhqui, the Aztec moon goddess, was excavated. Her unearthing further enshrines the lunar deity in a Chicana feminist episteme to recover, remake, and reinvent the self despite dismembering world violence. As Gloria Anzaldúa states, she is a skyward bridge: "I stare up at the moon, Coyolxauhqui, and its light in the darkness. I seek a healing image, one that re-connects me to others."[34] Whereas reviewer Hal Fischer argues that Minick's photo aesthetic "pits the mundane against the marvelous," it is quite the opposite; it reveals how the astronomical, archaeological, and science-fictional inform everyday Latinidades.[35] Similar to what Darko Suvin calls "cognitive estrangement," which "frames the world as constructed by human agency, revealing the potential for change," transformation in being, perception, and even relating to the universe belongs to East LA, and Haro makes this barrio futurist statement clear.[36] This interfacing with transplanetary relations is further punctuated by the third portrait completing this mural's heroic trifecta. The towering visage of John F. Kennedy appears above the teens, showering his radiance on them.

No longer fabricated in rolls of black velvet, Kennedy is reimagined through stucco; the mural positions the slain US president as the pinnacle of supernatural geniuses orbiting the barrio. At the highest reaches of the wall, he retains a privileged position, displayed above these teens like a north star. Celestial, if not deified, in his portrayal, Kennedy epitomizes the *beyond* as a symbol of futurity, a representation of the modern space program, and evidence of aerospace technological advancements that "[stand] as a monument to American ingenuity and the embodiment of [his] lunar aspirations."[37] Negotiating public service and private veneration, Minick's camera symbolically merges these urban homeboys with Mexican American seamstresses and garment workers of color. This photograph provokes a curious kind of image archive for Kennedy. The afterlife of his portrait belongs to the streets, the home space, and even the stars. But what to make of this Latinx investment in cultural memorialization of the late president? Is it a bid for Americanization? Or, as Haro's mural hints, a reach for the *beyond* (*más allá*)? The answer requires a brief look back at the Kennedy administration.

Viva Kennedy | Viva NASA

The relationship between candidate Kennedy and Mexican Americans begins with Texas. A set of social reformers emerged as political leaders, galvanized by a postwar America, answering to the educational opportunity afforded through the GI Bill, and heightened by newfound wealth through homeownership, vocational training, and other career pathways into the middle class. Under their purview, it was possible to jump-start entry into the electorate as a recognizable voting demographic. Initially, Mexican American political organizations responded to overtures from Richard Nixon's campaign: "Latino supporters had urged the Republican to make a strong appeal to the Spanish-speaking community" in the former California congressman's 1960 presidential bid.[38] According to historian Ignacio García, Nixon rejected this strategy. However, that prompted the Kennedy campaign to redirect outreach activities to a promising field of Mexican American Democrats. García concedes that there is little documentation indicating Kennedy's position, though the candidate's brother, Robert, agreed with the initiative.[39]

The campaign turned to Santa Barbara–born Carlos McCormick, who was tapped to handle "Latin American affairs."[40] His primary point of contact was San Antonio County Commissioner Albert Peña Jr. Peña agreed to spearhead this political imperative, but under a number of conditions, including the power to bypass the local Democratic Party with direct communications, high-level appointments for Mexican Americans in the administration, and elimination of the poll tax, a fee charged to all individuals intent on voting.[41] With Robert Kennedy's compromise, Peña leaned directly into the American GI Forum activities. The group's 1960 convention resulted in a number of civil rights resolutions and an enthusiastic reception for "Viva Kennedy" clubs, which targeted thirty-two states.[42] Although these clubs were dispersed and thus unevenly resourced, they found a groundswell of support throughout Texas and caught on with Mexican American communities in the RGV, even sidestepping the local Democratic chapter, which "feared the rising number of Mexican American registered voters . . . uncomfortable with their new assertiveness."[43]

The proliferation of Viva Kennedy clubs likely grew from a heterogeneous and politically frustrated Latinx public whose members were "civic-minded individuals, old reformers, hardcore Democrats, and novice individuals motivated by an impressive Democratic nominee."[44] Simply, there was something about Kennedy's national profile that registered with them. As García surmises, "He was a Democrat . . . sympathetic to Latin America, and . . . he was a liberal, and as such, sympathetic to the poor."[45] This confluence, combined with his Irish Catholic background and a First Lady fluent in Spanish, fueled a presidential image that was dynamic and manifold, certifying a Mexican American public as "Kennedy Democrats."

Hints of this unexpected political affinity appear in a photograph taken on November 21, 1963. One day before his murder in a Dallas motorcade,

Kennedy is documented by photojournalist Gustavo Garza at a dinner hosted by the League of United Latin American Citizens (LULAC) at the Rice Hotel in downtown Houston (figure 5.6).[46] Awarded an honorary membership in this historic organization, Kennedy is met with the ambient sounds of mariachi musicians singing "Kennedy! Kennedy!"[47] These joyous harmonies are painfully premonitory, however, unaware of the mournful corridos to come. Willie Lopez, who composed songs for Conjunto Florida, would grieve Kennedy in song with lyrics reflecting on the late president's *retrato* (portrait) on his living room wall, an appropriate sentiment given the ways in which a commemorative language unfurled in Mexican American home interiors and on rolls of black velvet.[48] Lopez's sentiment seconds what García remembered from his elegiac encounters: "It was not uncommon for me to see in the homes of friends or acquaintances old newspaper pictures of Kennedy prominently displayed alongside those of *la virgen de Guadalupe*. . . . Even my mother had one in our living room."[49] These recollections reaffirm how the mythos of Camelot and all that it represented was interred, housed, and audibly sounded, with renewed importance for Mexican American domestic expression.

That evening, bilingual translations also came in the form of First Lady Jacqueline Kennedy's opening remarks in Spanish, which were received "with wild cheers and applause."[50] Garza's photo of the grinning first family affirms a kind of racialized anointment bestowed by *gritos* (high-pitched Mexican shouts), Tejanx sights and sounds from the largest social reform organization for people of Latin American descent. Behind the pair is the mariachi band strumming their guitars, serenading these patriotic representatives of national patrimony, political visibility, and even the modern space program. Kennedy's appearance at the Rice Hotel was not his debut, however. A year prior he was there following his famed speech "We Choose to Go to the Moon." Before crowded stands at Rice Stadium on September 12, 1962, he famously said, "This generation does not intend to founder in the backwash of the coming age of space. We mean to be a part of it—we mean to lead it."[51]

His comments that autumn day were not limited to empty callouts about the infinite promise of space. He collated the future of human spaceflight with state politics, saying, "We meet at a college noted for knowledge, in a city noted for progress, in a state noted for strength, and we stand in need of all three."[52] This rhetoric was in part political stagecraft to invoke reminders that his running mate, Vice President Lyndon B. Johnson, was a longtime Texas civil servant. It was also informed by a two-day stint where the

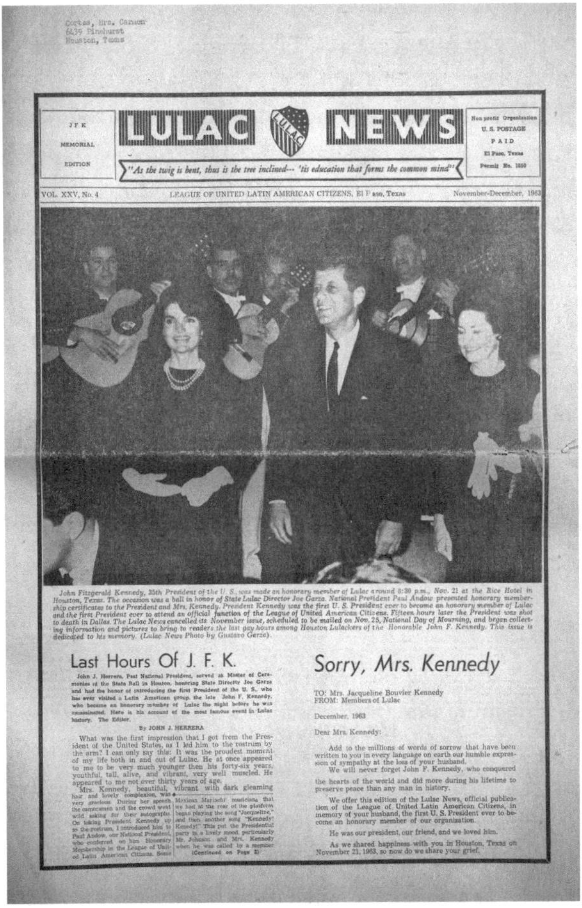

Cortes, Mrs. Carmen
6439 Pinehurst
Houston, Texas

JFK MEMORIAL EDITION

LULAC NEWS

"As the twig is bent, thus is the tree inclined--- 'tis education that forms the common mind"

Non profit Organization
U. S. POSTAGE
PAID
El Paso, Texas
Permit No. 1850

VOL. XXV, No. 4 — LEAGUE OF UNITED LATIN AMERICAN CITIZENS, El Paso, Texas — November-December, 1963

John Fitzgerald Kennedy, 35th President of the U. S., was made an honorary member of Lulac around 8:30 p.m., Nov. 21 at the Rice Hotel in Houston, Texas. The occasion was a ball in honor of State Lulac Director Joe Garza. National President Paul Andow presented honorary membership certificates to the President and Mrs. Kennedy. President Kennedy was the first U. S. President ever to become an honorary member of Lulac and the first President ever to attend an official function of the League of United American Citizens. Fifteen hours later the President was shot to death in Dallas. The Lulac News cancelled its November issue, scheduled to be mailed on Nov. 25, National Day of Mourning, and began collecting information and pictures to bring to readers the last gay hours among Houston Lulackers of the Honorable John F. Kennedy. This issue is dedicated to his memory. (Lulac News Photo by Gustavo Garza).

Last Hours Of J. F. K.

John J. Herrera, Past National President, served as Master of Ceremonies of the State Ball in Houston, honoring State Director Joe Garza and had the honor of introducing the first President of the U. S. who has ever visited a Latin American group, the late John F. Kennedy, who became an honorary member of Lulac the night before he was assassinated. Here is his account of the most famous event in Lulac history. The Editor.

By JOHN J. HERRERA

What was the first impression that I got from the President of the United States, as I led him to the rostrum by the arm? I can only say this: It was the proudest moment of my life both in and out of Lulac. He at once appeared to me to be very much younger then his forty-six years, youthful, tall, alive, and vibrant, very well muscled. He appeared to me not over thirty years of age.

Mrs. Kennedy, beautiful, vibrant with dark gleaming hair and lovely complexion, was very gracious. During her speech the cameramen and the crowd went wild asking for their autographs. On taking President Kennedy up to the rostrum, I introduced him to Paul Andow, our National President, who conferred on him Honorary Membership in the League of United Latin American Citizens. Some Mexican Mariachi musicians that we had at the rear of the platform began playing the song "Jacqueline," and then another song "Kennedy! Kenedy!" This put the Presidential party in a lively mood particularly Mr. Johnson and Mrs. Kennedy when he was called by a member

(Continued on Page 2)

Sorry, Mrs. Kennedy

TO: Mrs. Jacqueline Bouvier Kennedy
FROM: Members of Lulac

December, 1963

Dear Mrs. Kennedy:

Add to the millions of words of sorrow that have been written to you in every language on earth our humble expression of sympathy at the loss of your husband.

We will never forget John F. Kennedy, who conquered the hearts of the world and did more during his lifetime to preserve peace than any man in history.

We offer this edition of the Lulac News, official publication of the League of United Latin American Citizens, in memory of your husband, the first U. S. President ever to become an honorary member of our organization.

He was our president, our friend, and we loved him.

As we shared happiness with you in Houston, Texas on November 21, 1963, so now do we share your grief.

5.6 Gustavo Garza, *LULAC News* photo documentation of President John F. Kennedy and First Lady Jacqueline Bouvier Kennedy, November 21, 1963. *LULAC News*, Herrera Papers, MSS 0160, Houston Public Library, Houston Metropolitan Research Center.

president's meetings about the moon-shot program were accompanied by leading space scientists and five astronauts, Gus Grissom and Alan Shepard among them.[53] Tours of NASA's Manned Spacecraft Center facilities (the present-day Johnson Space Center) showcased "science-fiction-like gadgets" and "space machines," according to the press, and, in turn, countered Cold War pessimism with future promise.[54] Texas was there to help Kennedy beat the Soviets, and Houston was the city to do it.

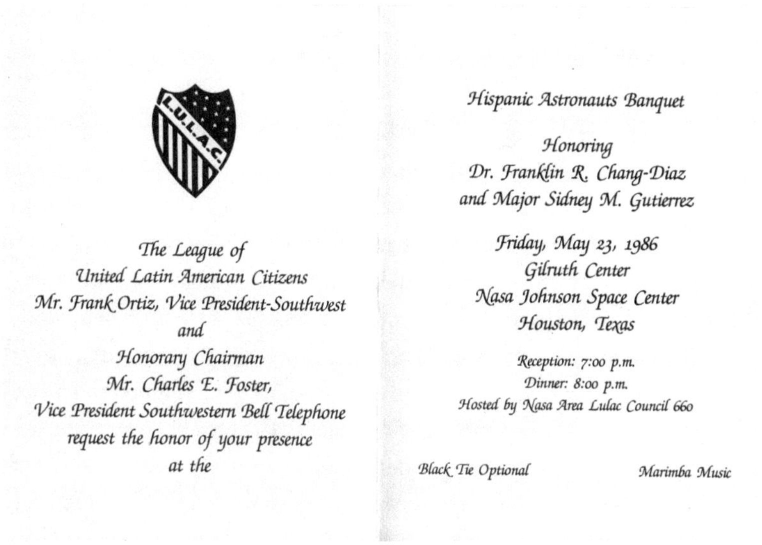

The League of
United Latin American Citizens
Mr. Frank Ortiz, Vice President-Southwest
and
Honorary Chairman
Mr. Charles E. Foster,
Vice President Southwestern Bell Telephone
request the honor of your presence
at the

Hispanic Astronauts Banquet

Honoring
Dr. Franklin R. Chang-Diaz
and Major Sidney M. Gutierrez

Friday, May 23, 1986
Gilruth Center
Nasa Johnson Space Center
Houston, Texas

Reception: 7:00 p.m.
Dinner: 8:00 p.m.
Hosted by Nasa Area Lulac Council 660

Black Tie Optional — Marimba Music

5.7 LULAC Astronauts Banquet invitation, May 23, 1986. LULAC Regional Papers, Council No. 660, box 1, folder 40, MSS 0353, Houston Public Library, Houston Metropolitan Research Center.

However, the Apollo program could not have been accomplished without people like Albert Peña Jr. and Carlos McCormick, whose fierce mobilization of Viva Kennedy clubs assisted Kennedy in securing the White House and, in turn, fostered his public vision to take humanity up there. And so LULAC's banquet was political theater enfolding a project of Mexican Americanization and civic engagement with defense and space industries. In this way, Kennedy sparked Latinxs across the US Southwest to reach for higher places, those conceived in state politics, inside the White House, and even on a perpendicular axis.

It is no wonder that LULAC would return to this ascendant formula with enthusiasm over aerospace and space exploration. It was, after all, modeled for them decades earlier, though now it had returned with a post-Apollo viewpoint. On May 23, 1986, Houston-based LULAC Council 660 hosted the Hispanic Astronauts Banquet at the NASA Johnson Space Center (see figure 5.7), where astronauts Franklin Chang-Diaz and Colonel Sidney McNeill Gutierrez were honored.[55] This grouping performed a kind of cultural patrimony mindful of a Kennedy inheritance of an electorate nourished from those grassroots Viva Kennedy campaigns and the realization of the Apollo missions. This banquet forwarded an organizational identification with tomorrow, an off-Earth vision that the slain president first imagined in Houston and for Houston.

However, the timing of the event was strange under such painful circumstances. The *Challenger* disaster had occurred a few months earlier on January 28, 1986. The entire crew perished in NASA's first major mission with multiple fatalities. This national trauma must have hung thick in the air and been awkwardly present, discomforting the night's honorees and the NASA Johnson Space Center staff. In short, this gathering met tragedy with stylish black-tie gala ensembles. The self-described "NASA Area LULAC Council" might have felt charged with or possibly emboldened to address this incident, assuaging public grief on behalf of Texans of Latin American descent more broadly.[56] Though these observations are more circumstantial than evidentiarily salient, it is worth considering how the *Challenger* disaster and LULAC's organizational identification with Kennedy could have been equal parts about claiming US citizenry and American patriotism as they performed loss under the auspices of the NASA organization and before other astronaut compatriots. Feeling for the nation in this way hints at the complex cultural work of Latinx grief, whether for a slain president or for fallen astronauts. Despite being omitted from the story of the space race, this multiethnic public had long mourned for a future promised to them as Kennedy Democrats, as voters, as Tejanxs, and even as women. After all, the *Challenger* mission accomplished something rare by including astronauts Judith Resnik and Christa McAuliffe, the latter of whom was touted as the first schoolteacher in outer space. On the ground, Viva Kennedy also achieved success in South Texas because of the work of Mexican American women like Estela Lone Treviño, who was elected as the vice president of the Edinburg chapter, a rare accomplishment in statewide races.[57] Her ascendance in the Democratic establishment does not discount those unnamed politicos whose "minor and interstitial acts . . . comprised Chicana technologies of resistance" in "tactical *movidas*" (movements).[58] Their involvement and participation in protest struggles remain unknown because movement history privileges heteromasculine actors, according to feminist of color scholars. García's work gleans Latina engagement with the postwar political landscape and requisite flashpoints formed around citizenship, Americanization, and pillars of Camelot-era policies, including space exploration. That intersection would intensify in South Texas decades later as the competition in the private aerospace industry took center stage and dimmed any optimistic outlook on the skies with calamity thundering overhead.

An air of rivalry guided commentary from the senior mayor of Brownsville, Texas, Trey Mendez. On February 15, 2023, state legislators gathered at Texas Southmost College, a two-year junior college located just opposite Matamoros, Mexico.[59] Here the ambitions of the outgoing city custodian were less than humble. He boasted about a nearly $20 million investment of American Rescue Plan Act funds, intended to stimulate the economy during the COVID pandemic. Mendez's plans were to expand the fiber optic networking of the RGV, a region "twice named one of the least connected in the country."[60] A subsidiary company of Lit Communities, dubbed BTX Fiber, would bring high-speed broadband telecommunications infrastructure, in an odd contradiction of Mendez's earlier contention that Brownsville is the "innovation capital of South Texas," overlooking its economic impoverishment. However, his spin to state policymakers about a city on the cusp of a tech boom got an assist from an unlikely player: Elon Musk.

In 2012 the billionaire tech giant started to procure acreage in nearby Boca Chica Beach, a Gulf Coast natural resource near a major shipping channel, the Gulf of Mexico, and Las Palomas wildlife refuge (more on this later). The site was crucial for Musk's fast-growing ambitions. His spacefaring company, SpaceX, required a private spaceport to produce, test, and launch rockets to accomplish his major goal of "mak[ing] humans a multiplanetary species."[61] By the time Mendez spoke to Texas lawmakers, Musk was already a fixture in the state. Initially SpaceX set up camp at the site of a former aerospace start-up called Beal Aerospace in McGregor, a small town near Waco known for housing munitions and weapons of war at the Bluebonnet Ordnance Plant, an ironically named arsenal, if only for its tribute to the state's flower.[62] With "197 acres, a test stand, and five buildings for $45,000 a year" under his belt, Musk tested early reusable rocket prototypes outgrew the McGregor facilities.[63] As a result, his focus turned to South Texas. His choice was an easy one. His activities in the state ranged from science and technology to public policy, "work[ing] with the legislature to rewrite beach access laws so the public beaches could be shut down during launches," and he had "offered more than $15 million in incentives" with then-Governor Rick Perry's goodwill.[64] In Musk's defense, his intentions were anything but inconsistent.

Through breaking ground on the aptly titled Starbase in 2014, Musk effectively renamed the coastal town as New Star City. As a result, SpaceX radically renovated this sleepy beach retreat. Musk employed thousands of workers, which had an economic impact on the housing market. This financial uptick was motivation enough for the aspiring Brownsville mayor, who was seen posing with the billionaire in social media posts. Mendez stressed, "Texas has been an historical leader in space. Texas is one of the two states in the U.S. that actually can do a launch. . . . Do we want to keep being the leaders? I think the answer to that is 'yes.' So, I would just ask you, please continue to allocate funding for space. Please continue to allocate incentives for companies that are looking to relocate to Texas."[65] His political gambit was anxiously relayed, as privatized aerospace programs were picking up speed in Alabama, California, Colorado, and Georgia. Although the city of Brownsville secured a partnership with another start-up, 9Point8 Capital, and thus expanded aerospace investments in the area, Mendez's plea to protect the state's "piece of this pie" echoed sentiments long recognizable from those Viva Kennedy chapters, whose roots were deeply entrenched in the RGV.[66] In much the same way that Mexican American voters sought electoral power, Mendez was grafting a new terrain for South Texas, one aided by "progress," technological innovation, and Texas history. Though Mendez's speech was tonally ambitious, not unlike Kennedy's space booster rhetoric, its intent appealed to these lawmakers' competitive spirit, asking them to reclaim their legacy as inheritors of aerospace ingenuity. His talk both endorsed and venerated what a techno-oligarchy had done for the local economy. This infusion of cash and private influence reshaped the city's cultural affairs with consequences for RGV civic identity.

This alignment of public good, real estate speculation, and economic self-interest commenced in a 2022 promotional video produced by the city of Brownsville cordially inviting Musk to the eighty-fifth anniversary of Charro Days, a commemorative event in which residents of Brownsville and nearby Matamoros, Tamaulipas, Mexico, honor an exchange between two nations. The festival is a celebratory showcase of folklife and foodways with performances of equestrian sports and displays of rugged showmen who parade in *traje charro y mariachi* adornment.[67] This multiday and multisite affair draws attendees from across nations and floods the streets with popular amusements including culinary vendors, ornate floats, and musical concerts. More important, the engagement flaunts the area's bounty of Tejanx pride.

The video is a public appeal as the city's civic elites invite Musk to a charro national pastime in exchange for a photo op. "Students came on buses, it was beautiful," noted Jessica Tetreau, city commissioner of Brownsville's District 2. "[They] performed with the intent to thank and invite Elon Musk for being a part of our community and being so generous to us. He's given to every organization that exists here in Brownsville. . . . Thank you for being not only our friend but thank you for being our family."[68] Her hyperbole alludes to the family, brokering a kind of kinship discourse based on neighborly promises. This adoration for the space baron is paired with "beautiful" visuals showing off the RGV's chief regional export: *ballet folklórico*. As an art form that gained popularity in the postwar United States, where Cold War anxiety and the golden age of science fiction composed an appropriate backdrop for transnational Mexican dance in the 1950s, this expression was essential for those in search of "a strong sense of group aesthetics and identity."[69] Thus, the city flexes its cultural strength in the form of twenty dancing children to appease this tech giant (see plate 57). Presented before two pillars of Musk's private industries, Starbase and Tesla, these Mexican American children add border panache to the grounds of his facilities where spacecrafts are designed, manufactured, and tested. A Tesla even appears in the frame tricked out with floral accents and an *abanico* (hand fan), transforming a piece of Musk's aerodynamic technology into an image that resembles the *danzantes* (dancers). Another border art imaginary comes into focus, a transplanetary-relational inflection of low-tech and high-tech technology from fuselages pointed at the sky to the swings of dresses imitating ocean waves. Musk's regional industrialization is made over and glamorized in *ballet folklórico* drag.

Soft fabrics and hardened spacecrafts accent a video that depicts twenty girls breaking into traditional dance, moving awkwardly over the graveled pavement, and struggling to cast beats as the renovated grounds absorb the punch of their footwork. Their traditional jewel-toned dresses create intense chromatic contrasts with Starbase in its muted palette of black and gray hues. A collection of handmade signs and banners in pink, blue, and green declaring "Thank you, Mr. Musk" add personal touches, countering the campus's dampened pigment and steely surfaces with a *convivencia diaria* (daily life interaction), an endearing expression of neighborly belonging.[70] Their *cuadros* (suite) adds color and vibrance to a scene of test-firing ranges and liquid oxygen fuel experiments, a deadly arsenal leading to brilliant, but harmful, explosions in the skies. As one headline in the *Texas Monthly* summarizes, "It's No Surprise SpaceX Blows Up Rockets in Texas. That's Why It Came Here."[71]

Although this *zapateado* (rhythmic dance) may appear tactical, it recalls a performance history in which these dancers were instrumentalized to mediate ethnoracial and transborder politics for Texas's aerospace entrepreneurs, corporate investors, and Latinx publics.[72] In 1976 Johnson Space Center (JSC), the same site at which National Welfare Rights Organization protesters contested the absurd federal spending on the Apollo programs, celebrated Hispanic Heritage Week. A report in the September 24, 1976, issue of the *Roundup*, the JSC's newsletter, included a photo pictorial of decorated "folk dancers" performing a *son jarocho* number to the distinctive Veracruz sound for which it is named. NASA attendees were apparently entertained by the "elaborate headdresses recall[ing] Mexico's Indian heritage."[73] The *Roundup*'s characterization is inaccurate, confusing *danza Azteca* with this regional dance, the implication being that the introduction of the dancerly body is homogeneously exotic, spectacularly amusing, and frozen in time. Because these "Mexican dancers liven [the] Hispanic program," as the headline reads, NASA staff consumes Latinidad through channels that are ancient despite visual evidence to the contrary.[74]

The impact of this program must have resonated, as the "Spanish-American contributions to our nation's space effort" are combined with dances that were "colorful and very professional . . . blend[ing] the traditional with a subtle interweaving of modern trends in the art" for the 1977 audience.[75] Unlike in prior years, information on key NASA personnel of Latin American descent is collated in a pamphlet entitled *Viva NASA*. This title cleverly references "Viva la Mexico," an outcry sparked by the Mexican Revolution, and merges it with the space agency. In this way, author Domingo Nick Reyes gives NASA a similar declarative power, imbuing it with an audible repertoire of dissent and empowerment. The publication is a work of historical recovery. Reyes identifies the earliest engineers and scientists of color instrumental in foundational aerospace experiments, ranging from Latinxs employed by the National Advisory Committee for Aeronautics (NACA), the predecessor of NASA, to Robert Goddard's experiments at White Sands Missile Range in New Mexico.[76] Documentation of the event suggests that his pamphlet was distributed, perhaps as a keepsake and even as an activist document magnifying racial disparity in the aerospace workforce. *Viva NASA* circulated alongside talks and lectures by television personality Elma Berrera and University of Houston history Professor Arturo Rosales. Their presence augmented "colorful" dance with data and evidence to elucidate the uncredited yet undeniable presence of Latinxs in the modern space program.[77] Reyes's gambit was seconded the following year with another Hispanic Heritage reception.

The September 1978 events at the JSC included a public lecture from College of the Mainland history Professor Manuel Urbina II.[78] His slideshow referenced the Mesoamerican past and included images of Maya pyramids, noting that they "once used 'to look at the sky.'"[79] Urbina's assertion added

Hispanic Day enlightens crowd

"We can thank Spanish tradition for water laws and income taxes, among other things," said Dr. Manuel Urbina of the College of the Mainland.

Urbina was principal speaker at the Hispanic Heritage Day program put on for the space center Sept. 15, in Bldg. 2. Employees and visitors filled the auditorium to view slide shows, hear speakers, and be entertained by dancers and singers in the Spanish tradition.

In one slide the flag of Mexico flew alongside the American flag, both projected on the auditorium stage. "Here we see the essence of Hispanic heritage," Urbina said. "These flags represent the cultural traits that make us able to unite our efforts and make these a grand United States of America."

Dr. Gerardo Cabrera and his company followed Urbina with a presentation of trajes (dress) and lifestyles of Guatemala. One of his slides showed Guatemalan pyramids, once used "to look at the sky."

"I wonder if they didn't have their NASA, too," Cabrera said.

More slides portrayed women at work, children at work, and "transculturalization:" workers commuting by bicycles on dirt roads while listening to pocket radios, Guatemalans attending Latino churches in the morning and worshiping idols in the afternoon.

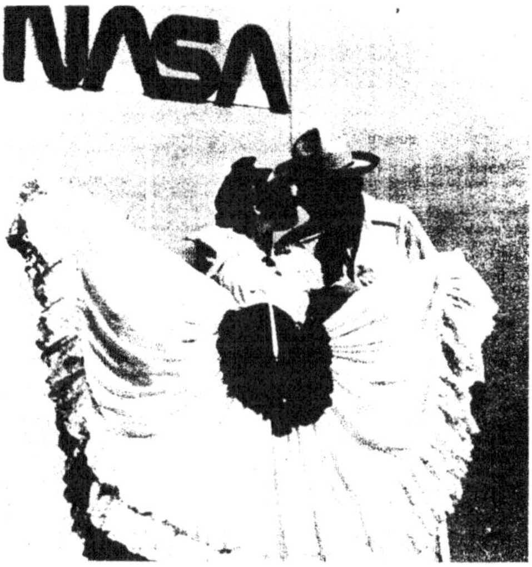

But the showstopper was the Ballet Folklorico de la Universidad. In white traditional costumes these "law students, chemical engineers, economics and business majors" tapped their feet dancing Hispanic percussion to music performed by a 3-piece band: harp, mandolin, and guitar.

The trio played "La Bamba" and with the dancers created the rhythm of a long-lived culture. Their tapping feet were an integral part of the music, and each song moved the audience to rich applause in appreciation.

When the Rondalla choir walked through the auditorium, an unexpected pleasure, their youthful voices and costumes completed the illusion of a trip to a far away land.

Saturday, Sept. 16, marked the anniversary of Mexico's independence from Spain, and Hispanic Heritage Week was designated by the President as a time for the U.S. to reflect on the history and culture of Latin America, and the contributions of Hispanic people to the hegemony of this civilization.

The space center program provoked consciousness of Hispanic roots in all who attended.

5.8 Johnson Space Center's *Roundup* newsletter coverage of its Hispanic Heritage Day program, including a *ballet folklórico* performance, September 29, 1978.

a transplanetary-relational outlook at that lectern by reconfiguring the ancient Americas within the foundational knowledge systems that permitted the science on which NASA is based. Thus, a "look at the sky" had also been the province of Mesoamericans, who searched aerial tableaux and conducted astronomical study prior to European conquest. With a visual position undergirding his presentation, Urbina dares his audience to look up and look *beyond* the *ballet folklórico* dance set to the chords of "La Bamba" before them, as *Roundup* reports (see figure 5.8). Indeed, "Viva NASA" was a collective call that Urbina and Reyes made, summoning their attendees to reimagine a border region that was always attuned to outer planetary seeing and thinking. Though the city of Brownsville arranged for its own troupe of dancing middle-school girls to entice a billionaire tech giant with attention to folkloric heritage and cultural tradition, it unknowingly confirmed how Mexican dance and space technology shared a complicated if not tangled history in ways that people like Urbina and Reyes intuitively understood from events decades prior.

Ballet folklórico is a Trojan horse, a carefully crafted performance exhibition in which the experience of dance is also about many things: the elision of NASA's Latinx workers, the historical contribution of Mesoamerican Maya astronomy, and even the clever spectacle to redraw Musk's connection to a small Texas border town. If "Chicanos turned to Mexican expressive cultural forms as sources of knowledge and inspiration," as Olga Nájera-Ramírez argues about *ballet folklórico*, then those young women outfitted in waves of jewel-toned fabric and lacy appliqués have the capacity to build nations, confront towering aerospace technologies, and thus bridge worlds.[80] In this way, Mexican dance traditions have always been modern, high-tech, and ascendant in orientation. *Danzantes* and other Latinx performers have been a consistent presence especially in the way that these aerospace organizations, public and private, ameliorate their reliance on ethnoracial labor, land, and, most important, sky. This conjunction can be observed in the way Musk allegedly employed a mariachi band to celebrate the hire of a "dozen geeks" in "low-rent office space" at the opening of his SpaceX start-up company in El Segundo, California.[81]

It is unsurprising that Musk returned this invitation at the request of twenty dancing schoolgirls with an appearance at Charro Days' complementary festival, Sombrero Days. His participation drew crowds eager to snap a photo with the tech giant and his son. Online photos document him devouring an *espiropapa* (Mexican street snack made of potato) and posing for selfies with locals in a way that added RGV authenticity to the exchange.[82] The public's excitement served as a kind of acquiescence to the billionaire's occupation of the region, consenting to his undeniable authority in economic and creative fields in the area. In this festival, SpaceX was an omnipotent presence as a cosponsor but also as a Latinx cultural influencer. The company participated in the festival with a float colored in the same monochrome palette as the science campus.[83] Its platform read "Starbase" in white block lettering, replicating the iconic signage from his facility at Boca Chica Beach. The SpaceX brand was a noticeable disruption of the vibrant hues for which Charro Days are known as it masked a fiesta aesthetic with a dampened pigment. Topping the float was a facsimile of a Raptor 2 engine—new technology with enough thrust to power 510,000 pounds of space rocketry. Its sophistication replaced any romantic references to the burro-powered wagon, invented by paisanos but discarded here as archaic and antiquated technology. The exhibition of Musk's mock-up on the streets of Brownsville brought cutting-edge rocketry fueled by liquified natural gas (LNG) and chemical resources from oil and gas wells in the US Gulf Coast under a Mexican and immigrant purview. Musk's boisterous and entertaining float billowed smoke as it paraded the machinery aiding in the cutting-edge of extractive colonialism.

As Musk's staff performs, waving company flags and maracas and wearing black velvet sombreros, they adapt the cultural symbols and heritage resources from a region that was a transborder, transnational, transplanetary, and even sacred landscape to the Esto'k Gna (Carrizo Comecrudo) tribe. By masking collusion and collision, the float descends onto the cheering Mexican and Mexican American audience, with a miniaturized and portable star base that rolls forward, asking residents to see what's before and ahead of them but not to look up. To turn vertically, this multiethnic public might recognize the starkly dimmer, ominously technological, and aesthetically estranging adaptation of their folkloric expression as a counter to the *cuadros* suite of dancing children. Appearing more David Cronenberg than Walt Disney, the arrival of SpaceX—replete with a salutary señorita in a metallic-accented *charra* dress and TV monitors broadcasting rocket launches—projects a future for Brownsville that is scientifically advanced yet chrome plated. Missed are the environmentally ravaged surrounds, unstable housing markets, and predatory loan lenders to come. Though Tejanx tastes are remade in the image of a private space company, this campaign for RGV's future would place nearby Boca Chica Beach as ground zero for a makeover of intergalactic proportions. That float was an important local step in a broader campaign Musk long fantasized about as building blocks of a "Mars Colonial Fleet" and an "Interplanetary Transport System."[84] His remarks from the International Astronautical Congress in 2016 in Guadalajara suggested that a private spaceport was needed for uninterrupted experimental launches, and that Boca Chica would be that port. However, signs of dissent came in the form of local RGV activists and artists prepared to upset any surrender of cultural resources and natural reserves by compliant state and local politicos.

Come to My Window

On the evening of February 15, 2022, Rebekah Hinojosa was awakened from sleep. Four police officers swarmed around her house and pounded on her door.[85] Without any regard for her person or state of undress, police took her into custody and she spent the next twenty-six hours in jail, charged with a class B misdemeanor. Her alleged crime: defaming a mural in downtown Brownsville. "Gentrified stop Space X" reads the vandal's text. The graffiti effacing the vibrant six-thousand-square-foot mural by Teddy Kelly was a telling rebuke of Musk and the artwork (see plate 58).[86] Kelly's signature abstract geometric shapes, pastel tones, and shadowed lettering added the illusion of depth, like an embossed signature announcing the arrival of something new, fresh, and Instagram ready. "BTX," it reads, abbreviating Brownsville, Texas, into a cleverly marketed three-character shorthand for the town. The mural, commissioned by the city in 2021 under the direction of Brownsville Community and Government Affairs Director Ramiro Gonzalez, foreshadowed a civic effort "to 'recover spaces for artistic expansion,'" if not to revitalize the depressed business district just across from the bridge, a border checkpoint on the way to Matamoros.[87] By hiring a graphic artist like Kelly with Mexican roots and commercial appeal, the rebranding efforts by Gonzalez and associates caused some to ask, "Will Elon Musk Austin-ify Brownsville?"[88] As Kelly's bold statement signaled in washes of pink and purple, this was just the beginning.

The arrival of SpaceX, and Latinx artists' responses to it, ignited like liquid oxygen combustion. No response was more inspired than Alexandro Gonzalez-Hernandez's muralism. His work lives in the open air—visible in refinished facades of businesses and homes and even a customized street van. Practicing under the pseudonym POPC_ULTURE, the artist drew local media attention over *House of Space* (2021), a commission for which San Benito resident Willie Rosales Jr. wanted his past experiences of star watching in Marfa, Texas, to visually permeate his residence.[89] Gonzalez responded with murals that combined pop art sensibility with technophilic touches of local celebrity. Tesla, NASA, and Starship Mars, a heavy launch vehicle, punctuate adoring vignettes about the nearby Starbase. Even the *Valley Morning Star* reported that visitors from Weslaco, McAllen, and Mission were turning the *House of Space* into a tourist attraction, perhaps regarding the rocket imagery on Rosales's garage as a viewing site or, at the very least, a backdrop worthy of a selfie. Such unbridled devotion to all things SpaceX is clear in the homeowner's assessment of Musk as "a generous man" and "the future . . . example of improvement."[90] This tribute to the space titan is undeniable, with two portraits of him blanketing the backside of one structure. Here Musk appears as either astronaut or tech giant visionary. Even the famed logo for NASA is adjusted to read ELON. This corporate investor and aerospace industrialist is portrayed as the new face of RGV civic arts—a savior through whom local Mexican and Mexican American creative economies flourish in a region poised to go to Mars.

Of course, this mural commission was not Gonzalez-Hernandez's first tribute to the SpaceX founder. Elements of its high-contrast aesthetic and pop art style appear in his exterior reworking of Los Elizondos, a commercial building in downtown Brownsville. Appearing the same year as *House of Space*, this work uses a darkened base coat to offset a vibrant and nearly ethereal depiction of Musk in a cosmic glow. His grin is earnest and unassuming, an inviting portrait that neutralizes public dissent, making him appear as a trustee, or even a protector, of this economically impoverished area. Again, as Rosales puts it, Musk is "the future." In a Warholian exercise of color and repetition, Gonzalez-Hernandez patterns Tesla-steering astronauts cruising beyond the Kármán line. In a tactic that recalls Haro's 830 Hicks Avenue mural, he uses the building's facade to communicate to residents with a speculative direction. "Boca Chica to Mars," declared in thick white lettering, is both an announcement and a command from mission control. Just as Haro's mural told commuting motorists "Look Beyond Yourself" in East LA forty years earlier (see figure 5.4), Gonzalez-Hernandez presents Musk as the rightful inheritor of Kennedy's Apollo dreams.

Gonzalez's *Boca Chica to Mars* was a companion artwork for Diane Garza's Milliken Garza Gallery, which opened a photo exhibition next door under the same name. Presenting astrophotography, rocket launch photo documentation, and portraits of spacecraft technology, the show focused on the local efforts of RGV image makers loosely organized as the SpaceX Boca Chica Group. Many of these creatives, like Pedro De La Fuente Silva and Carlos Nunez, add a Mexican American spin to the space art lexicon. They exert a visual cultural authority over Starbase activities in ways once governed by the NASA Artists Cooperative Program. These creatives are distinct from their counterparts in the formative years of NASA. Their location in South Texas offered these photographers an opportunity to record a private aerospace industry in its infancy without federal interference. This unique arrangement allowed people like De La Fuente Silva and Nunez the chance to shape Musk's burgeoning private enterprise. Thus Garza's show capitalized on the region's art-science abundance; for others, this exhibition affirmed that the photographers responsible for picturing SpaceX in news media, in private collections, and among space enthusiasts around the world were Mexican American.[91] With over four hundred attendees buying photography and viewing Tesla cars parked in the historic Livery Building, where stables once stood, the mural and exhibition were more than Musk worship. This moment was an art-historical inauguration enunciating the arrival of the next space age.[92] Indeed, as Gonzalez-Hernandez proclaimed, the RGV was headed to

Mars, and its burgeoning creative enterprise was serious business. His art, more than Kelly's, put on display the grave entanglements among local South Texas art, capital, and commerce, as well as the conflictual reception among some border residents bristling against this technogiant. As a public artist, he concedes that this rapid change and crisis of cultural identity were not without drawbacks. He told the *Texas Monthly* in 2021, "People were happy because the economy could go up, but not happy because the rockets were exploding. But I believe it's more good than bad."[93]

The way Brownsville's public registered its dissent was apparent in the Kelly mural vandalism. This outcry was manifold because it not only targeted a gentrifying RGV catering to "newcomers coming from MIT and Stanford" but also contested the economic arrangement underwriting the artwork.[94] Again, Kelly's $20,000 commission was paid by the Musk Foundation. Though Mayor Trey Mendez shrugged off public criticism about appointing a relative "outsider" to revitalize downtown (one mural was always earmarked for a local creative, and another was completed by Mexican artist Sofia Castellanos in 2021, he argued), this was no ordinary artwork. Any perception of anti-Musk discourse might dissuade future investment and undermine city trustees' good-neighbor diplomacy. That threat might even have motivated the mayor to post Hinojosa's mug shot on his social media account, call her community organizing work "anti SpaceX," and add her personal information in what some called an ill-conceived doxing plot.[95] Hinojosa's lawyer called his actions "retalia[tory]," after which the post was taken down.[96]

However, the implication of this conflict was never about salvaging the city's BTX rebranding campaign. For activist, mayor, and muralist alike, this incident illuminated a growing tension between those who praise Musk as a savior for South Texas and those who do not. Residents who refused to accommodate SpaceX as a friend of the region faced expulsion, humiliation, possible doxing, and even incarceration. Certainly, policing and detention were realities pervading this border town. However, it was the local government's prompt reaction on behalf of this corporation that was most profound, suggesting that had strong penalties not been imposed against Hinojosa, the city's new benefactor might have been unhappy—or, worse, might have left. To be a part of Musk's "multiplanetary" project came at the expense of not only land and environment but also free speech and bodily autonomy, sites of settler colonial violence that South Texas feminists and queers of color knew all too well. Rather than contest the present, they renewed a commitment to the possible.

Consider Celeste De Luna's *Fugitive Alien Break In* (2019) (see plate 59). Her screen print was among a range of Chicanafuturist works that were the focus of the group exhibition *Project MASA V: Mars Needs More Women* at the Centro Cultural Aztlán in San Antonio. Cofounded by Luis Valderas and Paul Karam in 2005, the MeChicano Alliance of Space Artists (MASA) imbued recognizable Chicanx cultural tropes—Catholic sacred icons, United Farm Worker emblems, barrio graffiti writing, foodways—with a speculative imagination and biting social satire.[97] Like Ernest Hogan's gravity-defiant Guerrilla Muralists in *Cortez on Jupiter* (see chapter 2), Project MASA points the way to a renegade barrio futurity for imagery and media that the science fiction novelist first contemplated in 1990.

Less formal art collective and more situational grouping, Project MASA engineered exhibitions, initially showcasing Latinx talent in ethnic-specific art locales with slapdash charm and political urgency. Together they broke the code of self-contained Chicanx iconography and rewired these semiotics for alien communication. Later shows illuminated interdisciplinary, performance, and fashion-based engagements in nationally acclaimed venues like the Queens Museum, Leslie-Lohman Museum, and Blue Star Contemporary.[98] The fifth iteration, curated by Cathryn Merla-Watson and Iliana Pompa, featured nineteen *frontera mujeres* (border women) organized in what Karen Mary Davalos calls an "errata exhibition" by which the structures of patriarchy and their resonant privileges in art and cultural production are contested and transformed. In turn, feminist ideas and creative protocols in cooperation and collectivity are recentered for a world empowering to Chicanas and Latinas.[99] Any exclusionary measures of cisgender women in the cultural circuits of Tejanx visuality and the histories of science, technology, and speculation are subordinated, proving that tomorrow also belongs to women of color. By forwarding a "collective critical discourse" in the spirit of museum interventionist "dissent," the curatorial framing of Merla-Watson and Pompa assembles Latina creatives who work on behalf of and in defense of the planet and cosmos broadly.[100]

An image maker like De Luna, who earned her MFA from the University of Texas–Pan American in Edinburg in 2007, exerts newfound confidence in the print medium, taking her audience to the front lines of Musk's South Texas Ground Tracking Station, with 3.9 meter S-band antennae gifted by NASA.[101] Viewed from among the nopales nestled in the composition's foreground, the composition is bisected by a barbed wire fence stretching across the print's middle. De Luna's piece recalls border art screen prints by the likes of Malaquias Montoya, Rupert García, and Sam Coronado. However, her approach transforms familiar cultural tropes of immigrant detention, fencing, walls, and carceral motifs. By pointing to vertical alignments, she reveals South Texas as a transplanetary-relational nexus. In keeping with Project MASA sensibilities, she draws from a speculative art repertoire of monsters and folklore. A creature centers the composition's activity. This Chupacabra resides on the fencing and thus tests the foreboding signage reading "do not enter" and "space-x," telling the trespasser to keep out. Caught mid-break-in, this "fugitive alien," as the title details, is literally riding the fence, making it ambiguous which side the Chupacabra belongs to. As an amorphous and mythical creature of conflicting nationality (first spotted in Puerto Rico according to some, and in South America according to others) and point of origin (terrestrial or extraterrestrial), it is a charged symbol that connects land and sky, Earth and stars, island and mainland.[102] The Chupacabra transgresses borders and traverses planets, succeeding in something that the nopales cannot. It moves in fugitive ways that upset the local and national measures of insider/outsider, homegrown/foreigner, or, in terms of Brownsville politics, pro-SpaceX/anti-SpaceX. By elevating a character of inherent criminality to a protest symbol, De Luna encourages ways to think like an alien, to empower what Matthew Goodwin calls "la conciencia Chupacabras" (or Chupacabra consciousness) and thus to work on behalf of "a vision of radical inclusivity, as well as being tolerant of ambiguity and perplexity," though not to be without "a tense and frightening sensibility."[103] For De Luna, the creature's trickery trolls the space campus in plain sight. Riding high, it stokes fear, anxiety, and paranoia, perhaps mocking another SpaceX disaster just three years prior.

In 2016 a SpaceX Falcon 9 rocket exploded on its launchpad in Cape Canaveral, Florida.[104] It was carrying a $195 million Israeli satellite, partly supported by Mark Zuckerberg's Facebook (now Meta) company, that was meant to broadcast the internet to developing nations.[105] Rumors ran amok, pitting the high-tech space industrialist against residents. Some speculated that "a projectile, maybe even a bullet or UFO," did it.[106] "If not an extraterrestrial," De Luna seems to ask, "why not a Chupacabra?" Did an *alien* agent threaten the company? Her visual efforts reside in the double meaning of *alien* as "extraterrestrial" and "undocumented immigrant," which quotes the wordplay of Project MASA. If a UFO had the power to stir company fears over the unknown, what other tricks might it have up its sleeve? Postrevolutionary printmakers in Mexico incited social change or, at the very least, stirred political awareness through works on paper in the first half of the twentieth century, and De Luna does a similar thing for an era of late capitalism and post-NAFTA at the precipice of the first Trump presidency. She elucidates how fear and racialized anxieties about the alienness of a South Texas border landscape cannot be so easily gated out. These emotive registers that disturb and encroach are affective resources to empower the minoritarian Other. De Luna appeals to her fellow Chupacabras, encouraging a fugitive epistemology that feels in its alien skin and takes frightening forms as "a projectile, maybe even a bullet or UFO."[107] Yet, for other Latinx artists, the consequences of SpaceX and its brutal scarring of the planet were no laughing matter.

Artist Nansi Guevara's small-scale mixed-media installation from *Project MASA V: Mars Needs More Women* is a natural bookend to De Luna's print. Less punning and more cunning, her piece *Colonization of la Boca del Rio* (2022) is historically deft, socially charged, and planetarily enmeshed (see plate 60). By combining painting with photography, cloth, and other vernacular architectural forms like altar making, she unveils environmental harm and the irreversible contamination of the US Gulf Coast from above. Her acrylic painting on canvas shows a composition representing two stark realities and timelines: the fading memory of citrus labor below and an imposing spaceship rocketing above the RGV landscape mid-launch. Her horizontal canvas, a bifolded vignette, interconnects historic traumas: residential dispossession, extractive colonialism, and land prospecting. She contemplates the schisms of white supremacy and racial capitalism as they extend from the foundations of the lower RGV to the burgeoning aerospace industries, thrusting local residents toward environmental destruction. From below, a farmer and his burro toil among the citrus groves, underscoring how a European settler colonialism occupied "an economically worthless and culturally backward desert" and thus expanded profits in a citrus belt dubbed the "Magic Valley."[108] This coinage dates to settler discourse in promotional railroad pamphlets for the Southern Pacific Line in the 1920s, calling "the combination of soils, climate, and irrigation" advantageous to "mak[ing] plants grow as if by some supernatural power."[109] Without any regard for the disenfranchised Mexican farmhands, these citrus barons implicitly acknowledged that these hands cultivated both fruit and "magic," making these fields ripe for speculation in both senses of the term.

If Mexican labor was responsible for the fertile and profit-earning grounds, why not spell casting? Guevara poses this question for the here and now with historic images of Anglo colonial settlers appropriated from marketing brochures and promotional materials from a century earlier. They are reproduced in her critique of South Texas suburbia. These homeowners represent the benefactors of Musk's newly minted technocratic leisure class. No longer a part of an agricultural grower system, they turn not to the resource-rich ground tilled by Mexican laborers as their forebears did but to the sky. Instead, new developments and refurbished beach homes fashioned in a monochromatic palette conversant with Starbase's dulled hues dot the landscape. This portrayal of a future RGV is drab, uniform, and fluent in the aesthetic vocabularies of this industrialist's aerospace brand. Teslas and electric charging stations ornament manicured lawns. A silver trailer references temporary housing for SpaceX workers, whose mark on the environment is visible in the eruptive smoke from another rocket launch. That propulsive fuselage enunciates the arrival of another space age predicated on Texas skies, native lands, immigrant labor, and ecosystems in peril. Astronautics' foundations are predicated on the Mexican magic of the valley from decades ago.

The threat of cultural erasure animates a pair of lenticular photos that cast memories of *la playa de la gente* (the people's beach), which fade and transform. The viewer gazes at framed images that flank the painting; with lateral movements, altering reflections glimmer. One gleam reveals an empty view of Boca Chica Beach, where the artist dances on the shore. Arms out, she embraces the coastal winds and boundless stretch of waterways connecting the Gulf Coast to Mexico and the Caribbean. The other gleam is a grassy sand dune, tranquil seashore, and unencumbered sky disturbed by invasive technologies and armed agents of detention and deportation. The beach is a hologram for a Tesla parking lot, Starship Mars spaceport, and border zone. A marauding patrolman in the foreground looks up, and his vertical viewpoint is a curious extension of the post-9/11 security state, a complicit defender of anti-immigrant law or banisher of "alien" invaders. Guevara instrumentalizes the lenticular medium to empower a window on collusion between ICE and SpaceX, making Boca Chica Beach a place where coordinated efforts among corporate capital, art philanthropy, border defense, and interstellar interests coalesce.[110]

By installing a replica of a ceramic *capilla* (outdoor shrine) against a backdrop of reflective fabric imitating sunlit radiance, Guevara points to the last remaining vestige of South Texas Valley Mexican tradition unmoved and untouched by the gentrifying powers of Musk's private aerospace corporation. The work, part monument and part memorial, responds to the endangered ethnoracial cultural footprint of *la playa de la gente*. Guevara's creative statement implies that in the lower RGV, racial trauma and spatial dispossession are correlated experiences. However, a colonial project that began in nineteenth-century citrus groves now reaches up toward orbital zones, intensifying the consequences for Tejanx residents in the latest stage of the space race and technological dominance over the skies. De Luna, Guevara, and other RGV creatives find themselves entangled in a national defense industry and corporate aerospace enterprises in ways that demand rebuttal. They strike back with public-facing counters that refuse to cede ground (and sky) to a hall of Musk celebrity murals or gallery shows that revel in this booming space art marketplace. Rather, they seek social transformation and transplanetary-relational knowledges from insurgent curatorial initiatives that rage against future planetary harm with Chicana feminist and queer of color opposition.

These tactical art activist projects form the center of Guevara and Monica Sosa's exhibition *Nuestra Delta Mágica* (Our magical delta). It opened on April 1, 2023, in a former office space arranged by cosponsors cdcb (come dream. come build.), an affordable housing nonprofit organization servicing the unhoused and economically impoverished in the RGV. Curators Guevara and Sosa mounted wall didactics to tell previously untold details about border publics severed from homelands, mother tongues, and clean ecosystems. Reproductions of ephemera and other archival records combine with wall labels, creating a Latina feminist knowledge system in which archivality is no longer the apparatus of the state but rather a "counterarchive" of insurgent Chicana feminist knowledge.[111] A pantheon of revolutionaries—Dolores Huerta, Gregorio Cortez, JT Canales, and Jovita Idar—appear as an RGV hall of disobedience. These profiles complement wall shelving, which contains books about the historical atrocities forming the US-Mexico borderlands, like an open library displaying the bibliographic foundations for this curatorial approach to a Latina space feminism. This pop-up show brings book, history, and feminist imagery together to materialize the literary building blocks of Latinx women's resistance in nineteenth- and twentieth-century Texas. Here weapons of defense, protection, and even joy are mined from the library. This insurgent ethos is doubly operationalized in the activist photography and paraphernalia seen on the opposing wall.

Banners taken from actions organized by the Carrizo Comecrudo Tribe of Texas and the Sierra Club, reading "Stop Destroying Our Sacred Lands" and "Stop LNGs / SpaceX," make Musk's private space corporation part of a broader imperialist project to not only colonize Mars but also eradicate Indigenous lifeways from lands deemed imperative to this goal. Among the banners is a comparative photograph taken by Guevara documenting these instruments of social protest. The large-scale picture records a political demonstration at Starbase in January 2023. Guevara's lens presents a counterimage against the glossy camerawork and celebratory bravado of Brownsville city officials commodifying the 2022 Charro Days as a neighborly offering to Musk. Her photo fits awkwardly around regional camera clubs, like the SpaceX Boca Chica Group, electrified by this newfound space boosterism. Instead, what hones her artwork is gritty and less refined. She shows overcast skies of a ravaged beach town in the winter offseason. A semitruck carrying LNG (liquid natural gas) is overlaid with the empowered fist of Indigenous activist Tony Briones. His clenched hand vaults above a SpaceX rocket venerated by city of Brownsville civic elites. His gesture in strength and protest subverts the visual domination of Musk's rocketry looming over the coastal skyline. Here the Carrizo Comecrudo people will overcome. They reclaim sacred land, air, and water, defying state authorities who discipline their bodies as illegal, criminal, or trespassing. This crowd looks up with the intention of tearing down. For Guevara, the volatile reality and disturbing underside of SpaceX operations are a painful reminder of colonial violence.

The photo is a callback to Mario De Biasi's documentation of women of color activists condemning the waste of tax dollars spent on the Apollo 11 mission at the Manned Spacecraft Center in Houston circa 1969 (see figure 2.2).[112] More than half a century later, Native, Mexican American, and Latinx activists refuse to recoil in the face of a different kind of threat as private aerospace operations, in order to best position the corporate monetization of a space tourist industry, allegedly poison the waterways and ecosystems long traveled by Indigenous ancestors. Guevara's politically engaged and planetary minded camera not only documents the front lines of social protest from the wetlands of Boca Chica Beach but consequently places this urgency as external to the everyday happenings of RGV residents and racialized publics.

In the exhibition Guevara also emphasizes the Mexican American home space to this conflict. To crystallize this interiorization of outer space and settler colonial violence, she and Sosa add elements of domestic material culture to the gallery, enhancing the potential of contemplative moments about labor, space exploration, and home. A television broadcasting the 2003 documentary *Valley of Tears* is parked before a couch. The documentary's subject is a 1979 migrant worker strike in Raymondville, a small town fifty miles north of Brownsville; the film demonstrates how day laborers picking onion crops worked in solidarity with the United Farm Workers, extending the organization's reach to South Texas.

Plush throw pillows, lacy doilies, and fabric flowers add *domesticana* embellishments to the exhibition design, destabilizing the clinical and sanitized visual experience typical of the art gallery environment. Borrowing from installation practices by Amalia Mesa-Bains, Maria Brito, and Leyla Cárdenas, the curators construct a domiciliary face for Chicana art and protest.[113] According to Guevara, "Exhibits can be intimidating, and so I also wanted this [show] to have elements of the home to make people a little bit more comfortable but also to point out that this is happening. . . . [It] affects us inside our home."[114] Her impulse is eerily reminiscent of those aforementioned photos by Camhi and Bernal that link sites of domestic tranquility to the Apollo program, Cold War geopolitics, and planetary attentions to borders from the ground to the sky. Homemaking in this way elucidates the creative practices little recognized under the racist, cis, and heterosexist taxonomies of art history, which overlook "the signs of making do [as] both an affirmation of the domestic life and a resistance to the subjugation of the women in the domestic sphere," as Mesa-Bains writes.[115]

Like a metaphorical skylight offering an ascensional aperture linking this world to others, the curators plot homey furnishings that crystallize transplanetary relations in a kind of tactical *movida* where decorative end tables and fabric window treatments accent walls, rooms, artworks, and political viewpoints that bend and break at space booster propaganda in the region. *Cortinas* (curtains) are fulcrums between the domestic setting and the aerospace industry, because indoors and outdoors are interdependent realms as exploding rockets and rumbling grounds intrude on private refuge and recreation in the RGV. Whether one considers the black velvet keepsakes eulogizing President Kennedy in Mexican American interiors pictured in the 1970s or the venerated portraiture of a billionaire rocket baron remaking facades of the South Texas built environment decades later, the means of making *home* are traced by allusions to security, an elusive position contingent on what is happening on the ground and, more important, in the sky.

From the show, one might also consider the installation work of queer of color mixed-media artist Josué Rawmírez. Combining art and activism with his profession as a public housing advocate, he negotiates the pitfalls of mortgage lending and market forces perpetuating housing unaffordability in Brownsville.[116] To make this atrocity tangible, he turns to bandit signs, those nuisance advertisements cluttering the South Texas cultural landscape's vacuous corners and recessed medians. These brightly hued and attention-grabbing placards prey on homeowner insecurity with fast-cash schemes and flashy promotions. A set of flowery curtains in the pop-up gallery opens to Rawmírez's *House Not Home* (2023), tucked into a discreet former office nook (plate 61). Tearing apart this material signage and reworking it into a large-scale installation, he fabricates the exterior and front sidewalk of a house from a disassembled array of commercial graphic discards. Loan signs declaring "I Buy Houses," "Credit Loans Available," and "¡Llame Hoy!" (Call me today!) are plentiful. This aggregation of found material suggests how predatory lenders are parasitic and replicated, like an analogue adware for vulnerable bilingual consumers in everyday Brownsville.

Rawmírez's concise cuttings expose 956 as a visible and recurrent marker in the work. Its bold typographical print and even handwritten authenticity suggest how a phone prefix from the region tactically deploys familiarity and local identity to scam local homebuyers and even home sellers. Masquerading as being "from the Valley," these companies have their covert disguises removed, and their unethical get-rich-quick schemes are exposed. Simply, houses cannot be homes when homemaking itself is under the surveillance of real estate prospectors who target low-income neighborhoods for quick sales or prepare areas ripe for new developments, aiding Musk's efforts to accommodate SpaceX engineers and staff by turning Boca Chica Beach into a rebranded company town: New Star City. Though Rawmírez's work asks, "Who's the Bandit?," the outcome of his exposition is punning.[117] By negotiating "the bandit" and its Spanish translation, *bandito*, he exposes how a racist archetype of Latinx criminality and borderlands lore is actually a fitting title for the region's aerospace industrial capitalists, city investors, and government elites. The immigrant futures promised behind these annoying advertisements are fallacies designed to distract from the culprits ultimately benefiting from a system of housing precarity, gentrification, and dispossession. His piece reaffirms the exhibition's larger initiative to interrogate the material consequences of SpaceX with great costs for RGV residents.

Free Falling

Rawmírez's installation in its reworking of nuisance signage littering the vacuous and unused strips of public space shares aesthetic questions and theoretical ideas with LA-based interdisciplinary artist Clarissa Tossin. As a precursor to Guevara and Sosa's insurgent curatorial effort, her show *Falling from Earth*, formally organized by Miranda Lash for the Museum of Contemporary Art Denver in 2022, also predominantly featured found materials. In 60-by-84-inch paper weavings called *Future Geography* (see plate 62), she composed complex works on cardboard braided and patterned after Indigenous aesthetics from her native Brazil. Salvaging discarded Amazon boxes gathered from friends and family, she sifted through these corporate-branded packing materials. This litter combined with large-scale reproduction of astrophotography, allowing Tossin to rework scientific information bits mined from NASA satellite imaging. Her assemblages materialize Indigenous cosmovision with the telescopic optic advancements studying the universe. By making these practices interrelated, *Future Geography* is a kind of mapping project with a hyperobject scale. That is, by reopening an artwork composed from lo-fi discards to the vastness of the universe, Tossin uses NASA coordinates to yield broader transplanetary-relational axes.[118] The enormity of these celestial pathways is woven into her "future geography" not in a way that applauds the violence of resource extraction but rather critically confronts it by pointing upward. These linkages to e-commerce, mass consumption, and shop on demand are unexpected yet pronounced correlations in another Tossin artwork that exposes how aerospace industrialist Jeff Bezos is anticipating steps toward the moon contingent on Amazon operations and lunar outposts.[119]

Based in Van Horn, Bezos's West Texas private space company, Blue Origin, is something of a regional savior to the blighted rural town.[120] Like Musk, Bezos is monumentalized in murals by public artists of Mexican descent. However, unlike Musk, his ties to the state and Latinidades are less circumstantial and more anchored in his youth. From the age of four, Bezos was raised in New Mexico by his adoptive father, Miguel, a refugee who fled Cuba after the Cuban Revolution.[121] In fact, his hispanophone surname is adopted. Bezos spent summers on his grandfather's ranch in South Texas, an experience that the billionaire likely referenced in his decision to purchase 331,859 acres in Culberson County on the west side of the state.[122] Corn Ranch, north of Van Horn, would become his new home, giving him greater proximity to his spaceport, where experimental rocket launches like New Shepard helped this e-commerce tycoon plan for what he foresees as his ultimate goal, "the ring of Shackleton Crater."[123] In taking aim at the moon's south pole, Bezos intends to engage in lunar mining and harvest ice found there and potentially refuel rockets and other spacecraft, using the planetary body to provide "logistics support, mineral compounds for developing structures, and near-continuous sunlight for power generation."[124] While his mission may sound like the musings of a science fiction writer, its serious intention and scientific plausibility were enough to alarm Tossin and refocus her eye on Earth's satellite. Under this regime, she grimly summates that the moon is set to become a "giant gas station."[125]

Tossin's attentions to Bezos's company are both satirical and incisive, making her a perfect addendum to *Project MASA V: Mars Needs More Women* by proxy. Her commentary about "Amazon" sifts through the transnational traffic of language and translation. In English, *Amazon* refers to the global online retail giant and, simultaneously, the world's largest tropical biosystem, which interconnects Brazil with other countries in northwestern South America. In Portuguese, however, the term is less fluid, more specific. The rainforest is called Amazonia, and so for Brazilians, *Amazon* does not translate in the same way.[126] This failure of corporate marketing places South American consumers apart from their US counterparts, and thus the brand falters because of the linguistic error. Despite the company's reach through numerous shipping warehouses in the country, the e-commerce giant is powerfully rebuked by Tossin for its textual malfunctions. The smiling logo seen through the woven shipping boxes is perhaps her mocking grin. It is also an interrogation of a business whose sincerity is revealed to be nothing more than a bandit sign. Like Rawmírez's paper house, the promise of home is a facade. Whether one considers the Amazonian rainforest or delicate biodiversity in South Texas, colonial extractive violence, harmful mining, and deforestation are the upsetting outcomes of a kind of lawless corporate banditry hidden behind Bezos's friendly signage.

Rawmírez and Tossin come together in an art activist outcry over the consequential environmental disaster caused by privatized aerospace companies in competition over not only science and technology but also airspace. Where these "future geographies" will go is anybody's guess, but the idealism of a space age sparked by Kennedy's vision for the Apollo age wanes for queers of color and Latina feminist creatives confronting the dire consequences of a privatized space industry in their backyards, rattling the walls of their homes after another rocket comes crashing down to pummel wetlands, annihilate avian sanctuaries, and dust cars with fallout. As Tossin's work declares, a box is not simply a box. Behind its folds are e-commerce's discards, evidence of high-speed consumptive behaviors and instant buyer gratification. Much in the same way that layers of trash envelop Earth like a damaged parcel rerouted to a planetary sender, that earnest smile grinning behind a corporate brand comes with strings. Thus, artworks by Rawmírez and Tossin renew the urgency to look up and look beyond the sign: to broadcast, to remap, and to protect the planet and even the solar system from impending calamity.

Though the artworks that this chapter focuses on were made half a century after Apollo 11 landed on the moon, they recall a Latina feminist space consciousness long cultivated under the Kennedy administration, when the induction of the space race fostered a romance with Mexican American voters and, in particular, women, whose domestic interiors were plotted with black velvety promises of Camelot and whose private sanctuaries harbored desires to secure the country's future by getting to the moon first. This dedication aimed at not only being better than the Soviets but also being better Americans. For these reasons, the sharp departure from these aspirational trappings of citizen subjectivity in the twenty-first century in these pieces demonstrates the complex and sometimes contradictory role feminists and queers of color find themselves in while negotiating with aeronautical technology big and small. Positioned on the shaky ground (and sky) of "differential consciousness permit[ting] the practitioner to choose tactical positions," which Chela Sandoval relates to the "clutch of a car provid[ing] the driver the ability to shift gears," Latina feminists face Silicon Valley tech giants, needing to not only downshift but also maneuver into warp speed.[127] Like the *zapateados* of teen dancers stomping the grounds of Starbase in 2022, other and more potent propulsions were needed to work expediently in defense of precious environments, neighborhoods, and ecosystems under attack by such predation.

These protective stances "offer a critique of technology's detrimental impact on the environment and human bodies," as Catherine Ramírez argues about Chicanafuturism's capacity to "[interrogate] the promises of science and technology."[128] In response, these queer and Latina feminist space art activists mime the movements of De Luna's fugitive Chupacabra. They take strange shapes and carefully balance on that fence mediating the ways in which Chicana artists, for instance, have long created "picture[s] of a politicizing spiritual hybridity" attached to a "cosmic consciousness that modernist discourses have related to the realm of the unreal because it is seemingly unprovable," according to Laura Pérez.[129] While that cosmic language traffics in a broader speculative vocabulary of Chicana feminist art making, with creatives like Ester Hernández and Yreina Cervántez being of note, the artists in this chapter show how these dire material realities and environmental complications are reshaping what this next stage of aerospace industrialization means for RGV livelihoods. More than sensing the land, their transplanetary relational alignments support activist art making in a "shared experience of harm between people and things . . . [and] also the potential for the refusal and resistance to that often-systemic harm," as José Esteban Muñoz discusses about the brown commons.[130]

Harm among Mexican American and Latinx artists in this region is not unidirectional; it is also self-inflicted. Consider how the establishment of these private aerospace corporations is radically transforming impoverished areas of West and South Texas, creating new art market opportunities for astrophotography hobbyists, for muralists, and for purveyors of SpaceX photography shot by locals of Mexican descent. These art-science activities are also proffering exhibition forums from Tesla-embellished horse stables to remodeled storefronts. Whether funded by Musk's foundation or independently driven, these artists find themselves cast as heroes, defenders, trespassers, bandits, and villains in border zones organized around pro- and anti-billionaire space entrepreneurs. Ironically, these corporate entities need these local space boosters, as James Webb and H. Lester Cooke intuitively knew when they established the NASA Artists Cooperative Program in 1962 to sell the Apollo missions and capture the nation's imagination. Together, artist and aerospace industrialist broker dreams.

However, the paradox that Latina feminists and queers of color find themselves in enunciates the next chapter of space art history. A vocabulary of visual art indebted to the iconic depictions of rocket boosters, launchpads, mission control, and suited astronauts forms the basis for art-science exchange from which Latinx creatives benefit, though under the shadow of New Shepard and Falcon 9 rockets. As art activists like Guevara argue, such perceptions of public good are misleading. "I think the images are colonized for me," she argues about the new Latinx astronomical art making and international attention from corporate mass and social media on the region. "I don't think I will be making any futurism stuff."[131] Her outlook not only contrasts with this Texas-based art-science visual economy but also contests larger optimistic viewpoints in queer and feminist of color art histories.

As Anzaldúa wrote in the aftermath of the 9/11 attacks, "The human species' survival depends on each one of us connecting to our vecinos (neighbors), where they live across the street, across national borders, or across oceans. A calamity . . . can compel us to think not in terms of 'my' country or 'your' nation but 'our' planet."[132] Her hopeful address is emblematic of a Latina space feminist consciousness that thinks in a planetary way, forging other kinds of connections on a grand scale to, as this book argues, transplanetary relational axes. Certainly, Guevara's refusal to partake in a Chicanafuturism project is less about pessimism. With a political consciousness shaped by outer space, she cannot detach her home in the "Magic Valley" from the enormity of planetary injury, the poisoning of her neighborhood, and the trashing of the skies. The promise of "Boca Chica to Mars" wounds her. The harm done to her precious environmental surrounds is reason enough to assume "a critical optic," as Muñoz says, "to combat the force of political pessimism" through not only hope but the radical possibilities of feminist and queer of color dreaming.[133]

By reanimating glimmers of that jubilant girl dancing oceanside, Guevara returns to *la boca del río* (mouth of the river), where the Carrizo Comecrudo people believe the first woman was created. As guardians of her waterways and tributaries that feed, fertilize, and wash the land anew, these art activists work in defense of *her*, finding productive uses of harm in the contradictory waters of an economically revitalized region set awash with Teslas, charging stations, and unaffordable housing stained in monochrome tones. With eyes learned in transplanetary relational ways, she and her art activist community crystallize imagery to protect a vital source of nourishment, replenishment, and biodiversity. Together, they powerfully look up at an altered skyline to fight the technology commanding the skies and towering above them. To work in a mode of Latina feminist space knowledge is to ride that fence, trespass the gates, traverse the wetlands, and twirl on that beach. To be with *her*, *mujeres* (women) and queers like Hinojosa, De Luna, Guevara, Sosa, Rawmírez, and Tossin crusade for ecological and social justice with the stomp of their feet and the thrust of their fists. Here they dare to dream otherwise from this narrow sliver of South Texas that refuses to surrender, and with that, the battle over Earth's future is only beginning.

Notes

Introduction: Art at the Outer Limits of Latinidades

1 The original airdate of "Tourist Attraction" was December 23, 1963; it was directed by Laslo Benedek. It was preceded by an episode ironically titled "The Borderland," though this story was not on the disc that I retrieved.

2 Ginsburg, *Cyborg Caribbean*, 6.

3 This comment is not to overlook the white and colonial hegemony that characterized the history of science fiction literature. I am moved by scholars like Isiah Lavender III, who argues that "invoking race and racism in an outwardly white genre is necessary. Coloring science fiction *is* an absolute and radical commitment." Lavender, *Black and Brown Planets*, 10. His comments acknowledging how "skin color matters in our visions of the future" boldly put pigmentation and colorization into conversation, complicating discourses about alien races and other extraterrestrials (6).

4 Much art-historical assessment has been done not in scholarly monographs but in exhibition catalogs, especially on the topic of alternative futurisms over the past decade. Worthy of closer recognition are notable shows such as *The Shadows Took Shape*, at the Studio Museum in Harlem (2013–14); *Afrofuturism: A History of Black Futures*, at the National Museum of African American History and Culture (2023–24); *Past Futures: Science Fiction, Space Travel, and Postwar Art of the Americas*, at the Bowdoin College Museum of Art (2015); *Mundos Alternos: Art and Science Fiction in the Americas* (2017–18), at the University of California, Riverside, ARTSblock; *Fronteras del Futuro: Art in New Mexico and Beyond* (2022–23), at the National Hispanic Cultural Center Art Museum; and *Indigenous Futurisms: Transcending Past/Present/Future* (2020–21), at the Institute of American Indian Arts.

5 For more, see Whiting, *Pop L.A.*, 3.

6 Billie Doux notes, "Dexter's confrontation with General Mercurio seemed to focus on how Latinos are more comfortable touching and kissing other men than Americans. What was going on there?" Doux, "Outer Limits."

7 *Latinx* is a broader term referencing the process of US racialization for those people of Latin American descent raised in or living as long-term residents of the United States. As Arlene Dávila notes, "While many Latinx artists have roots or connections with their home countries, at the root of the Latinx identity is the 'neither here nor there' condition that places them at the margin of geographically bounded definitions of authenticity." A. Dávila, *Latinx Art*, 25.

8 Brown, *Black Utopias*, 2.

9 Marez, *Farm Worker Futurism*, 6; Ginsburg, *Cyborg Caribbean*, 69.

10 *Captain Video and His Video Rangers* was the first US TV serial in the genre and aired from 1949 to 1955. A spin-off series called *The Secret Files of Captain Video* aired on Saturday mornings from 1953 to 1954. My father, who was born in 1951, was a child at this time and likely viewed them in contemporaneous reruns, a treasure trove of bad media for him.

11 This is not to say that the NASA space art program was entirely devoid of participants of Hispanic descent like Mario Cooper, who was born in Mexico City and taught advertising art and illustration in New York universities, including Columbia and Pratt Institute. He also contributed drawings to the US Air Force Art Program and illustrated short fiction and mystery serials by the likes of Agatha Christie. Most striking in the archive are the artists once considered for this and other space art–related projects. Records suggest that Salvador Dalí was in contention to make work responding to the cape at the Kennedy Space Center. Artist Julio César Fernández had a watercolor included in the National Gallery of Art's *The Artist and Space* (1969), curated by H. Lester Cooke. Also, an artist in residence program at the Smithsonian National Air and Space Museum in 1977 considered diverse artworks by Puerto Rican conceptualist Rafael Ferrer, Cuban artist Juan González, and even Japanese sculptor Fumio Yoshimura. On Dalí, see National Gallery of Art, "Art Program Projects" (ca. 1962), ephemera, SC-008, Hereward Lester Cooke Papers, box 2, folder 5, National Gallery of Art, Washington, DC. On Fernández, see Julio Fernández file, correspondence from H. Lester Cooke to Fernández, NASA Art Program papers, Art Curatorial files, folder 15, Aeronautics Division, National Air and Space Museum, Washington DC. On Ferrer, González, and Yoshimura, see correspondence from Bill Good to Carolyn Martin, March 10, 1977, NASA Art Program papers, Art Curatorial files, folder 28, Aeronautics Division, National Air and Space Museum, Washington DC.

12 I borrow this citation from Ginsburg's astute observation and translation. See Toledano Redondo, "El Regreso," quoted in Ginsburg, *Cyborg Caribbean*, 75.

13 Alvarado et al., "Introduction," 5.

14 Gómez-Barris, *Extractive Zone*, xvi.

15 See, for example, P. Gonzales, *Mud People*.

16 Aparicio, "Latinidad/es," 113 (italics mine).

17 For more on the vertical border, see Cornejo, *Visual Disobedience*, 148–49.

18 Vogt, "Arterial Border," 193.

19 Gómez-Barris, *Extractive Zone*, 6.

20 Gómez-Barris, *Extractive Zone*, 7, 6.

21 Gómez-Barris, *Extractive Zone*, 7, 5. Her emphasis on aerial technologies supports an argument about technology and "colonial theft," adding that "digital technologies contribute to the diminishment of regional national sovereignty over natural resources by enabling a grand-scale view from above" (8).

22 Saab, *Objects of Vision*, 3.

23 Oxford English Dictionary, "trans- (*prefix*), Etymology," December 2025, https://doi.org/10.1093/OED/7495348567; Butler, "Lost Races," 185.

24 Galarte, *Brown Trans Figurations*, 12–13.

25 Galarte, *Brown Trans Figurations*, 13; Halberstam, *Trans**, 5.

26 Halberstam, *Trans**, 5.

27 Spivak, *Death of a Discipline*, 71.

28 Spivak, *Death of a Discipline*, 72, 73.

29 Ginsburg, *Cyborg Caribbean*, 3.

30 Morton, *Hyperobjects*, 1.

31 Morton, *Hyperobjects*, 1, 15.

32 Morton, *Hyperobjects*, 19.

33 Morton, *Hyperobjects*, 12.

34 Galarte, *Brown Trans Figurations*, 13.

35 Saab, *Objects of Vision*, 30.

36 Morán González, "Aztlán @ Fifty," 176.

37 Merla-Watson and Olguín, "Altermundos," 4.

38 Merla-Watson and Olguín, "Altermundos," 4.

39 C. González, "Latino Sci-Fi," 211.

40 Readers may want to consider Norma Ávila Jimenez's exhibition catalog, *El arte cósmico de Tamayo* (2010), which appraises famed Mexican abstractionist Rufino Tamayo through his astronomical iconography. A 2015 Bowdoin College Museum of Art exhibition catalog, *Past Futures: Science Fiction, Space Travel, and Postwar Art of the Americas*, edited by Sarah Montross, explicates US and Latin American postwar artists' speculative impulses, bringing figures like Raquel Forner and Roberto Matta into conversation with Robert Smithson and Nancy Graves.

41 For more, see Schreuders, *Paperbacks, U.S.A.*, 207.

42 Telotte, *Movies, Modernism*, 110.

43 On Schomburg, see Gustafson, *Chroma*. For more on Senarens, see Goodwin, *Latinx Files*, 7.

44 Merla-Watson and Olguín, "Altermundos," 4.

45 C. Ramírez, "Cyborg Feminism," 376. Here it is worth considering Patrick McCray's important study about adolescents' involvement in Operation Moonwatch after the launch of Sputnik in 1957. See McCray, *Keep Watching the Skies!*

46 Maher, *Apollo*, 145.

47 Topham, *Where's My Space Age?*, 19.

48 Maher, *Apollo*, 155.

49 Maher, *Apollo*, 158.

50 Maher, *Apollo*, 159.

51 Exceptions include works by Latin American artists Juan Downey, Rufino Tamayo, Raquel Forner, Enrique Castro Cid, Xul Solar, and Joaquín Torres-Garcia (among others). See Montross, *Past Futures*; and Estrellita Brodsky and José Falconi, cocurators, *Elsewhere(s): Other Worlds, Other Times, Other Territories*, Another Space, Chelsea, New York, March 21–June 17, 2022.

52 This premise underscores racial formation theory. For more, see Omi and Winant, *Racial Formation*.

53 A. Dávila, *Latinx Art*, 26.

54 A. Dávila, *Latinx Art*, 25.

55 Beatriz Cortez, interview by the author (with Matt Shindell), January 15, 2021.

56 Cortez, interview.

57 Van Tuinen, introduction, 6.

58 Morton, *Hyperobjects*, 15.

59 A. Dávila, *Latinx Art*, 15.

60 Stableford, "Science Fiction," 30.

61 Cortez, interview.

62 Stableford, "Science Fiction," 30.

63 See C. Ramírez, "Deus ex Machina."

64 Sandoval, "U.S. Third World Feminism," 3.

65 C. Ramírez, "Afrofuturism/Chicanafuturism," 190.

66 C. Ramírez, "Deus ex Machina," 157–58.

67 Strait, introduction, 10.

68 Womack, "Afrofuturism as Space and Being," 27.

69 Womack, "Afrofuturism as Space and Being," 24.

70 C. Ramírez, "Deus ex Machina," 159.

71 Marez, *Farm Worker Futurism*, 11, 10. "Terrestrial bondage" is from Weems, *Barnstorming the Prairies*, xiv.

72 Muñoz, *Cruising Utopia*, 97.

73 Muñoz, *Cruising Utopia*, 1.

74 Van Tuinen, introduction, 6.

75 Saab, *Objects of Vision*, 30.

76 Schneider, *Performing Remains*, 10.

77 Avanessian, "Asynchronous Present Past," 11.

78 Schneider, *Performing Remains*, 10.

79 At the time of this writing, a spate of scholarship has been published on Latinx speculation, though with emphasis on literary and film study. Consider Díaz-Basteris and Urcaregui, *Latinx Comics Studies*; Gil'Adí, *Doom Patterns*; Hudson, *Latinx Revolutionary Horizons*; Díaz-Basteris and Urcaregui, *Latinx Comics Studies*; and Zimmer, *First Contact*.

80 This image is not the artist's first foray into outer space. Consider her artwork *Tito's Gig on the Moon* (2002). For more on this piece, see C. Cortez, *Carmen Lomas Garza*, 96.

81 *El Paso Herald*, June 25, 1927, 15.

Chapter 1. Planet Anew: Toward a Transplanetary-Relational Approach

1 Véa, *Gods Go Begging*, 109. I would like to thank Stephen Hong Sohn and Nancy Carranza for pointing me to this text.

2 Véa, *Gods Go Begging*, 110.

3 This passage translates to "How do you say it, satellite? One of those Sputniks?"

4 Véa, *Gods Go Begging*, 107.

5 Véa, *Gods Go Begging*, 110. Cornelius's laughter may also resonate with the equally ridiculous vision of Latinxs in space, with comedian Bill Dana's performance as accidental astronaut José Jimenez on his album *Bill Dana on Earth* (1961) being emblematic of such buffoonery. Incidentally, Dana's racist portrayal was so popular that even astronaut Alan Shepard "used [standup] excerpts in his radio communications to Gus Grissom on his Liberty Bell 7 flight on July 21, 1961." Topham, *Where's My Space Age?*, 25.

6 Véa, *Gods Go Begging*, 107.

7 Bojórquez, quoted in Davalos, "Sputnik and the Avenues," 28.

8 Davalos, "Sputnik and the Avenues," 28.

9 Bojórquez, quoted in Davalos, "Sputnik and the Avenues," 28.

10 Saab, *Objects of Vision*, 49. While I am referencing Saab's work, there is lengthy scholarship on optical technology, optometry, lenses, and telescope history. The work of Jonathan Crary, Fred Watson, and James Elkins is most germane to this discussion and is referenced throughout this chapter.

11 Saab, *Objects of Vision*, 52.

12 Saab, *Objects of Vision*, 53.

13 Davalos, "Sputnik and the Avenues," 28.

14 Saab, *Objects of Vision*, 52.

15 Véa, *Gods Go Begging*, 107.

16 International Trade Administration, "Mexico Country Commercial Guide."

17 For more, see International Trade Administration, "Mexico Country Commercial Guide."

18 Cantú, "Valley Activists."

19 Morton, *Hyperobjects*, 19.

20 Saab, *Objects of Vision*, 49.

21 Morton, *Hyperobjects*, 19.

22 Gómez, *Nuclear Nuevo México*, 9.

23 Gómez, *Nuclear Nuevo México*, 10, 7.

24 Gómez, *Nuclear Nuevo México*, 7, 8.

25 Weems, *Barnstorming the Prairies*, ix.

26 Weems, *Barnstorming the Prairies*, 49.

27 Weems, *Barnstorming the Prairies*, 54.

28 Weems, *Barnstorming the Prairies*, xiv; Foucault, *Discipline and Punish*, 202.

29 For more, see Foucault, *Discipline and Punish*.

30 Gómez-Barris, *Extractive Zone*, 6.

31 Mirzoeff, *Right to Look*, 10.

32 Mirzoeff, *Right to Look*, 10.

33 Tsing, in Mitman, "Reflections on the Plantationocene," 8.

34 Haraway, in Mitman, "Reflections on the Plantationocene," 10.

35 Haraway, in Mitman, "Reflections on the Plantationocene," 10.

36 Gómez-Barris, *Extractive Zone*, 6.

37 Gómez-Barris, *Extractive Zone*, 8.

38 Gómez-Barris, *Extractive Zone*, 8.

39 Marez, *Farm Worker Futurism*. Marez's study revisits the temporary agricultural worker arrangements between the United States and Mexico, like the Bracero Program. The Bracero Program started in 1942 in response to labor shortages during World War II but persisted long after the war, ending in 1964. For more, see Rosas, *Abrazando el Espíritu*. Also see Loza, *Defiant Braceros*.

40 Marez, *Farm Worker Futurism*, 87.

41 Padilla, *Up from Puerto Rico*, vii. Also, Sánchez, "Puerto Rican Identity," 198.

42 Ginsburg, *Cyborg Caribbean*, 3.

43 Weems, *Barnstorming the Prairies*, xiv.

44 Weems, *Barnstorming the Prairies*, xiii.

45 Gómez, *Nuclear Nuevo México*, 8.

46 Saab, *Objects of Vision*, 55.

47 Saab, *Objects of Vision*, 55.

48 Watson, *Stargazer*, 66.

49 Watson, *Stargazer*, 66.

50 Saab, *Objects of Vision*, 52.

51 Watson, *Stargazer*, 61–62.

52 This is Watson's conclusion. See Watson, *Stargazer*, 68.

53 Saab, *Objects of Vision*, 52.

54 Watson, *Stargazer*, 71.

55 MacPhee, *Architecture of the Visible*, 15.

56 MacPhee, *Architecture of the Visible*, 15, 16.

57 MacPhee, *Architecture of the Visible*, 17.

58 MacPhee, *Architecture of the Visible*, 18, 17.

59 Saab, *Objects of Vision*, 52; MacPhee, *Architecture of the Visible*, 14, 15.

60 MacPhee, *Architecture of the Visible*, 14, 15.

61 MacPhee, *Architecture of the Visible*, 15.

62 MacPhee, *Architecture of the Visible*, 17, 18, 17.

63 MacPhee, *Architecture of the Visible*, 18.

64 Messeri, *Placing Outer Space*, 12.

65 Messeri, *Placing Outer Space*, 12; MacPhee, *Architecture of the Visible*, 18.

66 Gómez-Barris, *Extractive Zone*, 6.

67 Weems, *Barnstorming the Prairies*, xiv.

68 J. González, *Subject to Display*, 159.

69 See Mesa-Bains, "Domesticana."

70 Durón, "How to Altar the World."

71 Gomoll, "Performative Spirit," 359.

72 Gomoll, "Performative Spirit," 359–60.

73 Saab, *Objects of Vision*, 52.

74 Noriega, "On Museum Row," 479.

75 J. González, *Subject to Display*, 142.

76 Ybarra-Frausto, "Latino Wunderkammer," 115.

77 Newkirk, "'Far More Useful,'" 9.

78 Quoted in Newkirk, "'Far More Useful,'" 16.

79 Newkirk, "'Far More Useful,'" 24.

80 Nicholson et al., "History."

81 Nicholson et al., "History."

82 Nicholson et al., "History." Also, Thurston, "Professor Fuertes Dies," 119.

83 Thurston, "Professor Fuertes Dies," 119.

84 Newkirk, "'Far More Useful,'" 25.

85 To view, consider Brenner, *Wind That Swept Mexico*, 242–43.

86 For more, see *Pareja observa por un telescopio el cometa Halley* (1910), La Mediateca INAH, https://mediateca.inah.gob.mx/repositorio/islandora/object/fotografia:437725.

87 Watson, *Stargazer*, 61–62.

88 For more, see Vasconcelos, *Cosmic Race*.

89 Ramón Menéndez's *Stand and Deliver* could be read as a science fiction film on par with the boom of speculative cinema that characterized this period of filmmaking in the 1980s. With Edward James Olmos's turn as Gaff in 1982's *Blade Runner* notwithstanding, the conventions of the cinematic biopic about a Bolivian immigrant schoolteacher peddling a neoliberal message about Hispanic social uplift cloud its rendering in these generic terms, however. Science fiction is covertly coded in the movie. For instance, when Escalante reports for duty to teach Math 1A, Javier (portrayed by Patrick Baca) is seated in the front row. His studious fashioning in knit vest and glasses is accentuated with a literary prop. He reads Frank Herbert's *Dune*. But his eagerness on the first day of school is not rewarded: "I was the first one here," he protests when Escalante removes him from his seat. His chair is given away to presumably monolingual and possibly undocumented teens. Javier's alienness is exacerbated when his literal alienation in the classroom is audibly sounded

through homophobic catcalls and whistles. This scene intensifies dual alien experiences for the students at Garfield High School in East LA, where the queer and immigrant outsiders simultaneously occupy the social fringes, and a math classroom ironically touts NASA's achievements in the set design. These parallels are undeniable considering that Menéndez's true-to-life biopic takes place in 1982, the same year that Ridley Scott pontificated a dystopian future LA circa 2019 in *Blade Runner*. Menéndez's scene appears to ask something about citizenship legibility in a way echoed in Scott's treatment: To whom does this seat belong? The alien, the queer, or the undocumented?

90 Guzmán, *Nostalgia for the Light*.

91 In fact, Cornell University is a part of an international consortium scheduled to operate the Fred Young Submillimeter Telescope, named after an alumnus who donated more than $16 million to the project located in the Atacama Desert. Glaser, "Breakthrough Telescope."

92 Ramírez-Soto, *(Un)veiling Bodies*, 76.

93 Guzmán, *Nostalgia for the Light*.

94 Celia Alvarez Muñoz, email to the author, November 21, 2021.

95 See Tejada, *Celia Alvarez Muñoz*.

96 Brenner, *Wind That Swept Mexico*, 18.

97 Brenner, *Wind That Swept Mexico*, 18.

98 *El Paso Herald*, April 20, 1910.

99 Ames Gallery of American Folk Art, "Wonderful Worlds: The Visionary Paintings of Alex Maldonado," 1989, ephemera, curatorial object file, Smithsonian American Art Museum, Washington, DC.

100 In verso description of *Mexico (May 1910)*, n.d., photograph, curatorial object file, Smithsonian American Art Museum.

101 Ames Gallery of American Folk Art, "Wonderful Worlds."

102 Ames Gallery of American Folk Art, "Wonderful Worlds."

103 *El Paso Herald*, April 20, 1910.

104 "Alexander A. Maldonado, Naïve Painter, Dies," *Antiques and the Arts Weekly*, April 14, 1989, newsprint clipping, curatorial object file, Smithsonian American Art Museum.

105 "Alexander Maldonado," Mexican Museum, n.d., ephemera, curatorial object file, Smithsonian American Art Museum.

106 "Alexander Maldonado," Mexican Museum.

107 While my comments are mainly about the US-Mexico border region, other examples abound. At the time of this writing, a forthcoming article by Abel Méndez and Ángel Acosta-Colón identifies cave art in a remote part of southern Puerto Rico. The depiction of a star with a fiery tail was dated to

May 19, 1910, when Halley's Comet was visible to the naked eye, suggesting how "the intersection of science, sensationalism, and humor shaped the collective experience of astronomical phenomena" in early twentieth-century Puerto Rico. Méndez and Acosta-Colón, "Fear of Halley's Comet Visit," 6.

108 Spivak, *Death of a Discipline*, 72.

109 Eugene Keilin, "'Visiting Professor' Kennedy Pushes Space-Age Spending," *Thresher*, September 19, 1962, newsprint, UA 109, John F. Kennedy Space Effort Speech at Rice University records, box 1, folder 3, Woodson Research Center, Fondren Library, Rice University, Houston, TX. Also, "Last Hours of J. F. K.," *LULAC News* 25, no. 4 (November–December 1963), 1, newsprint, MSS0160, John J. Herrera Papers, Houston Metropolitan Research Center, Houston Public Library.

110 McCray, *Keep Watching the Skies!*, 15–16.

111 Rosson and Miller, "Space Art," 76.

112 Kessler, *Picturing the Cosmos*, 29.

113 Kessler, *Picturing the Cosmos*, 19.

114 Miller, "Space Art," 319.

115 Rosson and Miller, "Space Art," 82.

116 Rosson and Miller, "Space Art," 74.

117 Dreyfus, "Robert McCall Illustrator," 80.

118 Elkins, *Six Stories*, 87–88.

119 Dreyfus, "Robert McCall Illustrator," 103.

120 For one exception, see Petersen, *Space-Age Aesthetics*.

121 Streeby, *Imagining the Future*, 83.

122 Rosson and Miller, "Space Art," 75.

123 These sentiments were conveyed by the artist. Simón Vega, interview by the author and Matt Shindell, February 26, 2021.

124 Cornejo, "'Does That Come,'" 194.

125 Vega, interview.

126 For more on Salvadoran and other Central American diasporic artists' responses to the civil wars, see Cornejo, "'Does That Come.'" See also Cornejo, "Central America."

127 Vega, interview.

128 Vega, interview.

129 *Latin Americanized* is Vega's term for the aesthetic. Vega, interview.

130 Vega, interview.

131 Vega, interview.

132 Morales quoted in A. Robinson, "Coachella 2018."

133 Vega, interview.

134 Here I am indebted to Ana Patricia Rodríguez's "trans-isthmian critical practice" as it argues for "new provocative ways of reading Central American texts in specific and transhistorical locations, in relation to regional, hemispheric, and global contexts, and in intertextual relation to one another." A. P. Rodríguez, *Dividing the Isthmus*, 11. Borrowing from this foundation, I also illuminate those provocations keyed to transplanetary relationality and astronomical symmetry. This viewpoint shifts the terrestrial geopolitics centering the discursive and even physical terms from which her study of Central American diasporic literatures is posited. The terms and meaning of Vega's neologism grow more ascendant and speculative in use as renewed attention is paid to cultural texts like hers.

135 These thoughts are indebted to Tomás Ybarra-Frausto's concept of "rasquachismo," which is more directly considered in chapter 4 of this book. For more, see Ybarra-Frausto, "Rasquachismo."

136 Tang, "Contemporary Art," 376.

137 Gómez, *Nuclear Nuevo México*, 8.

Chapter 2. Barrio Futurity: Public Art in the Age of Apollo

1 Hogan, "Chicanonautica Manifesto," 406.

2 Hogan, *Cortez on Jupiter*, ix.

3 Hogan, *Cortez on Jupiter*, ix.

4 Hogan, *Cortez on Jupiter*, x.

5 Hogan, *Cortez on Jupiter*, 39.

6 Hogan, *Cortez on Jupiter*, 55.

7 Hogan, *Cortez on Jupiter*, 22.

8 The Mexican art collective La Gravedad de los Asuntos, composed of nine artists and one scientist, underwent physical training at the Yuri Gagarin Cosmonaut Training Center in Moscow's Star City in 2014. Through international cooperation, Mexican artist and cosmonaut came together in a series of conceptual, literary, and performance actions staged in parabolic flight. In rolling waves of twelve- to fifteen-second zero-gravity pulses, these artists escaped the laws of the physical world and created artistic expressions at the edge of Earth's orbit. Their work is reminiscent of Hogan's speculative musings in *Cortez on Jupiter* as it interrogates the terrestrial basis of Mexican creative expression and the terms of transnational if not transplanetary-relational transformation. For more, see R. Hernández and Stallings, *Mundos Alternos*.

9 Hogan, *Cortez on Jupiter*, 60.

10 Despite reaching celestial bodies, Quetzalcoatl's travels in three realms are horizontally ordered, as Gerardo Aldana y Villalobos points out, "into the cosmic regions of east, north, west, and south." Aldana y Villalobos, *Calculating Brilliance*, 66.

11 Marshall, "Calling Out and In," 101.

12 On Porras-Kim, see Marshall, "Calling Out and In," 118.

13 Hogan, *Cortez on Jupiter*, 16.

14 Philbrick, *Group Works*, 14.

15 Latorre, *Walls of Empowerment*, 69.

16 Cockcroft and Barnet-Sánchez, introduction, 6.

17 Consider Olowin, "Man, Controller."

18 Coffey, *Orozco's American Epic*, 262.

19 Cockcroft and Barnet-Sánchez, introduction, 7.

20 Goldman, "How, Why, Where," 23.

21 Goldman, "How, Why, Where," 23.

22 Latorre, *Walls of Empowerment*, 69.

23 Latorre, *Walls of Empowerment*, 73.

24 Latorre, *Walls of Empowerment*, 73.

25 See Goldman, "How, Why, Where," 30.

26 Latorre, *Walls of Empowerment*, 83.

27 For more on the term, see Oziewicz, "Speculative Fiction," 5.

28 Miller, "Space Art," 316.

29 Miller, "Space Art," 316.

30 Miller, "Space Art," 316.

31 Miller, "Space Art," 316.

32 Miller, "Space Art," 316.

33 Miller, "Space Art," 319, 316.

34 McCurdy, *Space*, 53.

35 Fineman, "Daydreams by Moonlight," 77.

36 Fineman, "Daydreams by Moonlight," 77.

37 McCurdy notes a famed 1952 diorama by Bonestell that was reproduced on the cover of a 1986 National Commission on Space report. It was paired with an illustration by fellow space artist Robert McCall. See McCurdy, *Space*, 57–58.

38 Crouch, "Saga of a Lunar Landscape."

39 Crouch, "Saga of a Lunar Landscape."

40 Fineman, "Daydreams by Moonlight," 79.

41 McCurdy, *Space*, 38.

42 Crouch, "Saga of a Lunar Landscape."

43 Newell, *Destined for the Stars*, 18.

44 This protest seconds another campaign organized by the Southern Christian Leadership Conference (SCLC). Historian Neil Maher argues in his groundbreaking monograph, *Apollo in the Age of Aquarius*, that "the space race and the social and political movements of the 1960s . . . were mutually dependent on one another for popular and political support . . . [as] they represented two factions in a national debate regarding the present and future course of the United States." Maher, *Apollo*, 2. Things came to a head in the summer of 1969 when Reverend Ralph Abernathy, SCLC president, led twenty-five low-income African American families and four haggard mules to Kennedy Space Center in Cape Canaveral, Florida, to confront NASA Administrator Thomas Paine just one day before Apollo 11's historic launch on July 15, 1969 (11). The members of the Poor People's Campaign who assembled before the launchpad represented the racial and economic schisms pitting astronaut against the hungry and scientist against pastor-activist. "I want NASA scientists and engineers and technicians to find ways to use their skills to tackle the problems we face in society," Abernathy said, illuminating the unrelenting poverty devastating people of color in search of economic justice (12). The contrasts could not be starker. Maher sums up, "Watching the Apollo countdown that week, [the majority of US citizens] viewed the spaceship as a technological wonder, [but] Abernathy and the poor families accompanying him to the Cape saw it instead as a political blunder that left unresolved more pressing problems back on Earth" (13). The actions of the Poor People's Campaign were national in scope and activated protestors who demonstrated at the Johnson Space Center in Houston.

45 Saunders, "Art After Apollo," 139.

46 Anzaldúa, *Borderlands/La Frontera*, 80.

47 Maher, *Apollo*, 24.

48 Muñoz, *Cruising Utopia*, 1.

49 Maher explicitly covers African American protest in relationship to NASA and federal spending. See Maher, *Apollo*, 29–30.

50 Cockcroft and Barnet-Sánchez, introduction, 10, 12.

51 Goldman, "How, Why, Where," 24; Barnet-Sánchez and Drescher, *Give Me Life*, xxi.

52 Goldman, "How, Why, Where," 44.

53 Beronius, "Murals of East Los Angeles," T15.

54 Davalos, *Chicana/o Remix*, 74.

55 Barnet-Sánchez and Drescher, *Give Me Life*, 34.

56 Hough, "Too Chicano?," 62.

57 Richard Haro, interview by the author, October 3, 2021.

58 Haro, interview.

59 Haro, interview.

60 Haro, interview.

61 Barnet-Sánchez and Drescher, *Give Me Life*, 92.

62 For more on this nonextant mural, see Hough, "Too Chicano?"

63 Haro, interview.

64 Haro, interview.

65 Barnet-Sánchez and Drescher, *Give Me Life*, 85.

66 Barnet-Sánchez and Drescher, *Give Me Life*, 85.

67 Sánchez-Tranquilino, "Murales del Movimiento," 85.

68 Barnet-Sánchez and Drescher, *Give Me Life*, 148.

69 Newell, *Destined for the Stars*, 16.

70 Newell, *Destined for the Stars*, 7.

71 Although this was addressed earlier in this chapter, it is worth acknowledging how McCall's *The Space Mural—A Cosmic View* at the Smithsonian NASM, appearing in the building's lobby at 146 by 46 feet, is an impressive accomplishment. Though smaller in scale, Haro's mural would come one year after McCall's NASM commission, demonstrating how these artists were attuned to the US space program, albeit from different perspectives and modes of audience address, at the same time. Some iconographic references remain intact, but their vertical sight lines evoke different relations to the Apollo program, one provoking nearly divine colonial dominance and the other an outlook that tethers East LA to the future.

72 Sobchack, *Screening Space*, 101.

73 See Lovegreen, "Aerial Homesteading."

74 Ades, "Arte Madí/Arte Concreto-Invención," 246.

75 Aranda and Figueroa, "Latin American Kinetic Art."

76 See Alonso, "Argentines on the Moon," 79.

77 For more on Guidice, see Scharmen, *Space Settlements*, 154–57.

78 Muñoz, *Cruising Utopia*, 12.

79 Spivak, *Death of a Discipline*, 73.

80 Wayne Alaniz Healy (with Patricio Villagomez), interview by Roberto Tejada, July 2007, UCLA Chicano Studies Research Center Oral Histories

Series, no. 19 (May 2021), 9, https://www.chicano.ucla.edu/files/Wayne_Healy_oral_history.pdf.

81 Healy, interview, 10.

82 Healy, interview, 9.

83 Healy, interview, 9.

84 Healy, interview, 10.

85 Healy, interview, 10.

86 David Botello and Wayne Alaniz Healy, interview by the author, October 4, 2021.

87 Healy, interview, 15.

88 A similar sentiment is also conveyed to Tejada but with more emphasis on aviation. See Healy, interview, 18.

89 Botello and Healy, interview.

90 Botello and Healy, interview.

91 Botello and Healy, interview.

92 Healy, interview, 16.

93 These sentiments are further discussed in Latorre, *Walls of Empowerment*, 84–85.

94 Latorre, *Walls of Empowerment*, 85.

95 Latorre, *Walls of Empowerment*, 85. Consider R. Rodríguez, *Next of Kin*. Also, R. Hernández, *Archiving an Epidemic*.

96 Latorre concurs. See Latorre, *Walls of Empowerment*, 84.

97 Botello and Healy, interview.

98 Ellis, "Los Angeles," 26–27. The photography is attributed to Jodi Cobb.

99 Ellis, "Los Angeles," 39.

100 Ellis, "Los Angeles," 39.

101 Ellis, "Los Angeles," 41.

102 Botello and Healy, interview.

103 James Loewen refers to Culver City as a "sundown town." Loewen, *Sundown Towns*, 112.

104 Loewen, *Sundown Towns*, 14.

105 Sides, *L.A. City Limits*, 86.

106 Sides, *L.A. City Limits*, 110.

107 Sides, *L.A. City Limits*, 82.

108 Botello and Healy, interview.

109 Botello and Healy, interview.

110 Sawyer, "Aerospace Folktales."

111 This text is found as a painted epigraph in *Moonscapes I.*

112 Bartels, "Arecibo Observatory." Though it is a visual citation here, the observatory was an energizing force that sparked Latinx creativity, most notably in the video art collaboration *The Great Silence* (2014), by writer Ted Chiang and artistic duo Allora y Calzadilla. The work poetically ruminates on how Arecibo's calling out to extraterrestrial life is akin to how the nearby *Amazona vittata*, an endangered species of parrot, is calling out into a cross-species ether in a decolonial strategy of communal care and environmental responsibility. These custodial impulses are all recalled in the *Moonscapes* mural. See Allora and Chiang, "Great Silence."

113 Crary, *Techniques of the Observer*, 46

114 Crary, *Techniques of the Observer*, 46.

115 Cosgrove, *Apollo's Eye*, x.

116 Véa, *Gods Go Begging*, 109.

117 Barnet-Sánchez and Drescher, *Give Me Life*, 95.

118 Barnet-Sánchez and Drescher, *Give Me Life*, 95. For more on *Por Vida*, see Galarte, *Brown Trans Figurations*, 4–6. Also, R. Hernández, *Archiving an Epidemic*, 44–45. On Silvia Rivera in transgender mural art, see A. Gonzalez, "Art at Its Greatest."

119 Barnet-Sánchez and Drescher, *Give Me Life*, 95.

120 Wofford, "Diasporic Returns," 954.

121 For more on the term *techno-dominance*, see Ginsburg, *Cyborg Caribbean*, 3.

122 Cosgrove, *Apollo's Eye*, xi.

123 For more, see Alan Bean Gallery, *First Men*. Despite this author's best efforts, the Bean Estate elected not to permit reproduction of his painting in this text.

124 Bean, quoted in Geeting, "Alan Bean," 91.

125 Healy, interview, 16.

126 For more, see Cullen and Fuentes, *Caribbean.*

127 See Saunders, "Art After Apollo," 139.

128 Saunders, "Art After Apollo," 139.

129 The US space program made a tremendous impact on Robleto, who recalls a serendipitous encounter: "I stayed home sick from school that day and flipping through the channels . . . I stumbled on a program about the golden record. . . . [T]hey said in its broader description that these were sounds sent to space, and my young mind with this terrible cold and vivid imagination misinterpreted that to mean rather than sending the signals that we had received a signal[.] And I thought NASA was releasing a 1–800 number to the public so that we

could hear the first signal from aliens. . . . [A]ll I remember hearing was static and very distinct crackling. Fast forward now over forty years ago, and a huge part of my life has been dedicated to that mistake." As the artist attests, hearing a strange frequency as a child opened him to otherworldly sources of creativity where an indistinguishable sound became the impetus for an art practice linked to NASA, the golden record, and questions about the beyond. Dario Robleto, interview by the author (with Matt Shindell), August 12, 2021.

130 Gambino, "Voyager's Golden Record." Also see Chua and Rehding, *Alien Listening*.

131 Robleto, interview.

132 See Kenin et al., "Poet Laureate."

133 Robleto, interview.

134 Becker and Brečević, "More than a Portrait," 49.

135 This vandalism was conveyed in Botello and Healy, interview.

136 Healy, interview, 16.

137 Stromberg, "Historic Chicano Mural."

138 Rafael Vargas-Suarez Universal, interview by the author (with Matt Shindell), February 19, 2021.

139 Vargas-Suarez Universal, "Scientific Data Resurrection"; Mexic-Arte Museum Records, Nettie Lee Benson Latin American Collection, University of Texas Libraries, University of Texas at Austin.

140 Vargas-Suarez Universal, "Scientific Data Resurrection."

141 Vargas-Suarez Universal, "Scientific Data Resurrection."

142 Vargas-Suarez Universal, "Scientific Data Resurrection."

143 This part of his practice was conveyed in Rafael Vargas-Suarez Universal, interview by the author, March 2, 2022.

144 Muñoz, *Sense of Brown*, 4.

145 Muñoz, *Sense of Brown*, 2.

146 According to Garcia, the exhibition was inspired by the oft-cited Carl Sagan quote: "The vastness [of the universe] is bearable only through love." Miki Garcia, interview by the author, March 22, 2022.

147 These details were shared by the artist in Vargas-Suarez Universal, interview.

148 Vargas-Suarez Universal, interview.

149 Goldman, "How, Why, Where," 44.

150 Botello and Healy, interview.

151 Saab, *Objects of Vision*, 52.

Chapter 3. Terraforming the Gallery: In Search of Central America

1 Ferreira, "How Latin America," 210.

2 As Matthew David Goodwin notes, Senarens published under the pseudonym Noname. For more, see Goodwin, *Latinx Files*, 7.

3 The revised and expanded 2015 edition of *Twentieth-Century Art of Latin America* refreshes the map as front matter without resolving the absence of Puerto Rico and the erasures of the Dominican Republic, Paraguay, and Central American countries.

4 Alvarado et al., "Preface," x.

5 Arias, *Taking Their Word*, 185.

6 "Canal Zone, November 25, 1952, Declassified BBcase Condon Report," May 7, 1969, 6, unclassified report, MS 412, box 2, James McDonald Papers, University of Arizona Special Collections.

7 "Canal Zone."

8 Newell, *Destined for the Stars*, 208.

9 McCurdy, *Space*, 52–53.

10 Berger, *Sight Unseen*, 76.

11 Newell, *Destined for the Stars*, 208.

12 For more on the blue-marble photograph as it relates to the environmental movement of the 1970s, see Maher, *Apollo*, 93.

13 For more on McCall's rendition, see Scharmen, *Space Settlements*, 255–57.

14 Alvarado et al., "Introduction," 5.

15 Messeri, *Placing Outer Space*, 107.

16 Messeri, *Placing Outer Space*, 152.

17 As Mike Ashley notes, these canals or channels were first identified in the mid-nineteenth century by Giovanni Schiaparelli, and Percival Lowell continued that pursuit. See Ashley, "Imagining Mars," 17.

18 Alvarado et al., "Introduction," 16.

19 Cornejo, "Decolonial Futurisms," 22.

20 Cornejo, "Decolonial Futurisms," 22.

21 Beatriz Cortez, interview by the author and Matt Shindell, January 15, 2021.

22 By *countersite*, I am referring to Foucault, "Of Other Spaces."

23 Cortez, interview.

24 Hayden, *Power of Place*, 21.

25 For more, see Lefebvre, *Production of Space*.

26 Hayden, *Power of Place*, 8.

27 Hayden, *Power of Place*, 9.

28 Hayden, *Power of Place*, 9.

29 Rivera, *Undocuments*, 4.

30 See Villa, *Barrio-Logos*, 5; Londoño, *Abstract Barrios*, 180.

31 See Rojas, "Enacted Environment."

32 Rojas, "Enacted Environment," 271.

33 Lara, *Latino Placemaking and Planning*, 45; Londoño, *Abstract Barrios*, 177. Also, Londoño notes how "consumer-friendly diversity developments and Latinx cultural expressions [are] rendered in brilliant, seemingly affirming chromatic colors" (5).

34 E. Hernández, "Remembering Through Cultural Interventions," 144.

35 E. Hernández, "Remembering Through Cultural Interventions," 148.

36 Rivera, *Undocuments*, 4.

37 Arias, *Taking Their Word*, 185.

38 Noriega et al., "Introduction," 17.

39 Noriega, "To Dwell," 25.

40 *Home* includes two artists of Guatemalan heritage, Andres Asturias and Jessica Kairé. We might also consider how the blockbuster survey *Our America/ Nuestra America: The Latino Presence in American Art* at the Smithsonian American Art Museum (2013) also featured the work of one Salvadoran artist, Muriel Hasbun, despite the vast presence of this population in the DC, Maryland, and Virginia area.

41 Noriega, "To Dwell," 30.

42 Gaspar de Alba, *Chicano Art*, 19.

43 For more, see Lorde, *Sister Outsider*.

44 Cornejo, "'Does That Come,'" 191.

45 Messeri, *Placing Outer Space*, 21.

46 Messeri, *Placing Outer Space*, 3.

47 Messeri, *Placing Outer Space*, 25.

48 Messeri, *Placing Outer Space*, 153, 16.

49 Messeri, *Placing Outer Space*, 152.

50 Schindler, *Far End*, xi.

51 Schindler, *Far End*, xi.

52 These are Kevin Schindler's conclusions. See Schindler, *Far End*, 3–4.

53 Schindler, *Far End*, 5.

54 Schindler, *Far End*, 8.

55 Decades later, the National Science Foundation and Association of Universities for Research in Astronomy (AURA) founded Kitt Peak National Observatory in the Quinlan Mountains to the south of the Lowell Observatory. The Kitt Peak observatory was established in 1958 on the second-highest point of the Tohono O'odham reservation, a site that also demanded laborious infrastructure. Photography from the *Tucson Citizen* documents Native Indigenous workers stooping over dug up earth and rock opposite Anglo engineers from Tucson and Los Angeles with contemplative stares and folded arms. Clearing and excavating land in this way add a settler colonial surveillance, "enabl[ing] management to adopt a sort of panoramic perspective on the field, viewing at a glance who was kneeling and working and who was standing and not working." Marez, *Farm Worker Futurism*, 87. This scene of racialized labor suggests how these Indigenous laborers were key to constructing the very channels invaluable to the scientific linkages AURA anticipated. From this roadway, sky data will consolidate, derived from networked laboratories in Arizona and New Mexico and the Cerro Tololo Inter-American Observatory in Chile.

56 "Flagstaff's Observatory," *Los Angeles Herald*, November 11, 1896, in Andrew E. Douglass, scrapbook, box 21a, AZ 072, Andrew Ellicott Douglass Papers, 1867–1962, University of Arizona Libraries, Special Collections.

57 Schindler, *Far End*, 10.

58 "An Observatory Moving to Mexico," newspaper clipping, October 10, 1896, in "Lowell Observatory in Mexico," box 21, AZ 072, Andrew Ellicott Douglass Papers, 1867–1962, University of Arizona Libraries, Special Collections.

59 "An Observatory Moving to Mexico."

60 "A Site Selected," *Mexican Herald*, November 24, 1896, in Douglass, scrapbook.

61 "The Great Telescope," *Two Republics*, December 16, 1896, in Douglass, scrapbook.

62 J. Ruiz, *Americans*, 5.

63 J. Ruiz, *Americans*, 3.

64 J. Ruiz, *Americans*, 6.

65 J. Ruiz, *Americans*, 14.

66 J. Ruiz, *Americans*, 14.

67 J. Ruiz, *Americans*, 15.

68 J. Ruiz, *Americans*, 14.

69 These headlines pervade Douglass, scrapbook.

70 Schindler, *Far End*, 1.

71 "Flagstaff's Observatory."

72 J. Ruiz, *Americans*, 4.

73 "An Observatory Moving to Mexico."

74 Douglass, "Lowell Observatory," 2.

75 "An Observatory Moving to Mexico."

76 Douglass, "Lowell Observatory," 1.

77 "Site Selected."

78 "An Arizona Telescope," *Paterson Evening News*, 1898, in Douglass, scrapbook.

79 Messeri, *Placing Outer Space*, 158.

80 Douglass, "Lowell Observatory," 1.

81 "Site Selected."

82 Douglass, "Lowell Observatory," 3.

83 Douglass, "Lowell Observatory," 3.

84 Douglass, "Lowell Observatory," 3.

85 Douglass, "Lowell Observatory," 3.

86 "The Lowell Observatory," *Two Republics*, December 22, 1896, in Douglass, scrapbook.

87 Douglass, "Lowell Observatory," 3.

88 For more on necropolitics, consider Mbembe, "Necropolitics."

89 M. Franco, "Invisible Labor," 108.

90 M. Franco, "Invisible Labor," 109.

91 M. Franco, "Invisible Labor," 98.

92 M. Franco, "Invisible Labor," 98.

93 J. Ruiz, *Americans*, 66.

94 J. Ruiz, *Americans*, 66.

95 "Tacubaya Observatory," *Mexican Herald*, February 12, 1897, in Douglass, scrapbook.

96 "Tacubaya Observatory."

97 "The New Astronomical Building," *Mexican Herald*, November 17, 1896, in Douglass, scrapbook. Also, Lowell Observatory Visitor Guestbook, 1894–1938, Lowell Observatory Archives, Flagstaff, AZ. The entry on March 1897 reads: "Pres. Diaz & Members of his cabinet & staff."

98 "An Arizona Telescope."

99 B. Cortez, "Memory of Plants," 191.

100 Also consider her collaborative work with rafa esparza in the show *Pasado Mañana* (Day after tomorrow; 2018) at Commonwealth and Council in Los Angeles, replete with dirt floors and a hydroponic garden. See Moon, "Beatriz Cortez and Rafa Esparza."

101 Morton, *Hyperobjects*, 1.

102 Anthony Aveni and colleagues argue, "Venus was one of the principal astronomical bodies taken into consideration in the total design of [El Caracol]"; they equally note, "The Caracol windows were placed to aid such observations specifically to preserve the direction of the most predictable disappearances of Venus before heliacal rise." Aveni et al., "Caracol Tower," 983–84.

103 Aveni et al., "Caracol Tower," 981.

104 Ricketson, "Astronomical Observatories," 219. Also, Aldana y Villalobos, *Calculating Brilliance*, 247.

105 Pitzer College, Office of Communications, "Pitzer College Hosts."

106 Beatriz Cortez, interview by the author, July 24, 2022.

107 Carrasco, "Alberto Ruz Lhuillier."

108 Milbrath, *Star Gods*, 265.

109 For more on how this mural relates to astronautic vocabularies in Chicanx public art, see chapter 2. Also, Latorre, *Walls of Empowerment*, 83.

110 Dean, *Culture of Stone*, 2. This observation is indebted to Claudia Zapata. Also consider Malville et al., "Cosmological Motifs."

111 Dean, *Culture of Stone*, 2.

112 Dean, *Culture of Stone*, 8.

113 The vandalism and its resolution were detailed in email communications. Ciara Ennis, email to author, August 1, 2022.

114 Carrigan, "Artist Rafa Esparza."

115 Muñoz, *Sense of Brown*, 121. It is worth noting that even Muñoz concedes that "there are certainly connections between brownness and mud that are actually exhilarating to think about" (121).

116 Aveni, *Skywatchers*, 249.

117 Green, "Rafa Esparza."

118 Aveni, *Skywatchers*, 249.

119 Aveni, *Skywatchers*, 250.

120 Shanks, "Adobe, Dust, and Water."

121 J. Franco, "No Amateurs," 83–84.

122 J. Franco, "No Amateurs," 83.

123 Khalili, "Magma," 402.

124 Khalili, "Magma," 402.

125 Illia, "Nader Khalili."

126 Consider McClain, "Making Bricks."

127 Londoño, *Abstract Barrios*, 9.

128 Whitney Museum of Art, "Whitney Biennial 2017."

129 The artist's words. See Whitney Museum of Art, "Whitney Biennial 2017."

130 Gaspar de Alba, *Chicano Art*, 19.

131 Muñoz, *Sense of Brown*, 10.

132 Muñoz, *Sense of Brown*, 2. For more on being antinormative, see Muñoz, *Sense of Brown*, 63.

133 Muñoz, *Sense of Brown*, 15.

134 Esparza claims that he has no personal relationship with or close affection for the Getty Center, a site he has visited only "three or four times" in his life as a Los Angeles resident. For more, see Hammer Museum, "rafa esparza."

135 Hammer Museum, "rafa esparza."

136 Muñoz, *Sense of Brown*, 118.

137 Muñoz, *Sense of Brown*, 118–19.

138 This fact was relayed by Getty performance programmer Sarah Cooper during our interview. Sarah Cooper, interview by the author, April 27, 2023.

139 This detail was the recollection of Sarah Cooper. Her memory differs from the artist's; he claimed a bloodied T-shirt was tied to the strings of the balloons to symbolize the strife and trauma he endured on this planet. Cooper, interview.

140 See chapter 2 of this volume.

141 Santilli, "Getty Center's Stone."

142 This summation was relayed during my interview with the curator. Laura Copelin, interview by the author, May 24, 2022.

143 For more on this topic in Anzaldúa's unpublished "werejaguar" short story on Maya mythology, see S. Ramirez, "Recovering," 66.

144 This observation was pointed out by Copelin. Copelin, interview.

145 Jacqueline Arias, interview by the author, May 23, 2022.

146 This family story was conveyed by Arias. Arias, interview.

147 For more on this point, see Womack, *Afrofuturism*, 32.

148 *Terra Forms* was cocurated by Kelly Franck, Sonya Landau, and Jacob Niemiec. The eight artists who participated were Arias, Pablo Cruz, Drew Grella, Chelsy Mata, Charlotte Rose Ruth, Perla Segovia, Jandey Shackelford,

and Sydney Yount. *Terra Forms*, brochure, December 3, 2021, University of Arizona and Museum of Contemporary Art Tucson.

149 McCurdy, *Space*, 174.

150 For instance, consider Robinson, *Red Mars*.

151 McCurdy, *Space*, 182.

152 McCurdy, *Space*, 174.

153 For more, see O'Doherty, *Inside the White Cube*.

154 Rafael Vargas-Suarez Universal, interview by the author (with Matt Shindell), February 19, 2021.

155 For more, see Bonansinga, *Curating at the Edge*.

156 Again, "non-place" is Cornejo's term. Cornejo, "'Does That Come,'" 191.

157 For an important summation of SB 1070 and its related impact on Arizona's immigrant and activist communities, see Vega, *Drawing Deportation*, 30–31.

158 M. Franco, "Invisible Labor," 107.

159 Marks, "Molas," 37.

160 B. Cortez, "Memory of Plants," 191.

161 B. Cortez, interview, January 15, 2021.

162 Messeri, *Placing Outer Space*, 21.

Chapter 4. It Came from Beyond the Border: Tequila Science Fiction and the Latinf/x Sensibility

1 Translating *comadres* is an imperfect endeavor, though the term conveys a close friendship akin to a sisterly bond.

2 See V. Ruiz, "Introduction," 1:1.

3 Smith, *Photography*, 10.

4 Smith, *Photography*, 9, 11.

5 Steiner, "When You Look at This," 142–43.

6 Ybarra-Frausto, "Rasquachismo," 8. Also consider how Ybarra-Frausto discusses the origins of the term linked to the *pepenador* (scavenger of scraps), which I argue could also apply to media discards. See Ybarra-Frausto, "Imagining," 9.

7 Sconce, "'Trashing' the Academy," 372.

8 Stableford, "Science Fiction," 29.

9 Sobchack, *Screening Space*, 55.

10 Sobchack, *Screening Space*, 88.

11 Sobchack, *Screening Space*, 136.

12 Sobchack, *Screening Space*, 136.

13 Schauer, *Escape Velocity*, 68.

14 Wolfe, *Known and the Unknown*, 24.

15 Wolfe, *Known and the Unknown*, 198.

16 Sobchack, *Screening Space*, 136.

17 Lucanio and Coville, *Smokin' Rockets*, 29.

18 Telotte, *Movies, Modernism*, 4.

19 Telotte, *Movies, Modernism*, 3.

20 Gunning, "Cinema of Attraction," 64.

21 Gunning, "Cinema of Attraction," 65, 66.

22 Gunning, "Cinema of Attraction," 66.

23 Gunning, "Cinema of Attraction," 70.

24 Gunning, "Cinema of Attraction," 65.

25 Heffernan, *Ghouls, Gimmicks, and Gold*, 11.

26 Heffernan, *Ghouls, Gimmicks, and Gold*, 10.

27 Gamboa, "No Phantoms."

28 Armando Norte (with Consuelo Flores), interview by the author, May 3, 2021.

29 Sconce, "'Trashing' the Academy," 372.

30 Sconce, introduction, 3. Also, Hills, "Para-Paracinema," 220.

31 Sconce, "'Trashing' the Academy," 381. Also, Greene, *Mexploitation Cinema*, 15.

32 Sobchack, *Screening Space*, 136.

33 Rancaño, "Why Latinos."

34 Ybarra-Frausto, "Rasquachismo," 8.

35 Indych-López, "Nuyorican Baroque," 75.

36 Ybarra-Frausto, "Rasquachismo," 8.

37 Ahmed, *Promise of Happiness*, 219.

38 Schauer, *Escape Velocity*, 68.

39 Velasquez, "Cabrales Showcases New Exhibit."

40 Angel Cabrales, interview by the author and Matt Shindell, August 6, 2021.

41 Cabrales, interview.

42 Cabrales, interview. For more on shuttle flights at White Sands Space Harbor, see Eckles, "White Sands."

43 Cabrales, interview.

44 Curtis, "ART."

45 See Amada, "Summer Sizzle Continues." Also, Curtis, "ART."

46 Cabrales, interview.

47 Cabrales, interview.

48 Cabrales, interview.

49 Cohen, "Juárez, El Paso Partner."

50 E. Avila, "Dark City," 53.

51 López, "Community Resistance," 460.

52 López, "Community Resistance," 459.

53 López, "Community Resistance," 459.

54 E. Avila, "Dark City," 53.

55 Vincent Valdez, interview by the author, February 1, 2024.

56 Valdez, interview.

57 Rubin, "Los Angeles Story," 16.

58 Valdez, interview.

59 Ry Cooder, letter to Vincent Valdez, 2004. Displayed in the exhibition *Vincent Valdez and Ry Cooder: El Chavez Ravine*, LA County Museum of Art, Los Angeles, November 12, 2023–July 21, 2023.

60 Cooder, letter.

61 The exhibition setting reminded Valdez of the phantom zone sequence from Richard Donner's *Superman* (1978), in which General Zod and his minions are sentenced to life imprisonment in a flat 2D ghostlike existence. "When you see this thin shard of glass at an angle hovering over the truck, it reminded me of that scene instantly thirty-five years later," he recalled. Valdez, interview.

62 E. Avila, "Dark City," 60.

63 R. Gonzalez, "Vincent Ramos," 86.

64 Vincent Ramos, interview by the author, November 25, 2022.

65 Vincent Ramos, email message to the author, November 13, 2022.

66 "Collecting impulse" refers to Baudrillard, "System of Collecting," 24.

67 See Cascone, "Artist Mined."

68 Stromberg, "Hollywood Myths."

69 Consider J. González, "Rhetoric of the Object," 82.

70 For more, see Jennifer González's related chapter on Mesa-Bains: J. González, *Subject to Display*, 120–63. See also Rosten, *Hollywood*.

71 Valli, "Grease."

72 Tompkins, "*Post-America L.A.*"

73 Tompkins, "*Post-America L.A.*"

74 Ramos, interview.

75 Eller, *Becoming Ray Bradbury*, 10.

76 Bradbury scholars are divided about the existence of Mr. Electrico. Their encounter may have occurred in Chicago, Tucson, or even Los Angeles. However, I include the anecdote given its reoccurrence in Bradbury lore. For more see Eller, *Becoming Ray Bradbury*, 14. Also, Ofgang, "Sideshow Magician."

77 Eller, *Becoming Ray Bradbury*, 9.

78 Eller, *Becoming Ray Bradbury*, 12.

79 Eller, *Becoming Ray Bradbury*, 17.

80 See Bradbury, *Dark Carnival*.

81 Eller, *Becoming Ray Bradbury*, 122.

82 Eller, *Becoming Ray Bradbury*, 123.

83 For more, see C. Ramírez, *Woman in the Zoot Suit*.

84 Eller, *Becoming Ray Bradbury*, 55. Incidentally, the biographer discusses Bradbury's on-again, off-again proximity to the local Latinx population in LA as cause for his "keen" observations and writerly acumen (96).

85 Ramos discusses this exchange further in Adams, "Vincent Ramos."

86 Ramos, interview.

87 Tompkins, "*Post-America L.A.*" The original name of the artwork is *A Science Fiction Film, 1959, 2009, 2019* (2009), though, in keeping with Ramos's wishes, it is referred to as *Planets Beyond Jupiter, 1959, 2009, 2019* (2009) in this text.

88 See Duncan and McKenna, *Semina Culture*.

89 See Noriega, "Your Art Disgusts Me."

90 Telotte, *Movies, Modernism*, 158.

91 This anecdote was relayed by Ramos to the author. Ramos, interview.

92 Schauer, *Escape Velocity*, 76–77.

93 Schauer, *Escape Velocity*, 76.

94 Angel Cabrales, interview by the author, October 10, 2022.

95 Schauer, *Escape Velocity*, 76.

96 Telotte, *Movies, Modernism*, 111.

97 Telotte, *Movies, Modernism*, 110.

98 For more about the Department of Justice's investigation into Uvalde police failures, unpreparedness, and inept response, see US Department of Justice, *Critical Incident Review*.

99 Morales, "Horror in Gloria Anzaldúa," 53.

100 hooks, *Black Looks*, 21.

101 Greene, *Mexploitation Cinema*, 19.

102 Gaytán, *¡Tequila!*, 17.

103 Gaytán, *¡Tequila!*, 19.

104 J. Ruiz, *Americans*, 15.

105 Gaytán, "Transformation of Tequila," 79.

106 Gaytán, "Transformation of Tequila," 70.

107 Gaytán, "Transformation of Tequila," 71.

108 Gaytán, "Transformation of Tequila," 70.

109 For more, see Parker, "'Star Wars.'"

110 hooks, *Black Looks*, 21.

111 Gaytán, *¡Tequila!*, 25.

Chapter 5. Rage Against the Machine: The Art of Latina Space Feminism and Protest

1 As Tim Fernholz notes, "The US Air Force spends hundreds of millions of dollars to monitor orbital junk, sending a heads-up to satellite operators of the [International Space Station] whenever they forecast a collision. . . . [It] remains a real risk that space agencies around the world pay attention to." Fernholz, *Rocket Billionaires*, 233–34. Also, Tatiana Reinoza discusses the collaborative portfolio of Enrique Chagoya and Alberto Ríos, entitled *You Are Here* (2000). The work pessimistically riffs on the blue-marble photograph taken by Apollo 17 and grimly unveils Earth's envelopment in "space junk." See Reinoza, *Reclaiming the Americas*, 92–93.

2 *Time*, July 2, 2018.

3 Berger, *Seeing Through Race*, 124.

4 Berger, *Seeing Through Race*, 124.

5 Berger, *Seeing Through Race*, 124.

6 *Time*, July 2, 2018, 4.

7 John Moore, *Crying Girl on the Border*, 2018, World Press Photo, https://www.worldpressphoto.org/collection/photo-contest/2019/john-moore-soy/1. Also consider Mark and Ralph, "Getty Photographer."

8 Forestieri, "Federal Government." Also, Toledo, "Mountain View."

9 Barr and Faulders, "US Considers."

10 Forestieri, "Federal Government."

11 Fernholz, *Rocket Billionaires*, 156.

12 Kluger, "Peggy Whitson," 11.

13 Saunders, "Art After Apollo," 140.

14 See Fernholz, *Rocket Billionaires*, 258.

15 Fernholz, *Rocket Billionaires*, 243.

16 Sandoval, *Methodology of the Oppressed*, 41.

17 Sandoval, *Methodology of the Oppressed*, 43.

18 Ginsburg, *Cyborg Caribbean*, 3.

19 At the time of this writing, Los Ojos, New Mexico, houses the Tierra Wools Cooperative, an all-woman co-op galvanizing the local artisan economy predicated on alpaca- and sheep-based fiber arts. For more, see "Los Ojos (Parkview)," and Centinela Traditional Arts, "Rio Grande Weaving."

20 H. Fischer, "Espejo," 15.

21 For an overview of Bernal's oeuvre, see Foster, *Picturing the Barrio*, 62.

22 Barthes calls the "punctum" an "accident which pricks me (but also bruises me, is poignant to me)." Barthes, *Camera Lucida*, 27.

23 Bernal's yoking of sewing and the universe shares visual characteristics with other artworks at that time, like Chicana artist Yolanda López's *Margaret F. Stewart: Our Lady of Guadalupe* (1978), an oil pastel painting based on a photograph of the artist's mother sewing industrial-brand wares for the Naval Training Center in San Diego. Her mother's glasses teeter at the bridge of her nose with a mandorla glowing around her. Margaret F. Stewart is a Chicana mother goddess, a contemporary Coatlicue, and a modern-day Virgen de Guadalupe. She sews her own starry cape, prepared to blanket herself with a fabric as luminous as the universe. See Dawsey, "Portrait of the Artist," 29.

24 For more, consider de Monchaux, *Spacesuit*.

25 Mesa-Bains, "Domesticana."

26 Wingate, "Louis Carlos Bernal's Photographs," 4.

27 Mesa-Bains, "Domesticana," 93.

28 J. González, introduction, 8.

29 *Los Angeles Times*, "Report to Be Given."

30 For more, see Ellstrand, "Reclaiming the Patria."

31 *Los Angeles Times*, "VFW Posts." See also *Los Angeles Times*, "Veterans to Show"; and *Los Angeles Times*, "Vets Auxiliary."

32 See Gunckel, *Oscar Castillo Papers*. On barrio urban imagery, consider Valadez and, likewise, Iturbide; see photographs in Ortiz-Torres, *Mex/L.A.*, 164–73.

33 Tillman, "Saturn's Rings."

34 Anzaldúa, "Let Us," 10.

35 H. Fischer, "Espejo," 15.

36 Byrne-Smith, introduction, 13. For more, see Suvin, *Metamorphoses of Science Fiction*.

37 Davenport, *Space Barons*, 174.

38 García, *Viva Kennedy*, 48.

39 García, *Viva Kennedy*, 44.

40 García, *Viva Kennedy*, 44–45.

41 García, *Viva Kennedy*, 45.

42 García, *Viva Kennedy*, 54.

43 García, *Viva Kennedy*, 50.

44 García, *Viva Kennedy*, 53.

45 García, *Viva Kennedy*, 55.

46 "Last Hours of J. F. K.," *LULAC News* 25, no. 4 (November–December 1963), 1, newsprint, MSS0160, John J. Herrera Papers, Houston Metropolitan Research Center, Houston Public Library.

47 John J. Herrera and John F. Kennedy, November 21, 1963, newsprint, MSS0160, John J. Herrera Papers.

48 For more on Kennedy corridos, see Gurza, "Kennedy Corridos."

49 García, *Viva Kennedy*, 4.

50 "Last Hours of J. F. K.," 2.

51 Eugene Keilin, "'Visiting Professor' Kennedy Pushes Space-Age Spending," *Thresher*, September 19, 1962, 1, newsprint, UA 109, John F. Kennedy Space Effort Speech at Rice University records, box 1, folder 3, Woodson Research Center, Fondren Library, Rice University, Houston, TX.

52 Keilin, "'Visiting Professor,'" 6.

53 Forrest Fischer, "President Hailed City as the Heart of Space Effort," September 12, 1962, newsprint, UA 109, John F. Kennedy Space Effort Speech at Rice University records.

54 F. Fischer, "President Hailed."

55 Council No. 660 Invitation to Hispanic Astronauts Banquet, May 23, 1986, ephemera, MSS0353, LULAC Regional Papers, Houston Metropolitan Research Center, Houston Public Library.

56 In the invitation this chapter describes itself as the "NASA Area LULAC Council." See Council No. 660 Invitation.

57 García, *Viva Kennedy*, 51.

58 Cotera et al., "Introduction," 11, 3.

59 Taylor, "Mendez."

60 Vincent, "BTX Fiber."

61 Davenport, *Space Barons*, 123.

62 Davenport, *Space Barons*, 30.

63 Davenport, *Space Barons*, 35.

64 Pappalardo, "It's No Surprise."

65 Quoted in Taylor, "Mendez."

66 R. Avila, "City of Brownsville." Also, "piece of this pie" is from Taylor, "Mendez."

67 City of Brownsville, TX, "Brownsville Community."

68 Quoted in City of Brownsville, TX, "Brownsville Community."

69 Nájera-Ramírez, "*Ballet Folklórico Mexicano*," 161.

70 City of Brownsville, TX, "Brownsville Community." Also, Ricourt and Danta, *Hispanas de Queens*, xi.

71 Pappalardo, "It's No Surprise."

72 Nájera-Ramírez, "*Ballet Folklórico Mexicano*," 162.

73 "Mexican Dancers," 4.

74 "Mexican Dancers."

75 "Hispanic Program," 4.

76 NACA (National Advisory Committee for Aeronautics) was established in 1915 before it was reorganized as the National Aeronautics and Space Administration in 1958. "Viva NASA," 1977, Domingo Nick Reyes Papers, box 3, folder 10, Benson Latin American Collection, University of Texas at Austin.

77 Prof. Arturo Rosales, Elma Berrera, and Hermilo R. Gloria, who served as the director of internal programs for NASA, are pictured in the newsletter above an image of women dancing *ballet folklórico*. See "Hispanic Program."

78 "Hispanic Day," 4.

79 "Hispanic Day."

80 Nájera-Ramírez, "*Ballet Folklórico Mexicano*," 171.

81 Fernholz, *Rocket Billionaires*, 249. Fernholz also observes that "the company consisted of little more than 'a carpet and a mariachi band'" (66).

82 Karlis, "Billionaire Elon Musk." Other news outlets reported Musk's much-anticipated visit and a possible appearance in a Tesla Cybertruck. See Arevalo, "SpaceX."

83 Film and media reports abound. Consider Janeidy, "SpaceX Starbase."

84 Davenport, *Space Barons*, 242.

85 G. Davila, "Brownsville Activist."

86 Moreno, "Brownsville Mural."

87 Moreno, "Brownsville Pays."

88 Solomon, "Will Elon Musk."

89 Cavazos, "House of Space."

90 Cavazos, "House of Space."

91 Pedro De La Fuente, interview by author, May 24, 2023, Brownsville, Texas.

92 Moreno, "Hope."

93 Gonzalez-Hernandez, quoted in Solomon, "Will Elon Musk."

94 Solomon, "Will Elon Musk."

95 G. Davila, "Brownsville Activist."

96 G. Davila, "Brownsville Activist."

97 For more on Project MASA, see Merla-Watson, "(Trans)Mission Possible." Also consider R. Hernández, "Alien Skins."

98 These shows included *Mundos Alternos: Art and Science Fiction in the Americas* (UCR ARTSblock, Riverside, CA, 2017–18), which traveled in a multisite format to the Queens Museum, Leslie-Lohman Museum, and New York Hall of Science in 2019. Also, Valderas and LA David's garments were included in *Threads Bare* at Blue Star Contemporary in San Antonio, February 4–May 8, 2022, with a nod to Valderas's *Cosmic Couture*, a fashionable iteration of *Project MASA*.

99 Davalos, *Chicana/o Remix*, 23.

100 Davalos, *Chicana/o Remix*, 24.

101 In 2015 UTPA merged with the University of Texas at Brownsville to become the University of Texas Rio Grande Valley (UTRGV). Keane, "SpaceX BFR."

102 Goodwin, *Latinx Files*, 108, 111.

103 Goodwin, *Latinx Files*, 108.

104 Davenport, "After 2016 Rocket Explosion."

105 Davenport, *Space Barons*, 239.

106 Davenport, *Space Barons*, 240. Aliens must have been up to their old ways. In 2023 SpaceX's rocket Starship detonated just minutes into its launch. Its debris showered the Gulf of Mexico, with the Federal Aviation Administration (FAA) claiming "no injuries or public damage had been reported." The

explosion was felt among local RGV residents, with artist Nansi Guevara taking to her Instagram Live to document the shaking. "It felt like a *temblor*, like an earthquake. I used to live in Mexico City for a little bit, and it reminded me of an earthquake." Guevara, "Space X Launch Made the Ground Shake," Instagram, November 18, 2023, https://www.instagram.com/reel/CzyjBVBL5O8/?igsh=MWUzaTFoNzVkYTdmMg==. On March 6, 2025, a test flight went awry, with the debris of another Starship rocket explosion showering Florida, the Bahamas, and Turks and Caicos Islands. See Matza, "SpaceX Rocket Explodes." Also, Dunn, "Explosions."

107 Davenport, *Space Barons*, 240.

108 Brannstrom and Neuman, "Inventing," 123.

109 Brannstrom and Neuman, "Inventing," 130.

110 "Border Patrol."

111 Smith, *Photography*, 9.

112 See Saunders, "Art After Apollo," 140.

113 For more on Latina domestic interior installation art, consider Noriega et al., *Home*. Also, Martínez, *María Brito*.

114 Nansi Guevara, interview by author, May 24, 2023, Brownsville, Texas.

115 Mesa-Bains, "Domesticana," 95.

116 For more on housing unaffordability in Brownsville, see G. Davila, "Housing Costs."

117 *Who's the Bandit?* is also the title of Rawmírez's solo exhibition at the South Texas College Library Art Gallery. See Rawmírez, "Who's the Bandit?"

118 These sentiments are conveyed in Tossin, "MCA Denver Conversations."

119 These sentiments were further conveyed in Tossin, "MCA Denver Conversations."

120 Consider "Locals Embrace."

121 Davenport, *Space Barons*, 62.

122 Davenport, *Space Barons*, 26.

123 Fernholz, *Rocket Billionaires*, 236.

124 Fernholz, *Rocket Billionaires*, 241–42.

125 Clarissa Tossin, Zoom interview by author and Matt Shindell, January 18, 2021.

126 Tossin, "MCA Denver Conversations."

127 Sandoval, "U.S. Third World Feminism," 15.

128 C. Ramírez, "Deus ex Machina," 159, 157.

129 Pérez, *Chicana Art*, 4, 46.

130 Gómez, *Nuclear Nuevo México*, 8. Also, Muñoz, *Sense of Brown*, 4.

131 Guevara, interview.

132 Anzaldúa, "Let Us Be," 20.

133 Muñoz, *Cruising Utopia*, 4.

Bibliography

Adams, Thomas. "Ep. 5 Vincent Ramos." Art Traffic, September 11, 2017. YouTube video, 1:16. https://www.youtube.com/watch?v=dr5zgPHI88w.

Ades, Dawn. "Arte Madí/Arte Concreto-Invención." In *Art in Latin America: The Modern Era, 1820–1980*, edited by Dawn Ades, 241–52. New Haven, CT: Yale University Press, 1989.

Ahmed, Sara. *The Promise of Happiness*. Durham, NC: Duke University Press, 2010.

Alan Bean Gallery. "*First Men*—Buzz Aldrin." Last revised November 28, 2023. http://www.alanbeangallery.com/first-men-buzz-aldrin?rq=First%20Men%20.

Aldana y Villalobos, Gerardo. *Calculating Brilliance: An Intellectual History of Maya Astronomy at Chich'en Itza*. Tucson: University of Arizona Press, 2022.

Allora, Calzadilla, and Ted Chiang. "The Great Silence." In *Science Fiction*, edited by Dan Byrne-Smith, 93–97. Cambridge, MA: MIT Press, 2020.

Alonso, Rodrigo. "Argentines on the Moon." In *Past Futures: Science Fiction, Space Travel, and Postwar Art of the Americas*, edited by Sarah Montross, 76–88. Cambridge, MA: MIT Press, 2015.

Alvarado, Karina O., Alicia Ivonne Estrada, and Ester E. Hernández. "Introduction: U.S. Central American (Un)Belongings." In *U.S. Central Americans: Reconstructing Memories, Struggles, and Communities of Resistance*, edited by Karina O. Alvarado, Alicia Ivonne Estrada, and Ester E. Hernández, 3–36. Tucson: University of Arizona Press, 2017.

Alvarado, Karina Olivia, Alicia Ivonne Estrada, and Ester E. Hernández. "Preface: Our Process as Subjects Within Diasporic Communities and Fields." In *U.S. Central Americans: Reconstructing Memories, Struggles, and Communities of Resistance*, edited by Karina O. Alvarado, Alicia Ivonne Estrada, and Ester E. Hernández, ix–xii. Tucson: University of Arizona Press, 2017.

Amada, Rich. "Summer Sizzle Continues at UAMA with 'Hot Art.'" University of Arizona News, August 11, 2000. https://news.arizona.edu/story/summer-sizzle-continues-uama-hot-art (no longer available).

Anzaldúa, Gloria. *Borderlands/La Frontera: The New Mestiza*. San Francisco: Aunt Lute Books, 2012.

Anzaldúa, Gloria. "Let Us Be the Healing of the Wound: The Coyolxauhqui Imperative—La sombra y el sueño." In *Light in the Dark/Luz en lo Oscuro: Rewriting Identity, Spirituality, Reality*, edited by AnaLouise Keating, 9–22. Durham, NC: Duke University Press, 2015.

Aparicio, Frances R. "Latinidad/es." In *Keywords for Latina/o Studies*, edited by Deborah R. Vargas, Nancy Raquel Mirabal, and Lawrence La Fountain-Stokes, 113–17. New York: New York University Press, 2017.

Aranda, Yto, and Pamela Figueroa. "Latin American Kinetic Art and Its Relationship with Electronic Art: Gyula Kosice and Abraham Palatnik." In *Proceedings of the 19th International Symposium of Electronic Art*, edited by Kathy Cleland, Laura Fisher, and Ross Harley, 1–4. Sydney: ISEA International, the Australian Network for Art and Technology and the University of Sydney, 2013.

Arevalo, Evelyn Janeidy. "SpaceX Is One of the Sponsors of the City of Brownsville's 'Mr. Amigo Charro Day Fiesta'—People Hope Elon Musk Attends the Parade in a Tesla Cybertruck." *Tesmanian* (blog), January 27, 2022. https://www.tesmanian.com/blogs/tesmanian-blog/mramigo.

Arias, Arturo. *Taking Their Word: Literature and the Signs of Central America*. Minneapolis: University of Minnesota Press, 2007.

Ashley, Mike. "Imagining Mars." In *Moving to Mars: Design for the Red Planet*, edited by Andrew Nahum, Justin McGuirk, Eleanor Watson et al., 17–20. London: Design Museum, 2019.

Avanessian, Armen. "Asynchronous Present Past." In *Speculative Art Histories: Analysis at the Limits*, edited by Sjoerd van Tuinen, 11–20. Edinburgh: Edinburgh University Press, 2017.

Aveni, Anthony F. *Skywatchers: A Revised and Updated Version of Skywatchers of Ancient Mexico*. Austin: University of Texas Press, 2001.

Aveni, Anthony F., Sharon L. Gibbs, and Horst Hartung. "The Caracol Tower at Chichen Itza: An Ancient Astronomical Observatory?" *Science* 188, no. 4192 (1975): 977–85.

Avila, Eric. "Dark City: White Flight and the Urban Science Fiction Film in Postwar America." In *Classic Hollywood, Classic Whiteness*, edited by Daniel Bernardi, 52–71. Minneapolis: University of Minnesota Press, 2001.

Avila, Rolando. "City of Brownsville Lays Groundwork to the Next Frontier." ValleyCentral.com, November 9, 2021. https://www.valleycentral.com/news/local-news/city-of-brownsville-lays-groundwork-to-the-next-frontier/.

Barnet-Sánchez, Holly, and Tim Drescher. *Give Me Life: Iconography and Identity in East LA Murals*. Albuquerque: University of New Mexico Press, 2016.

Barnitz, Jacqueline. *Twentieth-Century Art of Latin America*. Austin: University of Texas Press, 2001.

Barnitz, Jacqueline. *Twentieth-Century Art of Latin America*. Rev. and exp. ed. Austin: University of Texas Press, 2015.

Barr, Luke, and Katherine Faulders. "US Considers Using NASA Facility to House Migrant Children." *ABC News*, March 10, 2021. https://abcnews.go.com/Politics/us-considers-nasa-facility-house-migrant-children/story?id=76380512.

Bartels, Meghan. "Arecibo Observatory: A Year After Telescope's Collapse, an Icon Gets Continuing Cleanup and a New Documentary." Space.com, December 1, 2021. https://www.space.com/arecibo-radio-telescope-collapse-anniversary.

Barthes, Roland. *Camera Lucida: Reflections on Photography*. Translated by Richard Howard. New York: Hill and Wang, 1980.

Baudrillard, Jean. "The System of Collecting." In *Material Culture: Critical Concepts in the Social Sciences*, edited by Victor Buchli, 7–24. London: Routledge, 2004.

Becker, Karin, and Geska Helena Brečević. "More than a Portrait: Framing the Photograph as Sculpture and Video Animation." *Membrana Journal* 3, no. 2 (2018): 48–55.

Benedek, Laslo, dir. *The Outer Limits*. "Tourist Attraction." Season 1, episode 13. Aired December 23, 1963, on ABC.

Berger, Martin A. *Seeing Through Race: A Reinterpretation of Civil Rights Photography*. Berkeley: University of California Press, 2011.

Berger, Martin A. *Sight Unseen: Whiteness and American Visual Culture*. Berkeley: University of California Press, 2005.

Beronius, George. "The Murals of East Los Angeles." *Los Angeles Times*, April 11, 1976.

Bonansinga, Kate. *Curating at the Edge: Artists Respond to the U.S./Mexico Border*. Austin: University of Texas Press, 2013.

"Border Patrol to Work with SpaceX During Tests at Boca Chica Site." KRGV.com, October 7, 2019. https://www.krgv.com/videos/border-patrol-to-work-with-spacex-during-tests-at-boca-chica-site/.

Bradbury, Ray. *Dark Carnival*. Sauk City: Arkham House, 1947.

Brannstrom, Christian, and Matthew Neuman. "Inventing the 'Magic Valley' of South Texas, 1905–1941." *Geographical Review* 99, no. 2 (2009): 123–45.

Brenner, Anita. *The Wind That Swept Mexico: The History of the Mexican Revolution of 1910–1942*. Austin: University of Texas Press, 1971.

Brown, Jayna. *Black Utopias: Speculative Life and the Music of Other Worlds*. Durham, NC: Duke University Press, 2021.

Butler, Octavia E. "'Lost Races of Science Fiction' (1980)." In *Octavia E. Butler*, edited by Gerry Canavan, 181–86. Urbana: University of Illinois Press, 2016.

Byrne-Smith, Dan. Introduction to *Science Fiction*, edited by Dan Byrne-Smith, 12–19. Cambridge, MA: MIT Press, 2020.

Cantú, Aaron. "Valley Activists Wage Transatlantic Battle to Stop Natural Gas Exports from South Texas." *Texas Tribune*, April 12, 2024. https://www.texastribune.org/2024/04/12/texas-natural-gas-export-terminals-brownsville-europe/.

Carrasco, David, ed. "Alberto Ruz Lhuillier." In *The Oxford Encyclopedia of Mesoamerican Cultures: The Civilizations of Mexico and Central America*, 98–100. Oxford: Oxford University Press, 2001.

Carrigan, Margaret. "Artist Rafa Esparza Honors Latino Labor in Marfa, Texas." *Observer*, November 15, 2017. https://observer.com/2017/11/artist-rafa-esparza-honors-latin-american-labor-in-texas-at-ballroom-marfa/.

Cascone, Sarah. "An Artist Mined the Paramount Pictures Archives to Critique Mexican Representation in Cinema History at Frieze Projects." *Artnet*, February 14, 2020. https://news.artnet.com/market/vincent-ramos-latino-cinema-history-frieze-projects-1778856.

Cavazos, Elsa. "House of Space: San Benito Man Commissions Home Tribute to SpaceX, Elon Musk." *Valley Morning Star*, June 20, 2021. https://myrgv.com/life/2021/06/20/space-house-san-benito-man-commissions-home-tribute-to-spacex-elon-musk/#google_vignette.

Centinela Traditional Arts. "History of Rio Grande Weaving." Chimayo Weavers. Accessed November 19, 2023. https://www.chimayoweavers.com/pages/history-of-rio-grande-weaving.

Chua, Daniel K. L., and Alexander Rehding. *Alien Listening: Voyager's Golden Record and Music from Earth*. Princeton, NJ: Princeton University Press, 2021.

City of Brownsville, Texas. "Brownsville Community Invites Elon Musk to 85th Annual Charro Days." February 9, 2022. YouTube video, 3:19. https://www.youtube.com/watch?v=xdbBooYn9_Q&t=199s.

Cockcroft, Eva Sperling, and Holly Barnet-Sánchez. Introduction to *Signs from the Heart: California Chicano Murals*, 4–21. Venice, CA: Social and Public Art Resource Center, 1990.

Coffey, Mary K. *Orozco's American Epic: Myth, History, and the Melancholy of Race*. Durham, NC: Duke University Press, 2020.

Cohen, Cindy Graff. "Juárez, El Paso Partner for Transborder Biennial." *El Paso Inc.*, June 4, 2018. https://www.elpasoinc.com/columns/local_columnists/ju-rez-el-paso-partner-for-transborder-biennial/article_d5c7e672-6776-11e8-8bf4-4be201229767.html.

Cooder, Ry. *Chávez Ravine: A Record by Ry Cooder.* Perro Verde Records, 2005. CD.

Cornejo, Kency. "Central America at Self Help Graphics: Camaraderie and Artmaking in the City of Angels." In *Self Help Graphics at Fifty: A Cornerstone of Latinx Art and Collaborative Artmaking*, edited by Tatiana Reinoza and Karen Mary Davalos, 191–223. Berkeley: University of California Press, 2023.

Cornejo, Kency. "Decolonial Futurisms: Ancestral Border Crossers, Time Machines, and Space Travel in Salvadoran Art." In *Mundos Alternos: Art and Science Fiction in the Americas*, edited by Robb Hernández and Tyler Stallings, 20–31. Riverside, CA: UCR ARTSblock, 2018.

Cornejo, Kency. "'Does That Come with a Hyphen? A Space?' The Question of Central American-Americans in Latino Art and Pedagogy." *Aztlán* 40, no. 1 (2015): 189–210.

Cornejo, Kency. *Visual Disobedience: Art and Decoloniality in Central America.* Durham, NC: Duke University Press, 2024.

Cortez, Beatriz. "The Memory of Plants: Genetics, Migration, and the Construction of the Future." In *Timescales: Thinking Across Ecological Temporalities*, edited by Carolyn Fornoff, Patricia Eunji Kim, and Bethany Wiggin, 183–92. Minneapolis: University of Minnesota Press, 2020.

Cortez, Constance. *Carmen Lomas Garza.* Minneapolis: University of Minnesota Press, 2010.

Cosgrove, Denis. *Apollo's Eye: A Cartographic Genealogy of the Earth in the Western Imagination.* Baltimore: Johns Hopkins University Press, 2001.

Cotera, María, Maylei Blackwell, and Dionne Espinoza. "Introduction: Movements, Movimientos, and Movidas." In *Chicana Movidas*, edited by María Cotera, Maylei Blackwell, and Dionne Espinoza, 1–30. Austin: University of Texas Press, 2018.

Crary, Jonathan. *Techniques of the Observer: On Vision and Modernity in the Nineteenth Century.* Cambridge, MA: MIT Press, 1990.

Crouch, Tom. "The Saga of a Lunar Landscape." Smithsonian Air and Space Museum, January 22, 2010. https://airandspace.si.edu/stories/editorial/saga-lunar-landscape.

Cullen, Deborah, and Elvis Fuentes. *Caribbean: Art at the Crossroads of the World.* New York: El Museo del Barrio, 2012.

Curtis, Cathy. "ART: Kinetic Sculpture Show Lacks a Point: The Works Are Diverse Yet Quirkily Provocative—At Saddleback College, Meanwhile, a German Art Exhibit Leaves Viewers Asking Why." *Los Angeles Times*, February 4, 1991. https://www.latimes.com/archives/la-xpm-1991-02-04-ca-530-story.html.

Davalos, Karen Mary. *Chicana/o Remix: Art and Errata Since the Sixties.* New York: New York University Press, 2017.

Davalos, Karen Mary. "Sputnik and the Avenues: The Art of Chaz Bojórquez." *Archives of American Art Journal* 57, no. 2 (2018): 28–47.

Davenport, Christian. "After 2016 Rocket Explosion, Elon Musk's SpaceX Looked Seriously at Sabotage." *Washington Post*, February 26, 2018. https://www.washingtonpost.com/news/the-switch/wp/2018/02/26/after-2016-rocket-explosion-elon-musks-spacex-looked-seriously-at-sabotage/.

Davenport, Christian. *The Space Barons: Elon Musk, Jeff Bezos, and the Quest to Colonize the Cosmos.* New York: PublicAffairs, 2018.

Dávila, Arlene. *Latinx Art: Artists, Markets, and Politics.* Durham, NC: Duke University Press, 2020.

Davila, Gaige. "Brownsville Activist Speaks Out After Arrest over Anti-SpaceX Graffiti on Musk-Funded Mural." *Texas Standard*, February 25, 2022. https://www.texasstandard.org/stories/brownsville-activist-speaks-out-after-arrest-over-anti-spacex-graffiti-on-musk-funded-mural/.

Davila, Gaige. "Housing Costs Skyrocket as SpaceX Expands in Brownsville." KERA News, May 13, 2022. https://www.keranews.org/texas-news/2022-05-13/housing-costs-skyrocket-as-spacex-expands-in-texas-city.

Dawsey, Jill. "Portrait of the Artist: An Introduction." In *Yolanda López: Portrait of the Artist*, edited by Jill Dawsey, 9–39. San Diego: Museum of Contemporary Art San Diego, 2021.

Dean, Carolyn. *A Culture of Stone: Inka Perspectives on Rock*. Durham, NC: Duke University Press, 2010.

De Monchaux, Nicholas. *Spacesuit: Fashioning Apollo*. Cambridge, MA: MIT Press, 2011.

Díaz-Basteris, Fernanda, and Maite Urcaregui, eds. *Latinx Comics Studies: Critical and Creative Crossings*. New Brunswick, NJ: Rutgers University Press, 2025.

Donner, Richard, dir. *Superman*. 1978. Burbank, CA: Warner Bros., 2000. DVD.

Douglass, Andrew E. "The Lowell Observatory in Mexico." *Popular Astronomy*, no. 39 (1897): 1–7. https://repository.arizona.edu/bitstream/handle/10150/200045/Douglass%2c%20AE_The%20Lowell%20Observatory%20in%20Mexico_1897.pdf?sequence=1&isAllowed=y.

Doux, Billie. "*The Outer Limits*: Tourist Attraction." *Doux Reviews*. Accessed October 15, 2023. https://www.douxreviews.com/2018/09/the-outer-limits-tourist-attraction.html.

Dreyfus, Patricia Allen. "Robert McCall Illustrator." *American Artist*, March 1971.

Duncan, Michael, and Kristine McKenna, eds. *Semina Culture: Wallace Berman and His Circle*. Santa Monica, CA: Santa Monica Museum of Art, 2005.

Dunn, Marcia. "Explosions End 2nd Test Flight of SpaceX's New Mega Rocket." PBS News, November 18, 2023. https://www.pbs.org/newshour/science/explosions-end-2nd-test-flight-of-spacexs-new-mega-rocket.

Durón, Maximilíano. "How to Altar the World: Amalia Mesa-Bains's Art Shifts the Way We See Art History." *ARTnews*, March 27, 2018. https://www.artnews.com/artnews/news/icons-amalia-mesa-bains-9988/.

Eckles, Jim. "White Sands Missile Range Marks 75th Anniversary." *Las Cruces Sun News*, July 8, 2020. https://www.lcsun-news.com/story/news/local/2020/07/08/us-army-white-sands-missile-range-history-75-year-anniversary/5257217002/.

Elkins, James. *Six Stories from the End of Representation: Images in Painting, Photography, Astronomy, Microscopy, Particle Physics, and Quantum Mechanics, 1980–2000*. Stanford, CA: Stanford University Press, 2008.

Eller, Jonathan R. *Becoming Ray Bradbury*. Urbana: University of Illinois Press, 2011.

Ellis, William S. "Los Angeles: City in Search of Itself." *National Geographic* 155, no. 1 (1979): 26–59.

Ellstrand, Nathan. "Reclaiming the Patria: Sinarquismo in the United States, 1936–1966." PhD diss., Loyola University Chicago, 2022.

Fernholz, Tim. *Rocket Billionaires: Elon Musk, Jeff Bezos, and the New Space Race*. Boston: Mariner Books, 2018.

Ferreira, Rachel Haywood. "How Latin America Saved the World and Other Forgotten Futures." *Science Fiction Studies* 43, no. 2 (2016): 207–25.

Fineman, Mia. "Daydreams by Moonlight." In *Apollo's Muse: The Moon in the Age of Photography*, edited by Mia Fineman and Beth Saunders, 71–79. New York: Metropolitan Museum of New York, 2019.

Fischer, Hal. "Espejo: Reflections of the Mexican American." *Picture Magazine*, no. 9 (vol. 2, no. 3) (1978): 1–16.

Forestieri, Kevin. "Federal Government Could Use Moffett Field to House Unaccompanied Minors, Sparking Protests." *Mountain View Voice*, March 15, 2021. https://www.mv-voice.com/news/2021/03/15/federal-government-could-use-moffett-field-to-house-unaccompanied-minors-sparking-protests.

Foster, David William. *Picturing the Barrio: Ten Chicano Photographers*. Pittsburgh: University of Pittsburgh Press, 2017.

Foucault, Michel. *Discipline and Punish: The Birth of the Prison*. Translated by Alan Sheridan. New York: Vintage Books, 1995.

Foucault, Michel. "Of Other Spaces." *Diacritics* 16, no. 1 (1986): 22–27.

Franco, Josh T. "There Are No Amateurs in Far West Texas." *Third Text* 34, no. 1 (2020): 71–87.

Franco, Michelle Arevalos. "Invisible Labor: Precarity, Ethnic Division, and Transformative Representation in Landscape Architecture Work." *Landscape Journal* 41, no. 1 (2022): 95–111.

Galarte, Francisco J. *Brown Trans Figurations: Rethinking Race, Gender, and Sexuality in Chicanx/Latinx Studies*. Austin: University of Texas Press, 2021.

Gambino, Megan. "What Is on Voyager's Golden Record?" *Smithsonian Magazine*, April 22, 2012. https://www.smithsonianmag.com/science-nature/what-is-on-voyagers-golden-record-73063839/.

Gamboa, Harry, Jr. "No Phantoms." *High Performance* 4, no. 2 (1981): 15.

García, Ignacio M. *Viva Kennedy: Mexican Americans in Search of Camelot*. College Station: Texas A&M University Press, 2000.

Gaspar de Alba, Alicia. *Chicano Art Inside/Outside the Master's House: Cultural Politics and the CARA Exhibition*. Austin: University of Texas Press, 1998.

Gaytán, Marie Sarita. *¡Tequila!: Distilling the Spirit of Mexico*. Stanford, CA: Stanford University Press, 2014.

Gaytán, Marie Sarita. "The Transformation of Tequila: From Hangover to Highbrow." *Journal of Consumer Culture* 17, no. 1 (2017): 62–84.

Geeting, Karen. "Alan Bean: The Human Dimension of Outer Space." *Southwest Art* 14, no. 6 (1984): 90–95.

Gil'Adí, Maia. *Doom Patterns: Latinx Speculations and the Aesthetics of Violence*. Durham, NC: Duke University Press, 2025.

Ginsburg, Samuel. *The Cyborg Caribbean: Techno-Dominance in 21st-Century Cuban, Dominican, and Puerto Rican Science Fiction*. New Brunswick, NJ: Rutgers University Press, 2023.

Glaser, Linda B. "Breakthrough Telescope in Chile Renamed for Benefactor Alum." *Cornell Chronicle*, September 16, 2020. https://news.cornell.edu/stories/2020/09/breakthrough-telescope-chile-renamed-benefactor-alum.

Goldman, Shifra. "How, Why, Where, and When It All Happened: Chicano Murals of California." In *Signs from the Heart: California Chicano Murals*, edited by Eva Sperling Cockcroft and Holly Barnet-Sánchez, 22–53. Venice, CA: Social and Public Art Resource Center, 1990.

Gómez, Myrriah. *Nuclear Nuevo México: Colonialism and the Effects of the Nuclear Industrial Complex on Nuevomexicanos*. Tucson: University of Arizona Press, 2022.

Gómez-Barris, Macarena. *The Extractive Zone: Social Ecologies and Decolonial Perspectives*. Durham, NC: Duke University Press, 2017.

Gomoll, Lucian. "The Performative Spirit of Amalia Mesa-Bains' *New World Wunderkammer*." *Cultural Dynamics* 27, no. 3 (2015): 357–77.

Gonzales, Patrisia. *The Mud People: Chronicles, Testimonios and Remembrances*. San Jose, CA: Chusma House, 2003.

Gonzalez, Alex. "Art at Its Greatest." *Dallas Voice*, May 31, 2019. https://dallasvoice.com/art-at-its-greatest/.

González, Christopher. "Latino Sci-Fi: Cognition and Narrative Design in Alex Rivera's *Sleep Dealer*." In *Latinos and Narrative Media: Participation and Portrayal*, edited by Frederick Luis Aldama, 211–23. New York: Palgrave Macmillan, 2013.

González, Jennifer A. Introduction to *Chicano and Chicana Art: A Critical Anthology*, edited by Jennifer A. González, C. Ondine Chavoya, Chon Noriega, and Terezita Romo, 1–10. Durham, NC: Duke University Press, 2019.

González, Jennifer A. "Rhetoric of the Object: Material Memory and the Artwork of Amalia Mesa-Bains." *Visual Anthropology Review* 9, no. 1 (1993): 82–91.

González, Jennifer A. *Subject to Display: Reframing Race in Contemporary Installation Art*. Cambridge, MA: MIT Press, 2008.

Gonzalez, Rita. "Vincent Ramos: The Collector." *Aperture*, no. 245 (2021): 86–91.

Goodwin, Matthew David. *The Latinx Files: Race, Migration, and Space Aliens*. New Brunswick, NJ: Rutgers University Press, 2021.

Green, Kate. "Rafa Esparza." *Artforum*, November 21, 2017. https://www.artforum.com/columns/rafa-esparza-talks-about-tierra-sangre-oro-at-ballroom-marfa-236552/.

Greene, Doyle. *Mexploitation Cinema: A Critical History of Mexican Vampire, Wrestler, Ape-Man and Similar Films, 1957–1977*. Jefferson, NC: McFarland, 2005.

Gunckel, Colin, ed. *The Oscar Castillo Papers and Photograph Collection*. Los Angeles: UCLA Chicano Studies Research Center, 2011.

Gunning, Tom. "The Cinema of Attraction: Early Film, Its Spectator and the Avant-Garde." *Wide Angle* 8, no. 3–4 (1986): 63-70.

Gurza, Agustín. "The Kennedy Corridos: Tragedy Revives a Genre." *Frontera Collection* (blog), June 22, 2018. https://frontera.library.ucla.edu/blog/2018/06/kennedy-corridos-tragedy-revives-genre.

Gustafson, Jon. *Chroma: The Art of Alex Schomburg*. New York: Father Tree Press, 1986.

Guzmán, Patricio, dir. *Nostalgia for the Light*. Paris: Atacama Productions, Icarus Films Home Video, 2010. DVD.

Halberstam, Jack. *Trans*: A Quick and Quirky Account of Gender Variability*. Berkeley: University of California Press, 2018.

Hammer Museum. "rafa esparza: UCLA Department of Art Lecture." November 20, 2020. YouTube video, 2:22:46. https://www.youtube.com/watch?v=hfI9xJYegPc.

Hayden, Dolores. *The Power of Place: Urban Landscapes as Public History*. Cambridge, MA: MIT Press, 1997.

Heffernan, Kevin. *Ghouls, Gimmicks, and Gold: Horror Films and the American Movie Business, 1953–1968*. Durham, NC: Duke University Press, 2004.

Hernández, Ester E. "Remembering Through Cultural Interventions: Mapping Central Americans in L.A. Public Spaces." In *U.S. Central Americans: Reconstructing Memories, Struggles, and Communities of Resistance*, edited by Karina O. Alvarado, Alicia Ivonne Estrada, and Ester E. Hernández, 144–65. Tucson: University of Arizona Press, 2017.

Hernández, Robb. "Alien Skins: The Outer Spaces of Transplanetary Performance." In *Mundos Alternos: Art and Science Fiction in the Americas*, edited by Robb Hernández and Tyler Stallings, 36–51. Riverside, CA: UCR ARTSblock, 2017.

Hernández, Robb. *Archiving an Epidemic: Art, AIDS, and the Queer Chicanx Avant-Garde*. New York: New York University Press, 2019.

Hernández, Robb, and Tyler Stallings, eds. *Mundos Alternos: Art and Science Fiction in the Americas*. Riverside, CA: UCR ARTSblock, 2017.

Hills, Matt. "Para-Paracinema: The *Friday the 13th* Film Series as Other to Trash and Legitimate Film Cultures." In *Sleaze Artists: Cinema at the Margins of Taste, Style, and Politics*, edited by Jeffrey Sconce, 219–39. Durham, NC: Duke University Press, 2007.

"Hispanic Day Enlightens Crowd." *Roundup* 17, no. 19 (September 29, 1978), 4.

"Hispanic Program Emphasizes Spanish-American Contributions to Our Nation's Space Effort." *Roundup* 16, no. 20 (September 30, 1977), 4.

Hogan, Ernest. "Chicanonautica Manifesto." In *Altermundos: Latin@ Speculative Literature, Film, and Popular Culture*, edited by Cathryn Josefina Merla-Watson and B. V. Olguín, 406–9. Los Angeles: UCLA Chicano Studies Research Center Press, 2017.

Hogan, Ernest. *Cortez on Jupiter*. San Francisco: Strange Particle, 2014.

hooks, bell. *Black Looks: Race and Representation*. New York: Routledge, 2015.

Hough, Jessica. "Too Chicano? The Path to Knowledge and the False University." In *¡Murales Rebeldes! L.A. Chicana/Chicano Murals Under Siege*, edited by Erin M. Curtis, Jessica Hough, and Guisela Latorre, 58–79. Los Angeles: LA Plaza de Cultura y Artes and Angel City Press, 2017.

Hudson, Renee. *Latinx Revolutionary Horizons: Form and Futurity in the Americas*. New York: Fordham University Press, 2024.

Illia, Tony. "Nader Khalili, Noted Earth Architect, Dies at 72." *Architectural Record*, April 21, 2008. https://www.architecturalrecord.com/articles/4352-nader-khalili-noted-earth-architect-dies-at-72.

Indych-López, Anna. "Nuyorican Baroque: Pepón Osorio's *Chucherías*." *Art Journal* 60, no. 1 (2001): 72–83.

International Trade Administration. "Mexico Country Commercial Guide: Aerospace." November 4, 2023. https://www.trade.gov/country-commercial-guides/mexico-aerospace.

Janeidy, Evelyn. "SpaceX Starbase Participates at the City of Brownsville's 2022 Charro Days Parade." February 27, 2022. YouTube video, 2:01. https://www.youtube.com/watch?v=H76UaxjG6Zs.

Jimenez, Norma Ávila. *El arte cósmico de Tamayo*. Mexico City: National Autonomous University of Mexico, Editorial Praxis, 2010.

Karlis, Michael. "Billionaire Elon Musk Caught Deep-Throating Spiropapa in South Texas Town of Brownsville." *San Antonio Current*, February 28, 2022. https://www.sacurrent.com/news/billionaire-elon-musk-caught-deep-throating-spiropapa-in-south-texas-town-of-brownsville-28319033.

Keane, Phillip. "SpaceX BFR Test Site Back on Track." Engineering.com, November 2, 2018. https://www.engineering.com/story/spacex-bfr-test-site-back-on-track.

Kenin, Justine, Mary Louise Kelly, and Elena Burnett. "Poet Laureate Ada Limon Talks About Her Poem Engraved on a NASA Spaceship." *National Public Radio*, October 8, 2024. https://www.npr.org/2024/10/08/nx-s1-5046708/poet-laureate-ada-limon-talks-about-her-poem-engraved-on-a-nasa-spaceship.

Kessler, Elizabeth A. *Picturing the Cosmos: Hubble Space Telescope Images and the Astronomical Sublime*. Minneapolis: University of Minnesota Press, 2012.

Khalili, E. Nader. "Magma, Ceramic, and Fused Adobe Structures Generated *In Situ*." In *Lunar Bases and Space Activities of the 21st Century*, edited by W. W. Mendell, 399–403. Houston: Lunar and Planetary Institute, 1985.

Kluger, Jeffrey. "Peggy Whitson: NASA's Space Ace." *Time*, July 2, 2018.

Lara, Jesus J. *Latino Placemaking and Planning: Cultural Resistance and Strategies for Reurbanization*. Tucson: University of Arizona Press, 2018.

Latorre, Guisela. *Walls of Empowerment: Chicana/o Indigenist Murals of California*. Minneapolis: University of Minnesota Press, 2008.

Lavender, Isiah, III, ed. *Black and Brown Planets: The Politics of Race in Science Fiction*. Jackson: University Press of Mississippi, 2014.

Lefebvre, Henri. *The Production of Space*. Translated by Donald Nicholson-Smith. Oxford: Blackwell, 1991.

"Locals Embrace Blue Origin Mural in Van Horn, Texas." KHOU 11, July 18, 2021. YouTube video, 3:41. https://www.youtube.com/watch?v=LxBnoBFNoyA.

Loewen, James W. *Sundown Towns: A Hidden Dimension of American Racism*. 2nd ed. New York: New Press, 2018.

Londoño, Johana. *Abstract Barrios: The Crises of Latinx Visibility in Cities*. Durham, NC: Duke University Press, 2020.

López, Ronald W., II. "Community Resistance and Conditional Patriotism in Cold War Los Angeles: The Battle for Chavez Ravine." *Latino Studies* 7, no. 4 (2009): 457–79.

Lorde, Audre. *Sister Outsider: Essays and Speeches*. Berkeley, CA: Crossing, 2007.

Los Angeles Times. "Report to Be Given by Mexican Official." January 18, 1943.

Los Angeles Times. "Veterans to Show Atom Attack Film." March 10, 1953.

Los Angeles Times. "Vets Auxiliary Serves Breakfast." February 20, 1964.

Los Angeles Times. "VFW Posts Note Pearl Harbor." December 7, 1953.

"Los Ojos (Parkview), New Mexico." Sangres.com. Accessed November 19, 2023. http://www.sangres.com/newmexico/rioarriba/losojos.htm#.ZEEuuy_MIW2 (no longer available).

Lovegreen, Alan. "Aerial Homesteading: Aerofuturism in Interwar America." *Criticism* 57, no. 2 (2015): 235–57.

Loza, Mireya. *Defiant Braceros: How Migrant Workers Fought for Racial, Sexual, and Political Freedom*. Chapel Hill: University of North Carolina Press, 2016.

Lucanio, Patrick, and Gary Coville. *Smokin' Rockets: The Romance of Technology in American Film, Radio and Television, 1945–1962*. Jefferson, NC: McFarland, 2002.

MacPhee, Graham. *The Architecture of the Visible: Technology and Urban Visual Culture*. London: Continuum, 2002.

Maher, Neil M. *Apollo in the Age of Aquarius*. Cambridge, MA: Harvard University Press, 2017.

Malville, John McKim, Michael Zawaski, and Steven Gullberg. "Cosmological Motifs of Peruvian Huacas." *Archaeologia Baltica* 10 (2008): 175–82.

Marez, Curtis. *Farm Worker Futurism: Speculative Technologies of Resistance*. Minneapolis: University of Minnesota Press, 2016.

Mark, Michelle, and Pat Ralph. "A Getty Photographer Tells the Story Behind a Heartbreaking Photo He Took of a Migrant Girl Sobbing While Agents Questioned Her Mom at the Border, Which Just Won World Press Photo of the Year." *Business Insider*, April 12, 2019. https://www.businessinsider.com/photo-migrant-girl-cries-as-border-agents-question-mom-john-moore-2018-6.

Marks, Diana. "Molas: Displaying the Quotidian Before Andy Warhol." *Fashion, Style and Popular Culture* 3 no. 1 (2016): 35–49.

Marshall, Jocelyn E. "Calling Out and In: *In Plain Sight* and Queer Feminist Care at the Border(s)." *Public Art Dialogue* 13, no. 1 (2023): 100–22.

Martínez, Juan A. *María Brito*. Minneapolis: University of Minnesota Press, 2009.

Matza, Max. "SpaceX Rocket Explodes, Raining Debris from Sky for Second Time in a Row." BBC, March 6, 2025. https://www.bbc.com/news/articles/cj92wgeyvzzo#.

Mbembe, Achille. "Necropolitics." *Public Culture* 15, no. 1 (2003): 11–40.

McClain, Joseph. "Making Bricks from Regolith (Because There's No Home Depot on Mars)." Phys.org, June 2, 2016. https://phys.org/news/2016-06-bricks-regolith-home-depot-mars.html.

McCray, Patrick W. *Keep Watching the Skies! The Story of Operation Moonwatch and the Dawn of the Space Age*. Princeton, NJ: Princeton University Press, 2008.

McCurdy, Howard E. *Space and the American Imagination*. Baltimore: Johns Hopkins University Press, 2011.

Méliès, Georges, dir. *A Trip to the Moon*. 1902. In *Landmarks of Early Film*. Chatsworth, CA: Image Entertainment, 1994. DVD.

Méndez, Abel, and Ángel Acosta-Colón. "The Fear of Halley's Comet Visit in 1910 Is Preserved in a Cave in Southern Puerto Rico." Preprint, arXiv:2410.03259, October 2024.

Menéndez, Ramón, dir. *Stand and Deliver*. 1988. Burbank, CA: Warner Bros., 1988. DVD.

Merla-Watson, Cathryn Josefina. "(Trans)Mission Possible: The Coloniality of Gender, Speculative Rasquachismo, and Altermundos in Luis Valderas's Chican@futurist Visual Art." In *Altermundos: Latin@ Speculative Literature, Film, and Popular Culture*, edited by Cathryn Josefina Merla-Watson and B. V. Olguín, 352–70. Los Angeles: UCLA Chicano Studies Research Center Press, 2017.

Merla-Watson, Cathryn Josefina, and B. V. Olguín. "Altermundos: Reassessing the Past, Present, and Future of the Chican@ and Latin@ Speculative Arts." In *Altermundos: Latin@ Speculative Literature, Film, and Popular Culture*, edited by Cathryn Josefina Merla-Watson and B. V. Olguín, 1–36. Los Angeles: UCLA Chicano Studies Research Center Press, 2017.

Mesa-Bains, Amalia. "Domesticana: The Sensibility of Chicana Rasquachismo." In *Chicano and Chicana Art: A Critical Anthology*, edited by Jennifer A. González, C. Ondine Chavoya, Chon Noriega, and Terezita Romo, 91–99. Durham, NC: Duke University Press, 2019.

Messeri, Lisa. *Placing Outer Space: An Earthly Ethnography of Other Worlds*. Durham, NC: Duke University Press, 2016.

"Mexican Dancers Liven Hispanic Program." *Roundup* 15, no. 19 (September 24, 1976), 4.

Milbrath, Susan. *Star Gods of the Maya: Astronomy in Art, Folklore, and Calendars.* Austin: University of Texas Press, 1999.

Miller, Ron. "Space Art." *Spaceflight* 30 (August 1988): 316–23.

Mirzoeff, Nicholas. *The Right to Look: A Counterhistory of Visuality.* Durham, NC: Duke University Press, 2011.

Mitman, Gregg. "Reflections on the Plantationocene: A Conversation with Donna Haraway and Anna Tsing." *Edge Effects Magazine*, June 18, 2019, 1–19. https://edgeeffects.net/haraway-tsing-plantationocene/.

Montross, Sarah J., ed. *Past Futures: Science Fiction, Space Travel, and Postwar Art of the Americas.* Cambridge, MA: MIT Press, 2015.

Moon, Kavior. "Beatriz Cortez and Rafa Esparza: Commonwealth and Council." *Artforum*, May 1, 2018. https://www.artforum.com/events/beatriz-cortez-and-rafa-esparza-239877/.

Morales, Orquidea. "The Horror in Gloria Anzaldúa: Reclaiming the Monstrous." *Rio Bravo: A Journal of the Borderlands* 24 (2020): 48–55.

Morán González, John. "Aztlán @ Fifty: Chican@ Literary Studies for the Next Decade." *Aztlán* 35, no. 2 (2010): 173–76.

Moreno, Gaby. "Brownsville Mural Stirs Mixed Reactions in Community." ValleyCentral.com, September 20, 2021. https://www.valleycentral.com/news/local-news/brownsville-mural-stirs-mixed-reactions-in-community/.

Moreno, Gaby. "Brownsville Pays LA Artist $20k for Downtown Mural." ValleyCentral.com, October 6, 2021. https://www.valleycentral.com/community/brownsville-pays-la-artist-20k-for-downtown-mural.

Moreno, Gaby. "Hope Is on the Horizon for Downtown Brownsville." ValleyCentral.com, May 20, 2021. https://www.valleycentral.com/news/local-news/hope-is-on-the-horizon-for-downtown-brownsville/.

Morton, Timothy. *Hyperobjects: Philosophy and Ecology After the End of the World.* Minneapolis: University of Minnesota Press, 2013.

Muñoz, José Esteban. *Cruising Utopia: The Then and There of Queer Futurity.* New York: New York University Press, 2009.

Muñoz, José Esteban. *The Sense of Brown.* Durham, NC: Duke University Press, 2020.

Nájera-Ramírez, Olga. "*Ballet Folklórico Mexicano*: Choreographing National Identity in a Transnational Context." In *Dancing Cultures: Globalization, Tourism and Identity in the Anthropology of Dance*, edited by Hélène Neveu Kringelback and Jonathan Skinner, 161–76. Oxford: Berghahn Books, 2012.

Newell, Catherine L. *Destined for the Stars: Faith, the Future, and America's Final Frontier.* Pittsburgh: University of Pittsburgh Press, 2019.

Newkirk, Zachary. "'Far More Useful to the World': Astronomy at Cornell's Humble Beginnings, 1865–1920." Final paper for Professor Martha P. Haynes,

Department of Astronomy, Cornell University, December 15, 2011. http://zacharynewkirk.weebly.com/uploads/1/2/9/0/12903499/astronomy_paper_final_draft.pdf.

Nicholson, Phil, Jennifer Bailard, and Shianne Beer. "History of the Fuertes Observatory." Cornell Astronomical Society. Accessed October 30, 2023. https://www.cornellastrosociety.org/fuerteshistory.

Noriega, Chon A. "On Museum Row: Aesthetics and the Politics of Exhibition." In *Chicano and Chicana Art: A Critical Anthology*, edited by Jennifer A. González, C. Ondine Chavoya, Chon Noriega, and Terezita Romo, 470–83. Durham, NC: Duke University Press, 2019.

Noriega, Chon A. "To Dwell on This Matrix of Places." In *Home—So Different, So Appealing*, edited by Chon A. Noriega, Mari Carmen Ramírez, and Pilar Tompkins Rivas, 23–73. Los Angeles: Chicano Studies Research Center Press, 2017.

Noriega, Chon A. "Your Art Disgusts Me: Early Asco 1971–75." *East of Borneo*, November 18, 2010. https://eastofborneo.org/articles/your-art-disgusts-me-early-asco-1971-75/.

Noriega, Chon A., Mari Carmen Ramírez, and Pilar Tompkins Rivas, eds. *Home—So Different, So Appealing*. Los Angeles: Chicano Studies Research Center Press, 2017.

Noriega, Chon A., Mari Carmen Ramírez, and Pilar Tompkins Rivas. Introduction to *Home—So Different, So Appealing*, edited by Chon A. Noriega, Mari Carmen Ramírez, and Pilar Tompkins Rivas, 17–19. Los Angeles: Chicano Studies Research Center Press, 2017.

Normark, Don. *Chavez Ravine: 1949: A Los Angeles Story*. San Francisco: Chronicle Books, 2003.

O'Doherty, Brian. *Inside the White Cube: The Ideology of the Gallery Space*. Santa Monica, CA: Lapis, 1986.

Ofgang, Erik. "The Sideshow Magician Who Inspired Ray Bradbury—Then Vanished." *Smithsonian Magazine*, March 9, 2023. https://www.smithsonianmag.com/history/the-sideshow-magician-who-inspired-ray-bradburythen-vanished-180981764/.

Olowin, Ronald P. "Man, Controller of the Universe." In *The Inspiration of Astronomical Phenomena VI: ASP Conference Series*, edited by Enrico Maria Corsini, 217–19. San Francisco: Astronomical Society of the Pacific, 2011.

Omi, Michael, and Howard Winant. *Racial Formation in the United States*. New York: Routledge, 1988.

Ortiz-Torres, Rubén, ed. *Mex/L.A.: "Mexican" Modernism(s) in Los Angeles, 1930–1985*. Ostfildern, Germany: Hatje Cantz, 2011.

Oziewicz, Marek. "Speculative Fiction." In *Oxford Research Encyclopedia of Literature*, published online. Oxford University Press. March 29, 2017. https://oxfordre.com/literature/display/10.1093/acrefore/9780190201098.001.0001/acrefore-9780190201098-e-78.

Padilla, Elena. *Up from Puerto Rico*. New York: Columbia University Press, 1958.

Pappalardo, Joe. "It's No Surprise SpaceX Blows Up Rockets in Texas. That's Why It Came Here." *Texas Monthly*, May 3, 2023. https://www.texasmonthly.com/news-politics/spacex-rockets-boca-chica-damage-lawsuit/.

Parker, Ryan. "'Star Wars': Richard Pryor Once Bartended at the Mos Eisley Cantina." *Hollywood Reporter*, December 13, 2017. https://www.hollywoodreporter.com/movies/movie-news/star-wars-richard-pryor-once-bartended-at-mos-eisley-cantina-1066895/.

Pérez, Laura E. *Chicana Art: The Politics of Spiritual and Aesthetic Altarities*. Durham, NC: Duke University Press, 2007.

Petersen, Stephen. *Space-Age Aesthetics: Lucio Fontana, Yves Klein, and the Postwar European Avant-Garde*. University Park: Penn State University, 2009.

Philbrick, Ethan. *Group Works: Art, Politics, and Collective Ambivalence*. New York: Fordham University Press, 2023.

Pitzer College, Office of Communications. "Pitzer College Hosts the Cactus and Succulent Society of America." May 28, 2015. https://www.pitzer.edu/communications/2015/05/27/pitzer-college-hosts-the-cactus-and-succulent-society-of-america/ (no longer available).

Ramírez, Catherine S. "Afrofuturism/Chicanafuturism: Fictive Kin." *Aztlán* 33, no. 1 (2008): 185–94.

Ramírez, Catherine S. "Cyborg Feminism: The Science Fiction of Octavia E. Butler and Gloria Anzaldúa." In *Reload: Rethinking Women + Cyberculture*, edited by Mary Flanagan and Austin Booth, 374–402. Cambridge, MA: MIT Press, 2002.

Ramírez, Catherine S. "Deus ex Machina: Tradition, Technology and the Chicanafuturist Art of Marion C. Martinez." In *Chicano and Chicana Art: A Critical Anthology*, edited by Jennifer A. González, C. Ondine Chavoya, Chon Noriega, and Terezita Romo, 146–64. Durham, NC: Duke University Press, 2019.

Ramírez, Catherine S. *The Woman in the Zoot Suit: Gender, Nationalism, and the Cultural Politics of Memory*. Durham, NC: Duke University Press, 2009.

Ramírez, Susana. "Recovering Gloria Anzaldúa's Sci-Fi Roots: Nepantler@ Visions in the Unpublished and Published Speculative Precursors to *Borderlands*." In *Altermundos: Latin@ Speculative Literature, Film, and Popular Culture*, edited by Cathryn Josefina Merla-Watson and B. V. Olguín, 55–71. Los Angeles: UCLA Chicano Studies Research Center Press, 2017.

Ramírez-Soto, Elizabeth. *(Un)veiling Bodies: A Trajectory of Chilean Post-Dictatorship Documentary*. Cambridge: Legenda, 2019.

Rancaño, Vanessa. "Why Latinos Heart Horror Films." *National Public Radio*, October 31, 2015. https://www.npr.org/sections/codeswitch/2015/10/31/452298992/why-latinos-heart-horror-films.

Rawmírez, Josué. "Who's the Bandit?" South Texas College Library, March 22, 2022. YouTube video, 19:56. https://www.youtube.com/watch?v=99srU6kuFok.

Reinoza, Tatiana. *Reclaiming the Americas: Latinx Art and the Politics of Territory*. Austin: University of Texas Press, 2023.

Ricketson, Oliver, Jr. "Astronomical Observatories in the Maya Area." *Geographical Review* 18, no. 2 (1928): 215–25.

Ricourt, Milagros, and Ruby Danta. *Hispanas de Queens: Latino Panethnicity in a New York City Neighborhood*. Ithaca, NY: Cornell University Press, 2003.

Rivera, John-Michael. *Undocuments*. Tucson: University of Arizona Press, 2021.

Robinson, Alicia. "Coachella 2018: Palm-3 World Station Installation Evokes Cold War Aftermath." *Press-Enterprise*, April 15, 2018. https://www.pressenterprise.com/2018/04/15/coachella-2018-palm-3-world-station-installation-evokes-cold-war-aftermath/.

Robinson, Kim Stanley. *Red Mars*. London: HarperCollins, 1992.

Rodríguez, Ana Patricia. *Dividing the Isthmus: Central American Transnational Histories, Literatures, and Cultures*. Austin: University of Texas Press, 2009.

Rodríguez, Richard T. *Next of Kin: The Family in Chicano/a Cultural Politics*. Durham, NC: Duke University Press, 2009.

Rojas, James T. "The Enacted Environment of East Los Angeles." In *Chicano and Chicana Art: A Critical Anthology*, edited by Jennifer A. González, C. Ondine Chavoya, Chon Noriega, and Terezita Romo, 271–77. Durham, NC: Duke University Press, 2019.

Rosas, Ana Elizabeth. *Abrazando el Espíritu: Bracero Families Confront the US-Mexico Border*. Berkeley: University of California Press, 2014.

Rosson, Lois, and Ron Miller. "Space Art as a Modern Movement: From the Moon to Today." In *The Beauty of Space Art: An Illustrated Journey Through the Cosmos*, edited by Jon Ramer and Ron Miller, 73–91. Cham, Switzerland: Springer, 2021.

Rosten, Leo. *Hollywood: The Movie Colony, the Movie Makers*. New York: Harcourt, Brace, 1941.

Rubin, David S. "A Los Angeles Story." In *Ry Cooder/Vincent Valdez: El Chávez Ravine*, edited by David S. Rubin, 7–22. San Antonio: San Antonio Museum of Art, 2009.

Ruiz, Jason. *Americans in the Treasure House: Travel to Porfirian Mexico and the Cultural Politics of Empire*. Austin: University of Texas Press, 2014.

Ruiz, Vicki L. "Introduction: A Historical and Regional Overview of Latinas in the United States." In *Latinas in the United States: A Historical Encyclopedia*, edited by Vicki L. Ruiz and Virginia Sánchez Korrol, 1:1–7. Bloomington: Indiana University Press, 2006.

Saab, A. Joan. *Objects of Vision: Making Sense of What We See*. University Park: Penn State University Press, 2020.

Sánchez, Alberto Sandoval. "Puerto Rican Identity Up in the Air: Air Migration, Its Cultural Representations, and Me 'Cruzando el Charco.'" In *Puerto Rican*

Jam: Rethinking Colonialism and Nationalism, edited by Frances Negrón-Muntaner and Ramón Grosfoguel, 189–208. Minneapolis: University of Minnesota Press, 1997.

Sánchez-Tranquilino, Marcos. "Murales del Movimiento: Chicano Murals and the Discourses of Art and Americanization." In *Signs from the Heart: California Chicano Murals*, edited by Eva Sperling Cockcroft and Holly Barnet-Sánchez, 84–101. Venice, CA: Social and Public Art Resource Center, 1990.

Sandoval, Chela. *Methodology of the Oppressed*. Minneapolis: University of Minnesota Press, 2000.

Sandoval, Chela. "U.S. Third World Feminism: The Theory and Method of Oppositional Consciousness in the Postmodern World." *Genders* 10 (1991): 1–24.

Santilli, Chris. "The Getty Center's Stone Seduces Visitors." Concrete Construction, September 1, 1999. https://www.yumpu.com/en/document/read/10157768/the-getty-centers-stone-seduces-masonry-construction/4.

Saunders, Beth. "Art After Apollo." In *Apollo's Muse: The Moon in the Age of Photography*, edited by Mia Fineman and Beth Saunders, 137–45. New York: Metropolitan Museum of Art, 2019.

Sawyer, Drew. "Aerospace Folktales." *Aperture*, May 24, 2017. https://aperture.org/editorial/aerospace-folktales-sekula/.

Scharmen, Fred. *Space Settlements*. New York: Columbia University Press, 2019.

Schauer, Bradley. *Escape Velocity: American Science Fiction Film, 1950–1982*. Middletown, CT: Wesleyan University Press, 2017.

Schindler, Kevin. *The Far End of the Journey: Lowell Observatory's 24-Inch Clark Telescope*. Flagstaff, AZ: Lowell Observatory, 2016.

Schneider, Rebecca. *Performing Remains: Art and War in Times of Theatrical Reenactment*. London: Routledge, 2011.

Schreuders, Piet. *Paperbacks, U.S.A.: A Graphic History, 1939–1959*. San Diego: Blue Dolphin, 1981.

Sconce, Jeffrey. Introduction to *Sleaze Artists: Cinema at the Margins of Taste, Style, and Politics*, edited by Jeffrey Sconce, 1–16. Durham, NC: Duke University Press, 2007.

Sconce, Jeffrey. "'Trashing' the Academy: Taste, Excess, and an Emerging Politics of Cinematic Style." *Screen* 36, no. 4 (1995): 371–93.

Scott, Ridley, dir. *Blade Runner*. 1982. Burbank, CA: Warner Bros., 2007. DVD.

Shanks, Gwyneth. "Adobe, Dust, and Water: Rafa Esparza and Rebeca Hernandez's *building: a simulacrum of power*." *X-Tra* 20, no. 2 (2018). https://www.x-traonline.org/article/adobe-dust-and-water-rafa-esparza-and-rebeca-hernandezs-building-a-simulacrum-of-power.

Sides, Josh. *L.A. City Limits: African American Los Angeles from the Great Depression to the Present*. Berkeley: University of California Press, 2003.

Smith, Shawn Michelle. *Photography on the Color Line: W. E. B. Du Bois, Race, and Visual Culture*. Durham, NC: Duke University Press, 2004.

Sobchack, Vivian. *Screening Space: The American Science Fiction Film*. New Brunswick, NJ: Rutgers University Press, 1997.

Solomon, Dan. "Will Elon Musk Austin-ify Brownsville?" *Texas Monthly*, December 27, 2021. https://www.texasmonthly.com/news-politics/is-brownsville-becoming-btx/.

Spielberg, Steven, dir. *Close Encounters of the Third Kind*. 1977. Culver City, CA: Columbia Pictures Industries, Inc., 2007. DVD.

Spivak, Gayatri Chakravorty. *Death of a Discipline*. New York: Columbia University Press, 2003.

Stableford, Brian. "Science Fiction Before the Genre." In *The Cambridge Companion to Science Fiction*, edited by Edward James and Farah Mendlesohn, 15–31. Cambridge: Cambridge University Press, 2003.

Steiner, Christopher B. "When You Look at This, Think of Me." In *Real Photo Postcards: Pictures from a Changing Nation*, edited by Lynda Klich and Benjamin Weiss, 138–49. Boston: Museum of Fine Arts, Boston Publications, 2022.

Strait, Kevin M. Introduction to *Afrofuturism: A History of Black Futures*, edited by Kevin M. Strait and Kinshasha Holman Conwill, 10–15. Washington, DC: Smithsonian Books, 2023.

Streeby, Shelley. *Imagining the Future of Climate Change: World-Making Through Science Fiction and Activism*. Berkeley: University of California Press, 2018.

Stromberg, Matt. "Historic Chicano Mural Whitewashed in Culver City." *Hyperallergic*, April 22, 2025. https://hyperallergic.com/historic-chicano-mural-whitewashed-in-culver-city/.

Stromberg, Matt. "Hollywood Myths and Latinx Art Histories at LA's Frieze Projects." *Hyperallergic*, February 10, 2020. https://hyperallergic.com/541590/frieze-projects-los-angeles-paramount-2020/.

Suvin, Darko. *Metamorphoses of Science Fiction: On the Poetics and History of a Literary Genre*. New Haven, CT: Yale University Press, 1979.

Tang, Jeannine. "Contemporary Art and Critical Transgender Infrastructures." In *Trap Door: Trans Cultural Production and the Politics of Visibility*, edited by Reina Gossett, Eric A. Stanley, and Johanna Burton, 363–92. Cambridge, MA: MIT Press, 2017.

Taylor, Steve. "Mendez: Texas Needs to Invest More in the Space Industry." *Rio Grande Guardian*, February 15, 2023. Video. https://riograndeguardian.com/video-mendez-texas-needs-to-invest-more-in-the-space-industry/.

Tejada, Roberto. *Celia Alvarez Muñoz*. Minneapolis: University of Minnesota Press, 2009.

Telotte, J. P. *Movies, Modernism, and the Science Fiction Pulps*. Oxford: Oxford University Press, 2019.

Thurston, R. H. "Professor Fuertes Dies." *Cornell Alumni News* 5, no. 15 (1903): 119–20.

Tillman, Nola Taylor. "Saturn's Rings: Composition, Characteristics and Creation." Space.com, November 8, 2017. https://www.space.com/23235-rings-of-saturn.html.

Toledo, Aldo. "Mountain View: Dozens Protest as Feds Consider NASA Facilities to Settle Migrant Children." *Mercury News*, March 15, 2021. https://www.mercurynews.com/2021/03/15/mountain-view-dozens-protest-as-feds-consider-nasa-facilities-to-settle-migrant-children/.

Tompkins, Pilar. "*Post-America L.A.*" In *Almost Utopia: 18th Street Arts Center 2009 Program Annual*, 25. Los Angeles: 18th Street Arts Center, 2009. https://issuu.com/18thstarts/docs/almostutopia (no longer available).

Topham, Sean. *Where's My Space Age? The Rise and Fall of Futuristic Design*. New York: Prestel, 2003.

Tossin, Clarissa. "MCA Denver Conversations: Clarissa Tossin in Conversation with Miranda Lash." Vimeo, accessed January 5, 2023. https://vimeo.com/786679903.

US Department of Justice. *Critical Incident Review: Active Shooter at Robb Elementary School*. Washington, DC: Office of Community Oriented Policing Services, 2024. https://portal.cops.usdoj.gov/resourcecenter/content.ashx/cops-r1141-pub.pdf.

Valli, Frankie. "Grease." RSO Records, 1978. Vinyl.

Van Tuinen, Sjoerd. Introduction to *Speculative Art Histories: Analysis at the Limits*, edited by Sjoerd van Tuinen, 1–10. Edinburgh: Edinburgh University Press, 2017.

Vargas-Suarez Universal. "Scientific Data Resurrection." *Mexic-Arte Museum Community Arts* 2 (1996): 6.

Vasconcelos, José. *The Cosmic Race: A Bilingual Edition*. Translated by Didier T. Jaén. Baltimore: Johns Hopkins University Press, 1997.

Véa, Alfredo, Jr. *Gods Go Begging*. New York: Plume, 1999.

Vega, Silvia Rodriguez. *Drawing Deportation: Art and Resistance Among Immigrant Children*. New York: New York University Press, 2023.

Velasquez, Gaby. "Cabrales Showcases New Exhibit 'It Came from Beyond the Border.'" *Prospector*, October 27, 2016. https://www.theprospectordaily.com/2016/10/27/cabrales-showcases-new-exhibit-it-came-from-beyond-the-border/#.

Verne, Jules. *Around the World in Eighty Days*. Philadelphia: Porter and Coates, 1873.

Villa, Raúl Homero. *Barrio-Logos: Space and Place in Urban Chicano Literature and Culture*. Austin: University of Texas Press, 2000.

Vincent, Matt. "BTX Fiber Names New President amid Brownsville, Texas Broadband Network Build." Lightwave, November 30, 2022. https://www.broadbandtechreport.com/fiber/article/14286421/btx-fiber-names-new-president-amid-brownsville-texas-broadband-network-build.

Vogt, Wendy. "The Arterial Border: Negotiating Economies of Risk and Violence in Mexico's Security Regime." *International Journal of Migration and Border Studies* 3, no. 2–3 (2017): 192–207.

Watson, Fred. *Stargazer: The Life and Times of the Telescope.* Cambridge, MA: Da Capo, 2004.

Weems, Jason. *Barnstorming the Prairies: How Aerial Vision Shaped the Midwest.* Minneapolis: University of Minnesota Press, 2015.

Whiting, Cécile. *Pop L.A.: Art and the City in the 1960s.* Berkeley: University of California Press, 2006.

Whitney Museum of Art. "Whitney Biennial 2017: Rafa Esparza." June 5, 2017. YouTube video, 3:09. https://www.youtube.com/watch?v=CfiKE8CuuN4.

Wingate, Jennifer. "Louis Carlos Bernal's Photographs of TV Screens and Domestic Interiors." *Panorama: Journal of the Association of Historians of American Art* 10, no. 1 (2024): 1–10.

Wofford, Tobias. "Diasporic Returns in the Jet Age: The First World Festival of Negro Arts and the Promise of Air Travel." *Interventions: International Journal of Postcolonial Studies* 20, no. 7, (2018): 952–64.

Wolfe, Gary K. *The Known and the Unknown: The Iconography of Science Fiction.* Kent, OH: Kent State University Press, 1979.

Womack, Ytasha L. *Afrofuturism: The World of Black Sci-Fi and Fantasy Culture.* Chicago: Lawrence Hill Books, 2013.

Womack, Ytasha L. "Afrofuturism as Space and Being." In *Afrofuturism: A History of Black Futures*, edited by Kevin M. Strait and Kinshasha Holman Conwill, 19–28. Washington, DC: Smithsonian Books, 2023.

Ybarra-Frausto, Tomás. "Imagining a More Expansive Narrative of American Art." *American Art* 19, no. 3 (2005): 9–15.

Ybarra-Frausto, Tomás. "The Latino Wunderkammer." In *Amalia Mesa-Bains: Archaeology of Memory*, edited by Laura E. Pérez and María Esther Fernández, 112–17. Oakland: University of California Press, 2023.

Ybarra-Frausto, Tomás. "Rasquachismo: A Chicano Sensibility." In *Chicano Aesthetics: Rasquachismo*, 5–8. Phoenix: Movimiento Artistico del Rio Salado, 1989.

Zimmer, Zac. *First Contact: Speculative Visions of the Conquest of the Americas.* Evanston, IL: Northwestern University Press, 2025.

Index

Note: Locators in *italics* refer to figures and plates.